Travels
in the
Old South

Travels in the Old South

Selected from Periodicals of the Times

Edited by Eugene L. Schwaab
with the collaboration of
Jacqueline Bull

Volume II

THE UNIVERSITY PRESS
OF KENTUCKY

Illustrations courtesy of The Bettmann Archive, Inc.:
396, 498, 533; Margaret I. King Library: Frontis, 290,
293, 296, 323, 343, 346, 350, 401, 446, 509, 514, 530, 557;
New York Public Library: 287, 305, 353, 361, 389, 404,
412, 471, 477, 507, 525, 536, 540

ISBN: 0–8131–1229–X

Library of Congress Catalog Card Number: 70–119814   JUL 3 '74

Copyright © 1973 by The University Press of Kentucky

A statewide cooperative scholarly publishing agency
serving Berea College, Centre College of Kentucky,
Eastern Kentucky University, Kentucky Historical Society,
Kentucky State University, Morehead State University,
Murray State University, Transylvania University,
University of Kentucky, University of Louisville, and
Western Kentucky University.

Editorial and Sales Offices: Lexington, Kentucky 40506

A Decade
of Nationalism
1836–1845

Many of the new generation of travelers, like their predecessors, dealt with such subjects as the exploration of frontier areas, natural phenomena, religious and moral conditions and information useful to the emigrant or the land speculator. But the travelers of the 1830's and 1840's also wrote about subjects that had received little or no attention in earlier years. The Seminole War and the Texas Revolution took men into new places and provided new experiences to be related.

Clark, *Travels in the Old South*, III, 103

The Allen family were notable in the early history of agriculture in the United States. Samuel Allen, the supposed author of these selections, was the father of Anthony B. Allen and R. L. Allen, who together founded the American Agriculturist *in 1842, a journal still published today. Lewis F. Allen, a third brother, was a notable breeder of cattle and editor of the* American Shorthorn Herd Book. *In 1847 the brothers established A. B. Allen & Co., which became one of the country's major dealers in agricultural equipment.*[1]

NO. I

.   .   .

LOUISVILLE.—This is a fine city, built upon a high level bank of the river, and is about half the size of Cincinnati, and laid out in the same manner, the streets crossing each other at right angles. It has some good buildings, of which the Court House and new Methodist church are among the most elegant.[2] The rapids of the Ohio here extend $3\frac{1}{2}$ miles, with a fall of 24 feet, over a solid bed of limestone. These are passed except in high water, through a steamboat canal of about two miles in length, cut through the solid rock, reminding us, though without the length and depth, of the deep cut of the Erie canal at Lockport.[3]

Louisville has a considerable trade, and is pretty largely engaged in hemp manufactures, the whole process of which, is by machinery, driven by steam power. It is said that the manufacturing of cotton bagging does not cost over three cents per yard. This may seem very cheap, but a single power-loom will weave 250 yards per day with one hand to tend it, and all the other operations are equally facilitated. With hemp at $3 per cwt., the manufacturer can successfully compete with the imported fabric, and even without a protective duty, will soon drive the foreign article out of the market.[4]

CULTURE OF POOR SANDY SOILS IN KENTUCKY—Journeying from Louisville to Frankfort, our attention was attracted upon the road to a burley-headed negro, with a long beard somewhat grizzled with age, encased in stout cow-hide boots, hickory-colored jean clothes, and a huge, white felt hat, the wide brim cocked up before and behind in military style, giving him a rakish and

[Samuel Allen], "Sketches of the West," *American Agriculturist* 2 (May, December 1843): 66–69, 323–25; 3 (February, August, November 1844): 35–36, 230–32, 322. A part of the first sketch dealing with Ohio and all of the fourth sketch, which added little significant information, are omitted.

1. *American Agriculturist* 1 (April 1842): 2; 51 (January 1892): 2.
2. Designed by Gideon Shryock, the Jefferson County Courthouse was begun in 1839 but was not completed until 1860. Rexford Newcomb, *Architecture in Old Kentucky* (Urbana, Ill., 1953), pp. 116–17. The courthouse is still in use today (1973). The first Methodist Church was built in Louisville about 1816; by 1831 the city had four churches. Isabel M. McMeekin, *Louisville, the Gateway City* (New York, 1946), p. 190.
3. The Louisville and Portland Canal was begun in 1826 and completed in 1831 at a cost of over $700,000. Adams,

Dictionary of American History, 3:310. The deep cut at Lockport was seven miles long of which two miles was through solid rock. Ronald E. Shaw, *Erie Water West: A History of the Erie Canal, 1792–1854* (Lexington, Ky., 1966), p. 130.
4. In 1844 the directory of the city of Louisville listed two bagging factories and six cordage and rope factories with an annual capacity of 900,000 pounds of hemp. It also listed seven small rope-walks. J. Stoddard Johnston, ed., *Memorial History of Louisville from its Earliest Settlement to the Year 1896*, 2 vols. (Chicago, 1896), 1:275.

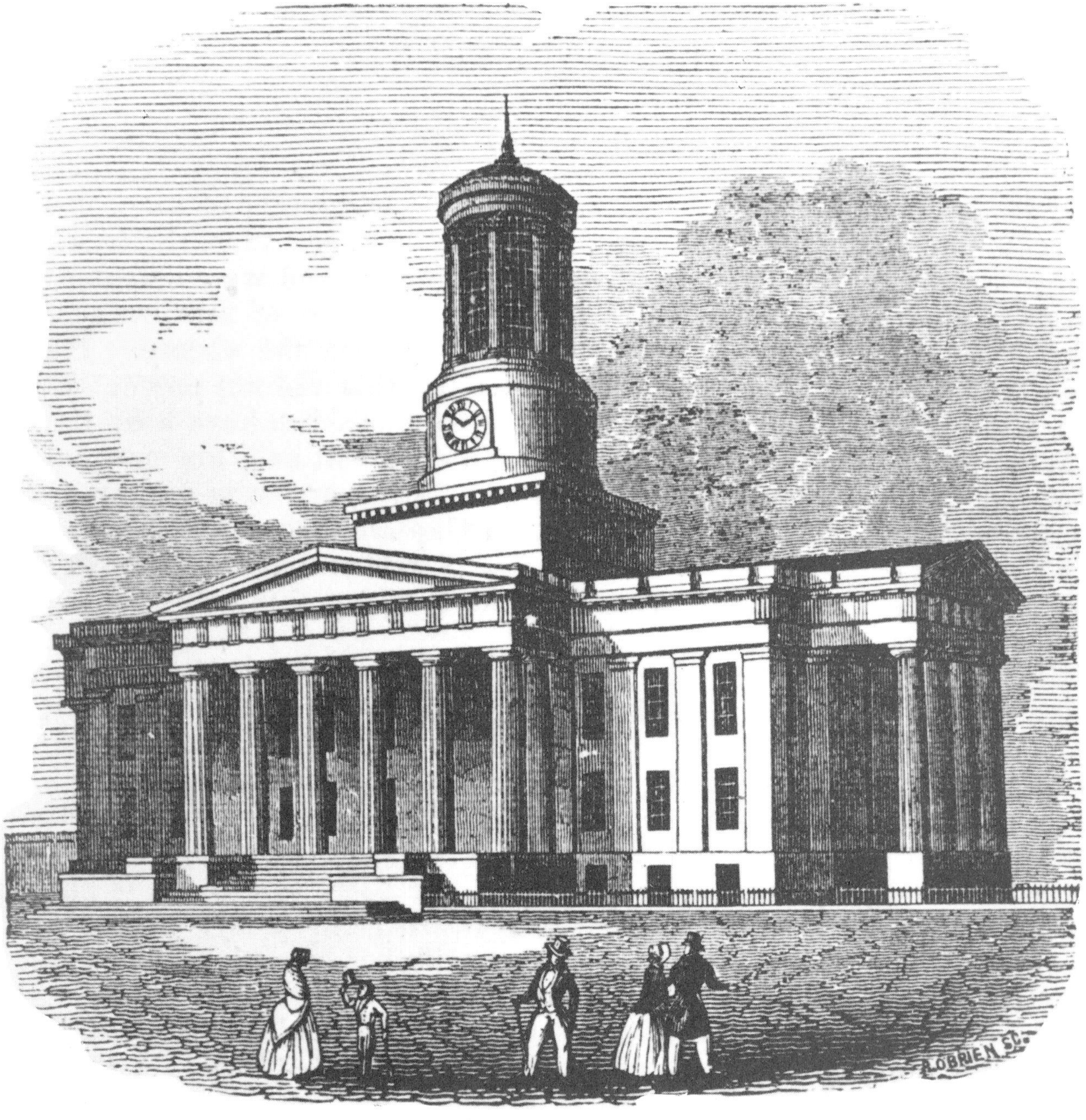

somewhat consequential appearance. He sat astride the bare back of the nigh ox of his team, hitched on to one of the smaller kind of Dutch wagons[5] filled with corn in the ear, and topped off with vegetables, and fresh killed pigs, and poultry "fixins" of various kinds, bound for the Louisville market. He flourished a tall whip, which was as thick as our arm, and braided from hemp of some six feet length. He sat him well, with a jaunty air, and was cheering on his patient team by singing in a lugubrious tone, to the popular old negro air of "Long time ago," probably an improvisatrized song, every stanza of which, in order to take fresh breath, and give vent to the exuberance of his feelings, he wound up in a chorus of loud cracks of his whip.

> Den goin' down to Loudeville,
> Long time ago,
> Where all de wagons chucky fill
> Stan' in a row;
> Crack! crack! crack!
>
> Ob pig and turkey chicken big,
> Long time ago,
> Who neber more his foot he dig,
> In garden ob Sambo;
> Crack! crack! crack![6]

Here the coach stopped to deliver a passenger, while another took the opportunity of questioning our ebony serenader.

"So then, Sambo, you have a garden it seems?"

"Yes, sartin, master give me garden, and one day a week to work him."

"And what do you raise there?"

Here he handed out sundry vegetables, and among others a huge carrot about as big as his leg from the hip down (not including his foot though), measuring it off with great pride.

"Pray how did you produce that?"

He placed his finger significantly upon his nose, and replied: "Master think him garden never grow nothin', poor dry soil; I wheel him on manure, I work him late, I work him arly."

As working "late and arly," as Sambo had it, when the dew is on the ground, is the very philosophy of tilling dry soils, and to our certain knowledge has been the means of doubling crops in several instances, without any addition of fertilizing materials, we began now to listen to the colloquy with great interest.

"Sambo, you are a genius to grow such carrots, a scientific agriculturist, did you ever read Davy or Tull?"[7]

"Tull," he replied with a grin, "who be he? Dog that tree de coon?"

"Not exactly, but do you produce other vegetables equally large?"

Here he put his finger to his nose again. "Pa'snip in the spring—him grow a might smart chance all winter."

"Very well, Sambo, very well, indeed; but now pray tell me how do you contrive to make such fat luscious-looking poultry there, as I see in the wagon? I fancy that they did not grow in the same way that your carrots and parsnips have here."

"I reckon not ezakly," said he, and burst into a loud laugh, and commenced dancing all round the coach.

"Well, you foolish fellow, we must be off in a

5. The Conestoga wagon was built by Pennsylvania Germans, who were popularly referred to as "Dutch." Perhaps this is the source of the term "Dutch wagon." James Truslow Adams, ed., *Album of American History*, 6 vols. (New York, 1944), 1:340.

6. This song is similar to one in Alan Lomax, *The Folk Songs of North America* (London, 1960), pp. 38, 55.

7. Sir Humphrey Davy was a celebrated English chemist. The reference here is probably to his book *Elements of Agricultural Chemistry*, published in 1813. *Century Dictionary and Cyclopedia*, 9:312. Jethro Tull was an agricultural writer. Among his works were *Horse-Hoing Husbandry*, published in 1731. *Dictionary of National Biography*, 19:1231–33.

minute, here is a *bit* (a shilling-piece) now tell me."

Taking the money handed him, he turned up the whites of his eyes, and commenced: "Master's corn-crib purty handy I reckon."

"Very likely, but that's not all."

"Beef liber might plenty, and pork crackalins."

"I don't believe you."

"Roast him possum then, sweet taters, and—"

Here everything was ready again, and our impatient driver put up his horses without waiting for the cautious Sambo to finish his method of fattening fowls, and the last we saw of him, he was again astride his favorite ox, singing out at the top of his voice:—

> What now you ask de pound for coon?
> Long time ago,
> Ah, massa, cheap at picayune,
> Times be so low.
> Crack! crack! crack!

Will any Kentuckian please to furnish us with the peculiar manner that the colored people so delicately fat their fowls, the knowledge of which to our great regret, we were cut off from obtaining of the redoubtable Sambo?

NO. II

PLANTATION OF MR. GREY.—One of the best plantations, especially for its farm-buildings, which we visited in Kentucky, was that of Mr. Benjamin Grey of Versailles.[8] The house, as is usual in the more southern states, stands near the centre of the domain on rising ground, and commands a fine view of the country around. It is in

8. Benjamin Gray's name does not appear in the history of Woodford County, but the will books of the county show that at the time of his death in 1856 he had forty-eight slaves and other property, excluding land, valued at $43,355. He provided that each of his seven children should receive property valued at $10,000. Woodford County Will Book P, pp. 272, 322.

cottage style, large and roomy, and flanked by thick, strong chimneys, built up outside of the gable ends. A pretty yard of smooth green-sward, decked with shrubbery and evergreens, is enclosed around with pointed white palings, and adjoining this is a noble park, formed by merely underbrushing and thinning out a few of the trees of the original forest. These are usually termed woodland pastures in Kentucky; yet in most instances, they better deserve the name of park, than many of those on noblemen's estates in Europe.

CROPS.—Mr. Grey's farm being principally devoted to stock, and what is rather unusual here, dairy products, the crops are but a secondary consideration. Hemp is the main one to which he gives his attention; and in addition to this, he raises a sufficiency of corn and the smaller grains for his own consumption. The rotation is much like that described in our first volume, under head of Tours in Kentucky.[9]

STOCK.—This is very fine indeed, Mr. Grey having been highly spirited in this matter. His Short-Horns are choice, and quite numerous. We particularly admired the cow Mary Ann, with the calf at her foot. She has a fashionable and airy form; an up-head, and deer-like action; handles well, and in addition to all these, we were informed that she is an excellent milker. Three heifers of her produce we also admired; the two youngest were strikingly like their dam. After the Short-Horns, we were shown a few good Cotswold, and South-Down sheep, imported direct from England by Messrs. Bagg & Wait of Orange Co., in this state. The stock-hogs are a cross of the Berkshire upon the Thin-Rinds (a grade Chinese), and they make excellent porkers.

FARM BUILDINGS.—These are among the most

9. Two articles based on a tour of Kentucky, "Kentucky Farming," appeared in the first volume of this periodical. *American Agriculturist* 1 (June, August 1842): 67–70, 138–40.

complete we have seen in any place, and we speak of them with the more pleasure, because they are blameably deficient in farm buildings throughout the whole southwest. The climate here, it is true, is warmer and much more open than at the north; but it is in this *very openness*, that consists the principal suffering of the stock. The ground during this time is muddy, cold and damp; and worse, consequently, for animals to repose upon, than when frozen dry, or covered with snow. Sudden changes are continually taking place. Mild weather prevails for a few days, relaxing the system; this is then followed not unfrequently by intense cold; the thermometer sinking in 48 hours from 55° or 60° above, to zero, and sometimes 8° to 10° below it. These sudden changes are very injurious to man and beast, and far more to be dreaded than the steady cold of northern latitudes; and for this reason, more attention should be paid to the warmth of their dress on the part of the people here, and to the housing of stock, than is generally done. It would lessen disease, add to their longevity, and give a handsomer, fuller, and more healthful physical appearance. But to return more immediately to our subject.

With the exception of the usually reserved gangway on the barn-floor, the lower story is devoted to stables. These are planked, and each animal is accommodated with a separate stall. Behind them is a shallow gutter, running the whole length of the stable, which conducts the liquid falling from the animals into a cess-pool in the yard, and is there absorbed by muck. The solid manure is also equally carefully saved and applied to the land, and notwithstanding the proverbial fertility of the soil of Kentucky, Mr. Grey assured us that he considered himself well paid in the increase of his crops for the labor employed in thus saving and applying his manure. Over-head in the barn are lofts for hay and straw; a straw-cutter to prepare them for feeding; cribs and bins

for grain; and a large square box with heavy wooden pounders, for the hands to pound up corn and cob into meal on rainy days when they can do nothing else. This cob-meal is usually mixed up with water, and allowed to stand till it ferments, and is then fed to the stock.

THE DAIRY.—This is a sufficiently roomy building, of one story, situated in a little dell a short distance from the mansion. One of the gable ends abuts against a nearly perpendicular cliff, out of which bursts a clear gurgling spring, that takes its course through the centre of the rocky floor of the dairy, and then finds its way into the valley below. Here is every convenience for making butter and cheese, in which Mr. Grey excels. We have dwelt thus minutely on the plantation, stock and buildings of Mr. Grey, because we consider them an excellent example to follow in Kentucky; and also for the purpose of giving our northern readers a general idea of the husbandry at the west, of which the great majority entertain the most indefinite notions imaginable.

MR. HART'S PLANTATION.—After taking an early dinner, Mr. Grey ordered up his buggy, and we started for Mr. Nathaniel Hart's.[10] This was some few miles off, yet in order to get there we paid no attention to the public roads, but took our way over gentle hill and dale, through woodland-pastures, and among fields containing a hundred acres or more in each, under a single fence. For the purpose of opening and shutting the field-gates as we passed, we were accompanied by an ebony urchin, as out-rider mounted on the bare back of a high-spirited gray nag, which he rode with no little address. This seemed quite a gala business for him; and bare-headed, with his

10. Nathaniel Hart's estate, "Spring Hill," was a land grant that had been in the Hart family since pioneer days. Part of the estate was a woodland surrounded by a high fence to protect its herds of deer. W. E. Railey, *History of Woodford County* (Frankfort, Ky., 1928), pp. 54–55.

thick wooly locks fluttering in the wind, and his shirt-collar wide open, he went grinning along, now advancing at a hard gallop, and anon closing up at a fast trot, swinging open and shutting to the gates, shaking his pate, and hallooing to every animal that he thought did not move with sufficient alacrity from our destined path.

"Yo! ho! So you no move, Misser Cow—then Pompey make you," and at her he charged, brandishing a long stick, like a Cossack of the Don with his spear, the gray nag at the same time laying back his ears, and opening his mouth, and showing his teeth, as if grinning in fiery sympathy with his redoubtable rider, and ready to devour the animal that so sluggishly obstructed the path. But one look from the cow, or whatever beast it might be, at the horse and boy, seemed quite enough; and without waiting further hints, they would shake their tails, then give them a slight curl, and set off at a round scamper, the triumphant Pompey following up their career a short distance, singing with high satisfaction:—

I tell you so, now Misser Cow;
Yo, ho, you go, bow wow, bow wow.

Mr. Hart's plantation is a very fine one, and he is one of the largest hemp-growers in Kentucky. He has done much to introduce a system of water-rotting hemp in ponds, which we think is the best and most simple of the kind yet tried.[11] He has promised us a description of this, with his late improvements, and we trust that we shall be favored with it soon, for the benefit of those desirous of preparing their hemp for market by the pond-water-rotting process. There is so much in common with Kentucky plantations, that it is unnecessary to dwell further upon particulars. Mr. Hart's stock of cattle is principally derived from the first importation of the Short-Horns into Kentucky, in 1817.[12] He keeps a flock of about 800 Merino sheep, which, low as wool is, he thinks make him as good, if not a better return, than anything else which his plantation produces. Sheep-husbandry is attracting much attention at present in Kentucky. It is a very superior region indeed, for sheep, and if the planters would go judiciously into the fine-woolled breeds, wool would soon become an article of large export with them, and a source of considerable profit. Let it be remembered, that the cheaper and better wool can be produced, the more there will be consumed of it; and the cheaper and better, woollen cloths will be furnished in return. We need not fear overstocking the country in our generation.

Mr. Hart keeps quite a herd of deer in his park, and several head of elk. These last, with their large branching horns, and lofty, erect heads, have a noble appearance. He formerly had a few buffaloes, but they became so troublesome in breaking down fences, and sallying out whenever they pleased, to the great terror of the country round, that he was at last obliged to kill them. Buffalo bulls get somewhat ferocious as they grow old, and are rather dangerous animals on the plantation. While in Kentucky, we picked up some comic anecdotes of their doings as they turned out; but a feather's weight in the other scale might have made them equally tragical; and upon the whole, unless enclosed within a fence that they could not break down, we should advise our friends to eschew keeping buffaloes.

11. In a letter of 2 August 1842 to Lyman C. Draper, Hart wrote that he was harvesting hemp from 150 acres with the intention of water-rotting it. Draper Papers, 2CC27. Microfilm in Margaret I. King Library, University of Kentucky; originals in State Historical Society of Wisconsin.

12. Lewis Sanders of Fayette County is generally credited with having been the first to import shorthorns directly from England to the territory west of the Alleghenies. Alvin H. Sanders, *Shorthorn Cattle* (Chicago, 1918), pp. 165–67.

Sketches of Kentucky

LEXINGTON.—From Versailles we rode over a beautiful undulating country, and in a short time arrived at Lexington. This is a very handsome town, of about 6,000 inhabitants, and presents the appearance of considerable opulence. The streets are regularly laid out, a branch of the Elkhorn meandering through the town, and in its clear course adding much to the beauty and variety of the place. A richer or more favorable agricultural district can not be found than that which surrounds Lexington in a circle of 60 miles. Added to this, it is healthy, and settled by a highly intelligent and enterprising population. In fact, the people here consider it as approaching Eden, and it is very agreeable to hear them amplify on its capabilities, which they do, and very justly, with an eloquence that can not be gainsaid. The Kentuckian yields to none in love of his country, and the western hemisphere may be travelled over in vain in search of one more deserving of being loved.

ASHLAND, SEAT OF THE HON. HENRY CLAY.— This beautiful seat and superb plantation,[13] of one of the most gifted and celebrated men of America, is about one and a half miles from Lexington, and is approached by an excellent Macadam road leading directly by it. We called there in company with a nephew of Mr. Clay, Mr. Pindell,[14] of

Lexington; who took us by a circuitous road, first showing us his own fine plantation, a little beyond that of Ashland. The buildings on it are handsome and commodious, and there was a choice collection of stock of all kinds, particularly of blood horses. One of the fillies, the name of which we have forgotten, struck us as being as promising an animal of her kind as we saw in Kentucky. Mr. P. had repeatedly exhibited her at their agricultural shows, and she had invariably carried off the first prize over all competitors.

A division-fence separates the property of Mr. Clay and Mr. Pindell, which we passed by a wide gate and came immediately into the woodland, or more properly speaking, park pastures of Ashland, the trees of which are mostly the reservations of the original forest. They are grand and majestic in their appearance, and give a dignity, comfort, and beauty to the landscape, which can not be too much admired. It was still in the month of January, but the winter being a mild one, the grass was yet green, and a lot of blood horses, and Short-Horn cattle were out feeding, and looking as fat and sleek as need be. The show of these, Mr. Pindell informed me, was not so good as formerly, Mr. Clay having been tempted, when high prices prevailed, to part with the greater proportion of his choicest animals. After taking a full view of the plantation, we came round to the stables, the most celebrated incumbent of which was a large French Jack, named Royal.[15] He was selected by Mr. Henry Clay, Jr., when he visited France, and was bred at Poitou, near the birth-

13. Clay made an agreement with Cuthbert Banks on 13 September 1804 to buy 125 acres of land. This was the first piece of the land that made up his estate, later known as Ashland. Clay continued to purchase land until 1830, by which time he had acquired over 400 acres. All of this land, with the exception of two acres surrounding the house, is now a part of the city of Lexington. James F. Hopkins and Mary W. M. Hargreaves, eds., *The Papers of Henry Clay*, 3 vols. to date (Lexington, Ky., 1959), 1:148–49; Glyndon G. Van Deusen, *The Life of Henry Clay* (Boston, 1937), p. 71.

14. Thomas Hart Pindell was the son of Dr. Richard Pindell and Eliza Hart Pindell, a sister of Lucretia Hart Clay. Sarah S. Young, comp., *Genealogical Narrative of the*

Hart Family in the United States (Memphis, Tenn., 1882), p. 9.

15. A Lexington newspaper reported: "Mr. Clay has just imported from Europe via New Orleans, two Jacks and four Jennetts, of a race never before introduced into the United States as far as is known. . . . One of the jacks, Royal, will stand at Mansfield, about two and a half miles from Lexington" *Lexington Intelligencer*, 3 June 1837. Mansfield was the home of Henry Clay, Jr.

place of the celebrated Montesquieu. Whether from this circumstance Royal has inherited any of the legal talent of the profound jurist we are unable to say, he not yet being gifted with the power of speech to explain himself, as was Balaam's ass of old;[16] but what, perhaps, is of more utility where [he is] stationed is, [that] he has the faculty of stamping his superior size and strength on a numerous progeny of mules, to the great benefit of the country around him.

When we called at Ashland, Mr. Clay was passing the last of his term at Washington in his senatorial duties; we, therefore, missed the advantage of seeing him at home on his farm, where he is universally acknowledged to rank as high as in the councils of the nation. He has ever been foremost in every good word and work in agriculture in Kentucky, and perhaps few have done as much to assist in developing and improving the resources of his native state.[17] No one was more ardent and persevering in the introduction and growing of hemp than Mr. Clay; in the introduction also of improved stock, and all other measures calculated to promote agriculture, which, although well known at home, yet, on account of his brilliant forensic talents, his labors and example in this department, have in a measure been overshadowed and kept hid from the nation.

The mansion-house at Ashland is roomy and handsome, and such as a refined country gentleman may have been supposed to erect for his own comfort and convenience. The grounds are ample and beautiful, abounding with what we most admire in winter, a profusion of lofty evergreens. The views from the spot are charming, embracing the town of Lexington just beyond, and a fertile country of considerable extent in quiet repose around. In the absence of Mr. Clay, his respected lady received us very politely, and we found her presiding with equal dignity and grace over the affairs of the household; where, to her honor be it spoken, and also in the general management of the plantation, she as eminently excels, as her husband in the Legislative Halls—proving herself an admirable wife for one whose public duties have so often called him away from his home.

We are fearful of trespassing upon the sanctity of private life by dwelling longer upon this theme, and will only add that we felt no less honored than gratified by our visit to Ashland, and, at our departure could not but breathe more strongly than ever the wish that its possessors may soon be transferred by the voice of this great nation, to that exalted seat which their eminent talents and virtues have so well fitted them to adorn and fill.

NO. V

Plantation of Mr. Benjamin Warfield.[18]—This we also found a very fine one, and under a good state of cultivation, and devoted principally to stock. There is the usual quantity of woodland pasture set off here, the residue of the land is devoted to a simple rotation of crops, being mostly corn and rye. The sod is broken up during the winter, or as early in the spring as possible, and planted with corn. Sometimes the ground is so rich that it will bear two or three crops in succession; but we believe Mr. Warfield generally allowed only one crop to be taken. This, as soon as the corn is

16. Num. 22:30.
17. Henry Clay was born in 1777 in Virginia, not in Kentucky.

18. Benjamin Warfield was one of ten children of Elisha and Ruth B. Warfield, who moved from Maryland to Kentucky about 1790. He was a breeder of blooded cattle on his farm on the Winchester Pike near Lexington (now in Lexington). Elizabeth M. Simpson, *Bluegrass Houses and Their Traditions* (Lexington, Ky., 1932), p. 107. In his will, filed in Fayette County in November 1856, he left almost 700 acres of land to his family. He had 14 slaves. In addition to this property, he left considerable amounts of stock in railroads and turnpikes. Fayette County Will Book W, p. 414.

glazed, he cuts up close to the ground, shocks it, and then sows the field with rye. In October they commence husking, and so continue on during the winter as they have time. As the grass fails, the husked corn-shocks are carted on to the field which it is designed shall be plowed, the next year, spread evenly over it in patches, and a large herd of cattle fed upon them. By this method the field shortly becomes abundantly manured, and is then broken up for the following year's corn crop. It is thus the Kentucky planters are saved the dirty and laborious process of digging up and carting out large quantities of manure from the barnyard, a system of northern farming not at all to their fancy, and to which they usually express a decided disgust. We have often laughed at the wry faces they made up on speaking of it, and replied that it was less laborious and unpleasant than they supposed; there was nothing like habit in these matters, and we Yankees took the drudgery as a matter of course. They are indebted in Kentucky to their superior mild climate for being able to manage these things more easily than we do. Their system of open feeding is a good one for them, and meets our hearty approval, except during heavy rain-storms, and the severest cold weather, when shelter there is quite as necessary as here. The rye gets so strong and rank a growth in the fall, that it can be pastured beneficially more or less all winter when the ground is frozen sufficiently hard to prevent poaching;[19] and then again, when the land has become dry in the spring, till the middle of April. After this the stock is taken off till it becomes ripe, when hogs are turned on to harvest it; the stubble is then plowed up for corn again, or suffered to remain in pasture if it has been previously sowed with grass-seed.

Stock.—This, of course, is Durham, and the foundation of Mr. Warfield's herd was the '17 importation, crossed on by the best later ones.

19. Rendering land broken or slushy by trampling.

They are choice and fine, and all have quite a family resemblance in the horn, which is very slender and somewhat longer than usual in this breed. His superior young cow Caroline has already taken seven premiums; she is extremely even and well shaped, and of good milking qualities, as indeed is his whole stock, this being a sina qua non with Mr. W. in breeding. We found Cossack[20] here, an imported bull, half brother to Mr. Jacques' (of England) celebrated Clemente, which won the first prize as a two year old at the Royal Agricultural Society's meeting at Cambridge, in 1840. We saw him in August, 1841, at the Yorkshire show at Hull, when he was second only to Mr. Bates' Cleveland Lad.[21] Cossack is a fine snug bull and remarkably well ribbed up. Shannon, bred by Mr. Sullivant,[22] of Columbus, Ohio, is a noble, airy, upheaded, active fellow. Mr. W. has many fine animals, and means to keep on breeding till his farm is completely stocked with first-rate thorough-bred Short-Horns. We also found here a fine stock of thorough-bred Berkshires and their crosses.

Returning to Lexington by way of Dr. Warfield's,[23] we took a look over his horses; and really

20. The shorthorn bull Cossack was imported by Henry Clay, Jr., in 1838 and afterward was sold to Captain William Warfield. Sanders, *Shorthorn Cattle*, pp. 206–7, 275–76, 302.
21. Thomas Bates began breeding shorthorn cattle in 1800 and continued breeding them until his death in 1849. His cattle became famous and brought very high prices for the period. Ibid., p. 69.
22. Michael L. Sullivant of Columbus, Ohio, was the second son of Lucas and Sarah Starling Sullivant, pioneer settlers of Franklin County, Ohio. He raised cattle, horses, and mules. He introduced the use of machinery and new methods of agriculture in the area and was one of the founders of the Ohio Stock Importing Company. In 1854 he sold his Ohio lands and bought 80,000 acres in Illinois at government prices. Andrew Denny Rodgers II, "*Noble Fellow*," *William Starling Sullivant* (New York, 1940), pp. 258–59.
23. Elisha Warfield, probably best known as the breeder of the famous horse "Lexington," was a brother of Benjamin Warfield. He owned a farm, "The Meadows," on the Bryan

a beautiful lot he has, and quite numerous. Those which pleased us most among them was a pretty troop of fifteen or twenty colts running wild in a large pasture, just like any other cattle. They were the produce of some of the most celebrated horses of the day; and with their fine forms, clean blood-like [*sic*] limbs, high spirit, and gay action, running, capering, and playing, like a herd of wild deer in their wide paddocks, presented as animating a sight as one will easily meet with in an enclosed country.

Plantation of Mr. James E. Letton.[24]—We had many other invitations, and a great deal to see in the neighborhood of Lexington, but some necessary business to attend to in Ohio, obliged us to depart; but arriving at Millersburg, we found that we could not pass without calling to see Locomotive,[25] lately imported by Mr. Letton, from Mr. Bates' celebrated herd at Kirkleavington, England. To do this we had six miles to thread out all alone, in a pretty blind way across the country. But a gentleman at the hotel where we stopped, drew a plain map of the route, and the landlord furnishing us with a smart bay filley, that from her spirit and action we set down at once for near thorough-bred, away we galloped. We pretty soon got into a large open park, then bearing to the left, and now taking to the right, and fording a wild crooked rivulet half a dozen times, opening and shutting as many

different gates as we passed from enclosure to enclosure, we at last arrived opposite a snug farm-house. Here we thought it was best to make an enquiry, when a very obliging young man came out and insisted on accompanying us to show the way to Mr. Letton's, although some two miles or more distant. We had not proceeded far, however, before we espied a person on a tall white pacer, making for the same gate as ourselves in an oblique direction. Coming up, this turned out to be Mr. L. himself, so after making a self-introduction, he hospitably invited us home.

The cultivation of this plantation is much like others before described; we shall therefore pass it over. In feeding his stock, Mr. Letton goes against the forcing system entirely, and means to treat his high-breds in the same way that any good planter and Christian man would his common farm animals. We accordingly found Locomotive running out in the field with the other stock, from which he was taken up at night and fed a little cut hay, mixed with coarse bran.

In the month of January stock appears to disadvantage and on first looking at Locomotive, one might say that his brisket is even too low, and his fore legs, perhaps a little too close together. On the other hand, his head and horns are fair, with an elegant arched neck; his back, loin, and quarter particularly good; straight, fine hind leg; twist well let down; and tail beautifully set on. To look at him behind, his barrel is superb, and his handling from beginning to end, fine, elastic, and without fault. Mr. Bates spoke very highly to us of the milking qualities and fattening propensities of his progenitors, and all we can further add, is, that he stands, and, though not perfect in himself (for what animal is?) he can not but be of eminent service to the stock of Kentucky, high-bred and superior, as all acknowledge it now is. When we looked over Mr. Letton's stock, his cows were all imported. We liked Miss Severs best. She is

Station Pike just outside Lexington; it contained almost 700 acres. The house was razed in 1960, and only the names of streets of the section recall its former glory. Simpson, *Bluegrass Houses*, pp. 105–13.

24. James E. Letton was born in 1807. According to family tradition, he was killed in 1841 in Carlisle, Kentucky, when a horse he had imported from France fell on him at an exhibition. *Kentuckian-Citizen* (Paris, Ky.), 2 November 1943.

25. Sometime between 1839 and 1841, "Locomotive" was imported by Letton. The bull was later the property of W. T. Calmes of Fayette County, Kentucky. Sanders, *Shorthorn Cattle*, p. 214.

superior in the brisket, and otherwise very good.

Mr. L. also brought over from England a couple of young stallions of the cart-horse breed. The black is a very handsome animal of his kind; indeed, one of the most so that we ever saw. The gray is larger, but somewhat coarser. The object in view is to cross them on the largest mares of the country, and the females of this produce breed to large-sized Jacks, for the purpose of insuring them stout 16-hand mules, for the heavy work of the farm and to sell south. Mules are so much tougher and hardier than horses in a hot climate, that it has become a great object to breed them of sufficient size to do the heavy work of the plantation. Under these circumstances, Mr. L.'s enterprise is highly commendable, and we wish him marked success in his laudable improvements.

Next to the horses, we were shown some fine large Leicester sheep, and some swine, a cross of the Berkshire on the Irish Grazier, which, had they a smaller ear, and one could be assured of the same hardiness, we should consider them almost equal to the pure Berkshire, We think this cross, anyhow, infinitely superior to all the Woburns we saw in Kentucky, or crosses of them.

On the road to Maysville, mounting the box alongside of the driver of the coach, whom we found quite an intelligent young man, as the horses started off, we were attracted by the superior power, form, and action of the leaders, and inquired where they were bred?

"At the north."

"Do you not find them superior to those in Kentucky?"

"Yes."

"In what respects?"

"They stand not only the cold, but the hot weather better than the native-bred horses here; have harder hoofs, and are more enduring; possess more power; better wind and bottom; and some-how or other seem to do their work quicker, easier,

and more comfortable to themselves and driver."

"Have you had much experience in driving northern horses alongside of the western ones here?"

"Three years."

"To what do you attribute the northerner's superiority?"

"Mostly in breed, but something in climate and food. The farmers here feed too much corn and rich rank pasture."

"I should judge from their action, your leaders would easily trot their mile in 4 minutes."

"Yes, that they would, in less time with a light load; for when I have had in my whole team of northerners, I trotted a mile with this great heavy stage in 4 minutes 22 seconds; which is at the rate of 14 miles an hour, and I can any time do it again."

Gentlemen may take this conversation for what it is worth; but now that Macadam roads are pervading Kentucky, if they would breed the proper sort of horses, adopt lighter vehicles, carrying only 6 passengers inside and 3 outside, they might travel 8 miles an hour, with as much ease as they now do 5 miles. Railroads are out of the question there for a long time to come; they can never pay, and it is to be hoped under these circumstances that greater attention will be paid to expediting their stage-coaches.[26] We have always thought coaching much more useful, and certainly quite as exciting, as the course. Young men in the interior want something to stir up their blood and give life and spirit to a country life. Suppose then they get up a few driving-clubs, for four-in-hand handsome match horses, put the driver in costume, mount one of their servants in the republican livery for a guard, and give him a French horn to

26. Though several enterprises for building railroads were underway in Kentucky before 1850, the period of real expansion came later. Charles Kerr, *History of Kentucky*, 5 vols. (Chicago, 1922), 2:736.

occasionally enliven the road. The stage-coach of Kentucky would thus soon become in great vogue and add much to the pleasure of a journey through this beautiful fertile country.

NO. VI

Plantation of Mr. Adam Beatty.[27]—Stopping two miles or so short of Washington, we diverged to Prospect Hill, the plantation of Judge Beatty, who has so much distinguished himself in Kentucky as a writer on agriculture and as a practical farmer. Though at an elevation of nearly 300 feet above the Ohio river, the land, in common with other large tracts at this elevation, is extremely fertile, frequently as much so as that lower down on the plains. We found the plantation in admirable order. It embraces about 400 acres, covering two hills, with a pretty valley between, through which meanders a clear rivulet, sparkling over a white limestone bottom. Plenty of excellent fencing stone abounded in the valley, and Judge Beatty had commenced the use of it for his enclosures. Wherever stone can be had in Kentucky, we found that it was rapidly taking the place of wood for fences, it is found so much more durable, and it is assuredly to be preferred on account of its greater strength and beauty, for nothing can be more unsightly than the crooked snaky fences so common the United States over.

Crops.—The main crop on this plantation is hemp, and for the better production of it, and also to maintain the fertility of the soil, Judge B. has an established system of rotation, the particulars of which, as it has lately undergone some modifi-

cation, we hope to publish hereafter from his own pen. Large quantities of corn are raised here, together with some wheat and the other small grains. With the exception of potatoes, roots are not much thought of, so destructive is the fly, and numerous other insects in the first stages of their growth.

Stock.—As Judge Beatty did not wish to embark in the business of breeding fine animals for sale, he has availed himself of the best grades, within his reach, which answer all purposes of general utility. Large, stout horses and mules are mostly used for the farm work; the cows for milk, and the cattle for fattening, are principally a high cross of the Durham, the swine a greater or less intermixture of Irish Grazier or Berkshire; and the sheep of pure or mixed Merino blood. We noticed a fine large stock of all these different animals, particularly the last, which upon the whole we believe were considered the most profitable stock kept upon the farm. Judge B. esteems sheep highly in another respect; and that is, for feeding off his grass and clover, and leaving the land in a better and richer condition than other stock can do for the succeeding crops. We regret to say, that this part of sheep husbandry is little thought of, not only in Kentucky, but even at the north, where our lands east of the mountains, owing to their general thinness of soil, require more skill and attention in keeping up and increasing their fertility, than those at the west.

We found many things in practice at Prospect Hill worthy of notice, but inasmuch as the best of these were embodied in a general way, in two articles upon Kentucky Farming in the first volume of this work,[28] it is unnecessary to repeat them. Suffice it to say, that in cultivating his plantation, Judge B. adopts all such improvements as a long course of scientific agricultural reading, and the

27. Adam Beatty was born in Maryland in 1777 and came to Kentucky in 1800. After studying law in Lexington, he moved in 1802 to Washington in Mason County. He served in the state legislature but is best known for his work in the improvement of agriculture. He wrote many essays and at least one book on the subject. *Dictionary of American Biography*, vol. 1, pt. 2, pp. 99–100.

28. *American Agriculturist* 1 (June, August 1842): 67–70, 138–40.

observation of the best practice in the United States have proved advisable for his particular section of the country. In the neatness of his farming operations, order, general good management, and average products from year to year per acre, we know of no place of anything like its size, which is superior to the plantation at Prospect Hill—and there are things here which must be seen rather than described, to be properly appreciated.

Hemp Factory.—On leaving Prospect Hill, Judge B. had the kindness to give us a drive in his carriage to Maysville, distant about seven miles. Here we found a large hemp factory, erected at a cost of $80,000, and capable of making a million yards of cotton-bagging per annum, beside large quantities of bale rope.[29]

We now left Kentucky on an excursion to Ohio and as far south as New Orleans and subsequently revisited a small part of it the following June. We were not only gratified by what we saw of this noble state, but received much valuable instruction on agriculture and the rearing of stock during our short journeying there. It is our intention to see more of this superior section of the country, together with other parts of the west and south, at the earliest opportunity which may offer to accomplish so desirable an object.

29. The schedule of manufactures for the 1850 census of Kentucky lists a bagging factory, operated by C. Schultz in Maysville, valued at $80,000. U.S., Bureau of the Census, *Schedule of Manufactures, Kentucky, 1850* (microfilm in Margaret I. King Library, University of Kentucky), p. 57.

RAMBLES IN THE SWAMPS OF LOUISIANA

*Benjamin Moore Norman (1809–1900) succeeded to the ownership of his father's book store in Hudson, New York. In 1837 he transferred the business to New Orleans, adding printing and publishing to his activities. He was a victim of the yellow fever epidemic of 1841; his health was permanently impaired, and in an effort to improve it he travelled extensively. He wrote two rather widely read travel books—*Travels in Yucatan *(1843) and *Rambles by Land and Water . . . in Cuba and Mexico *(1845)*. He died near Summit, Mississippi.*[1]

My dear Wec:— In looking over one of your old letters to-day, I was reminded of a promise which you swindled out of me when you were with me last, to give you an account of my vagaries for the season. I don't know that you are so generous as not to remind me of the obligation, and besides I

scorn to be beholden to any man's forbearance. So, if you will adjust yourself to a comfortable, and patient frame of mind "*et vacet annales nostrorum audire laborum,*"[2] then the things which I saw and the things which I did, and the way they were seen and done, you shall straightway hear.

You know my passion for pedestrious expedi-

B. M. Norman, "Rambles in the Swamps of Louisiana," *Arthur's Magazine* 1 (January 1844): 9–12.
1. Katherine Bridges, Librarian, Louisiana Room, Northwestern State College of Louisiana, to Jacqueline Bull, 24 July 1969.

2. Virgil *Aeneid* 1.373. A liberal translation of this phrase is, "and leisure to hear the story of our woes." H. R. Fairclough, *Virgil with an English Translation*, 2 vols. (London, 1940), 1:267.

tions. To gratify it and my curiosity at the same time I determined in my humble way, following the example of modern scientific travellers, to investigate the social, political, scientific and religious condition of the Louisiana Swamps.

It had become firmly impressed upon my mind, that if somebody did not do this it would never be done, and by parity of reasoning, if it was never done, that it would be because no one had done it. So without further deliberation or delay, save what was necessary to gather up my "plunder," which consisted of leather trowsers and hunting shirt, and the old companions, my gun and compass, I set forth on the third day of May last, from the Levee on board the "Grace Darling,"[3] determined to make my exodus from the comforts of civilization as heroical as possible by foresaking one of its noblest monuments for the unreclaimed and uninhabitable wilderness. After thirty-four hours contest with that wilful and most obstinate "Father of Waters," I very quietly withdrew from the lists at the beautiful town of Natchez. Here after refreshing myself with a bath, and a most memorable night's rest, for which I desire to be grateful as long as my days shall be in the land, I proceeded to make the inquiries which were to be preliminary to my further progress. They resulted in determining me to proceed westward through the forests or swamps, along the Washita, and thus up into Arkansas, and on to the frontier of Mexico.

It was on the sixth of May at high noon, the thermometer at 90° in the best superterranean shade in the vicinity of Vidalia[4] (a small town in

Louisiana opposite Natchez—whither I had proceeded to take my departure)—indorsed with my knapsack, my gun in hand, and "afoot and alone" that I started for the Washita, distant about thirty-five miles; for which journey I set apart in advance my three first days travel. My first twelve miles, lay along the borders of Lake Concordia,[5] a beautiful sheet of water not less than twenty miles in length. This used formerly to be the bed of the Mississippi; but since she changed her route, this part of her deserted channel has set up for a lake, in which it gets along "excellent well." Seldom have I seen more picturesque scenery than is presented from different points in the margin of this lake, so little known to the travellers on the "lower Mississippi."

The banks are studded with the comfortable looking residences of wealthy planters, who still hold fast to the scenes of their former prosperity, and present honourable repose.

I stopped for the night at the "Panola plantation," where I was received and entertained with a stout and princely hospitality. Early next morning I had breakfasted and was on the road, my route lay through a dry swamp, inhabited chiefly, as I discovered, by charred trees whose leafless and branchless trunks seemed to look at the heavens in grim defiance of all its destructive engineering of elements; they did not move, neither did they regard wind, rain or heat. There they stood, black, lifeless and unsocial, like the ghosts of the once beautiful forest, waiting their silent decomposition and restoration to the earth again. They reminded me of those hapless shades of the departed dead, whom Aeneas encountered on the banks of the

3. A 292-ton side-wheeler built at Louisville, Kentucky, in 1842, this boat was dismantled in 1848. William M. Lytle, comp., *Merchant Steam Vessels of the United States, 1867-1868*, The Steamship Historical Society Publication no. 6 (Mystic, Conn., 1952), p. 78.
4. Vidalia was the first European settlement on the western bank of the Mississippi River between Point Coupée and the mouth of the Arkansas. First settled by the Spanish in 1786, it was later abandoned. In 1801 Don Jose Vidal

established Concord Post. The name was later changed to Vidalia in his honor. *Louisiana Guide*, pp. 466–67.
5. Lake Concordia is an oxbow lake near Waterproof, Louisiana. It was the scene of the murder of a notorious highwayman in 1803 by a gang of highwaymen which included one of the Harpes. Ibid., pp. 596–97.

Styx waiting the lapse of the hundred years fixed for all "*mortis honore carentes*" before they can be permitted to pass the "*stagna exoptata*" to their new estate of being.[6] I trudged along diligently among their dingy ghostships until noon, when finding myself before a settler's hut, I determined to commend my appetite—which had been in training since six o'clock—to the hospitality of its inmates. I found a woman apparently thirty-eight or forty years of age, in an attire, the texture and cut of which must have commended themselves to her taste, chiefly if not entirely for their utility. It was one of those dresses which you may have seen, for I know you are a close observer of these things, so distressingly shapeless that there was no kind of use in putting a pretty figure into it, or making a pretty face look out of it. No power of abstraction could discriminate an angel's face, no power of imagination conceive an angel's figure in such a guise. She was sitting on the rough plank floor of the hut pounding corn, while her nerves were being disciplined by the protracted and tearless screams of a little tow-headed pretty faced child of sixteen months, rolling on the floor beside her. My appearance at the threshold, suspended the nervous discipline of the mother and the pounding of the corn simultaneously. The mother rose from the floor, and while giving my person a thorough inspection from head to foot, and walking around me twice to verify her impressions, permitted me to learn that her *man* was about the woods, that he would be in soon to dinner, that they had lived in these "diggins" fifteen years, during which she had been to the *settlements* but once, and her husband six or seven times. I felt for an invitation to partake of their approaching prandial festivities, but with only partial success. She said she was not

used to getting things for quality folks (as she took me to be—she afterwards informed me—by my glasses), and did not think she had anything good enough for me. I began to feel a little alarmed at this reception, but before I had occasion to urge my necessities, her "man" came in, whose acquaintance I was most happy to make, and perceive was more than king to her, but not more kind to me.

He directed "Mehitable" to stir around at once and get the dinner "fixens" ready, which were already in a state of forwardness. Baked corn and bacon were soon before us, and between my voracious appetite, and a miscellaneous conversation about Millerism,[7] and about my peregrinations which neither of us could understand, I made a very satisfactory dinner. I remember some of the remarks my kind host made, whilst putting on my knapsack, previous to my departure, and they did not quicken my digestion, about the Indians, alligators, wolves, snakes and other varmints, which I should find before I should proceed far upon my route, and then like a good talker who is satisfied with the impression he has made, very cordially bid me good bye. I forgot to say that he spake of some Indian mounds about five miles off my track, and that I had resolved at once to visit them. Traversing the swamp by devious paths and after a very fatiguing walk I reached them, but found nothing to reward my curiosity. These remains of the aborigines—like others I have visited in the south-west, are not all demonstrative. There is nothing in their appearance indicative of their history; and the imagination is provoked to as high activity by a description, as a sight of them. It was dark when I turned my back upon them, when for the first time it occurred to me that I had not

6. These two phrases are from Virgil *Aeneid* 6.330, 333. They are translated, "all those who are bereft of the honor of death," and the "longed for pool." Fairclough, *Virgil with an English Translation*, 1:529.

7. William Miller (1782–1849), leader of the Adventist movement, was born in Pittsfield, Massachusetts. His followers were known as Millerites and his doctrine as Millerism. *Dictionary of American Biography*, vol. 6, pt. 2, pp. 641–43.

bespoken any lodgings for the night. I was not long in debating the course I should pursue. I was immediately on my way back, to the hut of my recent acquaintance. But alas, it is oftentimes given to finite beings, to conceive of things which they cannot execute. Night was upon me before I recovered my path; after struggling more than an hour with the sharpcutting palmettos, the thick long grass and rank vegetation, and stumbling every tenth step over the half concealed logs which overlaid the whole country, and which had probably escaped the attention of the road inspectors, I felt myself quite fagged out, and compelled to take such shelter as the woods could furnish me. I had to reason with myself some time before I could realize that I must positively lie down here in this disgusting all-out-of-doors sort of a place with alligators and wolves, who have no more respect for the laws than if there were no such things, and who would think it a good joke to make sausage meat of me in the midst of my most important dreams without having even the civility to wake me to witness the performance. But my fatigue wrought the conviction which my reason could never have established, so I quietly cast about for the means of tabernacling most comfortably for the night in this dismal solitude. I soon found a large and exemplary looking cypress tree, at the base of which I proceeded to build a fire of such combustibles as were to be found in the vicinity. I had always understood that fire was the best *feraephotic* [8] known to the western traveller, and the tracks of the "varmints" I had observed in the forests had impressed upon my mind already more deeply than perhaps I should like to confess in a mixed assembly, the necessity of some prophylactics besides the gun that lay at my side. With my shirt drawn over my face to protect it from the moschetos, my feet towards the fire, my

8. This appears to be a coinage, meaning the effect of light on wild animals.

knapsack under my head, my gun at my side, and my trust in God, I laid me down at once to rest. I was almost instantly fast asleep. I dreamed that I was trying to ascend the Cordilleras with bare feet and they were so hot that I could not advance, stand still, or recede without burning me. Fortunately for me I did not wait to experiment longer upon the matter, but awoke, and pulled away my feet from the fire, which had taken to the grass and was eating its way along up towards me, and in a half minute longer would have enveloped one of my legs in the flames. It had already disposed of a part of my bed, from which I was at once obliged to migrate. I rose hastily and checked its farther progress, replenished my fire and composed myself again to rest. Near daylight my slumbers were again interrupted in a way which was near being more serious. I heard the crackling of brush and leaves which at first I supposed was occasioned by the fire, but on raising my head, I discovered a wolf taking advantage of my almost extinguished fire to pay me his early respects. I did not wait long to learn his object, indeed I had no curiosity about it, but gently raising my gun to my shoulder, I sent that "*varmint*" to kingdom come without giving him time to wink his acknowledgments. I did not like this interruption, I had heard that there were as many fish in the sea as ever were caught, so there may be as many wolves in the forest as ever were shot. However, as I was ready to attribute his impertinence to the condition of my watch fire, I repaired it once again, and having carefully reloaded my gun, resumed my nap where I left off.

I slept soundly until sunrise, and then rose as much refreshed as from any bed I had ever enjoyed in my life. My first business was to consult my compass, which had now become to me of vital importance. To my utter discomfiture it would not traverse. I shook it a little, then I looked beseechingly at it—it did not stir—what the deuce to do now? Here I was in the midst of this infernal swamp, so thickly shaded with trees that I could hardly see daylight, much less the sun, with nothing to give me any idea of my latitude and longitude, and utterly unable to distinguish North from South, or East from West. Not a sign of a human footstep, or of a human habitation was to be seen, while the tracks of wolves and alligators were to be seen all over the exposed soil, and their traces covered every log. Wild and poisonous vines obstructed my path at almost every step, all around too upon the trees I could descry the marks of former overflows of the adjacent rivers at least a foot above my head. It reminded me that the river was rising when I crossed it, a few days before, and that I should soon perhaps be compelled to betake myself to the trees, and substitute death by starvation, for that by drowning. These *unpleasant* imaginings were not at all ameliorated by the remembrance of a flock of buzzards which I had seen but the morning before holding grand carnival over the carcass of a dead alligator which was lying upon the banks of a stagnant bayou—and then to think too, that, surrounded and hedged in as I was by such a catalogue of menacing calamities, yet I was not probably twenty puffs of a steamboat from the plantation, where I had been so hospitably entertained but a few nights before, I was really alarmed at first at my condition. I now became sick to think, that I had been such an unmitigated goose, as to tempt the devil by such a fool-hardy expedition as this, right into the very jaws of destruction.

I put on my knapsack, and took up my gun, and started to go on in what I took to be an easterly direction, but had not gone far, before, I was reminded that I had eaten nothing since noon of the preceding day. I very soon brought a fine large bird to my feet who was dead before I had an opportunity of inquiring his name, and cooked and eaten before I had felt any curiosity to know it.

The effect of this breakfast was enchanting. My spirits mounted to the level of unconcern before I had half finished, and when I rose from my seat, I felt an involuntary impulse to sing which nothing but the consciousness of being alone among entire strangers enabled me to repress.

I was soon again upon my way, and for three days I journeyed to and fro, and up and down those swamps, being, as I described, but apparently approaching no nearer a better country, or a happier prospect for myself than I opened upon the morning after my first encampment. I finally resolved to build me a house of some kind, and settle down, until my strength should recruit, and, meantime to plan some new mode of extricating myself from the network of calamities, which compassed me about. I selected a place near the bank of what proved to be one of the largest bayous in the state, with a view of being taken up by some boat which might chance to pass by in the progress of events, and transport me from my involuntary seclusion. After gathering together some broken branches of trees and stripping the bark from the bodies of the logs that were lying about, I undertook my first experiment in the science of architecture. I found my work was going to do very well, for my present purposes. It did not aid me much when I contemplated it from a distance after it was finished, in realizing the notion that architecture is frozen music,[9] though if I had been compelled to remain in it during the winter, the result might have been different. I next went out and collected several armfuls of dry leaves for my bed, and large quantities of wood which I piled up near the entrance of my hut for my fire. When I found myself fully established as a householder I took a look at my larder, where I found one gray squirrel, and one

9. Goethe used this phrase in a letter to Eckerman 23 March 1829. Burton Stevenson, *The Home Book of Quotations*, 10th ed. (New York, 1967), p. 95.

red-headed woodpecker. I immediately set about dressing the squirrel and preparing a supper; everything went on prosperously, and I began to feel really happy. When I had finished my supper I replenished my fire, stirred up my leaves and went to bed.

My enjoyment of my new home was of a short duration. The following morning as I was loitering about in the woods in the vicinity of my cabin with my gun in my hand, picking wild berries here and there from the bushes, I heard a noise like that of oars moving in the row-locks of a boat. I ran in the direction from whence the noise came, and what did my delighted eyes fall upon but a boat rowed by two men coming down the stream towards me. I leaped for very joy, and yelled until the woods resounded with my voice, and the frightened birds returned the cry as they flew up in terror from their perches. The attention of the boatmen was immediately arrested by my noise. They pulled in their oars and at the same time reached down to the bottom of their boat, and the next thing I saw was a pair of rifles pointing at me, either one of which could have made a bridge for me between time and eternity, and walked me over it, before I could have uttered the shortest compliments to their promptitude. As they were not frightened, I was not. If they had been however, I fear they would have treated me as I did the wolf, shot me first, and asked my business afterwards. I soon made them understand my condition and receive me into their boat. I never experienced so much pleasure in looking upon any face of man as now upon these two boatmen. They soon observed that I was exhausted with fatigue, and one of them handed me a jug which he commended to me with a sort of welcome I do not know how to describe; to prove my gratitude to him, however, I appropriated about a half pint of its contents in satisfying my suspicions that it was real Monongahela.[10] They then handed me out some corn bread and bacon, with which I was soon very much refreshed. So absorbed was I in the discussion of these stores that I forgot to inquire the destination of my good Samaritans. You can, dear Wic—imagine my delight, when I was told that we were now passing through the bayou to the Lake Concordia, and that we would soon be within magnetic distance of the Seat of the Muses—the home of the Poet of Vidalia.[11]

10. This river, a tributary of the Ohio, has given its name to American whiskey. *Brewer's Dictionary of Phrase and Fable*, rev. ed. (New York, 1965), p. 617.
11. The "poet of Vidalia" has not been absolutely identified. However, Miss Katherine Bridges suggests that it probably was Thomas Bangs Thorpe, whose home was Vidalia. Thorpe, well known as a writer at this time, was in the habit of sprinkling his prose with poetry. Katherine Bridges to Jacqueline Bull, 24 July 1969.

COAL MINING IN VIRGINIA

Edmund Ruffin (1794–1865) was a pioneer in scientific agriculture and one of the outstanding citizens in the pre–Civil War South. He founded the agricultural journal Farmer's Register *in 1833 and edited it for ten years. His attitude toward slavery and secession is grimly delineated by the facts that he was accorded the honor of firing the first shot against Fort Sumter and that upon the collapse of the Confederacy in 1865 he committed suicide.[1]*

While in the neighborhood of the coal mines, I was desirous of descending into, and examing one of them; and my choice was directed to "Graham's Pits," partly by vicinity, and convenience, and still more by the advantage of the company of my old friend Edward Anderson, esq., who is one of the present owners.

The former owner, Graham,[2] a rich old Scotchman, seemed to have had a greater passion for opening new shafts, than resolution and perseverance to exhaust the coal to which each opened. The land is blackened and defaced throughout by the sites of numerous old shafts, and the heaps of slate and remains of refuse coal, which form naked and barren spots forever after. These shafts (or perpendicular pits, through which the coal is lifted), were sometimes within fifty or sixty yards of each other—and at any rate were very far more numerous than was necessary, even if they had been fully worked. But it has since appeared, that from no one shaft was half the coal raised, that might have been, by the means now used—and from many, very little was got out. It seems indeed, as if he dug shafts merely to ascertain the extent and state of the coal bed, and in many cases partially filled and abandoned them, as soon as the coal was penetrated.

I heard several remarkable cases of the ignorance that have sometimes existed in regard to what is beneath the surface of the earth, among persons above, in the immediate neighborhood; and here was one of the most remarkable. When the tract of land was about to be sold, after Graham's death, it was supposed that all these abandoned shafts indicated either exhausted workings, or "seams" of coal not worth working. Graham's mining operations had been superintended and directed entirely by a confidential slave of his own (whom he afterwards emancipated, and then paid $200 a year wages), and the laborers were also slaves; and they, only, knew anything of the condition of the coal. A gentleman who resided then, and still is, within two miles of the works, and who is an intelligent and judicious business-man (and who stated to me these circumstances) was desirous of joining in the purchase of the property; and was authorized by two capitalists to buy it for them and himself, at $40,000, if necessary, provided he could

[Edmund Ruffin], "Notes of a Three-Days Excursion into Goochland, Chesterfield, and Powhatan," *Farmer's Register* 5 (1 September 1837): 315–19.

1. *Dictionary of American Biography*, vol. 8, pt. 2, pp. 214–16.

2. Graham and Havans, merchants from Richmond, opened several pits in a search for coal of good quality. "But these gentlemen, who are neither chemists nor mechanicians, are content to grope their way without applying for advice to more enlightened man, for there is not one person throughout America versed in the art of working mines." Duke de La Rochefoucault Liancourt, *Travels through the United States of America . . . in the years 1795, 1796, and 1797*, 2 vols. (London, 1799), 2: 62–63.

obtain satisfactory accounts of the quantity of coal. The works were then suspended; but all information, from what seemed the best authority, seemed so well to establish that the coal was nearly exhausted, that he felt no longer any inclination to buy, at any price; and the whole tract, of about 1,000 acres, and through which the coal has been reached by shafts for more than a mile of distance, near the line of out-croppings, was sold for $13,000. The operations since, though far from being well conducted, and indeed attended by some causes of heavy loss, have at least shown that the coal is abundant.

A steam engine of ten-horse power is in operation at one of the shafts, drawing off the water accumulated in the old works. Two enormous buckets, each holding 170 gallons, are continually bringing up the water—and the artificial stream thereby formed, which is running continually to the river, and with a pretty equal volume after reaching some distance below, is large enough to turn a mill. The depth of this old shaft is 360 feet, and the water is still 160 feet deep, and will require yet a long time to be drawn off, by the means now in operation.

Two other neighboring shafts are now worked, the depth of neither exceeding 200 feet. The coal is dragged out of the "drifts" or working galleries in "corves," which hold from three to three and a half heaped bushels of coal. These corves are like little sleds, sliding on runners shod with iron. Each loaded corve is attached, at the bottom of the shaft, by hooks to one end of the rope, in place of the empty one sent down, and is rapidly drawn up by two mules, while another emptied corve descends at the other end of the rope. The mules move very rapidly in a circle, to work the drawing machinery, and are turned in the contrary direction at every ascent of a bucket, to reverse the movement of the ropes.

Before descending we had first to take the usual and very necessary precaution of changing our outer clothing for old jackets, trousers, shoes and hats (kept for the purpose) of a quality and fashion not to be hurt by any such exposure. This masquerade dress was not a little ludicrous—but it is so frequently resorted to here, that it is quite a thing of course, and attracts no notice. We had not to be let down the shaft in an empty corve, as is the usual course (and which I have tried elsewhere on a former occasion), as there is a steep sloping tunnel cut for a foot-way. The entrance is through a low and rough door-way, supported, as are the ceilings and sides of the tunnel, by "gearing" or timbers placed thickly for that purpose. The descent through the foot-way was at an angle of about thirty degrees, and is rendered not a little fatiguing by the stooping posture, made necessary by the low ceiling. However, a larger and better graduated foot-way is now constructing which will make the passage sufficiently easy. Each of us carried a miner's lamp, and our lights served to dispel the deep darkness but for a few feet around us. After descending some distance, we came to a hole through which we had to let ourselves down about four feet, into a lower passage. When we got to the coal, the gallery through which we passed was similar to the upper part of the foot-way, except being generally higher, rarely requiring one to stoop, in walking through.

The bed of coal is every where steeply inclined, or "dips" rapidly. The dip here is about thirty degrees, and in other mines it is often much more. Of course, from wherever a new shaft reaches the coal, drifts may be dug, according to their direction, either ascending, descending or horizontal. The plan is to make the first or main drift ascending, or following the greatest ascent of the seam, and to pursue it to the extremity (or out-cropping) of the coal, unless it is so distant that it would be cheaper to dig another shaft. After this main gallery is finished as far as is desired, a drift is carried across it, and near to the shaft, on a level bottom, or nearly so; and others are opened, in succession, similar and parallel to the first cross-drift, and about twenty to forty feet apart from each other. Each successive cross-drift is of course on a higher elevation than the preceding, and all discharge into the first main drift, which serves as the passage from all to the shaft. Afterwards, other drifts are carried parallel to this main passage, and of course, cutting nearly at right angles all the first parallel drifts. When all these galleries are finished as far as the workings are designed to extend, for one shaft, the whole seam of coal through that space is divided into square masses, or "pillars," of twenty to forty feet diameter, and the perpendicular height of the seam of coal.

The drifts are dug from three to five feet wide. When the miner has dug in about two feet (a little more or less, it may be, according to the degree of the solidity of the roof), and the side walls have been made perpendicular, he puts up on each side a prop of green timber, five to eight inches through, with a cross timber extending from over the top of one to the other—and so shaped at the joinings, that the cross-piece cannot possibly be made to slip off, by the enormous perpendicular pressure. These two uprights and one cross piece, when placed thus, and similar ones at every two feet, or thereabouts, form the frame-work of the gearing. Rived timbers about two inches thick are placed over the cross timbers, and close enough together to prevent any falling in of loose rock from above. These split pieces of course are across the cross-timbers or joist-pieces, and therefore run in the same direction as the drift. Other similar split pieces are also soon required, behind the upright side-timbers, as the coal, however solid at first, soon begins to moulder and crumble down, therefore requiring to be in some measure kept up by timbers. This plan of gearing would seem sufficiently laborious and costly, even if permanent;

but it is continually failing, and the timber of every drift requires renewal about once a year—and this not so much on account of rotting, as of the crushing and sinking of the timbers. As we groped along the drifts, I noticed one of the uprights bent to an angle, and splintered, in yielding to the pressure; and remarked to the overseer, who acted as our guide, that his timber there was too small. He answered, as cooly as if we were in day light, "No, it is only the creeping of the metals above our heads." I soon saw plenty of such cases of shivered and yielding timbers, and was surprised to learn that it was not a partial and particular effect, but a general and continued though usually very slow and gradual sinking of the roof, or "creeping" down, as they call it. The side-walls of coal crumble, and run out more or less into the galleries, or otherwise press the props inward. To prevent these being bent or broken inward, lower cross pieces (called "Sampsons") are put between them, to resist the pressure from the sides. But if nothing else gives way, the bottoms of the props gradually break into the foundation of coal or slate below, and sink lower then their original position, and thereby suffer all the gearing, and the roof, to come lower. So it is, however, the roof of a mine that is worked to its full height, and to enough extent, is continually "creeping" down, and generally "tumbles" or falls to the floor, before near all the coal has been removed.

But before any considerable and extensive sinking has taken place, new galleries and enlarged diggings have rendered most of the first diggings useless. After making drifts as above mentioned through the space intended to be excavated, the masses of coal left are "robbed," or reduced in size, throughout, and then are again so reduced a second time. Finally, if not prevented by a previous "tumble" of the superincumbent slate-rock, the whole of the coal, or as nearly the whole as may be, is removed, by beginning at the extreme limit of the working, and then coming on towards the shaft, leaving the roof with no additional timber support; and it usually falls in very soon after the space is emptied and abandoned. In such cases of final operations, a coal mine must present an unusually exciting scene; there being added to the usual matters of interest, the increased apprehension of danger—the rapidity of the excavation, by the concentration of numbers in small space—and successive abandonment of each portion—and by the continual sounds of cracking and crushing timbers, and falling in of masses of the stony roof, in places not many yards distant, and which were excavated by the miners but a few days, or perhaps but a few hours before.

The water, that is always met with in digging coal, if in a new work, is made to drain into a deep pit, under the shaft, whence it is drawn up in buckets, when enough is collected, by the same machinery that draws the coal. In some pits, it is so abundant that the drawing of water and of coal is necessarily carried on together, that is, first a vessel of water and then one of coal. But if there is an older and deeper mine close by, which has been abandoned, the water is easily led there, and thence drawn up, when necessary, by separate machinery, as is done here.

In going through the galleries, we passed different places where miners were "drifting," or digging galleries, and gearing them, to supply the corves which the "trainers" drew off to the shaft. The dragging of the loaded corves seemed to be heavy and oppressive labor. Each man, has a chain fastened by straps around his breast, which he hooks to the corve, and thus harnessed, and in a stooping posture, he drags his heavy load over the floor of rock. Every digger and trainer has his lamp—and their appearance well accords with the gloomy scene of their labors. However, the task may be light enough, though the operations are laborious; and so it would seem, from the fact that the

laborers are permitted to do extra work for their own gain, and that they do earn money in that manner. I even saw afterwards where they had opened two (not very deep) shafts to the coal, for their own private working—though their proceedings had been stopped, and certainly should not have been permitted to be commenced, on so distinct and independent a footing.

At one part of a gallery the carbonic acid gas was so strong that two of our lamps were extinguished, and the third, carried by the guide, was kept burning only by his holding it as high as possible. I had supposed before, that wherever lights would not burn, the respiration must be powerfully affected, and life endangered, by exposure of any length of time; but was surprised to hear that digging was sometimes executed in spots in which no flame could live an instant. But though laborers are not very sensibly affected by a certain degree of exposure, if they continue there long, they become very sick when they reach and breathe fresh air. Finding that the effects were not so powerful and dangerous as I had before supposed, I requested to be carried to where the gas was still stronger. It was generated in an old working of the lower seam, which communicated by some fissure with the lowest drift of this seam, and the working of which had been suspended on that account. I followed the guide to the lowest part of this descending drift. Our lamps, though nursed as carefully as possible, for experiment, went out when we had not reached the bottom by some seven or eight yards of distance. Still at the lowest point, and even when stooping so as to breathe with two feet of the floor, I did not perceive the peculiar smell of carbonic acid gas, nor was I sensible of any inconvenience, after remaining several minutes, except a slight sense of fulness in the head.

As this gas is continually extricated or generated in coal mines, and its great weight prevents its ascending, in still atmospheric air, its accumulation would make any mine unfit to live in, but for the ventilation which is produced by currents of air, directed at will through the galleries. By this means the gas is stirred up, and diluted by mixture of other air, and by throwing it into the ascending current, is continually thrown out of the mine.

A much more dangerous gas, hydrogen, or inflammable air, is evolved in some places and in some mines in large quantities. This comes in through crannies and fissures in the coal, and metal pipes are fixed for it to pass through and being lighted at the upper ends of the pipes, it burns continually, and thus is destroyed. But when it is permitted, by neglect or ignorance, to accumulate in the high galleries (to which its extreme levity carries it), as soon as the flame of a lamp touches it, the whole explodes like gunpowder, and spreads ruin and death around. Last year, in one of the newly worked mines in Chesterfield, this occurred, to such effect, as to cause the work to be stopped, and the value of the property to be lost—at least for the present time.

The seam of coal in the pit which I visited was about ten feet thick. The body here is divided by the interposition of a layer of slate (thirty or forty feet thick) into two seams—and in some mines there are many such separate seams, of various thickness. Seams not more than four feet thick are worked. In some places the interposed slate runs out, and the different seams of coal unite. Such is the case in one shaft of this tract (now unfortunately underwater), where the solid coal was forty-seven thick; and in Chesterfield, in Wooldridge's pit, it was more than fifty feet thick, and in Heth's still more.[3] Neither of these mines are now worked;

but other shafts are now sinking to the same thick seam, which is reached at the depth of about six hundred feet. The operation is [sic] these very deep mines, and in such thick seams, are far more interesting than such as I saw, and which I should have been glad to witness. In them, the coal is blasted by gunpowder, instead of being dug by picks and by hand labor entirely—the loaded sleds are drawn by mules to the shaft—and thence steam engines draw the coal up to the surface.

Where the coal is in two separate seams, the upper is first worked, over a sufficient space and then that beneath is taken out, in like manner, not affected by the filling in, which is still in progress, or finished, of the seam above.

It was on this property that the singular accident occurred about two years ago of filling the whole of a working of the upper seam with water from James River. The mines were then rented out; and the tenant sunk a shaft in the low-ground near the river, and actually extended his excavation under the river, where it is perhaps two hundred yards wide, until within twenty-nine yards of the opposite bank. Still it would have been safe; but for the pillars being left too weak, and the settling of the roof permitting the water above to find entrance, and of course overflowing the works.

After coming out of the pit, I saw the manner in which the coal is carried to the boats on the canal. For this object, the design is very good, and the facilities great—but the execution though recently much improved, is very bad.

A railway has been made from each of the two working shafts to the canal. From the highest, the railway has just been continued across the canal and low-ground to the river—the whole of it being about 600 yards in length. This continuation will permit boats to be loaded when the canal navigation

3. Abraham Wooldridge, Archibald L. Wooldridge, Jane Elam, and Charlotte Wooldridge chartered the Midlothian Coal Company in 1835. The Wooldridge Brothers and John Cobb chartered the Rosewood Coal Mining Company in 1837. Archibald Wooldridge and John Heth chartered the Persons Coal Iron and Manufacturing Company in 1837,

the same year the Wooldridges chartered the Chesterfield Coal Mining Company. Francis Earle Lutz, *Chesterfield: An old Virginia County* (Richmond, Va., 1954), p. 192.

is interrupted, which has been frequently the case, to the great loss of the colliers. The descent will permit the cars of coal to run rapidly the whole distance to the canal—and to the river when required—by the force of gravity alone. The cars carry twenty-seven bushels of coal. Mules are quickly attached at either end. The railway extends on long beams, which turn on a hinge or pivot, over the canal. At the end, there are strong bars of iron curved to fit against and to stop the wheels of the car, and the beams are prevented from yielding to the weight of the car by being confined by a rope. The end of the car (or tail-board), is held by hinges at top, and is kept close by an iron bar, or latch, extending quite across, and fitting into catches at both ends. When in its place, the rope is cut loose, the outer ends of the railway-beams sink, with the car, so as to be considerably inclined; and the latch is struck, and the pressure of the coal against the tail-board throws it open at bottom, and the load slides out into the boat, which had been placed below.

The railway string-pieces are made of scantling four inches by five, and without any iron where the road is straight. Thin iron is on the rails through the length of a curve made to the shaft. I should suppose that there would have been *economy* in having the whole railway lightly ironed, both to prevent wearing away the angles of the rails, and to keep the cars more securely on the track.

The inclination of the railway is so steep that it is necessary to expand considerable power, on part of the route, to retard the rapidity of the cars, by a mechanical contrivance, to regulate which (and to empty the load) a man rides down on the car. On one occasion, the man became alarmed, and leaped off, leaving the car to run down without the usually and necessary obstruction, and such was its acquired velocity, that it bent one and broke off the other of the strong iron bars, intended to stop its course, and leaped across the canal, without

touching the water, and stuck into the bank on which it struck. If the inclination of the railway was better graduated, and a straight course adhered to throughout, it would be quite practicable, on a double track, to make the descent of the loaded cars operate to bring back the empty ones, and so dispense with any other power than gravity. Or if this plan was not simple enough, and mule-power was still preferred to bring back the cars, and hand-power to retard the descent of the loads, still it might be so fixed (as at the Mauch Chunk mines in Pennsylvania),[4] that the mules might *ride down*, on the loaded car, so as to be on the spot to return immediately with the car as soon as emptied. This would save half the travel of the mules, prevent all delay in waiting for their arrival, and also the need for the hand who now rides them down to the canal, or river.

As farming is not the main business of the proprietors of this naturally fertile tract of land, and moreover (as one of them said to me), as colliers are to a proverb negligent of every source of comfort and of profit, except the coal or ore they are in pursuit of, it would be out of place here to describe or criticise the agricultural operations of this estate. It is enough to say, that the farming operations, and state of the farm, present, in all respects, the most perfect contrast imaginable to those of the proprietors' near neighbor Richard Sampson. But, on the other hand, my friend A. assures me that his management is capital on his fine estate on the Appomattox, where farming is the sole object; and that he means to do wonders there next year, and thereafter, as a live-stock

4. In eastern Pennsylvania between Allentown and Wilkes-Barre, the Mauch Chunk settlement was begun in 1815. Coal has been mined here at least since 1820, though its existence was known much earlier. Writers' Program, Pennsylvania, *Pennsylvania: A Guide to the Keystone State* (New York, 1940), pp. 75, 504. Hereafter cited as *Pennsylvania Guide.*

breeder and grazier—all of which operations I hope hereafter to see, and to award to them due credit and praise.

There was however one ditching operation of Mr. Anderson's, on a large scale, which well deserves notice, and imitation, under similar circumstances. An excellent saw and corn mill is turned by water drawn from the canal, at an annual rent. The fall is twenty-two feet, and of course, it was necessary to dig a canal, or race, as deep, from the mill-wheel to the river, several hundred yards. This would have been a heavy job, if executed by spades and barrows; but was effected with great ease, in the following manner. The track was laid off, ten feet wide, and well coultered[5] by a team of oxen. Water was then turned on from the canal, in sufficient quantity, and the current soon swept a passage along the coultered surface, and carried off all the earth as low as it had been well loosened, into the river. The coultering was then begun again, upon the sub-soil, and the current of water being still kept flowing, it washed away every slice almost as fast as it was loosened by the coulter. In this manner, the layers of cutting or digging were made entirely by the coulter, to the full depth required, and the current of water served for the whole lifting and removing power. It being in summer, the flow of water was not hurtful to the team, or ploughman. The sides of the canal were thus carried down as nearly perpendicular as possible, but they have since crumbled in, so as to be sufficiently sloped, and to have width enough at top, the water from the mill serving to carry off all the crumbled earth as fast as necessary.

There was another excavation in progress, which attracted my notice particularly. This was a tunnel which was intended to pass through a

5. A coulter is a knife or a steel disc which is attached to a plough, making a vertical cut in the ground to form the furrow slice.

hill, for the purpose of leading pure water from a well, to supply the steam engine. The water drawn from the coal mine cannot be used for this purpose, as it is strongly impregnated by copperas, and would corrode the boilers—and indeed all the water from wells and springs over the bed of coal is vitiated in like manner; though in but a slight degree. When I went into the tunnel, as far as finished, it had reached thirty-seven yards under the hill. It was dug horizontally through clay and sometimes through sandy and water-yielding earth, about four and a half feet high, and four wide. The man who was digging it advanced the work three feet a day, gearing as he proceeded, as is done in the galleries through the coal. He worked, generally, seated on a low stool, and with a short and light pick, the cutting ends of which were chisel-shaped, and not more than half an inch wide. With this pick, he cuts in about two feet, a narrow opening at the bottom of the tunnel, and the whole width across; then makes a similar narrow perpendicular cut at one side; and then, by striking in wedges, brings down the earth, thus undermined, in large masses. Another hand draws out the earth in a coal-corve. The examination of this tunnelling satisfied me of the practicability and safety with which a like work might be executed through solid marl, wherever required by the great thickness of, and labor otherwise necessary for removing the superincumbent earth. Still, this operation is so slow, that it would be cheaper to dig away twenty feet of over-lying earth, rather than to tunnel beneath it. Notwithstanding, the knowledge of this process, and, still more, of the mode before described of discharging the cars of coal into boats, may be perhaps advantageously applied to the loading vessels with marl on tide water, when that becomes a business worth pursuing—as it most certainly will be, at some future time.

SKETCHES OF SOUTH CAROLINA

These sketches present an intimate and revealing picture of the interior life on a famous rice plantation in the low country area of South Carolina.

NO. III. 'MERRY CHRISTMAS'

The merry days of good old Christmas are still observed in the Palmetto State. While the rest of the world are whirled onward from generation to generation, leaving the times and customs of antiquity far in the distance, and almost forgotten, the loyal landholders of the South remain quietly at home, rejoicing in the undisturbed possession of the heritage of their fathers. It matters not to them that the spirit of improvement holds the reins of the age, and is driving on over the manners and mysteries of our worthy sires; they gaze and admire, perchance, but are still untempted to try its speed or to trust themselves to its destiny.

Even in the far upland country, among those who have wandered from the ancient homesteads into the deep pine forests, is the keeping of fasts and holydays religiously observed. There, in the long solitude which no season breaks; where winter succeeds to summer with hardly a change upon the surrounding landscape; where neighbors intrude not, nor thoroughfares, with their rumbling coaches and loaded wains, and bustling market-men ever come; and where even the factor's visit, to bargain for the yearly crop, is almost doubtful; there the annual return of days of leisure and merriment is never disregarded. Easter, Lent, Candlemas, Shrovetide come and go, each recognized by these honest descendants of the High

Church cavaliers,[1] and each respected as its merits claim. They are the land-marks of the year, these red-letter days of the calendar; the way-stones, without which old Time would lose the reckoning of his circuit, and be plunged into the thickets and quagmires which beset his journeyings. Long before they come in sight are they thought of and looked after by the heedful housewives, who guide the households; and to pass them without the proper ceremonies which custom and church have prescribed from immemorial antiquity, would be little better than high treason to the government of Heaven.

It is not here, however, that one can expect to find Christmas holydays in all their glory. The upland planters, in these days of diminished profits upon their staple product, are too poor to make a show, even upon their festivals. The currency, on which their's more than any other calling of our people is dependent, has made sad havoc in its changes, with their wealth and income; and like the subjects of a vacillating tyrant, they have suffered more from the whims and caprices of power, than they would have done from the equitable enforcement of the most rigid laws. All over the State the upland cotton-growers are

---

"Sketches of South-Carolina, Number Three: 'Merry Christmas'; Number Four: 'Slaves and Slavery,'" *Knickerbocker Magazine* 21 (March, May 1843): 222–29, 333–48; 22 (July 1843): 1–6.

1. Historians have referred to this theory of the settlement of the southern coastal region as the "cavalier myth" or "cavalier tradition." Clement Eaton, *Freedom of Thought in the Old South* (Durham, N. C., 1940), p. 48; Clement Eaton, *Mind of the South* (Baton Rouge, La., 1964), p. 191; Wesley F. Craven, *The Southern Colonies in the Seventeenth Century, 1607–1689*, The History of the South (Baton Rouge, La., 1949), p. 247.

poor; their debts are unpaid; their crops unsold, their labor unproductive; and if a change come not soon, they must without exception be reduced to abject penury.

On the rice plantations, however, it is not so. Like the soil of the Sea Islands, these rich river bottoms yield a product which competition can never force below its real value. The landholders of the low country are affluent, living in all the luxury which taste and refinement can bestow; and though composing but a small proportion of the great mass of the population of the State, they are its representatives abroad, and its excellence and glory at home. It is here that Christmas days come arrayed in their holly-green of the olden time. The ancient mansions ring with the joyousness of light-hearted youngsters, from the merry greetings of its first daybreak to the magic ceremonies around the cake which crowns its twelfth night. All business and care are banished from the household; the plans and calculations of other days are religiously laid aside; the work of the field is suspended; the routine of duties which move the numerous operatives of the plantation from day to day is broken up; the plough and spade, and delver lie in the long sheds in unmolested repose; and every movement in master and man indicates the return of the planters' jubilee.

The preparations for Christmas are noticeable long before its coming. The first frosts of November, banishing all fear of the malarious atmosphere, give the signal for return from the summer's wanderings; and carriage after carriage, with distended boots and cumbrous luggage, may be seen winding along the heavy road, or turning into the narrow pathway which leads to the secluded plantation. Then come the arrangements for the season; and while the ladies of the manor direct the changes in the mansion, the master investigates the doings of men and overseers abroad. The check-book is hastily looked over and laid

aside for a more thorough examination; the storehouses are visited, and their contents measured with a careful eye; the old and sick are greeted within their cabins, and tokens of remembrance bestowed on the deserving; and praise or blame, reward or punishment is meted out to the anxious people of the field, as each has done his duty. Within doors all is bustle and confusion. Carpets are to be laid, curtains hung, tables waxed, beds corded, and the paraphernalia of household preparations hastened forward to completion. Days, and sometimes even weeks, hardly bring about the contemplated changes; and while the planter rides about his grounds, or saunters with dog and gun into the neighboring woods, the busy housewife luxuriates in her undisturbed control over the metamorphoses in the domicil.

As the festival approaches, visiters from the city begin to make their appearance. The advocate, who claims an acquaintance with his host in college days; the factor, whose mill has husked the rice and whose ware-houses have stored it for many years; the superannuated beau of the maiden-aunt, whose yearly visits have almost encouraged her to deem him an accepted suitor; the parish member, the chance acquaintance at the Springs, the distant cousin; all find a reason to spend the Christmas holydays at the plantation, and all are welcomed and cared for with unstinted hospitality. My invitation had come from a son of one of the Georgetown planters; and though I resolutely declined to accept it, on the ground of important business which could not be postponed, it would not avail, and on the morning of the twenty-fourth of December we started for the country.

It was as bright a day as the most fastidious wooer of nature could ask. Our horses had been sent to the other side of the river the previous evening, and at the first sound of the ferryman's horn we were at the landing and on board. In a moment the boat was pushed off from her moorings, the mules began to pull, the driver to halloo, the chains to creak, and the wheels to dash; and the old hulk, heading hard up the stream, moved slowly and heavily into the sluggish current. I confess to no romance on board a horse-boat, though in more senses than any other sea-craft, she may be said to "walk the waters like a thing of life";[2] yet there was something that morning in the beauty of the scenery around the Ashley, which I can never forget. The frost of the night had covered the thick surge-grass,[3] which extends for miles along the banks, with myriads of icicles, whose tiny points glowed and sparkled in the dawning, making the marshes seem like fairy pearl forests. The city, stretching from river to river, without a single elevation, lay in her repose graceful as a swan upon the waters. The dense woods of James's Island in the far distance, apparently unlighted by a single ray of morning, and the bleak sides and mounted ordnance of Castle Pinckney,[4] frowning just before us; the crowded shipping around the wharves, and the solitary brigs in the offing; the tall spire of old St. Michael's catching the first rays of sunlight; the streaks in the east, brightening as morning advanced and mirrored in the waters; the smoke curling upward from the chimneys; and high above all, the buzzards wheeling their lazy flight through the air; all made up a picture not brighter or fairer, but beautiful as the Morning ever shows to him who

2. George Gordon, Lord Byron, *The Corsair*, canto 1, sect. 3, line 11.
3. Dr. Paul Tabor, Athens, Georgia, has suggested that this might be a corruption of the name "sedge grass." John W. Bonner, Jr., Special Collections Librarian, University of Georgia, to Jacqueline Bull, 7 April 1969.
4. James's Island is one of the islands in the harbor of Charleston. Castle Pinckney, on a small island in the harbor, was begun when war with France was feared in the 1790s. It served as a prison for Federal troops during the Civil War. Robert Mallory, *Charleston: A Gracious Heritage* (New York, 1947), pp. 3, 83, 103.

loves to meet her in the glen or on the waters, and to greet her, the rosy-fingered, like an old school-boy friend.

.   .   .   .

The sun had set, and it was full night; the stars winking and glimmering above us, serving us with light sufficient only to see the road, and to make the long moss from the oaks seem like sheeted ghosts as we rode rapidly on, when we came to the gate of the wild-orange hedge which enclosed the plantation. Alighting from my horse, my companion wound a stirring note from the conchshell which hung by the post, when presently the old portress, with lantern and keys, issued from her lodge in the grove, to give us admittance. "Is this Deacon Cooper's plantation, Mammy?" inquired my merry companion, in a tone of mock gravity, as the old servant swung open the gate; "does Deacon Charles Cooper live here?"

"Why! Massa Charles! Massa Charles!" exclaimed the old woman, as the voice struck her ear; and then throwing the light of the lantern into his face, she cried out in assurance, "It is Massa Charles heself! How do, Massa Charles? How do? Me so glad to see you, Massa Charles! Me know you come hom' Christmas to see old Dinah! Old Massa be 'lighted to see you, Massa Charles! He been talking 'bout you a' day long!"

"And how are they all at the house, Mammy?"

"Well, Massa, bery well! Dey all spending Christmas eve in de old hall. Massa got gemmen an' ladies, an' minister, an' doctor, an' eber so many buckratos, an' having a great time dis eve! Won't Massa Charles com' in and see old Dinah?"

"Not now, Mammy! I'll come and see you to-morrow! We will leave the horses here for Chestnut to take care of, and will walk up to the house": and so, fastening our horses to the gate, while old Dinah went on talking, we proceeded up the avenue.

The plantation of Major Cooper was situated upon the rich peninsula, which the Pedee rivers form above the point of their junction. The rice-fields, diked into regular plots of twenty acres, lay contiguous to each other on the banks of the stream, where they could be alternately flowed and drained as the crops might require. On a gentle elevation, some half a mile back, commanding an extensive view of woodland and water, with its broad esplanade of massive oaks in front, and its terrace of evergreen and shrubbery sloping from the rear toward the streamlet that bounded it in the distance, stood the irregular pile of buildings which composed the manor-house. Courts, piazzas, wings with their gable ends and quaint turrets, kitchens, cottages, sleeping apartments disconnected from the main buildings, and quiet little domicils under the trees, were mingled together in so strange a confusion, that, but for the guiding of my companion I should have sought in vain the entrance to such a labyrinth. As we approached the central mansion, and the largest of the group, bright lights appeared gleaming from the windows, and uproarious shouts of laughter fell upon our ears.

Excited by expectation, my friend suddenly opened the door, near which we had stood for a minute, and the scene that burst at once upon us was beautiful as a vision of angels. In the midst of a group of uncles, aunts, cousins, and neighbors, all seated in a circle around a large room, were half a dozen girls, the oldest of whom might have been twelve years, playing blind-man's buff. The grandfather of them all, a placid, gentlemanly man, whose head was white with the touch of time, but whose heart was young as in the days of childhood, presided over the game, and was the arbiter in all cases of dispute. The others sat quietly by, aiding the petted youngster in her efforts to escape, and watching the groping of the blinded one, as she carefully followed the footsteps of the timid hiders,

or darted suddenly upon some more daring one at her side. Clustered in the corners and behind the chairs and tables, were the colored boys and girls, evincing in their laughing eyes and merry shouts the interest they took in the sport, and ever and anon darting across the floor in the increasing spirit of the game. Our entrance suspended but for a moment the mirthfulness of the party, and after the cordial greeting and hearty welcome had been given, the merriment went on. Game succeeded game; "hunt the slipper," "hot cockles," "puss in the corner," "who has the bird," treading on the heels of one another, until a late hour of the night. It was a family picture, beautiful as earth can produce; the mingling of old hearts and young, bound by the ties of affinity through three generations. It was beautiful; and my recollection is now hallowed by the thought, that one, the oldest and gentlest of that fairy group, who, when the play was finished, so sweetly and mournfully sang the Christmas ballad that tears fell from many eyes, is now, on this next returning anniversary of the Saviour's birth, doomed to be mute on earth, but hymning his praise in heaven. As we separated for the night, my hostess, whose stately figure, then somewhat bent beneath an easy weight of most venerable years, must once have been queenliest among even the beautiful forms of the South, came and bade me anew a hearty welcome to the Christmas gathering. My quarters were in a neat little cottage, some distance from the suite of rooms occupied by the family, and the servant who accompanied me thither, and who, according to a custom seldom dispensed with in the old mansions of the South, slept in the room on his blanket beside my bed, was unusually intelligent and communicative. I was not a little interested in his account of himself and his fellow-servants, and with the devotion he manifested to the family of his master. "But do you not want your freedom,

John?" I asked in reply to one of his expressions of love to his master and home. "Would you not like to be your own man?"

"An' what me do den, you tink, s'pose me had me freedom? Who tak' care of me when me sick? Who provide for me when me old? No! no! Me no want me freedom. Massa tell me an' Ben we might hab our freedom spose we go North and live wid him every summer when he com'; but me tink it a over, and me say, No, massa; Ben an' me stay here wid you." And I afterward learned that such has been the case. After the protective laws were passed in South Carolina, forbidding slaves to be brought into the state,[5] Major Cooper offered to two of his slaves their freedom and money to commence business, on condition that, for the same wages they could get elsewhere, their services should be rendered to his family every summer during their northern visit. They asked two days to reflect upon the proposal, which were granted. On the third morning, presenting themselves, before the Major, he asked: "Well boys, what do you say? Ben, will you go north?"

"No, t'ank you, Sir! d'rather not!"

"John, will *you* go?"

"Yes Sir, me go north when *you* say so; on 'spress condition, that me come back when *me* say so!"

"Ah, John, that will never do; I want you to go north and stay. Eh?"

"Den me say," was the quick reply; "den me say, like Ben, *No Sir!*"

I was awakened the next morning before sunrise by the chanting of a Christmas hymn beneath my window. Perceiving that John had left the room, I arose, and looking cautiously from the corner of the lattice, that I might not be discovered, found that a group of little negro girls, dressed in their favorite colors of green and white, were rendering their morning salutations to the various members of the family. The words of the hymn ran nearly thus:

> Brightly does the morning break
> In the eastern sky; awake!
> Cradled on his bed of hay
> Jesus Christ was born to-day.
> Let a merry Christmas be,
> Massa, both to me and thee!

This was sung, with a slight variation, two or three times; and then whispering together for a moment, the blithe party scampered off to another chamber to repeat the same ceremoney. I learned afterward from John that this was an old custom on the plantation, which the master, who was a great stickler for the merits of all ancient manners, would never allow to be dispensed with; and that, beginning beneath his own window, it was repeated until all had been awakened by the Christmas welcome.

I was pleased with this little relic of good old English days, among a people separated from the mother country in political connection for more than half a century, and in custom and habit a far longer time. But I was still more pleased to find another custom was in favor, and that even in this land, far away from the young vrouws and mynheers who are his special favorites, Santa Clause makes his annual round. Spirit of Peter Stuyvesant! Bless thee for the mantle of protection thou didst throw over thy guardian saint! Shade of Oloffe Van Kortland![6] rest thou in paradise, for wooing

5. Several laws were passed in South Carolina making it illegal to bring slaves into the state either from another state or from the West Indies or Africa. The first of these laws was passed in 1787. Elizabeth Donnan, *Documents Illustrative of the History of the Slave Trade to America*, 4 vols. (New York, 1965), 4:494.

6. Oloff Van Cortlandt is pictured in Washington Irving's *A History of New York* as dreaming of a visit from Saint

to this distant land the household divinity of thy ancestors! Manes of the burghers of New-Amsterdam! Thrice honored be your memories, that the idol of your worship, supplanting every saint of latter days, outliving every saint of olden time, from year to year increasing in his sway, is now the spirit of our land, bringing pleasant gifts to the children of bondmen and free, and making joyful hearts in the house of master and of slave!

After breakfast, the whole family attended public worship. I never saw a more perfect picture of beautiful repose than that small church and burial-ground and rectory (all combined and embowered within a space that the eye could take in at a single glance) presented to the beholder. The church was constructed of a rough gray stone, which gave it the antique appearance one likes to see about places of worship in the country. The sunlight, streaming upon the long east window, lighted it up with a glowing refulgence, while the strongly-defined shadows marked out the rude tracery of the low tower, and the heavy work of the massy buttresses, patched with green and yellow moss, which glowed bright as emerald. Within, all was simple and purely classic in its style and order; and the worshippers assembled were representatives of some of the oldest families of the state. Remote from kindred, and from all the friendships that were the growth of the fair fields and green hill-sides where my boyhood and youth had roamed, and from the sacred places where I had meditated and learned God's praise, I had never found so much satisfaction in the worship. How sank the Christmas service of the beautiful litany that day in all our hearts! How rose the feelings of gratitude, when the deep organ began to breathe forth its solemn sounds, and the youthful voices

Nicholas. Cortlandt, who died in 1684, was a Dutch colonist and magistrate of New York. *Century Dictionary and Cyclopedia*, 9: 1026.

to join the diapason! And as the eyes were fixed on the picture over the altar, of our Saviour

Bearing his cross up rueful Calvary,

what deep emotions filled every bosom!

. . .

NO. IV. 'SLAVES AND SLAVERY'

No sketches of any Southern State of the Union can faithfully present its features to the reader without bringing into view the great population of slaves. Of South Carolina is this especially true, for there not only do the bond-men outnumber the free, but the customs of society, the laws, the daily pursuits, the very habits of thought and expression, and life, are all inwrought and interwoven with this great institution so intimately, that it is recognized in every movement and forced upon you at every hour. The bell that sends its loud summons over the city at night and morning; the twilight reveillé of the city guard; the clanking of the musket under your window in the depth of midnight; the trained-bands mustering at every alarm of fire; the loud cry of the watchman sounding from ward to ward at each quarter of the hour until it dies far away in the distance; all declare to you that you live and walk and sleep in a land of slaves. You see it in the market, where the German soldier strides up and down through the long, crowded avenue the live-long day. You hear it on the bustling mart, in the excited exchange, through the rattling streets. You find it every where; and at the buoyant party or the social dinner, in your morning stroll or evening siesta, there is upon you a restraint awkward and irksome beyond endurance.[7]

And yet if the picture can be varied by lighter shades, why not so regard it? The heart which

7. A full discussion of these regulations is given in Richard Wade, *Slavery in the Cities* (New York, 1964), pp. 80–110.

would oftentimes be repelled from the hideous deformity of human misery, is attracted by some fair proportions which ally it to its species, and by gazing upon what does not revolt the feelings, becomes itself partaker of the untoward lot, and bound by new ties to aid the sufferer. For myself, it has not been in the shocking descriptions of itinerant enthusiasts or the revolting vignettes of newspaper and pamphlet that I have found my sympathies most awakened for the slave; but in his quiet cabin, at his allotted task, by the way-side or on the water, where I have learned his happy nature, and recognized him as a fellow-man and brother.

There is no one trait of character which the colored race possess that is so remarkable as their *habitual cheerfulness*. Wherever you find the negro, in city or country, at the house or plantation, eating his scanty meal in the pine forests of North-Carolina, or following the lumbering wheels of the Kentucky wagon to the distant market, at play or work, hungry or satiated, he is ever disposed with philosophic equanimity, to make the best of his condition. Even at the auction-sale, that place of all others where slavery appears in its naked deformity,[8] he rarely loses his hilarity; and if he can but manage to be sold at a price below his real value, he is abundantly contented. Were it not that the better feelings of one's nature suffer so rude a shock at these marts of human flesh, the contest that is constantly going on between the auctioneer and slave, the seller and sellee, would be sufficiently amusing. To bring a low price; to stand his master in a sum so small that he shall feel no necessity to overtask his laborer, is the constant object of the party being sold; while the auctioneer is equally strenuous to gain the highest offer. The one of course recommends; the other

8. Wade says that the public auction "became for the enemies of slavery the symbol of the whole regime." Ibid., p. 201.

depreciates; the latter extols the capacities and excellence, the honesty and virtues of the slave he offers, while the former meets him at every step with the flattest contradictions.

"Here, gentlemen," cries the auctioneer, "here is something you don't often see! Look at this man and woman, and just see those children! The finest lot I ever offered for sale! What will you give?"

The last words are not out of his mouth, when men, women, and children cry out simultaneously:

"Aint a fine lot! aint a fine lot!"

"Well, gentlemen," continues the auctioneer, "come, give us a bid! This is a prime fellow!"

"Aint a prime fellow!"

"Why, yes you are a prime fellow, Caesar!"

"No! aint a prime fellow, either!"

"What's the reason you are not a prime fellow? What's the matter?"

"Got a lame leg, and never able to finish my task in time, Sir. Massa knows me aint a prime fellow!"

"Oh, pshaw! nonsense, Caesar! You're lazy, that's all the difficulty. What will you give, gentlemen? One hundred dollars! Only one hundred dollars for this prime lot of negroes!"

"Aint a prime lot! Aint a prime lot!"

"One hundred dollars! One hundred and fifty! fifty! fifty! One hundred and fifty dollars!—only one hundred and fifty! Why gentlemen, you don't know what you are losing. Look at that woman! Isn't she a prime wench? Only one hundred and fifty dollars a-piece for this prime lot of negroes!"

"Aint a prime wench! aint a prime wench! aint a prime lot! aint a prime lot!" comes up in tones so shrill and rapid from the parties to be sold, that the auctioneer is oftentimes forced to cease his recommendations, and to cry only the prices that may be offered.

In this contest between the seller and the slave, it often happens that the latter, by insisting upon his defects, gains the advantage, and is sold far down below his real value. Then the congratulations of his fellows upon his success, after he has left the stand, know no bounds, and the fortunate chattel becomes the hero of the morning.

I remember stepping, last summer, into the "Vendue Range"[9] (the chief market for slaves in Charleston), while a large sale of plantation-hands was going on, to look up a person whom I wanted to see. As I came within the enclosure, an old man had just been. put upon the stand for sale. My attention was drawn toward him from the extreme decriptitude he manifested, as he stood, withered, bowed down, and almost helpless, upon the table of the auctioneer. A shudder seemed to run through the crowd of buyers, in seeing so aged a person exposed for sale; and even the auctioneer himself, little accustomed as he was to manifest a sympathy for his victims, seemed shocked as he reluctantly cried out: "Well, gentlemen, what will you give for the old man?" A moment's silence followed, when a gentleman taking compassion upon the poor fellow answered: "I'll give you ten dollars for him!" "Knock him off! knock him off!" cried several voices; "don't keep the old man up there!" and the auctioneer knocked him down at ten dollars. No sooner had his hammer struck the board, and the words "sold! take him down!" fallen upon the old man's ear, than a perfect metamorphosis took place in his whole appearance! Straightening himself up, with a nod of gratitude to his buyer, he clapped his hands together with a hearty "Good! good! me hab easy times now!" and with an agility that a moment before would have seemed miraculous, sprang from the stand to the ground, and running to a corner of the Range, received the congratulations of his fellows upon his successful and well-managed ruse.

That there are *instances* of extreme personal abuse of the slaves, of wanton cruelty in their treatment, of reckless violation of domestic ties, and of egregious wrong for base and mercenary purposes, cannot be denied. Unlimited power is always subject to abuse. But to represent these instances as examples of the whole, and to draw from them conclusions against the great majority of the masters, is manifestly unjust. It is not from the physical condition of the slave that the great argument against the institution is to be drawn. Custom all over the world is infinitely stronger than law, and custom in the slave States prescribes less labor from the servant and better treatment from the master, than in any free country in the world. Lord Morpeth[10] remarked, with his characteristic simplicity and plainness, after he had passed several weeks upon the plantations of the Cooper and Ashley rivers: "I am an Englishman, and cannot be expected to yield my strong predilections for free labor; but yet I will frankly say, that I have never seen in Europe, a class of peasantry, exposed to so few deprivations, or apparently so happy in their condition, as are the slaves of South Carolina." The testimony of every unprejudiced traveller over the Southern States has ever gone to corroborate the same; and he, who doubts that, as a class, the slaves are cheerful, contented, and happy, should mingle with them during their work-hours upon the plantation, or visit them in their humble cabins, or listen to their merry laugh ringing from house to house in the afternoons of summer, or through the winter evenings.

It is not in the physical condition of its subjects that the great argument against the institution of slavery is to be found. It is the moral and intellectual degradation in which the slaves are found,

9. The wharves of the Clyde Line steamships occupy the site of the old slave market on the Vendue Range. *South Carolina Guide*, p. 204.

10. George W. F. Howard, Lord Morpeth, an English statesman, was chief secretary for Ireland, 1835-1841. *Century Dictionary and Cyclopedia*, 9: 515.

and which is not incidental only, but essential to the very existence of the system, which constitutes the true argument against it. Here is its weakness; here lies the whole gist of its wrong. It stupefies the soul, and does it purposely. It blinds the eye of reason, and shuts truth from the heart. It pampers the body, and starves the mind. And the very last trace of God's image in his creature man is defaced and blotted out. For all this the master is not to be blamed, but the system; and hundreds of thousands of good men at the South mourn over it as an evil which they cannot cure. Let us thank God that they *do* so mourn it, and, like brethren good and true, lend them our hearts and hands to banish it from our land!

The slaves upon the plantations are far more ignorant then those who live in the cities. The latter, from their constant intercourse with the whites, become shrewd, acute, and oftentimes very intelligent. Indeed, it is not unfrequent that the favorite house-servants are taught to read and write, and even to cipher in the fundamental rules of arithmetic. As a general thing, however, their intelligence is manifested in conversation only; and the efforts made to instruct them in what Mrs. Malaprop calls the "obnoxious sciences,"[11] are entirely thrown away. Especially in *numbers*, even in those simplest combinations which we teach our children in their earliest years, are they ignorant beyond belief. My attention was first called to this surprising deficiency in their knowledge, in the first settlement I ever made with my laundress, a very respectable, middle-aged woman, whose conversation and manners were much above her class. "Well, Minta," I asked, "how much do I owe you now?" She replied by stating, that on such a day she had washed a dozen and two pieces,

11. A careful examination of Richard Sheridan's play *The Rivals* does not reveal this quotation. Perhaps the writer meant that this was a phrase Mrs. Malaprop might have used.

on another a dozen and three, on another a dozen and one, and so on, reckoning by a dozen and fractions of a dozen and leaving me to make up the amount. She then enumerated the moneys she had received; as, for instance, once a dollar, next half a dollar, then seven-pence, then four-pence; specifying *coins* each time, until I had put upon paper the full sum she had received. Casting up the several columns and subtracting the difference, I said: "You want just one dollar and sixty-nine cents, Minta, do you not?"

She looked at me with a half-amazed stare, and replied: "Me don't know what you mean, Massa!"

"Why I mean that I owe you one dollar and sixty-nine cents!"

"Me don't understand you, Massa; me don't know what you mean!"

Supposing she had made some mistake in her own reckoning of the bill, I again enumerated the items and stated the result, but with no better fortune than before. Minta still replied: "Me don't understand you, Massa!"

"Well, Minta," I said at last, as the only hope of an amicable settlement, "tell me what you think I owe you, and I'll pay it."

She reckoned a moment upon her fingers and said: 'You owe me, Massa, *one dollar, half a dollar, seven-pence, and four-pence*.'

"Well done, Minta!" said I, "that is just what I told you myself!"

"No, Massa!" was the characteristic reply; "you no tell me dat! *You say sixty-nine cents; me say half dollar, seven-pence, and four-pence!*" And yet Minta was a house-servant more than usually bright and intelligent, and had always lived in Charleston.

Among the market-men and women, however, and in the mechanic trades, there is generally great quickness in reckoning and making change, and rarely an error in the result. Some few, indeed, extend their knowledge even beyond, what the necessities of their business require, and become distinguished in their caste as literary *savans*. I once saw a communication which had been sent for insertion to the editor of a southern literary magazine, and which, malgré the orthography, contained all the elements of a well-told tale, that had been composed and written by a slave. Above all others however, in the literary line, stands BILLY the Jew; the blackest, raggedest, shrewdest, quickest, richest, and honestest slave in the whole State of South Carolina. Billy is not only a Jew in name but by descent, and claiming through the African Israelites, the paternity of Abraham, he is admitted to the rights and enjoys all the privileges of the wealthy synagogue. In Hebrew and Arabic, Billy is an accomplished scholar; and there are few who excel him in a thorough and critical knowledge of the Old Testament scriptures. With the true instinct of his race, he has hoarded up from his little earnings no small amount of money, but with a penuriousness that one can hardly understand, he utterly refuses to purchase his freedom, and daily performs his allotted task. To one curious in such matters, Billy has secrets in regard to the African Jews that would while away many a long summer's day, and which a golden key would not fail to unlock for the benefit of his generation.

But these instances of intelligence are found only in the city. Over the whole territory of the South, the slave is elevated in intelligence and intellect but a little above the brutes that perish. Every avenue to knowledge is shut out from him. His place of residence, his origin, his country, his age, his rights, he knows nothing of. Alas! he knows not even his destiny! There is his task, and he performs it; there his food, and he eats it; there his humble cabin, and he lies down to sleep. But the *spirit* within him, the home prepared for it by a SAVIOUR's love, the GOD who bends the blue sky above him, he knows not of. For the wealth of worlds I would not be the owner of such a slave. Not that I *blame* the master, for with the kindest feelings of a brother's heart I *pity* him. And if the petition of an erring soul can reach the sanctuary of the Great Spirit above, in the utter inability of human reason to devise a remedy for this great evil, mine could only be "GOD look in mercy alike upon the master and the slave!"

It was as beautiful an evening as a lover could ask, the second day of April, 1842, that I bade my friend Dana good-bye, and started in my sulky for a tour over the land of Nullification. I left Charleston in the evening, that the wearisome task of crossing the river might be over, and the earlier start upon my journey be made the following morning. Tarrying at the house of a fine old planter during the night, who amused me until nearly cock-crowing with his long stories of revolutionary days, I arose, after a very slight refreshment from sleep, and was on my way toward Georgetown an hour before sunrise. It was a toilsome way enough, the road running parallel with the sea-shore the whole distance of sixty miles, just far enough inland never to catch a glimpse of the water, and leading you over a dreary pine barren, where neither house, cultivated field, nor flowing streamlet occurred to divert your attention for the whole day. It was pleasant enough at first to feel one's self alone in those boundless forests of pine; and for an hour or two of the early morning I was sufficiently amused by the novel sight of some young alligator splashing into the water from the road-side as the noise of my wheels awoke him from his siesta, or of a huge moccasin darting away beneath the dense reeds and lily-pads of the swamp, or of the ever-varying, myriad-toned music of the mocking birds who filled the air with their melody. But by degrees, as the sun began to rise above the trees, and the heavens to assume that brazen face which characterizes a southern sky, the never-changing scenery about me grew dull and wearisome, and I found myself looking forward in the hope of finding some place by the roadside where my horse might slake his thirst. No such place, however, appeared; on and onward we jogged over that apparently unending level of creaking sand, without one sign of human industry or human life. As matters began to grow serious, and my weary steed to manifest symptoms of dissatisfaction which could not be mistaken, a kind Providence sent a fellow-being along my path, in the shape of the most hideous, tattered, and woe-begone negro I have ever seen—my first specimen of a plantation servant. The poor fellow's face and garments, however, sadly belied him; for upon my salutation of "Boy, good morning; can you tell me where I can find water for my horse?" he touched his rimless hat and most civilly replied:

"Oh, yes, Massa! dere is fine water just back ob you!"

"Back of me?" I replied. "Strange I did not see it!" and turning my horse to retrace the path, the negro discovered my greenness, and laughing, said:

"Why, Massa, you 'ab no bucket to water de horse!"

"Bucket?" I inquired in astonishment! "Bucket? What do you mean, boy? What *do* you mean?"

The poor fellow could scarcely contain his gravity, while he replied, pointing to the bottom of the sulky: "Sure, Massa 'ab no bucket! Massa no bin long in Carolina to tink water he horse widout bucket! Every body hab bucket on carriage in Carolina!"

Here was indeed a perplexity of which I had never dreamed, and to extricate myself from which more than surpassed my share of even Yankee shrewdness. I could not think of driving fourteen long miles back to my morning resting-place in the heat of that torrid sun, nor of going forward the twelve miles to my first stopping place on the

Georgetown road; and yet, from all the information I could gain from the negro, these seemed the only conditions upon which horse or driver were ever again to meet with the proprieties of civilized existence. In utter despair I looked up to my informer, with a respect I had never bestowed upon tattered garments before, and asked: "Boy, what *am* I to do?"

"Don' know, Massa! Neber see a carriage wid'out bucket afore! Don' know, Massa!"

Though my informant had hitherto evidently been greatly amused at my perplexity, the despair of my countenance, or his pity for the jaded beast, now awakened his sympathies; and after scratching his head—a manipulation which the negro invariably performs when he is in trouble—he suddenly rolled the whites of his great eyes up to me and said with quickness, "Me tink, now, Massa! Me tink how Massa water he horse!" and plunging into the woods, presently returned with his *hat* filled with water. It was a capital thought, and the promptitude of its execution would have done honor to a Connecticut pedler. My dilemma was over; the negro's hat of water was a goblet of ambrosia to my steed; and the tattered son of Ham became in my eyes fair as a messenger of the gods.

Between the Ashly and Santee rivers, a distance of more than thirty miles, there are upon the main thoroughfare but three dwelling-houses. Upon the banks of the latter, one begins first to see something of the wealth of the Carolina rice-plantations. For many miles up and down the North and South Santee rivers, which are here separated but a single mile, are cultivated those deep rich bottoms, annually flowed and inexhaustible in resource, which are the glory of the State. The lordly owners of these manors pass the winter months in superintending the affairs of the homesteads, gathering about them all those luxuries which minister to ease and pleasure, of which none better understand the value, or select with more taste, than do these descendants of king Charles's cavaliers, and entering with a zeal and alacrity into those rural sports which are the zest and glory of a southern country life. Finer horsemen, more skilled marksmen, on the plain or in the forest, hardier frames for pugilistic feats, or a quicker eye and prompter hand for a game at fence, the world cannot produce. They are generally men also of liberal learning and generous dispositions; frank, hospitable, and courteous; and, bating a tithe of that hot-blood chivalry upon which they are too apt to pride themselves, noble and humane in all their impulses.

One marks every where at the South the eminently kind relations which exist between master and servant. To every man born and bred upon the plantation, the negro seems essential, in a thousand respects with which a northerner can have no sympathy. I saw nothing of what we call prejudice against color in all my travels. In infancy the same nurse gives food and rest to her own child and to her master's; in childhood the same eye watches and the same hand alternately caresses and corrects them; they mingle their sports in boyhood; and through youth up to manhood there are ties which link them to each other by an affinity that no time or circumstances can destroy. An illiterate, rough planter, who was by no means remarkable for the kindness he showed his servants, said to me one day: "I travelled last summer all over Iowa territory, and I didn't see a nigger in two months. To be sure, I felt kind o' badly, but it couldn't be helped; so I made the best of it, thinking all the time I should be home again bye and bye. Well, Sir, I got back again as far as Zanesville in 'Hio, where there was a general muster and a heap of people; and pretty soon I heard a banjo; thinks I, there's some of *our folks*, I know; and sure enough there was two niggers and a wench going it powerful; and the way I went up to em and got hold of their hands, and says I, 'How are you, my good fellows? how are you, girl?' and the way I

shook and they shook, was a caution to abolitionists, I tell you?"

Georgetown *District* is the wealthiest portion of the State; but a more miserable collection of decayed wood domicils and filthy beer shops than are clustered together to make up the *town*, it would be difficult to find. Indeed, unlike the free States, the wealth of the South lies almost entirely in the country; the towns, unless Charleston form an exception, being made up of artizans and traders.

    ·   ·   ·

As you advance inland from Georgetown, and begin to enter the cotton country, the scenery is completely changed. The huge live oaks, draperied with moss, the peculiar characteristic of the sickly lowlands, all disappear, and with them depart nearly all the evidences of wealth or taste or refinement. Instead of princely mansions surrounded by old parks and highly cultivated plantations, one sees nothing but low, piazza'd domicils, in fields bare of vegetation, and the appendage of miserable hovels scattered at short distances here and there for the field-hands. In the low country the rank growth upon the marshes affords some compensation for the want of green fields of grass; but in the up country every shade of greenness is lost in the interminable red clay-fields which spread out every where around you. It was new to me that the upland grasses could not be cultivated below Virginia, but so it is. Every where, by the road side, in the court-yard, over the fenced fields, and in the forest, the bosom of mother earth is bared before you; and to one accustomed to the green mantle with which she robes herself in New England, the sight is almost shocking. Equally so was another sight, with which, however, I soon became familiar, but which at the outset startled my sense of decency to a degree; I refer to the nudity of the young negroes. Up to ten and eleven years of age, the colored children of both sexes run about entirely naked; and in the more secluded plantations they may be seen at even a later age, without a fig-leaf of covering to their jetty limbs. I beg my friends, the abolitionists, will not set this down as a new instance of the cruelty of the masters, as I had repeated and indubitable evidence of its being a habit of determinate choice upon the part of the children, as to defy every effort to break it up. That it manifests the state of utter degradation to which the slaves are reduced, I do not deny; for everywhere in lowland and highland, country and city, nothing is more evident than the mental and moral degradation of the negro.

As the value of the lands and the wealth of the inhabitants decrease, while you journey toward the back country, so also does the intelligence of the people. I never met in my whole life with so many white persons who could not read nor write, who had never taken a newspaper, who had never travelled fifty miles from home, or who had never been to the house of God, or heard a sentence read from his Holy Word, as I found in a single season in South Carolina. Like the inhabitants of Nineveh, many of them could not discern between the right hand and the left. What wonder then that the hosts of Yankee pedlers until driven out by the sumptuary laws,[12] fattened upon the land! "What do you think I gave for that?" asked an ignorant planter in Sumpter district, while pointing to a Connecticut wooden clock which stood upon a shelf in the corner of the room. "I don't know," was my answer; "twenty dollars, or very likely twenty-five!" "*Twenty-five dollars*, stranger!" replied the planter; "why, what do you mean?

12. There were no laws in South Carolina regulating pedlers until December 1843. However, it has been suggested that since the law was introduced into the legislature in July 1843 the writer of this article may have been familiar with discussions on the subject. Letter from Beverly Boyer, Assistant Librarian, Law Library, University of South Carolina, to Jacqueline Bull, March 14, 1969.

Come, guess fair and I'll tell you *true!*" I answered again that twenty-five dollars was a high price for such a clock, as I had often seen them sold for a quarter of that sum. The man was astonished "Stranger" said he, "I gave one hundred and forty-four dollars for that clock, and thought I got it cheap at that! Let me tell you how it was. We had always used sun-dials hereabout, till twelve or fourteen years ago, when a man came along with clocks to sell. I thought at first I wouldn't buy one, but after haggling about the price for a while, he agreed to take sixteen dollars less than what he asked, for his selling price was one hundred and sixty dollars; and as I had just sold my cotton at thirty-four cents, I concluded to strike a bargain. It's a powerful clock, but I reckon I gave a heap of money for it!"

In fact, during those years when the staples of Carolina sold for nearly thrice their intrinsic value, and wealth flowed in an uninterrupted stream through every channel of industry, the plantations of the South became the legitimate plunder of Yankee shrewdness. It was no meeting of Greek with Greek in the contest of wits, but a perfect inrush of shrewd, disciplined tacticians in the art of knavery, upon a stupid and ignorant population. The whole country was flooded with itinerant hawkers. There is scarcely an article in the whole range of home manufactures upon which fortunes were not made during those times of inflated prices of the southern staple products. Through the mountain passes of Buncombe county there flowed a stream of pedlers' carts, wagons, carry-alls, and arks, which inundated the land. Indeed, so great at length became the evil, and so overmatched in the contest of wits were the planters of the uplands, that the legislature passed laws forbidding a Yankee pedler to enter the State.

It is this deplorable ignorance, which is prevalent over a large portion of South Carolina, that constitutes the most insuperable obstacle to the removal of slavery. Among the more wealthy and intelligent of the population, juster sentiments prevail in regard to that great evil; but their opinions and wishes are greatly overbalanced by the masses of the middling classes. They, wedded to the customs of their fathers beyond all hope of improvement; vegetators upon the soil cleared and prepared by their ancestors; ignorant, idle, and overbearing; driven by thriftless modes of agriculture, and the impoverishing system of slave-labor, to penurious economy, and scouting every suggestion of manual toil as servile and degrading; *they* compose the great barrier around the institution of negro servitude, which the tide of public sentiment never reaches, and which the advancing intelligence of other portions of the world cannot soon affect. To them, hedged in by the antiquated prejudices of a barbarous age, alike unfitted to know and unwilling to receive the new truths of humanity and religion, the negro seems the connecting link between man and the brute. Of their own origin and destiny they know and care little; of him who toils for them, less; and it is vain to hope, until the States between them and the free people of the North shall have broken down the system which curses alike the owner and his soil, that the intelligence of an independent and virtuous people can never reach them.

In these Sketches, which are now brought to a close, I have endeavored to represent the condition of South Carolina as I saw it. Of slavery I have said what I believe, and of its white population what I know to be true. There, as elsewhere in a world tainted by evil injustice too often embitters the cup of life. But it is not the slave, bending to his irksome task, nor he who toils under the heat of a southern sky alone, who drains it to its dregs. The chalice is commanded to the lips every where. And deeply has the writer drank, from the hands of those who profess to be guided by the divine precepts of Christ, banded as they were to subvert oppression and wrong, to southern institutions, a draft of injustice more poisonous than the bitterest potion of slavery.

Sketches of South Carolina

Vessels bearing some of the richest cargoes ever stowed in a hold were wrecked on the dreaded Florida Keys. Before the cession of Florida to the United States, salvagers would take their recovered ships and cargo to Nassau and Havana for adjudication. In 1825 Congress passed a law requiring salvage to be brought to some port of entry within the territorial United States, and a federal court was established in 1828. The abuses attendant upon the disposal of salvage at Key West, as described in this selection, motivated Congress to regulatory action. In 1847 it passed a law requiring any person who wished to engage in wrecking to obtain a license from the judge of the district court of Florida. This afforded the opportunity to bar from salvage operations any person deemed to be of undesirable character. The improvement in conditions resulting from the establishment of controls is described in a later article in the same journal, Hunt's Merchants' Magazine.[1]

"There be land-rats and water-rats, land-thieves and water-thieves. . . . And then there is the peril of the waters, winds, and rocks."—*Merchant of Venice.*[1.3.22]

THERE is no portion of the American coast more dangerous to the mariner, or where more property is annually wrecked, than on the Florida Reef. Its contiguity to the gulf stream, and forming a sort of Scylla to that Charybdis, the Bahama Islands, are the main causes which make it so dangerous to, and so much dreaded by seamen. Lying in the way, as it does, of much important commerce, many ships of the largest class are compelled to encounter its dangers, and run the risk of an inhospitable reception upon its rocky shores and sunken coral reefs.

There is, on an average, annually wrecked upon the Florida coast, about fifty vessels,[2] a very great proportion of which are New Orleans, Mobile, or other packets. The great destruction of property consequent upon this state of things, and the hope of gain, have induced a settlement at Key West, where, to adjudicate upon the wrecked property, a court of admiralty has been established. A large number of vessels, from 20 to 30 are annually engaged as wreckers, lying about this coast to "help the unfortunate," and to help themselves. These vessels are in many instances owned in whole or in part by the merchants of Key West; the same merchant frequently acts in the quadruple capacity of owner of the wrecker, agent for the wreckers, consignee of the captain, and *agent for the underwriters.* Whose business he transacts with most assiduity, his own, or that of others, may be readily inferred.

A residence of a few years on the Florida reef, enables me to speak with some knowledge of the manner in which business is usually conducted about those parts; and to a community suffering as much as this does, I think a statement of facts may

"Wrecks, Wrecking, Wreckers, and Wreckees, on Florida Reef, by a late Resident of Florida," *Hunt's Merchants' Magazine* 6 (April 1842): 349–54.

1. "Key West, Florida," *Hunt's Merchants' Magazine* 26 (January 1852): 52.

2. A report from Key West covering the period 1844–1854 ranges from a minimum of twenty-three vessels in 1852 to a maximum of fifty-eight in 1854. The figures are not in a steady progression. "Statistics of Wrecks at Key West, Florida," *Hunt's Merchants' Magazine* 32 (May 1855): 627.

prove useful. The commercial world need then no longer remain inactive in seeking a redress of grievances in consequence of an ignorance of their existence.

I am sure the manner in which wrecked property is saved, and adjudicated upon in Key West, cannot be known to the underwriters, or they would take some measures to put an end to many of the evils they endure under the present state of things.

The whole coast, from near Cape Canaveral to the Tortuga, is strewed with small wrecking vessels, either sloops or schooners, that anchor inside of the reef, *out of sight* from vessels at sea, because if they were seen by the unfortunate vessel who is making unconsciously too near an approach to the shore, they would apprise her of her danger, so that she would stand off to sea, and thus the victim would not be sacrificed. That the wrecker hails with delight the wreck of a vessel, is not to be wondered at. His gains are enormous; it is his business, and his interests are so much at stake that all the softer feelings of humanity soon die away in his bosom, and he hails the stranding of the unfortunate vessel with delight. It is not to be supposed, then, that he will, seeing a vessel coming ashore, sail for her and make known to her the danger she is encountering, but rather that he will endeavor by every means in his power, if not to allure her, at least not to caution her. To the praise of the wreckers be it said, that they never have refused to listen to the calls of humanity, even when doing so has often been to their loss. The cases are numerous where they have left their wrecking ground, and carried wrecked passengers upwards of a hundred miles, furnishing the passengers with food and passage free of charge. The wreckers have been accused of raising false light to deceive vessels at sea. As a general rule I do not believe this charge is true, and the strongest reason I have for disbelieving it is, that it is not to their interest to do so.

As soon as a vessel sees a light on Florida shore, she knows she is as near to land, if not nearer than she ought to be, and of course would immediately haul off from the danger. The practice of the wreckers is quite the reverse. No lights are allowed to be burning in their vessels except in the binnacle, and this light is most cautiously guarded, lest vessels at sea should descry it, and thereby discover their proximity to land. Every morning at break of day, the whole of the reef is scoured by some one or the other of the vessels, in search of "a prize" that may have come on the rocks at night. If a vessel is discovered on shore, and two wreckers descry her at the same time, every stitch of canvass is set, in order to be the first to board her and relieve her; if it is calm, the small-boats are manned, and they pull as if for life. This looks charitable, but the charity begins at home. The captain of the wrecker jumps on board the unfortunate vessel, and inquires for her captain; and now commences a series of impositions upon the underwriters. "Captain," says the wrecker, "are you insured?" "Yes; well— to the full amount." "I suppose you know," says the wrecker, "that if you go into Key West to get repaired, that the expenses are enormous, and your owners will be obliged, according to the rules of the underwriters, to pay *one third* of the repairs; *whereas, if the vessel should be so unfortunate as to be a total loss*, the insurers pay all, and that makes a clean and short business of it." "Certainly," says the wrecked captain, "that is very true, but I am bound to do the best I can." "All right, sir, but what can you do? you are hard and fast—the tide is at its height (probably it is then dead low-water), and you had better let me take full charge, for if not got off this tide, she'll bilge the next. I am a licensed wrecker." The license is produced, signed by the *judge of the admiralty court*, at Key West. Of course this is all right, at least so the wrecked captain thinks, or pretends to think. "But," continues the *unfortunate captain*, "if my vessel earns no freight, I earn no wages." "Very true," answers the complacent wrecker, "and I pity your unfortunate case; it is truly deplorable that such injustice is done to such a worthy class of men, and as I shall make something handsome by saving this property, if you give me and my consorts* the full business of wrecking the vessel, I could afford to pay you your wages, and make you a handsome present of three or four thousand dollars." "But will this all be right?" asks the wrecked captain. "Certainly; *you can if you please hand the three or four thousand dollars to the underwriters*—that is left to yourself; if you say nothing about it, of course I shan't—I dare not—I should lose my salvage if I did." Enough. The bargain is fixed, the captain has an order on the merchant for the cash, the stranded vessel is in the command of the wrecker, and there need not now be any fear that the owners will have to pay *one third* for repairs— the vessel will soon be beyond repair. As to the underwriters, they have seen all they will of the bonus paid the captain. An appearance of an effort to get the vessel off, must be kept up among the passengers and the crew, who have heard none of the foregoing conversation, which generally takes place in the captain's private state-room. "Come boys," cries the wrecker captain to his crew, "we must go to work as soon as the tide serves to get her off"; in the mean time, all hands turn to, to lighten her. By all hands is meant all the wrecker's crew. Some of them have already charitably informed the sailors that they have lost their wages by the loss of the vessel, of course they work no more. The hatches are opened, and the articles taken out till she lightens. By this process she is driven still further on the reef; and when by lightening her she has got so far on that it is impossible to back her off, an attempt is made "*to*

*Consorting is for several vessels to go shares, and station themselves on different parts of the reef, and when one gets a wreck, he sends to the others to come and help.

pull her over." To this effect an anchor or two is carried off from her bows, and dropped on the reef; the windlass is then manned, and all hands put to work to drag her over, aided by her sails. It is soon found that is impossible, and she is now in the middle of the reef, beyond hope of getting forward or backward, and here she bilges.

In unloading, one would suppose it was to the interest of all parties to save the property in as good a condition as possible—but it is not; the wreckers' interest is to have it a little wetted, inasmuch as a very large per centage as salvage is given on property saved wet, compared to that on the dry—50 per cent, sometimes, on wet, and 7 to 10 on dry. And although the property is taken dry from the stranded vessel, some of it gets damaged on board the wrecker; a great quantity being put upon the decks of these small vessels, for each puts on board as much as he can, as they are paid by the quantity of goods saved and their value, and not by the number of loads. The passage from the wrecked vessel to Key West, is frequently boisterous, and always dangerous.

The goods when they are landed at Key West, are consigned to some merchant—probably, as before stated, the owner of the wrecker. The captains of the wrecked and the wrecker are now of course "hail fellows well met." The latter recommends his own merchant to the former, as his consignee; the merchant invites the captain to his house, makes no charge for his stay, and the captain, in the next paper, publishes a card of thanks for the merchant's "*disinterested hospitality.*"

All now is going on swimmingly. The marshal advertises the goods (and here let me say, that the *present* marshal discharges his duty like a man and a christian), the auction sale comes on, and thirty to forty thousand dollars worth of goods are sold on an island containing about five or six merchants, nearly a hundred miles from any inhabited land. Who is to blame? Not the marshal—the law points out his duty, and he pursues it. The advertisement generally consists of publication in a paper, the subscribers of which number about three hundred, nearly all wreckers, owned and supported by the merchants of the Key; and a few written advertisements stuck up around *the island*, added to this, completes the publication. The marshal can do no better; it is not that it is an unfair sale that is to be complained of, but the whole system is to be reprobated.

The day of the sale arrives. Who are the bidders? The aforesaid five merchants! How easily *might* these merchants agree not to run the one the other on his bid, and thus a whole cargo, worth thirty thousand dollars, might be divided among them at the cost of about two thousand dollars each, or less. It is true, sometimes advertisements are sent to Havana; but sometimes also the sales take place before the merchants from there have a chance to get over to Key West, and *sometimes* this may be known when the advertisement is sent; but then the sending to Havana will have a good appearance when represented to underwriters and absent owners.

Methinks I hear the reader asking, where, all this while is the captain of the wrecked vessel, and what is he about during this interesting epoch? I have often asked the same question, and found him sometimes in one of the grog-shops, or busily engaged in getting rid of his bonus by card-playing.

I have known purchases made of valuable goods at these auctions, where the top was a little wet, and all the rest perfectly dry; they were bought by the wrecker, who knew how far the wet extended, because he brought them up on the deck of his vessel, and one end of the box lay by accident in the lea-scuppers. A package of beautiful ready-made clothing of this kind, I saw once sell for about $150 or $200, and before it was removed from the ground, one third was retailed out at $250. The profits on the whole must have been enormous.

The captain of the wrecked vessel often employs a proctor in the court of admiralty to defend absent underwriters and owners, and so cripples the proctor by compelling him (by so instructing him) to admit the wreckers' libel, that no justice can be done for those abroad, because they are trusting to a captain who is already bought up, and who is actually fighting against their interest, though seemingly for it.

The whole system from beginning to end is manifestly wrong, and ought to be changed. Underwriters are imposed upon by their own agents the captains, and then they blame the wreckers and people of Key West. The latter, living as they do upon wrecks, and every one on the island being dependent upon them more or less as a means of subsistence, naturally work for their own interests in preference to that of others. And for this the wreckers are blamed. It must be remembered they are men; and tempted as they are, I often wonder they do not act worse than they do. They have very large sums invested generally, and are at a great expense; is it natural then they should frighten away the bird when she is about to light in their net? As regards the merchants there, they live by buying cheap and selling dear, and they must make hay while the sun shines.

He who censures a law or practice ought to be prepared to point out some mode of redress. I will conclude this article by doing so.

In the first place, the underwriters should have a vessel or two on the reef, or a small steamboat would be better. These crafts should be constantly going from one end of the reef to the other, and while one was scouring the lower portion, the other should be on the upper. They should all have lights at night at their mast-heads, which could be distinguished from the light-houses, when not under way; their moving when sailing would be a sufficient notice that they were other lights than that of the beacon; in cases of fog, let them toll a bell or fire guns occasionally. The expense of a steamboat is raised as an objection to its employment. This is indeed penny wise and pound foolish. The ribs of many a noble ship would not now be lying in "Rotten Row," at Key West, could a steamboat have been procured to haul her off when she was but slightly on the rocks. *Nine times out of ten* ships and cargoes that are made total losses, might be saved by a steamboat taking off her deck load, and hauling her off by her steam-power. Again; in cases of wrecks, the steamboat, if strongly constructed, could lay alongside as well as a sloop or schooner, if not better, and she might take off her cargo and carry it on shore six times where a wrecker could once; and in case a vessel was ashore in a calm, then the steamboat could go when no sail vessel could. A wrecker when he gets a load starts with it for *Key West*, a distance often of upwards of a hundred miles, and it is a week ere he returns. Small warehouses might be built on the islands, about five miles apart, where the goods could be safely stowed till all were out of the vessel, and then it need not be carried to Key West, as there is no necessity of adjudicating upon it; thus all this expense and sacrifice of property, which is very great, might be saved. A steamboat, or two, would save in this way to the underwriters annually from two to three or four hundred thousand dollars, and the cost would be a mere trifle compared with the expense of others, as the best of wood all along the coast is to be had for the cutting. Captain Housman,[3] who resided on, and owned most of Indian Key, intended to have a steamboat as a wrecker, and had engaged with a builder to

contract for one for him, but heavy losses deterred him at that time from pursuing what to him was a favorite plan, and his death subsequently put an end to the scheme.

The captains of the steamers, when they missed a wreck (which would seldom happen), could see after the goods and act as agent for the underwriters, or get some one who could and would attend to it for them faithfully, and not leave it to a bought-up captain. No doubt the underwriters who read this will say they have tried this plan to a certain extent. It is true they appointed *the owner of wreckers*, a merchant in Key West, their agent, *without pay*, and bought a wrecker to be put under his charge. The result was, he converted her into a wrecker, and claimed salvage for all she saved. Cheap work is generally badly done—so this turned out. If the underwriters want an agent in Key West, they must pay him well, and then their business will be well attended to.

Another remedy I would point out for the existing evils is to make more ports of entry along the reef and thus break up the Key West monopoly. One port might be made at Cayo Biscayno,[4] and another at Indian Key. This would create competition, and one would watch the other with a jealous eye, and expose any improper conduct.

Again, the judge of the court of admiralty should not be selected from among the lawyers of Key West, who have been for years acting for the wreckers, and received large fees from them. The connection is too close between them, and the underwriters do not stand quite so good a chance.

Never let your captains leave cases to arbitration on Key West; for ten to one the persons selected will be part secret owners of the wrecking vessels to whom they are going to award salvage; if not, then probably they have the supply of them, or

3. Captain Jacob Houseman was a wrecker and storekeeper on Indian Key. Located about halfway between Key Biscayne and Key West, Indian Key was used as a trading post to the Indians by the Spanish. Marjory Stoneman Douglas, *Florida: The Long Frontier* (New York, 1967), p. 148; Federal Writers' Project, Florida, *Florida: A Guide to the Southernmost State* (New York, 1939), pp. 330–31. Hereafter cited as *Florida Guide*.

4. Key Biscayne is an island off the coast of Florida opposite Miami. *Webster's Geographical Dictionary* (Springfield, Mass., 1966), p. 552.

they are otherwise too much interested to decide impartially.

Establish an honest agent at Key West—send him there with a good salary, or else allow him a good per centage on the amount of all goods saved, after expenses are deducted; this will make it to his interest as well as his duty to oppose unnecessary expenses. Let there be established a board of underwriters, in case he has a salary to pay him, and let each insurance office pay the board in proportion to the losses they suffer.

There is annually paid by the insurance offices about $6000 for proctors' fees among the *several* lawyers. Concentrate this in *one*, and make him act as agent, then you will have an agent and no additional expense. I proposed this plan years ago to the underwriters, but they did not seem to regard it.

Have no property sold in Key West except perishable. Have it shipped to Havana, Mobile, New Orleans, Texas, Charleston, Savannah, or wherever it may bring the most by a fair competition.

Let the judge of the admiralty court reverse his practice, and give high salvage where a vessel is got off without damage to her and her goods, and low in proportion to the bad state they are saved in. This will make it to the interest of the wreckers to save vessel and cargo in as sound a condition as possible.

Let the underwriters abolish the system of making owners pay for one third repairs—this loses many a noble vessel that would otherwise be saved. Pay captains their wages, wreck or no wreck, where they have done their duty. Don't leave them to choose between starvation of their family and the wrecker's "bonus." So also with the sailors, don't cut off their wages, and so lose their services when most wanted. This is most miserable policy.

An immense deal of merchandise which is saved wet, if it could be immediately washed and dried, would be comparatively but little injured. Whereas by the present mode it is stowed away, much of it in the hold of the vessel, in a hot tropical clime, there to sweat on a voyage of one hundred miles, where it is not uncommon for calms to make it several days. To thus wash and dry the goods, these houses on the shores I have recommended would be very useful. The sweating of the goods entirely rots them, so as to make them almost valueless.

The present system of paying salvage according to the value of the goods saved works unjustly, because all are entitled to the same protection of their property under these circumstances. But whether to remedy this evil would not work a greater, I will not pretend to say.

SOUTHERN LADIES

Although here and there the prose is stilted, this is essentially a dignified and unaffected plea for sectional understanding as well as a fairminded appraisal of southern ladies by a simple Maine schoolteacher.

As we travel from one extremity to another of the U.S. we feel a glow of proud complacency and self gratulation, that this is our own native land. Our country, how extensive her territory, rich her resources, abounding in fertile lands, and exhibiting a spirit of enterprise peculiar to the people of this great republic.

A northern sky may temper this glowing zeal, or a Southern kindle with it, other and less useful passions, still an American is an American, find him where you may, North or South, East or West. The same is true of the ladies, with some slight shades of dissimilarity, arising from difference of education and means of information. At the South is a mixed population more so than at the North. Often the father is a foreigner, the mother a native American and vice-versa. Sometimes one parent is from the North, the other a Southern, differing more or less in their tastes and habits, which mingle and combine in the fostering care of their little ones. Again, there are the Creole-ladies, natives of the South, Creole applying to all born in the South, without distinction. Then there are ladies from the North, who have emigrated in early life, with their parents; come out as youthful brides, or as more sober and venerable matrons. Some have come to visit relations and spend a winter, become entangled willingly or reluctantly in Cupid's meshes and found a resting place for life. Others have come as teachers, in private families, assistants in Boarding Schools, in music &c. Then there are the Brunette ladies, of dark complexion,

P., "Southern Ladies," *Portland Transcript* 2 (12 July 1838): 115.

peculiar to the South, though not universal, for there are native Southern ladies of as fair complexion as any at the North. Some of these are connected with the first families in the South, exhibit in their conversation and manners, all the sprightliness and flow of soul peculiar to Southern ladies. Their black tresses and dark flashing eyes give burning pungency to their quick repartees, while the social circle is enlivened by the sweetest strains of music, and a generous prodigality of the luscious and bountiful productions of the sunny South.

I am acquainted with several of this class of ladies, of excellent education, and refined manners, whose pens have enriched the poet's corner with the daintiest luxuries of the poetic muse.

Then again are the French ladies, whose conversational powers are well known to be unrivalled, unequalled. These, whether abiding, generation after generation, among their own people, or intermixing with the American population, still evince all their suavity of manners, cheerful gaiety, and inexhaustible flow of language. While the children of the latter, partaking of their warm and generous natures, moderated by the less ardent temperament of their Northern, or European sires, develope mingled peculiarities of character, unknown at the North, where there is a less mixed ancestry from all parts of the civilized world.

The name of a Southern lady, in the minds of some, is associated with wealth, effeminacy and luxuriance in dress and living. While at the South, there is less poverty in proportion to the number of the wealthy than at the North, still there are the same gradations, and the same classes of the intelligent, the wealthy, the ignorant, the improvident, the moral and the abandoned in vice. Few beggars, or suffering poor are seen strolling about the cities or country, and those only of intemperate, reckless habits, or imbecility of character.—While there are some ladies at the North, who have been trained only to drum a piano, to sit strait and look pretty, is it surprising that in the South there should be some such self-conceited shadows and gilded toys in the parlors of the aristocracy? While such personages are found all the world over, still there are in the South the daughters of the plain, substantial planter, who have been raised in all the homespun style of country life, domesticated as well as refined, affable, intelligent, and commanding respectful attention, honorable esteem and durable friendship. Then there are young ladies of wealthy parents, who from indiscretion, prejudice, or parsimonious habits, have too much neglected the education of their daughters, though of such parents there are but a despised few, fast decreasing as the institutions for intellectual improvement increase and become more convenient.

I have met with some ladies in the South of excellent education, whose parents could not read or very imperfectly. These parents, husband and wife, once worked together, as they have told me themselves, in the corn and cotton fields; cut down the wild cane-brakes, and ploughed and hoed together in the first days of matrimonial bliss, taking the little sleeping babe with them into the field, for fear of harm while absent in their cheerful labors. By industry and economy, they have become wealthy, have sent their sons to college and their daughters to the boarding school or convent.

Again, there is a striking dissimilarity in different parts of the South. In one city, Natchez for instance, the body of the people are of Northern extraction; hence the manners, the diversions, the style of the buildings, the moral, religious and literary institutions, &c. are all Northern. In another, say Baton Rouge, there are more French, and French customs prevail. In N. Orleans, one part of the city is American, the other French; each retaining its national peculiarities. So that a stranger will find much to interest, amuse, and instruct, in studying the different and mixed peculiarities and anomalies of character, and find much room for charity, when he sees the progressive state of improvement all through the southern country.

A New-Englander abroad will learn to appreciate the privileges, social, moral and religious, of his distant native home, and will eagerly lend his aid in promoting the welfare of society in his adopted state. And so it is, nearly all the male and especially female teachers, in the schools, Colleges and Ladies Boarding Seminaries at the South, are natives of New England. I would not attempt a comparison between N.E. and the South, but I would fearlessly say, that to many of the descriptions of southern effeminacy, hot headed recklessness, indolence of habits and want of enterprise, there are many noble exceptions. Here is one. The mother of the late representative in Congress from Mississippi, the Hon. J. F. H. C. resides near Natchez.[1] A pious and noble souled lady, she is loved by a large circle of the most respectable of the community, of all sects and parties. Her quiet and spacious mansion is the resort of the youth to admire and venerate; of the matured in life, for counsel and esteem; of the aged for mutual solace and reciprocal regard. Her son is worthy of her. Elevated to the State Legislature at 21, he has remained in public life until this year, and could only be ousted by a *Portlander*, of unusual popularity. It is very probable that he and the Hon. S. S. P,[2]

1. John F. H. Claiborne served in the House of Representatives in 1835–1837. *Dictionary of American Biography*, vol. 2, pt. 2, pp. 112–13.
2. Sergeant Smith Prentiss was admitted to the bar in

will be next elected, he was anticipated at the last election. But I am no dabbler in politics. Suffice it to say, he is a son worthy of such a mother, a gentleman and scholar of energy and enterprise.— Engaged as he has been from early strife in the excited atmosphere of political life,[3] I was gratified and astonished when he told me at his mother's house and in the presence of several others, that he could say, what few other Southerners could say, that he, *a native of the South, had never thrown a card, been on a racetrack, or fought a duel.* Such a man, a Mississippian, would do honor to any mother, to any State. There are ladies at the South, natives too, who with luxurious plenty around them, are good mothers, good housewives and good christians. That there are no more is not strange, considering the history of the country, and the present comparatively few facilities for improvement, mental, moral, and in the business of house-wifery, now receiving so much attention from some Northern writers.

In the South is a fair field for the exercise of female influence by ladies emigrating from the North. From the success of some of my female friends, from this and other States, I can confidently encourage any Ladies, of good acquired and natural abilities, to improve the first opportunity, by means of visiting friends, &c. to go South and teach in private families, or Female Boarding schools, where their labors will be easy, genteel, and well rewarded. They will thus see a little of the country, and return if they choose, well paid and independent—With the needle, a lady in the South, will find an abundant and lucrative employment. Every respectable lady from the North, is welcomed with tokens that reach the heart, by the fair daughters of the sunny South.

P.

Mississippi in 1829. He followed Claiborne in the House of Representatives, serving until 1839. Ibid., vol. 8, pt. 1, pp. 191–92.
3. The printer apparently transposed "strife" and "life."

A TOUR THROUGH KENTUCKY AND TENNESSEE

Henry Ruffner (1790–1861) was first a student, then a teacher, and ultimately the president of Washington College in Lexington, Virginia. He was active throughout his life in improving the Virginia educational system. He was also an ordained Presbyterian minister, who preached regularly. Although an unimpeachable southerner, he had an antislavery attitude.[1]

.   .   .

From Cincinnati I went to Louisville in the mail packet, General Pike,[2] which made the voyage in about thirteen hours. The scenery on the river varied little from that above. Most of the villages present themselves perched on high, naked and crumbling banks, amidst fields, out of which, and about which, the fine forest trees have been diligently destroyed.

The nakedness of the banks is exposing them to be undermined by the current, and the waves thrown up by the steamboats. The soil is of a loose sandy description, and is underlaid by a deep bed of sand and gravel. When the river is sufficiently high to cover the shelving bars of gravel at its margin, the current comes in contact with the steep part of the bank, and washing out the sand underneath, causes frequent slides and falls of the soil from above; the lighter materials are swept away by the current, while the heavier gravel is washed down to the shelving beach, which is thereby enlarged from year to year. This effect is much hastened by the steamboats, which cast out on either side an oblique line of billows that roll and break against the shore. When the dash of these waves is carried against the friable soil of the banks, the effect is more destructive than that of the current. The only remedy—and that should be promptly applied—seems to be, to plant willows and other trees of quick growth and tenacious roots, and to fortify their position with a layer of stones.[3]

The most thriving town between Cincinnati and Louisville, is Madison, on the Indiana shore. Near this is the South Hanover college and theological school. The institution was founded some years ago on the manual labor scheme. The cheapness of education here, as well as the merit of the instructors, soon attracted a large number of students. The manual labor department was here as elsewhere attended with much difficulty, and has failed to yield all the advantages that were anticipated. Still it is deemed so far beneficial, as to be worthy of continuance; but it is now left to the option of the students whether they will labor or not. Two or three years ago, a destructive tornado passed over and almost ruined the college buildings.[4]

Henry Ruffner, "Notes of a Tour from Virginia to Tennessee in the Months of July and August 1838," *Southern Literary Messenger* 5 (January–April 1839): 44–48, 137–41, 206–10, 269–73.
1. *Dictionary of American Biography*, vol. 8, pt. 2, pp. 217–18.
2. The *General Pike* was built at Cincinnati in 1835. W. G. Lyford, *The Western Address Directory* (Baltimore, Md., 1837), p. 463.

3. Charles Ellet's report in 1852 on flood control was the first official study of this subject by the federal government. Ellet called attention to the caving river banks and recommended the construction of reservoirs to control floods; he noted that an even flow of water would greatly assist efforts to plant trees along the banks and thus would control erosion. Charles Ellet, Jr., *The Mississippi and Ohio Rivers* (Philadelphia, 1853), pp. 303–6.
4. In 1833 Madison was described as "a flourishing post

The only instance of gambling which I saw on my whole tour, occurred on the General Pike, shortly after we left Cincinnati. A party at a card table played a few games for money. But another card party, among whom no bets occurred, excited my attention. The boat was scarcely under way, before an elderly lady, large and fair to look upon, came into the gentlemen's cabin, and looked about as if she wanted somebody or something. She addressed several gentlemen; and soon, she and three of them sat down to cards. They shuffled, and cut, and dealt out, and played away; till some of the gentlemen showed signs of weariness: but not so the lady; she held them to it more than two hours, until the party was broken up, by the setting out of the dinner table. No sooner was the cloth removed, after dinner, than the same elderly good looking lady came forth again, looking round and round, till she gathered up the party for another set to. They shuffled, and cut, and dealt out, and played away, till late in the afternoon, when two of the gentlemen fell back in their chairs, and yawned, and finally got up. When the lady saw this backing out, she turned to the third gentleman by her side, and detained him with some questions on the subject of card playing and a proposal to show him certain mysterious manoeuvers with cards, which he admitted himself to be ignorant of. She seized the pack, shuffled, divided, dealt out, lectured, explained; shuffled, dealt out, lectured, explained, in continuation—putting her finger first on one card, then on another, as she commented thereupon; whereof I understood nothing; but whereat I was

amused, nevertheless, when I observed the indefatigable earnestness of the lady, and the listless patience of her auditor. When the supper table was set, the lecture ended. No sooner was the table cleared, than forth came the self-same lady once more, and the self-same operations of the forenoon and the afternoon, were repeated and reiterated and gone over, times innumerable—the shuffle—the deal—the cut—the turning up the trump—the playing out, &c. Now it so happened, that the lady sat at the card table with her back almost touching my berth; and being of considerable dimensions, she debarred me of access to my place of repose. When I became very sleepy about ten o'clock, I politely requested the company to allow me space to enter my dormitory. They promptly complied—the lady rose, and pushed the table forward a little, and drawing her chair after it, she turned about, and finding by inspection that I could pass and drop my curtain, she sat down and resumed the game. I crept in, and dropping my curtain close to her back, doffed my garments and lay down; but the rustling of cards within three feet of my ears, and the frequent pronunciation of the words, "ace-queen-knave-trump-trick"—and other terms of the card playing vocabulary, kept me awake for some time. Finally these sounds had a lulling effect—dreamy thoughts stole upon me—thoughts of card playing ladies—"an old age of cards," as Pope has it [5]—till I fell asleep with this sort of reflection: "Well, Mrs. D. (for I had heard her name), if I were a Drake, I should not choose you for my duck."

Our boat landed about eleven o'clock at night, and lay till morning. When I got out and looked about, I found on the bank, the city of Louisville, and along the shore the greatest sight of steamboats that I ever beheld. They lay as thickly as they could crowd, with their noses to the land, for the space of half a mile, many of them vessels of

town." It had 2,500 inhabitants and a promising future as a trade center. In the same year it was stated that a college on the manual labor system was to be established. John Scott, *The Indiana Gazetteer*, 2d ed. (Indianapolis, Ind., 1833), pp. 81, 111-12. Actually Hanover College was founded in 1827. Federal Writers' Program, Indiana, *Indiana: A Guide to the Hoosier State* (New York, 1941), p. 381.

5. Alexander Pope, "To a Young Lady," line 243.

large burden, giving evidence at once, that here was the greatest commercial port on the Ohio.

The river is here of great breadth—more than half a mile at the falls, and somewhat less for some miles above and below. The falls, or rather rapids, are made by a ledge of rock, swelling up in the channel, but most on the Kentucky side, so as to force the current towards the Indiana shore, where it runs with violence, when the river is low, down a sluice about a mile long; but when the river is much swollen, it spreads over the whole space between the banks, and affords a safe passage to boats over the rapids. At other times, the canal on the Louisville side must be used.[6]

Louisville is neither so large nor so handsome a city as Cincinnati, nor has it such pleasant scenery about it. Several streets next to the river are compactly and handsomely built; but there are as yet few public buildings of any note. They are erecting an edifice, however, which, in point of magnificence and solidity, will exceed any thing of the kind on the western side of the Alleghany. They call it the court house, but it will give ample room and verge enough to accommodate the legislature also, and I heard it suggested that its dimensions were made so large with this view. Nor does there seem to be any sufficient reason why the seat of government should not be located in Louisville, which stands indeed on one side of the state, but midway between the extremities. Steamboats and railways will make this great commercial depot the chief point of convergence, and afford easy intercourse with all parts of the state. This building is a fine grey sandstone from the Kentucky river, and presents a front of more than 200 feet.[7]

The country about Louisville is an extensive plain of dark rich soil. The town was formerly unhealthy, from the pestiferous effluvia of ponds and marshes in the vicinity. Those nearest the town have been drained, and Louisville is now *almost* as healthy as the towns of the upper Ohio. But the situation will never permit it to be a *very healthy* place in the autumnal season. The city now contains 25,000 inhabitants, and it is growing with such rapidity, as to threaten Cincinnati with rivalship in population, as it now rivals that "queen of the west" in trade.

On the Indiana side, are the towns of Jeffersonville, above the falls, and New Albany below. The latter is a thriving place, pleasantly situated near the only hills apparent from Louisville, over which it has some natural advantages, but which it can never rival for want of an equal start. Capital and population have fixed on Louisville as their seat—having made their location, they will keep it. Experience proves that a city once become populous, and wealthy, will in the ordinary course of events triumph over natural disadvantages; and by means of capital and industry, maintain its superiority over neighboring towns more favorably situated. Where natural advantages are very great, they may nevertheless, in the end, attract capital and population from their ancient seats.

CHAPTER III
From Louisville to West Tennessee

The Galt house[8] in Louisville furnishes the traveller with excellent accommodations, administered too with a promptitude in the servants and a kind-

6. The development of steamboat transportation on the Ohio River, the opening of the canal in 1830, and the development of railroads in Kentucky all caused Louisville to grow commercially during this period. The first iron foundry, built in 1812, was joined by other such industries to make Louisville an important place for building and equipping steamboats. The manufacturing of tobacco products and soap, meat packing, lumber, and steam flour mills added to the versatility of the city's commerce. Johnston, *Memorial History of Louisville*, 1:79–83.

7. In 1792 Louisville was considered as a possible location for the state capital. In 1866 the question of the removal of the capital to Louisville was discussed in the legislature but defeated. Collins, *Historical Sketches*, 1:169, 186; 2:181.

ness of manner in the landlord, that make one's abode there doubly agreeable. Southern gentlemen on their way, up and down, often tarry some days in the Galt house for their pleasure alone. In a shop on the opposite side of the street, I drank of the "Blue Lick water," brought from the Blue Licks in the upper part of the state. It is sulphureous, but mainly distinguished for a strong mixture of salt, of which the muriate of soda, or common salts, is distinctly tasteable. It is reputed to have very salutary effects; but it is certainly not as agreeable to the palate as our sulphur waters in Virginia.

From Louisville, the traveller to Nashville has generally the choice of a conveyance by steamboat or by stage. The low state of the waters now, made the success of a voyage up the Cumberland rather problematical; so I took passage in a stage coach, on the third day after my arrival at Louisville.

Our way down, for twenty miles, lay through the broad level tract on which Louisville stands. The soil is exceedingly rich, but cursed with ponds full of rank and rotting vegetation—the potent nurseries of musquitoes and fevers. The country is aptly named "The Pond Settlement."[9] We stopped in the midst of it at a whiskey tavern to change horses. Here we saw some of the *pale faces* of the settlement. They told us that the annual visitation of fevers and agues had already begun. When we asked one of them, whether the ponds could not be easily drained, he answered, "yes, very easily; but a good many of the settlers are opposed to draining them." "What!" said I,

"opposed to draining these festering ponds! Do they wish to be sick every year?" "It seems so," said the pale face—but he spoke with an indifference of manner, which showed that he felt little concern on the subject. "How use doth breed a habit in a man!"[10] These people have grown so accustomed to ponds, musquitoes and fevers, that they take them quietly, as things in the due course of nature.

The next stage brought us to the bank of the Ohio at the mouth of Salt River,[11] which, though gentle as a lamb where it meets with the superior Ohio, is said to be as violent as a brawling bully at a distance from its mouth, and consequently to require a navigator with strong arms and a stout heart to stem its current. This has furnished the Kentucky bruisers with a striking figure of speech: when they would terrify an adversary with a lively apprehension of rough usage, they threaten to "row him up Salt river."[12] We descended the steep muddy banks to a boat, and were rowed not *up* Salt river, but *over* it—an operation that would have been pleasant enough, had not the festering ooze of the banks saluted our nostrils with a compound of villainous smells, drawn forth steaming hot by the cloudless sun of July. After this nasal treat, I was not surprised to hear that the hamlet on the southern bank, where we dined, is a sickly place. In fact, no place on the Ohio, below Louisville, can be called positively healthy; though some

8. Built in 1835, the first Galt House was a well-known hotel for many years. It burned in 1865 and was rebuilt four years later. Newcomb, *Architecture in Old Kentucky*, pp. 126–27.
9. Filson's map of Kentucky (1785) shows Pond Creek and a group of ponds below Louisville; Mitchell's map (1846) shows this creek and a large pond in the southern part of Jefferson County below Louisville. No "Pond Settlement" has been located.

10. William Shakespeare, *Two Gentlemen of Verona*, 5.4.1.
11. Salt River empties into the Ohio at West Point, Kentucky.
12. This phrase, according to Bayard Taylor, American poet, 1825–1878, originated in the Ohio River boatmen's practice of threatening refractory crew members with being turned over to men who worked in the salt works on the river. It was also supposed to refer to river pirates, who found its tortuous course a good hiding place for their loot. William S. Walsh, *Handy-Book of Literary Curiosities* (Philadelphia, 1892), p. 986.

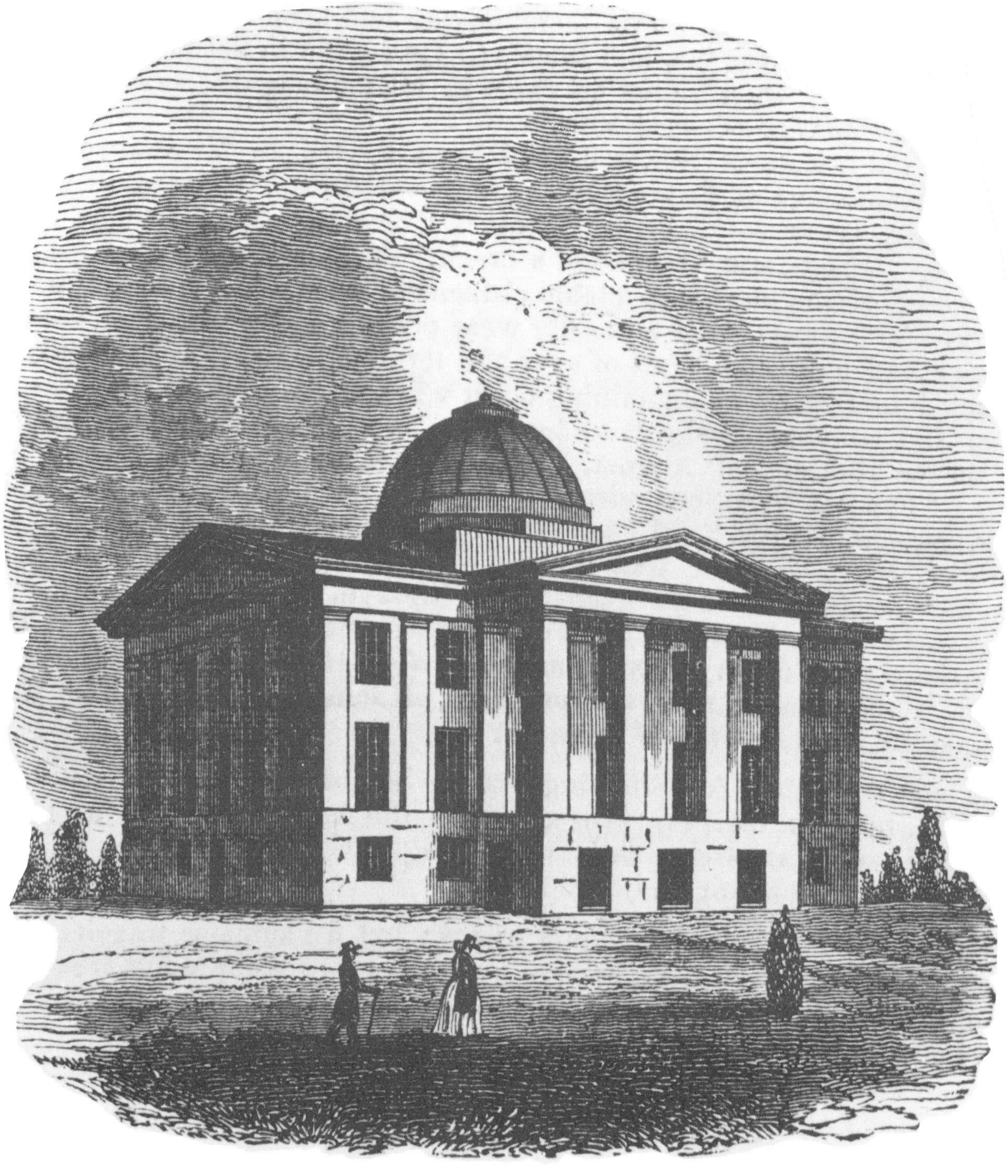

situations are comparatively so. All will become less sickly, when the lands shall be drained and cleared of the overshadowing forests. Were the settlers to spare the valuable trees, and destroy the others, and to cut ditches through their low wet lands, they might generally enjoy the blessing of health, while they reaped the exuberant harvests of their teeming soil.

Below Salt river, we soon began to ascend the hills which here border the Ohio; and after mounting some five or six hundred feet, above our former level, we found ourselves in a broken limestone country of indifferent soil, which became more sandy as we advanced into the less broken parts of the interior; while the trees dwindled to a new growth of saplings, or if not this, an elder generation of black-jacks—till, what with the yellowish white sand and the scattered dwarfish trees, and the peculiar character of the annual plants growing among them, the country assumed the genuine aspect of *The Barrens*,[13] as the early settlers descriptively named this wide region. But the soil, unlike most men, performs more than it promises; flourishing fields of corn surprise the traveller with its vigorous growth and healthy green, on a soil which in its natural state would seem to be scarcely worth cultivation.

As we advanced, the ravines made by streams flowing into the Ohio on our right, gradually disappeared; and the country spread out into a great plain, somewhat variegated by hills and vales; but again showing only some hills at a distance, with slight undulations near the road, without streams of water, but with frequent ponds of dirty water—an ugly sight to one accustomed to vallies and clear brooks. For the space of more than one hundred miles across the country we met with only two brooks. We crossed the Green and Barren rivers, which seemed to be fed by subterraneous streams; for the flat region of ponds about them, leaves the rain water no choice but to go up into the clouds again, or to sink down into the earth. The country is full of caverns and sinkholes. In some of the latter, as before remarked of Greenbrier, streams of water issue at one side and flow into a cavern at the other; seeming to have made for themselves these holes, through which they could take a peep at the upper world as they pursued their underground way. Where a natural breach occurred in the limestone, and left only earth above these streams, the loose matter would gradually fall in and be carried away.

Near Bowling Green, the road passes directly over a mill in a cavern, out of which a stream flows and then enters another cavern a few yards distant. In this country, too, is one of the largest caverns in the world,[14] if reports be true, as I heard them on the way; it is said to have been explored nine miles, and yet no end discovered! But it appears not to be remarkable for any thing but its vast extent.

We arrived at Elizabethtown to supper, the first day; but we were not permitted to take lodging there. We had to go on, and to sleep in the coach, as we best could. Happily there were but three of us, one to a seat. Mine was the fore seat, broad but

13. Filson said that "the Barrens" area was "very good land, and level. It has no timber, and little water, but affords excellent pasturage for cattle." John Filson, *The Discovery, Settlement and Present State of Kentucky* (Wilmington, Del., 1784), p. 20. On the map in this volume an area between the Green and Salt rivers is called "Green River Plains." Elihu Barker's map of 1796 designates an area below the Green River as "Barrens." Kentucky has both a county and a river named Barren in this vicinity.

14. Mammoth Cave was first discovered by white men about 1800. During the War of 1812 saltpeter was mined there for the manufacture of gunpowder. The area became a national park in 1936. Federal Writers' Project, Kentucky, *Kentucky: A Guide to the Bluegrass State* (New York, 1939), pp. 309–10. Hereafter cited as *Kentucky Guide*.

short; whereupon I spread the breadth of my back, with a fellow traveller's pormanteau under my head, and my lower members doubled and erected to a perpendicular, with the knees up. Thus I slept, and the better, after a hot day, for being fanned with the night breezes. About once an hour, I had to rise and unfold my cramped limbs; which being presently restored to their wonted animation, I folded them up again to their perpendicular attitude, and soon rocked and fanned away to the silent realms of Morpheus. I note this incident of my journey, that I may commend this mode of sleeping to stage passengers, who can have a whole seat for their bed. It is far preferable to the more common custom of going to bed in a tavern at eleven o'clock, and of being called up at one—just as a body begins to enjoy a sound sleep after a fatiguing day.

But, N.B. (that is, *noty beny*, as I have seen it written), if you measure six feet or more in length, choose rather the middle seat for your bed; as my next neighbor, who was very long, found the length of that seat an advantage. At first indeed, he tried the doubling process as I did, but the seat being narrow and round backed, and open on both sides, he was frequently jolted off; until he put his head upon the coach window on the one side, and his feet through the opposite one; thus he could maintain his position, without being cramped. He only complained a little of the hardness of the wood used in making the coach-frame; but the interposition of a cloak made it somewhat softer.

The second night we reached Bowling Green, in the midland region of the Barrens. The soil rather improved in appearance, but owing, I suspect, to its thinness upon the surface of the rock, the crops in many places, were of inferior quality. Dry hot weather soon exhausts the moisture of these thin layers of soil, especially where the rock lies in horizontal strata, as it does in this country. Vegetables are then precluded from striking deep

root, as they may in the crevices of inclined or broken strata.

The horizontal stratification of the rocks in this country, was most strikingly apparent in a range of hills on the right, which seemed to constitute the western boundaries of the Barrens. As the road gradually approached them, I was struck with the regular formation of a hill, which swelled out on the side of the adjoining ridge, in the perfect shape of a half cone; the base curving round in a semi-circle more than half a mile in extent, in the manner of a natural wall of limestone; then after a gradual slope of soil, a second wall of rock with a smaller curve; then another slope of ground contracted the hill; and so in succession, a wall and a slope, like a terraced garden, till the lessening semi-circles terminated in a small round top, higher than the ridge out of which this regular half cone projected. The hill had been cleared of trees, except such as grew about the walls. It made an appearance at once beautiful and grand. Should some wealthy proprietor, one hundred years hence, build his mansion on the top, he might by some additional planting and by trimming and cultivating the smooth slopes, convert this hill into the most splendidly elegant residence in the world. It's height I would suppose to be about three hundred feet, and the view from the top must be of great extent.[15]

Bowling Green is a small but neat village.[16] All the villages which we saw on this route are small; but the country is of late becoming populous.

When the wave of emigration first reached the

15. "The city rises in a series of narrow streets, up to a central square with a thinly planted park as its core; it rises farther to the top of a hill on which . . . is the Western State Teachers' College [now Western Kentucky University]." Ibid., p. 306.
16. Collins wrote that the population of Bowling Green was 815 in 1830. No other figures are available until 1870, when the federal census first carries a figure for this town. Collins, *Historical Sketches*, 2:265.

Barrens, it suddenly stopped before a wide tree-less waste of apparently barren soil. When the vicinity of settlements, checked the custom of yearly burning the dried grass of the Barrens, a crop of young trees sprang up and in ten or twelve years settlements began to be made. The unexpected productiveness of the soil, and the extension of the young forest, caused a rapid succession of new settlements. The whole country is now peopled, though not as densely as it may and will be. But for me this country has no attractions. Without mountains, without valleys, without brooks, without large trees—but a great plain with deep sink holes and shallow basins of dirty pond water, and puny woods of the black-jack pattern—it has no charms for my eyes, nor has it any invisible qualities to make compensation.

On the third day we entered the state of Tennessee, at a point near which the waters of Green river part from those which flow into the Cumberland. The character of the country changed immediately; streams of water flowed through vales, and the soil assumed a reddish cast, except the alluvian of the vallies, which was darker. The color of the soil, I suppose, occasioned the name of Red river to be given to the stream, of which we crossed the head waters. Then ascending a ridge, we dined at the Tyree springs,[17] a small watering place, whose water has a muddy sulphureous taste, but, I suspect, very little medicinal virtue. Here, however, we found forty or fifty visiters, who seemed to be trying to enjoy themselves. We then descended into a valley of limestone with a soil black and rich, but in many places too thinly laid over the rock to be very productive in a dry season. This valley conducted us to the Cumberland, a little above Nashville. We crossed the river

17. Tyree Springs, twenty miles north of Nashville on the road to Franklin, Kentucky, was probably the state's best-known watering place. Eastin Morris, *The Tennessee Gazetteer* (Nashville, Tenn., 1834), p. 165.

on a good bridge at the city, and ascending the bluff to the public square, we were put down at the city hotel.

I may as well here, as elsewhere, notice a certain custom of boarders at public houses—a custom which I observed at almost every place in my tour, but more particularly in Tennessee. It may be thus described in general:

You arrive, a stranger at a public house; you wish to see men and things, so you keep yourself a good deal about the bar-room and door. Near meal-time, you observe the company increase; young men and middle aged men come in; and the minutes wear away, they become restless, pacing the room near the door that leads to the dining hall, and seeming frequently to listen, as if they watched for tokens of a coming person or event. If ignorant of this custom, your curiosity is excited to learn the cause of their movements and gestures. Wait a little, and you will see them simultaneously rush through the door, and hurry into the dining room, almost before you hear the dinner bell. You and other strangers begin to follow. Before you have time to enter the dining room, you hear a thundering of chairs, succeeded instantly by a sharp confused clatter of plates, dishes, knives and forks. When you enter the room, you find all the most convenient seats at the table, occupied by a set of men, with heads down and mouths open; and pieces rapidly disappearing from their plates by the quick three-fold operation of a cut—a gape—and a swallow. You may take your seat where you can, and eat as you list— what is it to them? They see you not, their eyes are on their plates—they hear you not, their ears are filled with the music of the knives, forks, and glasses. By the time you are fairly underway with your meal, you again hear the frequent grating of chairs on the floor as they rise and depart.

Now I have but two remarks to make on this custom:

1st. It is *unmannerly*, thus to push in before strangers to the table, to take all the first places, and to snatch all the choice dishes: and, 2nd, it is *beastly*, to rush, seize, gulp down a meal, like a pack of famished hounds. I turn to a more pleasant theme.

Nashville has a commanding situation on a rocky hill, against which the river has run, by means of a horse shoe bend, until it has worn and torn off the point, so as to form a precipitous bluff, perhaps one hundred and fifty feet high. The top is broad and level enough for a large public square containing the court house and market house.[18] Around this and on the sides of the hill, most of the town is built, or rather was built; for the late additions have been made principally on the hill further from the river, where the ground—or rather the rocks—rise still higher and form, half a mile from the square, a lofty round top, where groves of stunted cedars draw a scanty nourishment from crevices in the limestone.

The buildings are generally neat, but not remarkable for size or elegance. Three or four churches, all apparently new, are constructed in a chaste style of architecture, unless we except an unfinished Baptist church, which is deformed, externally, with a superfluity of corrupt Gothic appendages.[19]

The hill which lifts the town to the air, also exposes it to the summer sun, which in a dry hot season like this, makes the bare rocks and walls glow with a heat that issues nightly without being exhausted, and increases daily until rains or long nights bring relief.

I was struck most agreeably with the open benevolent countenances of the people about the streets. None of your care-worn, shy, suspicious-looking faces, so frequent in northern towns. I felt at once that I might freely address any and every man, on any matter that interested me, and be sure of his polite, and even kind attention. Nor did my few days' acquaintance belie these first impressions. They are a sociable, hospitable, orderly and moral population. I never saw more quiet streets, and more uniform good behavior. A population of this character cannot be idle, though I observed less signs of a painful and bustling industry, than is usual in northern towns. There are no large manufactories, except a rolling-mill.

Here are a number of flourishing schools for both sexes: and in the vicinity is the Nashville University,[20] the chief literary institution of the state. It is, however, as yet, merely a college, with eighty or one hundred students. It was once richly endowed with lands; but the legislature so managed this valuable fund, that the institution has enjoyed but a small portion of what the lands might have yielded. Popular legislatures are often very unfit trustees for seminaries of learning.[21]

Just below the town there is a saline sulphur spring, the water of which is very similar to the Blue Lick water that I drank at Louisville. I found it a very salutary drink in hot weather, and not unpalatable, though persons unaccustomed to

18. The Cumberland River is referred to here. The city itself occupies a bowl-like area, with the state capitol and other government buildings occupying a hill in the center. *Tennessee Guide*, pp. 179–80.

19. This description compares in general with that of Morris in 1833. *The Tennessee Gazetteer*, pp. 108–24.

20. Nashville University was a forerunner of George Peabody College for teachers. Allan M. Cartter, ed., *American Universities and Colleges*, 9th ed. (Washington, D.C., 1964), p. 1072.

21. By an act of Congress, 18 April 1806, certain disputed lands were ceded to the state of Tennessee with the specification that the state should appropriate 100,000 acres in the lands reserved for the Cherokee Indians for the use of two colleges and an additional 100,000 acres for the support of academies (one in each county). In issuing grants of land, the state was to set aside 640 acres in every six square miles for the use of schools. U.S., Laws, Statutes, etc., *Public Statutes at Large* (Boston, 1845), 2:381–83.

mineral waters, would be apt to loathe such a strong compound of salts and sulphureous gas. Warm baths are also made of it, and these are both pleasant and medicinal. The spring was known of old to the French settlers of Louisiana. Their hunters made salt of it: hence it came to be called the French Lick.[22]

In addition to a navigable river, the commerce of Nashville will soon be facilitated by four or five Macadamised roads diverging from it. These are now in a process of construction. The one by which I travelled southwards is finished eighteen miles to Franklin, and will soon be extended twenty three miles further to Columbia.

The aspect of the country on this route is pleasant. Low winding hills, crowned with woods of a dark green foliage, part the vallies of the different rivers and brooks. The borders of the Cumberland are diversified with rich low grounds, and high rocky bluffs. The vale of the Harpeth about Franklin, is of a tamer character, but is broad and very rich. Duck river again, on which Columbia stands, exhibits, on a smaller scale, the bold scenery of the Cumberland. This town, like Nashville, is built on a rocky hill; and so is Shelby-ville, thirty eight miles eastwardly, also on Duck river.

All the towns of West Tennessee are laid out after the same model: a public square in the centre containing the court house, and streets crossing at right angles. Nashville, the oldest and largest, seems to have been the prototype.

From Shelbyville I directed my course towards McMinville, in the Barrens, north-east, about forty miles. Here the Cumberland mountains are in full view, not more than five miles off. This is a village of four hundred inhabitants. Hence to Sparta, in a line somewhat more northward, the distance is twenty-six miles. This village, about as large as McMinville, is also in the Barrens, and within two miles of the mountain, where the road by the Crab Orchard passes over to East Tennessee.[23]

Having thus indicated my route, I will now make some general observations on West Tennessee. Of the "Western District," between the Tennessee and Mississippi rivers, I saw nothing, and have therefore little to say. It is represented to be a plain, with small differences of level; the higher parts are generally dry and in part healthy; the lower, flat, marshy, subject to general inundation in wet season, and of course infested with musquitoes and fevers. The soil is mostly rich, and human industry may do much to alleviate the natural evils of the country.

Middle Tennessee,[24] between the river and the Cumberland mountains, is crossed, north and south, by a belt of rich dark loamy soil, on a deposit of recent limestone, full of shells, beginning in the valley of the Cumberland, and extending into Alabama. This belt is about forty miles, more or less, in width, and the richest line of it is marked by the position of Nashville, Franklin, Columbia, and Pulaski. Westward of this tract, the sand-stone appears, where the descending waters have cut deep ravines in their course to the Tennessee. Here the country is comparatively rugged and poor. On the eastern side, the soil gradually be-

22. French Lick Springs was located on the outskirts of Nashville. Morris, *The Tennessee Gazetteer*, pp. 122–23.

23. An 1830 map of Tennessee shows a road running from McMinnville via Sparta to Crab Orchard, then on to Kingston, Knoxville, etc. H. S. Tanner, *The Traveller's Pocket Map of Tennessee* (Philadelphia, 1830). Crab Orchard, referred to later in this sketch, was the location of a gap in the hills of Bledsoe County. Located 136 miles east of Nashville, it was a post and stage stop. Morris, *The Tennessee Gazetteer*, p. 36.

24. Middle Tennessee was especially active in the importation of fine stock and in stock breeding. One farm in the area contained 5,000 acres, most of which was in pasture; race horses were raised, and there were 2,300 head of sheep and about 700 horses, mules, and cattle. Gray, *History of Agriculture*, 2:854–55.

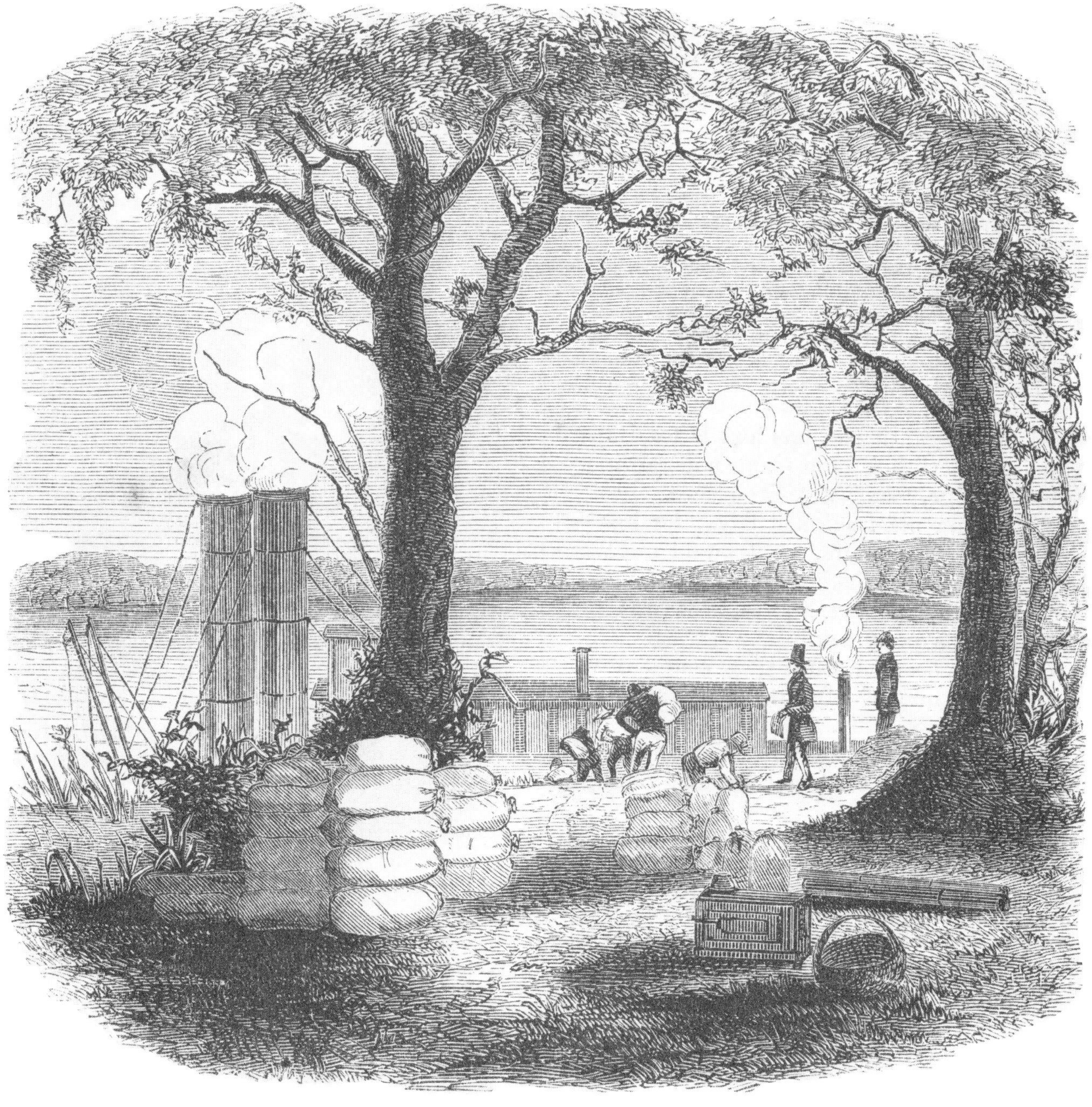

353

A Tour through Kentucky and Tennessee

comes more sandy and less dark, but continues to be for the most part rich and productive, till you approach the Barrens, which is a plateau of level country, elevated about four hundred feet above the rich country below. Here a bed of gravel and sand covers the limestone, except where the waters have washed out vales and exposed it again. The high flat surface of this table land is too poor for cultivation. These Barrens may extend some twenty miles from the base of the Cumberland mountains.

The rich lands are not generally of first rate productiveness. The staple crop is maize; and fifty bushels to the acre is above the average product. Wheat does tolerably well; but twenty bushels to the acre are esteemed a good crop. Cotton often fails, and must be abandoned. Grass does not flourish well in so dry a soil, where meadows cannot be watered. The country is not well watered; the streams do not purl with twinkling surface over beds of gravel; they are evaporated by the scorching sun of July, and the farmers (as one of them told me) have to go sometimes twenty miles to mill.

I do not like the climate. The country slopes northwestwardly from the mountains; it is exposed, therefore to the unmitigated blasts of the coldest wintry winds; then in the summer time, the tropical winds of the gulph meeting and struggling with the northern current on the parched expanse of the great prairie, is turned upon this country with its hot breath; or falling short, leaves the inhabitants becalmed under a burning sun, to snuff the hot steam of their limestone rocks. Hence, the climate is often, in winter, as cold as New England, and in summer, as warm as the West Indies. The spring season is exceedingly variable; one while opening the buds with genial heat, then suddenly destroying the embryo fruit and tender plants with a wintry blast from the

northwest. These are faults of climate, common to the middle and southern states; but I suspect, that the position of west Tennessee gives them here a sensible aggravation. The suspicion is confirmed by the fact, that while the spring naturally begins two or three weeks earlier than in middle Virginia, the frosts continue to occur to as late a period.

Yet, notwithstanding these objections, he would look in vain, who desired to find a country, where nature has upon the whole, offered much higher rewards to human industry, than in the belt of fine lands under consideration. The esteem in which it is held by its densely settled occupants, is evinced by the high prices of farms, and many other tokens of ease and plenty among the inhabitants. He must feel like a prosperous farmer, who can be induced to change his location only by the offer of forty or fifty dollars an acre, even where no very expensive improvements have been made; when a steamboat would in a few days, carry him to regions where every acre sold, would purchase him eight or ten acres of the richest virgin soil.

To me, a mountaineer, there is another objection to this fine country as a residence. Though its surface is varied by low hills, not a mountain is to be seen, even in the distant horizon. I would not choose my abode, where the rising and the setting sun shoots his rays along the surface of the plain. I prefer to see him rise over the mountain top, and to send down his rays through tall pines upon the dewy herbage of the valley, and in the summer evenings to sit in the shadow of the western mountain, while his golden light steals up the side of another in the east. The advantages of such a locality extend beyond the pleasures of the imagination. Here are the abodes of rosy health; and here the farmer's cattle, range through the herbage of unbought pastures. The rich counties of Tennessee are not very healthy; the finest situations on the rivers are too generally infested with *malaria*, which makes the occupants pay dearly for their advantages. Sallow complexions are common; but still there are many exceptions.

In a moral view, Tennessee exceeded my expectation, although two of her lately enacted laws gave me favorable impressions of what I might expect. These were the law against those fashionable instruments of murder, pistols, daggers, and bowie knives, and the law to prohibit the selling of spirituous liquors by retail.[25]

During a ride of more than four hundred miles, through the most populous parts of the state, with frequent stops and sojourns in the most public places, I saw but one drunken man (and he was from Virginia, and had been in the army). I rarely heard profane language; I saw no riotous or disorderly parties; and no quarrelling or fighting, except a sudden affray between two students at a dancing school in Nashville. Even these fiery boys only boxed each other a little, to the great terror of the girls, rather than to their own hurt.

But while the population generally seem to be characterized by mildness, sobriety, and good order, I observed a marked distinction between the inhabitants of the rich lands, and those who live in the Barrens and in the sandy tracts adjacent to them. The former seem to be a compound of Virginians and Kentuckians. The mixture appears to have invigorated the one and mitigated the other, in this climate. A good result. But no sooner had I entered the sandy soils, and especially the Barrens, than I seemed to have discovered a people a century old, not in respect to their individual longevity, but in their ideas and habits. Their "speech bewrayed" their origin; I soon recognized old *Noth-Cahlinur*, in their nasal mushy pronunciation. Among these ancient denizens of the sands, Arkwright's machinery had not invaded the prescriptive rights of the spinning wheel and loom; nor had a windsor chair yet showed his rounded form among the old *split-bottoms*, with low seats and tall perpendicular backs. Here the honest country women still enjoy the summer luxury of bare feet, and make no extravagant use of soap and water. Yet, among them all, I saw a manifest spirit of kindness and good nature. If not as wise as serpents, they are, however, as harmless as doves.[26]

The cause of education is making rapid progress in Tennessee, particularly the education of daughters. To prove this, I will mention a few facts. Besides the numerous schools at Nashville, I found at Franklin, eighteen miles distant, an academy for males, and three seminaries for females, with more than two hundred scholars: at Columbia, twenty-three miles further, a flourishing academy for young men, in the neighborhood, and in the town, two large edifices, nearly finished; the one a college for youth, the other a seminary for young ladies: at Shelbyville, in the next county, besides a male and a female academy in being, they had just filled a subscription of twenty-five thousand dollars for a college. Even at the small town of McMinville, in the Barrens, they had an academy for each sex.[27] In east Tennessee, there are also many seminaries of various ranks and merits, the chief of which is a college at Knoxville.[28] The legislature has also provided a fund for common schools by means of a new bank, with branches diffused over the state.[29] This banking

25. Tennessee, Laws, Statutes, etc., *Public Acts of Tennessee, 1837–38* (Nashville, Tenn., 1838), pp. 186–87, 200–201.

26. Matt. 10:16.

27. Morris, *The Tennessee Gazetteer*, gives interesting comments on these schools under the names of individual towns.

28. A forerunner of the University of Tennessee, this institution is more fully described later in this selection. See also Cartter, *American Universities and Colleges*, p. 1090.

29. Tennessee, Laws, Statutes, etc., *Acts Passed at the*

scheme seems to have been ill devised; but perhaps good as well as evil may result from it.

As to the quality of the education given in all these schools, I can say nothing, except to express a suspicion that it is generally too superficial; but this fault is not confined to Tennessee; and where a good thing is so widely diffused, the effect in the aggregate must be highly beneficial. Superficial education will also lead to a more thorough system.

Yet Tennessee contains a numerous population, especially in the sandy and barren regions, who are very ignorant, and who, as might be expected, are opposed to the patronage of literary institutions by the state. The mental condition of this class may be illustrated by two anecdotes. I breakfasted one morning at the tavern of a late senator of Tennessee, when his son, a youth of eighteen, was setting out to join his school-fellows in turning the master out of doors, until he should treat them to a barrel of cider! I was also told of a case, a few years ago, on the Cumberland. The boys tied their teacher to a board and ducked him in the river, till he promised to treat!

CHAPTER IV

From West Tennessee, by the eastern route to Virginia

From Sparta I crossed the Cumberland mountains by the main road from Nashville to Knoxville. These mountains part from the more eastern ridges of the Alleghanies, between Virginia and Kentucky, where they divide the waters of the Tennessee from those of the Kentucky and Cumberland rivers. They run by a straight course through the state of Tennessee, on the southern border of which they are broken by a chasm, affording the great Tennessee just room to press its contracted waters through, with a swift but unbroken current. The

First Session of the Twenty-third General Assembly of the State of Tennessee (Nashville, Tenn., 1840), pp. 65–75.

mountains extend into Alabama, till they gradually sink into the lowlands near the gulf.

The Alleghany mountains generally, are cut into sharp ridges and spurs, with narrow vales between them, or else broad vallies of limestone separating the chief parallel ridges. The Cumberland mountain, is of a different character: it is a single ridge with two broad plateaus or tables of land on the western side. In the preceding chapter, I described the Barrens of Tennessee, as a broad level space of sandy country, about four hundred feet above the rich limestone district of Middle Tennessee. This is the first plateau of the Cumberlands. You no sooner reach this upper level from below, than you see what is called the mountain, rise before you in a long straight line, broken at intervals by ravines which discharge the mountain streams. This line of mountain is in fact the great bank of the second plateau, elevated about one thousand feet above the former. In ascending to its top from Sparta, I observed that the horizontal limestone lay six hundred feet or thereabouts in depth above the lower plateau; then eighty or one hundred feet of sandstone—then as much limestone again; but finally all was sandstone to the top. This being attained, the road passes over a plain as broad as the Barrens below—that is, about fifteen or twenty miles. The surface is cut at intervals by ravines, but no sharp ridges occur. The road crosses the plateau diagonally, and the whole distance across, from Sparta to the eastern base, is about forty miles. The soil on the top is very poor, too poor to nourish stout forests, such as clothe the mountains of Virginia. Yet some families endeavor to extract a living from these dry sands. Chalybeate springs and a pure atmosphere, attract some visitors from the lower country in the hot season. I found a house, at the distance of nine miles from Sparta, that was filled with boarders, who drank the water of a fine chalybeate, spouting from the rocks in a ravine shaded with evergreens. It is only in a few ravines that I saw the Rhododendron, the Kalmia, the Hemlock (Pinus Cadadensis), and other evergreens, so common in our mountains.

After travelling a few miles further over this plateau, I began to see the eastern ridge of the mountain stretch along the horizon. It rises about five hundred feet above the plateau, running in a single straight line parallel with the western bank of the plateau, and broken at intervals of some miles with gaps. The road leads to one of these gaps, and passes through with scarcely an ascent, at a large farm called the Crab-Orchard. The soil improves in the neighborhood of the ridge; the sandstone ceases, and limestone appears again, seeming to constitute the body of the ridge. But this is not the recent shell-limestone of West Tennessee; it is the old blue limestone, in shapeless masses, so common in the valley of Virginia; and it shows that here, as well as elsewhere, the mountains are older than the plains.

Immediately on passing through the gap, the road begins to descend into the great valley of East Tennessee. The descent is much less than the total ascent on the opposite side because the great valley is a much higher country than the low lands of the west.

To my sorrow I missed the sight of a remarkable curiosity, in descending the mountain; because I did not hear of its existence, until I had left it far behind. Near Nance's tavern, on the mountain side, a brook falls in a single cascade, to the depth of at least three hundred feet, into a narrow gloomy ravine.[30] The bottom is said to be a wild romantic place, overshadowed with precipices and trees, where the visitor's sense of loneliness is increased to awe, and almost to terror, by the perpetual dash of the torrent, that seems to fall from the skies into this dusky glen. The scene inspires that sort of horror, which freezes the veins in reading stories of robbers, caves and deeds of blood, in solitary places. Such a deed was actually committed here, two or three years ago. A traveller known to have on his person a large sum of money, stopped at the tavern, and out of curiosity, clambered down the rocks by himself into this wild chasm. Not returning to the house, he was sought for, and his body found with the marks of murder on it, but no money. He lies buried where he so mysteriously lost his life; and now the visitor, who descends to see this romantic water-fall, must stand by the grave of the unfortunate stranger, who "sleeps alone."

From the mountain to Knoxville, the road passes through a country of little interest to a traveller. There are vales of limestone land, more or less fertile, and watered by springs; the hills are dry and gravelly, and covered with oaks, sometimes goodly timber; but too often especially about the Clinch river, miserable scrubs of the black jack pattern. The Clinch is a pleasant sort of river, one hundred yards wide, with some fertile low grounds. At Kingston,[31] I looked for a fine water scene, at the junction of the Clinch with the great Tennessee; but I was disappointed: the junction, more than a mile below the village, is hidden from view by the dry gravelly hills of black-jacks—the very image of tame poverty.

Through the one street of the village, the road strikes off into the dry gravelly hills of black jacks, avoiding both rivers, and threading the intermediate country. The season was hot and dry; I was weary of the sandy plateaus of the mountain,

30. This probably refers to Ozone Falls, often mentioned in the early travelers' accounts. An inn was located here, but histories of this area do not record the murder related. Helen Bullard Krechniak and Joseph Marshall, *Cumberland County's First Hundred Years* (Crossville, Tenn., 1956), pp. 133–34.

31. Kingston, the seat of Roane County, was established in 1799 on the land of Robert King. Morris, *The Tennessee Gazetteer*, p. 82.

and fatigued with travelling from Nashville on horseback; I longed for interesting scenery; I looked from the tops of the dry hills for a sight of the great Tennessee—but I saw nought except other dry gravelly hills of black jacks; from other hill tops, I looked again—and I saw—ditto, ditto. I was in a state of mind to be easily disgusted; and disgusted I was. Disgust leaves as durable impressions as pleasure. I have, and through all my days I shall retain, in my imagination, vividly pictured, the perfect image of *dry gravelly hills covered with black jacks.*

Farther up the country towards Knoxville, the hills were less tame and barren, the lands between them more spacious and fertile. A few miles below Knoxville, I was at length gratified with a sight of the Holstein, the chief branch of the Tennessee, but much smaller than the main river below the Clinch. The Holstein has a clear lively current, winding among hills, and bluffs, and low grounds.

On approaching Knoxville, I was struck with the conspicuous appearance of the college, seated on the flattened summit of a round hill below the town.[32] The chief edifice, resembles a church. This occupies the centre of the area; around three sides of which are ranges of low dormitories. The institution is attended by eighty or ninety students. Classical studies are said to be pursued here with more success than the sciences.

I was disappointed in my expectations of Knoxville—I mean its external appearance. I had expected to find the chief town of East Tennessee, something more than three hundred houses scattered over the hilly ground about two neighboring creeks.[33] Near the upper and larger of these

creeks, there is a street which for a hundred yards is almost compactly built. Unfortunately for this, the most populous quarter of the town, the creek is a mill-stream; dams have collected a large mass of stagnant water, and consequently the neighborhood is annually infested with fevers. The yearly visitation had already begun, when I arrived there about the 3d of August. From recent notices in the papers, the sickness appears to have been unusually severe, owing probably to the extraordinary drought. I found in this instance a confirmation of the remark formerly made, that opposite sides of stagnant waters are not equally affected by the pestilential vapors. The eastern, which is the leeward side of this creek, is more sickly than the western; because the western winds prevail, and blow the miasma, towards the east.

My stay in Knoxville was too short to furnish me with notes on the character and manners of the inhabitants. Information leads me to believe that they are moral, sociable and hospitable, with all the essentials of true politeness, but with less refinement of mind and manners, than may be found in some older towns.

My venerable friend, Judge White,[34] of the United States Senate, advised me to pursue a route to Abingdon in Virginia, less direct, but more pleasant, than the one usually travelled, through the Sequatchy valley.[35] A stranger, he observed, would

32. East Tennessee College was established in 1807. "The College edifice stands on a retired eminence in the western suburbs of the town, commanding a fine view of the river Holston." Ibid., pp. 84–85.
33. The population of Knoxville was first given in the 1850 census as 2,076. U.S., Bureau of the Census, *The*

Seventh Census of the United States: 1850 (Washington, D.C., 1853), p. 574.
34. Hugh Lawson White, born in North Carolina in 1773, moved in 1785 to that part of North Carolina which became Knox County, Tennessee. He was judge of the state supreme court, 1801–1807 and 1809–1815 and was elected to the United States Senate to fill the vacancy caused by the resignation of Andrew Jackson in 1825. He was reelected in 1829 and in 1835, resigning on 13 January 1840 because he could not obey the instructions of his constituents. *Biographical Directory of the American Congress*, p. 2002; *Dictionary of American Biography*, vol. 10, pt. 2, pp. 105–7.
35. Sequatchy or Sequatchee River is a branch of the

find more interesting objects on the southern route by Dandridge, Greenville and Jonesborough; and would moreover find the less frequented way, more shaded from the scorching rays of the sun, in such hot dry weather as then prevailed. Disagreeable intelligence from home induced me, desirous as I was to take the most pleasant route, nevertheless to pursue the most direct: so I went to Rogersville by way of Rutledge, in the long narrow vale of Sequatchy. The road enters this vale a few miles above Knoxville, and pursues the middle of it in a straight course for the space of forty miles. The vale is about two miles, often less, in width. The Chesnut ridge separates it from the valley of the Clinch on the north-western side, and a range of hills less bold and regular from the valley of the Holstein on the opposite side. It maintains strictly the character of an Appalachian valley, in its direction, its almost uniform width, its limestone soil, and its being crossed by streams of water, which here cut the south-eastern hills and flow into the Holstein. It is nearly all under cultivation; the road lies between an almost uninterrupted succession of fields, with scarcely a tree to shelter the traveller from the fierce blaze of the sun, in dog-days. For a while the pleasant features of the scene, and the repose which seemed to reign among the inhabitants of this secluded valley, amused me; but the tedious uniformity of the whole, united with the fatigue of travelling, and the ceaseless glow of the sunshine, made it so wearisome at last, that I almost wished for a mile or two of the dry gravelly hills covered with black jacks. On the second day of my journeying through this quiet length of valley, I saw before me an evident sign of change, in the loftier swell and closer approximation of the mountains ahead; the valley seemed to divide—a narrow portion of it

ran up between the high mountains, another turned to the right: this latter was my route, and conducted me again to the valley of the Holstein. The scenery was now both various and pleasant. The road wound up again among the hills, and led me, by ups and downs, and turns of all sorts, among fields, rocks and hills, to Rogersville, two miles from the river.

Near the village I observed among the gray limestones, some rocks of extraordinary color. On breaking off some fragments, I found them to be a calcareous breccia[36] composed of small crystalline fragments, brown and white. On alighting at the village tavern, I observed that the windows were full of polished specimens of this breccia, exceedingly various and beautiful. Some were white, a little discolored with brownish grains; some black, but dusted with grains of lighter hue; most of them, however, were variously made up of brown and white pieces, round or angular, of different sizes and shades of color; often brilliant, and often displaying an intermixture of shells, and other animal remains, with the native stone. Some of them resembled, a good deal, the variegated marble of which the pillars in the capitol at Washington are made. Inexhaustible quarries of this marble might be opened about Rogersville. Some of it may find a market, by water carriage, down the Tennessee; but it is too remote from the seats of luxury, to be much used for ages to come, beautiful though it be. As yet but one stone cutter finds employment by it; he makes tombstones, and some articles of furniture.

Rogersville is a small village of sixty or seventy dwellings.[37] Its marbles are its only distinction from ordinary villages. From this to Kingsport at the confluence of the north and south branches

Tennessee River rising near Crab Orchard. Morris, *The Tennessee Gazetteer*, p. 146.

36. Calcium fragments of rock.
37. Rogersville, the seat of Hawkins County, was established in 1786. *Tennessee Guide*, p. 310.

of the Holstein, the country presents nothing remarkable, except that the mountains in view assumed a bolder and more picturesque appearance. The road traverses an arable country of good limestone land, but hilly, as such lands commonly are. Kingsport is but a poor village;[38] the scenery about it is, however, the finest on the whole of this route through East Tennessee. The ridge that separates the vallies of the Clinch and Holstein has been in view all the way from Kingston; but it has now risen to grandeur, and puts on quite a dominating aspect. Between the branches of the Holstein another ridge presents itself, and would seem, after running down from Virginia, to terminate here; but on turning your face southward, you observe a high ridge, arising from the rivers at their point of junction, and stretching away quite loftily towards the southwest; showing itself on examination, to be only the last mentioned ridge, continued, after a breach had been made for the south Holstein. From Ross's bridge over the north branch, a very sweet scene presents itself. You see the rivers meet a few hundred yards below, their banks shaded with fine trees; and an island just below the junction, with its thicket of willows and other trees, half hides and half displays the united waters, as they steal away under the shady foliage of the banks. This pretty scene was to me the more refreshing, because I saw it on a calm summer evening after riding wearily under the beams of a scorching sun.

Near the bridge is the residence of its wealthy proprietor, the Reverend Frederick A. Ross,[39]

whom I name here as worthy of commendation for two enterprises, which, if imitated by East Tennesseans, will greatly improve the condition of their remote valley. He has erected on the North Holstein a cotton mill with one thousand spindles. What is probably of more importance, he has planted thirty acres of the Chinese mulberry, to which the soil and climate of East Tennessee are well adapted; and so flourishing are the young trees, that by next year they will feed worms enough to make at least a thousand pounds of silk.

Being now on the border of Virginia which I entered by way of Blountville, I will stop to make some observations on the country of East Tennessee.

On my return from the west, I would fain have passed through Cherokee on the southern border of East Tennessee, and the borders of the adjacent states. This last remnant of the once great territory of the Cherokees, embraces the south-western extreme of the Appalachian mountains. All reports agree in representing it as a beautiful country of hills and vallies; the hills sometimes gravelly and rather poor, but clothed with vegetation; the vallies rich and watered by perennial springs. The climate is the most temperate in the United States, and the whole region highly salubrious. Here the peach, the melon, and the grape, acquire their most delicious flavor: maize, yams and all the products of mild climates flourish abundantly. The mulberry could not find a more congenial soil and climate. The high hills and mountains will pro-

38. Kingsport is located in an area of the state which has been settled since 1761; however, it did not develop into a city until early in the twentieth century. In the pioneer period it was an important shipping port because of its location on the Holston River, a tributary of the Tennessee. Ibid., pp. 279–82.

39. Ross was born at Cobham, Cumberland County, Maryland, in 1796; as a young man he moved to Tennessee in the area near Kingsport. He studied theology under the Reverend Robert Glenn; was licensed to preach at Glade Springs, Washington County, Virginia; and was ordained as an evangelist at Rogersville, Tennessee, six months later on 5 October 1825. His home, Rotherwood, near Kingsport, became a showplace. In his later years he lived in Huntsville, Alabama, where he died on 13 April 1882. J. E. Alexander, *Brief History of the Synod of Tennessee, From 1817 to 1887* (Philadelphia, 1890), pp. 120–22.

duce the grains and fruits of the north; the low warm vallies will mature some of the most valuable products of a tropical climate.

No wonder that the Cherokee loved his fatherland, when it was so lovely in itself, and was moreover the seat of his tribe and the dwelling place of his fathers, from times beyond the reach of tradition. All that can attach mankind to the earth, attached him to the woody hills, the rich vales and the clear fountains of this beautiful region. No wonder that this, the most civilized of the Indian tribes, clung with fond affection to the delightful home which God had given to them: but the white man coveted, and would have it, because he could take it by force. A fraudulent treaty had been made,[40] and was now, at the time of my journey in the process of execution by military coercion. The Georgians had already cast lots for their portion of the spoil, and threatened bloodshed if it were not immediately surrendered. Troops of soldiers were hunting the Indians, and driving them like cattle to the encampment. Like cattle, the Indians submitted, and were peacefully gathered, preparatory to their removal. I was deterred by the confused state of the country, from taking this southern route on my way home.

The valley of East Tennessee, comprehending the space between the Cumberland mountain and the great Unaka or Iron Mountain[41] on the southeast, is from forty to sixty miles wide, and two hundred long. It terminates in the hills of Cherokee, on the southern border between Tennessee and Georgia. It is but a continuation of the great valley of Virginia, spreading to a greater breadth by reason of the many waters which converge and form the Tennessee; thus joining in one, several vallies before separated by continuous mountains. The country is hilly, the atmosphere pure and healthful. There is much good soil, but not much of first rate fertility.

The people are generally moral, sober, and plain in their manners; education is more attended to than in most parts of the south. Several institutions besides the one at Knoxville, have the name of colleges: they are rather academies, where many youth of the country obtain some knowledge of the classics and of several branches of science. The comparative poverty of the inhabitants is apparent to a traveller. Few handsome houses or other indications of wealth and luxury, present themselves. Though nature bestows the gifts of the earth with sufficient liberality, the productions of art are difficult to obtain, owing to the remoteness of this valley from all the great marts of trade. The navigation of the Tennessee and its upper branches is long and difficult; the roads toward the Atlantic are long and rough. Livestock is therefore the principal export. With this single resource, and a heavy freightage on imports, the farmer may acquire the necessaries and some of the comforts which are obtained by exchange; but the elegancies and luxuries are generally beyond his reach. Cotton mills, by aiding domestic industry; and the culture of silk, by furnishing a valuable staple of easy carriage; would improve the circumstances of the people. A rail road to Charleston, and another to the James river canal, with an improved navigation of the rivers, would complete the means, by which East Tennessee might ere long become as prosperous and delightful a valley, as any of the thousand vallies of the Appalachian mountains. At present this is not the country for any one who aims at the rapid accumulation of wealth. The inhabitants seem to be aware of this.

40. Probably the Treaty of New Echota, signed on 29 December 1835, whereby the Cherokees agreed to give up all their land east of the Mississippi and move to the West within two years. Adams, *Dictionary of American History*, 4:97.

41. The Unaka Mountains are a section of the Great Smokies; they separate Cherokee County, North Carolina, from Monroe County, Tennessee. Heilprin and Heilprin, *A Complete Pronouncing Gazetteer*, p. 1881.

Hence there is little of the activity and bustle, the eager enterprise and noisy driving of business, visible in many parts of the United States. Considering the density of the population, it is the most quiet country that I ever saw. This indicates both poverty and contentment. If the people are not rich, still they are evidently not miserable.

A farmer who lives in rural plenty below Knoxville, related to a party of us who lodged at his house, an anecdote that may illustrate the philosophic contentment, which many in this country feel in their quiet abodes. A man who lived in a secluded nook in the mountains, came to his house; and when he saw the farmer's large stock of cattle, and other constituents of rural wealth, he turned to the proprietor and said:—but I should remark that the mountaineer habitually uttered his words with a loud droning accent, making pauses to gather breath, and closing every sentence with a long drawn—hah! by way of emphasis. Turning to the farmer who was a magistrate, he drew forth this speech. "Why—squire—what in the world do you want with all these cows—hah? And such a parcel of horses—hah? And I see you have two wagons—hah? you can't use so many things—hah! And there you have a barn yard—full of stacks—hah! Too much trouble—squire—hah! Why I hav'nt a quarter as many things as you have—and I have too much—hah! I have three cows—and two horses—and a wagon—hah! I mean to sell one horse—and the wagon—hah! I can make enough to eat and wear, without them—hah! All that's over what one needs—is useless trouble—hah! That's my notion—hah! Ain't I right squire—hah?" This speech of the droning mountaineer, expresses the philosophy of many in this quiet country—and in other countries too.

I entered Virginia on the evening of a sultry day. I was fatigued with my long travel on the open roads of Tennessee—exhausted with a perpetual sweat of three hot weeks—sore with the effort to keep an umbrella over my head. I had seen clouds pour out showers at a distance, but not one had shed refreshment on my debilitated frame. This afternoon a heavy shower had fallen before me, and what was extraordinary the road entered a forest; in the evening a delightful coolness was diffused through the atmosphere. As I entered the forest at dusk, that musical tribe of insects, the *catydids*, began to chirp merrily on the trees. The woods grew darker; the air freshened to a delightful temperature; the notes of my shrill musicians grew shriller and multiplied, till every tree and bush and leaf, seemed to quiver with the sound. Thus was I ushered into the limits of my native state by dark woods, that rang with the sharp strains of a million joyful *catydids*.

The next morning on paying my bill, I had palpable evidence that I had crossed the line. Tennessee *shin-plasters*[42] were rejected; Tennessee bank notes were gently declined—but a Virginia bank note, brought me silver dollars in change! During a ride of four hundred and fifty miles from Nashville, I had seen nothing in circulation but Tennessee bank notes (mixed occasionally with an Alabama note), down to the denomination of six and a quarter cents; and shin-plasters of all sorts and of all sizes, from a dollar downwards, and manufactured by all sorts of persons, from the wealthy merchant to the market butcher and the petty shopkeeper. This latter generation sprang into being immediately on the stoppage of specie payments by the banks.

·   ·   ·

42. Shinplasters were fractional currency issued by banks and businesses until the time of the Civil War. Adams, *Dictionary of American History*, 2:321.

SOUTHERN GARDENS AND AGRICULTURAL INDUSTRY

The weekly Southern Sportsman *was edited by Thomas Bangs Thorpe and R. L. Brenhan during its short lifespan of twelve weeks. Its editors hoped to attract the financial support of the literate and sporting plantation element of the South, but the unannounced, abrupt demise of the periodical after so brief an existence is mute evidence that the hoped-for sustenance was not forthcoming.*[1]

To a person who has resided but a short time in a country far from his native home, and who there finds usages widely different from those in the midst of which he was brought up, can sometimes, although a stranger to its various sources of industry, perceive, by simple comparison, radical evils, which the force of habit, and often common routine, hide from the observation of those who are the most seriously concerned; however, in this case, it is only with extreme reserve, that a stranger ventures to submit his reflections to the public. This is precisely my position, in the observations I purpose delivering, on the cultivation and produce of land here, which a residence of some years in the rural districts of other Agricultural countries, has enabled me to frame. I will first speak of Horticulture, a pursuit which engrosses the time and capital of so many planters in the vicinity of this city.

Garden grounds in this region generally comprise an extent of 15 or 20 acres or more, from the river inland, with a narrow front of no more than from one to four or five acres. Immense labor is necessary to cultivate these, for a garden, vast tracts, and render them fruitful, by irrigations, weeding, &c., &c.—many expensive means are employed to collect the daily produce, which, from

the field, is brought to the bank of the river, and from this point conveyed to the town. But before its conveyance thither, it is necessary to count all its different species; divide them into small lots, according to the expected demand in the market; distribute to each *negro-merchant* the quantity entrusted to him, that he may give to his master a just account on his return home. These preliminaries being settled, the small craft, loaded with vegetables, is despatched about the middle of the night, under the charge of the negro-merchant who is generally selected from amongst the best slaves. Whatever may be the state of the weather, it is always necessary to convey the products to the river bank, and there count and despatch them.

The negroes, on their arrival to the town, arrange the vegetables on the market-place; when the sale is ended, usually before noon, they carry again to their boats the articles which remain unsold, and with which they are obliged to return to the plantation, in order to render up a strict and minute account of the quantities disposed of, and those which remain. But what is thus daily brought back, almost always exceeds by much that which is sold, and being of no further value to the owner, can only be applied to feed the animals on the plantation, or perhaps be thrown away. This state of things is thus repeated from day to day, and year to year, causing incalculable loss, on which I intend to make a few remarks, and strive to indicate the defects from which it flows.

B., M.D., "Southern Gardens and Agricultural Industry," *Southern Sportsman* 1 (5 June 1843): 96.
1. Milton Rickels, *Thomas Bangs Thorpe: Humorist of the Old Southwest* (Baton Rouge, La., 1962), p. 73.

So many small boats being every night despatched to the town, whatever may be the weather and season, we can easily foresee the continual dangers to which they are exposed, either from sudden squalls, or from the waves sometimes running very high, occasioned by the steamboats coming near them—very happy, indeed, when the pilot condescends to turn his helm a little, in order not to sink a frail skiff, which cannot avoid them.

The health of the negroes thus employed, is undermined, both by these nocturnal expeditions, being exposed to all the inclemency of the weather, and by another more fatal cause, that is to say, the use of ardent spirits, to which almost all this class are strongly addicted. This is a double evil for the planter, who, without any possibility of preventing it, furnishes the means of this abuse, and who, at the end of a few years after, sees his best slaves perish, or seriously deteriorate, from the united influence of this night labor, and its closely connected wretched excess.

There is another evil operating on the negro, and resulting from his familiar acquaintance with the increasing crowd of white people, which overflow the markets with the products which they buy at second hand, from the gardeners, or even from the negroes themselves. At the end of some years, the slave who has been thus hail fellow well met, with uneducated and low men, becomes more and more prone to lay aside those habits of respect and submission, which his condition imposes on him.

Thus the negro has lost, under triple account of health, good behavior and docility. Let us add the daily punishments, caused by his continual faults, and so very painful to his master to inflict. These observations, which I could easily multiply at will, suffice to prove the necessity, in my opinion, of a reform in the fruition of this species of industry. I will pursue this subject.

The planters fancy they have done a great deal, when they have prepared their grounds for a large harvest; but I do not know any of them endeavoring to improve and vary their products. Every season has for them its peculiar kind of tillage, and we see them all together produce the same mass of vegetables. What is the inevitable consequence of this? a ruinous superabundance; for, this glut of produce, the greater part of which is returned on their hands, and becomes almost perfectly useless, has cost in tillage, sowing, weeding, irrigation, gathering, transporting to the river, apportioning, conveying to the market, and at last bringing back again, without any profit whatever—this rejected part exceeding, to an enormous extent, the quantity which has been disposed of. Let us, however, suppose that there is an equality between the portions of the sold and returned. That would only prove that the gardeners had just realized the half of their fond anticipations. They had thrown away half of their time and expense for nothing at all. A dead loss!! It is well known that at every period of the year there is a paucity in many articles of garden produce, whilst at the same time there is a glut in others. The inclemency of the season opposes the due development of those; granted, but should not the genius of the Horticulturist, as in Europe, find resources to contend successfully against the influences of the season? On that continent, how frequently do we see a handsome revenue issue from the proper cultivation of a single acre of ground? There everything is foreseen, every resource is put in requisition, to extract the last susceptibility from the smallest particle of soil. By means of irrigation, and judicious manure, the earth's fecundity is inexhaustible. There, every species of fruit and vegetable is improved by the mode of culture, either in selecting sun or shade, low or elevated situation, according to the nature of the plant, or by skilful graftings; in short, by every means which necessity, or the ceaseless activity of man, furnishes to his hand.

Would it not be better for each planter, under

his own hand, his own eye, to put into improved cultivation one or two acres, or more, where everything might be looked after, with respect to greenhouse, hot-beds, commodious means of available irrigation, coverings, &c., &c., in order, by strict attention, to improve the quality of his products, and thereby augment their price in the market? A certain portion of this precious reserve might even be advantageously consecrated to the exclusive raising of fruits, either too much neglected, or entirely overlooked; or exotics, to this time unknown in this country, whose produce might raise the Horticultural character of Louisiana, and redound to the individual fame of the cultivator. I am perfectly convinced that many delicious fruits might be naturalized here, with much ease, and a little expense, were we but once to give our minds to the subject; and I should be happy, if the suggestion thus thrown out, be adopted by others, more interested and experienced in those affairs than myself.

The half of the remaining land might be indiscriminately cultivated, as at present, which would produce amply sufficient for the demand, as we have seen by our former statement, in which it appears that the larger portion was far too abundant for sale. There would then remain an entire half of the land, in which labor has been the hardest in every respect, and more particularly in that of carriage. Might not this portion be advantageously devoted either to a simple meadow, from which all weeds and noxious plants should be rooted out, in which animals could be bred; or to a plantation of fruit trees, the species of which might be improved by graftings or other means, and better still to both a meadow and a plantation of fruit trees, under whose genial shade the domestic animals might find a shelter from sun and rain? I plainly foresee the objections which may be urged against this plan. I may be told that the negro is too careless, too limited in his intelligence,

to admit of his being employed in works like these, at once both delicate and exacting? Besides, the grounds would be subject to perpetual robbery, the thief being attracted by the greater value and scarcity of the produce? Other objections might be adduced, but I shall not stop here to examine their validity (which, by-the-bye, do not appear to me difficult to surmount); since, from what I said at the beginning of this article, I merely skim the surface of the subject, with much reserve as to my own powers of discrimination, and I should be loth to commit myself in the discussing of the particulars, which would destroy the effect of what I have advanced, that may be deemed entitled to consideration.

It is certain that all kinds of industry experience, at different epochs, more or less distant, general modifications, which are either in constant progress, or are the fruits of a change dictated by the state of the market consumption. Now, when the want of these modifications makes itself felt, it would be positively unwise to refuse to adopt them. There is one principle, which we ought never to lose sight of—that in every species of industry, the question is not the amount of produce we can raise, but what is necessary to supply the public demand at the period. If we depart from this we are liable both to blame and loss. It is puerile to complain of the immense masses of produce which remain unsold; the fault is ours, and our want of prudent foresight.

I will conclude this communication with a reflection, which has often forced itself on me, whilst I have stood on the banks of the river, and contemplated the innumerable quantities of garden produce prepared for night embarkation. I have asked myself the question, whether some means of obviating this evil could not be found, for example, by a collective or private enterprise of boat or boats, which, at stated intervals, might every day come to different landing places, and carry away to town the produce of each planter, which might be regulated according to the known wants of the market, having regard at the same time to economy in the vegetables, and the due interest of every proprietor. But I bound my remarks on this last particular, by simply indicating the means, without attaching any other importance to it. But are not the evils of the system which I have brought to light, sufficiently prominent to demand some serious and immediate remedy? This is for the consideration of those parties who are alone interested with respect to property and capital, and to them it addresses itself for their examination and decision.

B., M.D.

OUR VISIT TO NATCHEZ

Internal evidence strongly suggests that the author of this selection was Thomas Bangs Thorpe, one of the editors of the Southern Sportsman. *Among other indications, the initial* P *probably stood for "Pardon Jones," a character Thorpe employed in his humorous fictional writing, one well known to his readers.*

Thomas Bangs Thorpe (1815–1878), was born in Massachusetts; for his health he moved to Louisiana about 1835. A man of many talents, he painted, wrote humorous stories, was active in politics, and was a skilled sportsman. In 1853 he moved to New York, where he was a regular contributor to the leading periodicals of the day. When the Civil War broke out, despite his earlier affiliation with the South, he served on the Union side.[1]

We were always encouraged to believe that Natchez and its vicinity possessed great natural and artificial beauties, but we had very little conception of the country; or the improvements it possessed until we made personal observation. The bold bluff on which reposes in so much quiet the most beautiful city of the South, is one of the most striking peculiarities that meets the eye of the traveller on the Mississippi. It rises up with singular and startling effect from among the low lands with which it is surrounded, and is exaggerated by the contrast. Persons travelling upon our Northern waters, are struck with the picturesque appearance of the towns and villages that line their banks; rising from the water's edge, the houses ascend the sides of the hills like steps, and seem to be almost the creation of fairy hands. These beautiful places, upon near inspection, prove that "distance lends enchantment to the view,"[2] and that they possess little merit save that of accidental and beautiful location. The opposite of this is the case with Natchez; its "landing" is, like all such places, full of boats, small houses and great ones; placed together with an eye to trade alone, and crowded with drays, dust, boxes, barrels and business. But ascend the steep road that leads from it, and place yourself firmly on top of the "bluff," and where

[Thomas Bangs Thorpe], "Our Visit to Natchez," *Southern Sportsman* 1 (15, 29 May 1843): 68, 88.
1. *Dictionary of American Biography*, vol. 9, pt. 2, p. 509.

2. Thomas Campbell, "The Pleasures of Hope," pt. 1, line 7.

will you find a more singularly beautiful city or landscape? Before you stretches out like a panorama, the Mississippi and the productive lands of Concordia,[3] marked by the divisions of plantations and work of the plough; the small houses of the negroes nestle among groves of the quick-growing China tree,[4] or are hid from view by the remains of the primitive forest. Far up and down the majestic river are exhibitions of life and industry; the powerful steamer passes swiftly by; the richly loaded flatboat, quietly and mysteriously disappears; huge trees, that shaded, perhaps, the wild savage of the Upper Missouri, or formed the protection for a children's party on the lovely banks of the Ohio, tumble about in the current of the river, and pass on, to be caught in some swift eddy of the Louisiana shore, there to be used in the hot fires of the sugar house, or, escaping all obstructions, find a grave in the depths of the Mexican Gulf. Inland, opens the city of Natchez, composed of beautiful streets and rural residences. In this respect this city has few equals; and we would pay a tribute to the master spirits that originally "settled on the bluff" and started their improvements in so much better taste, and inspired those who followed them with the same spirit, than can be found in any other city or village in the South and West. Everywhere the stranger is met with elegant and tasteful display. The mansions of the rich, hid with foliage, festooned and trimmed, and variegated, full of gravelled walks and choice flowers, finds a fit companion in every little cottage, however poor, that has, too, its flowers and modest trees, and little vines; showing that the prevailing taste is elegant, and appreciates those ornaments that are Nature's most beautiful, and yet within the reach of the poor and the rich alike.

The country around Natchez is broken, and the soil, like all lands of the kind in the South, very rich, and covered with the finest forest trees. We have travelled through some of these beautiful specimens of Nature's handy-work, before the axe had made a single waste, and we were struck with the great beauty of the groves of trees which met our eye everywhere, and we could not help expecting the palace of some wealthy landholder would suddenly peep out among the trees of the distant landscape. Around Natchez, though one of the oldest settled countries in the Union, these beautiful natural groves have been spared, and every road leading from the city is lined with elegant mansions, the abodes of luxury and taste, hid partially from view by the rich magnolia and oak, the frowning gum and delicate beech. In the immediate vicinity of these mansions are all the delicate shrubbery and flowers that grow with such profusion in the South—a perfect fairy land; and yet, for want of time, what we saw was said to be the least remarkable of all the improvements in the vicinity of Natchez.

. . . .

An hour brought us to the quiet village of Washington,[5] which seemed, upon our entrance, to be in enjoyment of the slumbers of a gentle *siesta*—so quiet was the air of repose which rested over her unpeopled streets, and hovered around the sweet cottage homes, peeping through clustered verdure upon the deserted thoroughfare, like a coy maiden, stealing from her retiracy an anxious glance upon the "great world" told of, but all unknown to her, and of all things most pined for. We arrived at sunset at the house of a friend—one of those we delight in esteeming—the architect of his own fortune, and glorying in the knowledge

3. Concordia Parish, Louisiana, is directly opposite Natchez.
4. The chinaberry. William Carey Grimm, *The Book of Trees*, p. 449.

5. Between 1802 and 1820 Washington served as Mississippi's second territorial capital and its first state capital. It was the first station on the Natchez Trace east of Natchez. *Mississippi Guide*, p. 333.

that it was won by the sweat of his own brow, stern integrity, justice in all things, and by the uniform practice of that *self dependence*, which gives ever evidence of its possessor's determination to succeed in his undertakings, and assurance that success *must and will be his*. He has a warm heart and open hand—a friendly thought and kindly word for all—and is, in all things, worthy the tribute we here give to his worth. We met here several of the best practical planters of Adams and Jefferson counties, and until a late hour of the night, feasted on the converse of experience, upon things Agricultural, receiving many important hints, some new truths, and much general information, upon this most important subject.

The morning of the 19th was chill and lowering, but as the day advanced it grew pleasanter, and finally became Spring-like and cheering. About 10 o'clock we reached Fayette, the County seat of Jefferson.[6] The village was already crowded, while from various quarters others were constantly arriving. We strolled over to the Academy, just in the suburbs of the village, and occupying a beautiful location, shaded densely by a grove of pines. A bower of considerable size was arranged for the convenience and comfort of the ladies, while outside the enclosure, in various directions, stood the different kinds of stock, arranged in proper order.

It was a glorious day for "old Jefferson"; her sons and daughters were here congregated, to show by their kindly words, and kinder smiles, the efforts intended for the advancement of their community, in that knowledge which is the truest wealth. We passed an hour pleasantly, in strolling at will over the grounds, making a hurried examination of the stock, implements, manufactures, &c., exhibited, which, although not extensive, gave high evidence of the pride, enterprise and ingenuity of the citizens. At 11 o'clock, an admirable address was delivered by Professor K. Montgomery, Esq., one of the Vice Presidents of the Society.[7] An address better adapted to the occasion, could not, we think, well be conceived; for, while it contained many home truths, and hints of importance, and words of cheer, for those engaged in the good work, a vein of quaint humor and quiet satire, gave it that zest, too frequently lacked by addresses concocted for such occasions. It was received with gratification by all. . . .

       ·   ·   ·

The exhibition then commenced of the stock, manufactures, &c. Of the former, we have never seen a finer exhibition in the South, and doubt greatly whether, as to quality, it could be much exceeded elsewhere. The principal manufactured articles were presented by Mr. John Robertson, who is now engaged in erecting a factory, some ten miles east of this village. A pair of blankets, shown by him, and made from the wool of sheep raised in this immediate vicinity, exceeded anything we had previously met with of American manufacture, and we are somewhat familiar with such things, as our Jefferson friends can testify. Samples of Canton Flannel, and Webbing, of fine quality, were also shown; a Hearth Rug, beautifully and richly dyed, of tasteful pattern; and last, a piece of Cotton Bagging made from an *inferior article of Cotton;*[8] this was an admirable article, and *must*

6. Fayette is about twenty-six miles northeast of Natchez. Heilprin and Heilprin, *A Complete Pronouncing Gazetteer*, p. 637.

7. This may be a misprint for Prosper K. Montgomery, who was born in Adams County, Mississippi, in 1808 and died in Jefferson County in 1886. The diary of Susan Sillers Darden, 1854–1861 and 1865–1877, now in the Jefferson County Library, Fayette, Mississippi, contains many references to him. Mrs. E. O. Greathouse, Librarian of Jefferson County Library, to Jacqueline Bull, 2 October 1969.

8. Hemp bagging and hemp rope were generally used for covering cotton, but from time to time efforts were made to substitute cotton bagging because of the high price of hemp. Gray, *History of Agriculture*, 2:705–6.

take, with all who acknowledge the necessity of advancing the consumption, by all possible means. Its width was about 35 inches, and weighing about 17 ounces to the yard, of double and twisted warp, and can be manufactured, provided the planter furnishes his *inferior* cotton, which answers as well as the best, at the moderate rate of 8 cents per yard. This experiment should by all means be pushed to the perfection of which it is susceptible, by the enterprising citizens of Jefferson. She has led the way in this matter, as also in that of using hoop iron for baling, and we doubt not slight effort will keep her *ahead* in the *good work*, for which she deserves high praise.

We have not space to detail our observations in relation to the entire exhibition, and shall close by adding a few remarks in relation to the distinguishing features of the occasion, and appending a list of the premiums awarded, so far as ascertained before our departure. At one o'clock a bountiful dinner was served in the shady corner of the enclosure; it were needless to observe that full justice was done this part of the exhibition of *Old Jefferson's fatness*. An hour after, an exciting scene occurred upon the trial of several splendid saddle horses. . . .

.   .   .

We close by observing that the exercises of the occasion closed by a brilliant party at Truly's[9]—and, as may be supposed, it was *truly* interesting, for the fairest of old Jefferson's daughters were there gathered. We shall forward you the regular reports of the Committees so soon as received.

Your friend, P.

9. The old Cameron House, a tavern on the Natchez and Port Gibson Post Road, was kept by James Bennett Truly until his death in 1845. Mrs. E. O. Greathouse to Jacqueline Bull, 19 June 1969.

AN EXPEDITION INTO THE EVERGLADES

George Henry Preble (1816–1885), who rose to the rank of rear admiral in the United States Navy, came from a seafaring family of Portland, Maine. His father had been a sea captain and his uncle a commodore. He himself became a midshipman in 1841 and served in the Indian Wars in Florida shortly thereafter. The diary from which this selection is taken was written during that period of service. Later Preble served in the Union Navy in the Civil War and upon his retirement wrote on naval and other aspects of American history.[1]

The following pages are a verbatim transcript of a penciled memorandum of events made by me from day to day while on an expedition across the Everglades, around Lake Okeechobee, and up and down the connecting rivers and lakes, in 1842.

. . .

The expedition, my diary of which follows, was commanded by Lieutenant John Rodgers,[2] who died only last May a rear-admiral. The second officer in seniority, Lieutenant William L. Herndon,[3] the father-in-law of President Arthur, as is well known, went down in the steamer "Central America," preferring "certain death to the abandonment of his post," and of the remaining officers, only myself and Passed Midshipman Samuel Chase Barney (who is no longer in the service) are living. It is to be presumed that all, or nearly all of the seamen, and rank and file of marines, have passed away.

Those "dug-out" canoes which formed *our homes* for the sixty days the expedition lasted were hollowed cypress logs, about thirty feet long and four feet wide, propelled by paddles, and steered by a broad rudder. At the stern was a locker about six feet long, which held our stores and ammunition, the latter sealed in glass bottles for preservation from dampness. On the top of this locker the officer spread his blankets, and it formed his bed at night; the men sleeping on their paddles and thwarts,—a hard life at the best. Each canoe was provided with a tent, a small square-sail made of ordinary cotton sheeting, and an awning.

. . .

Feb. 4, 1842.—At Indian Key, preparing for an Expedition into the Everglades; also rigging and fitting ship, having stepped a new foremast.

Feb. 12.—Left the Brig "Jefferson" at Key Biscayne at 4 P.M., in command of five canoes and twenty-two men; arrived at Fort Dallas[4] at 7 P.M.,

George Henry Preble, "The Diary of a Canoe Expedition into the Everglades and Interior of Southern Florida in 1842," *United Service* 8 (April 1883): 358–78. Material from pages 373–78 is omitted.

1. *Dictionary of American Biography*, vol. 8, pt. 1, pp. 183–84.
2. John Rodgers, a native of Maryland, was appointed midshipman in 1828 and was promoted to the rank of lieutenant in 1840. Between 1840 and 1843 he was engaged in the Seminole War. He died in 1882 having attained the rank of admiral. *National Cyclopaedia of American Biography*, 5:14.
3. William Lewis Herndon also received an appointment as midshipman in 1828, becoming a lieutenant in 1841. After a distinguished career, he was lost when his ship went down on 12 September 1857. Ibid., 4:201.

4. Fort Dallas was established by army troops in February 1838 at the mouth of the Miami River. It was abandoned in June 1858. Prucha, *Guide to Military Posts*, p. 70.

and camped for the night on the left-hand bank of the river opposite. At 8 P.M. a detachment of canoes from the "Madison" came up, and camped on our right.

Feb. 13., *Sunday.*—Capt. Rodgers came up at daylight and assumed command of the scout, arranged as follows: Staff, Lieut. John Rodgers Com'dg the Scout; Rob. Tansall, 2d Lt. of marines, Adjutant; Negro John, wife, and child, and John Tigertail, Indian Guide. 3 Canoes, 4 Sailors, 7 Marines.

1st Division, U.S. Sch. "Madison": Lieut. W^m. L. Herndon Com'dg; Passed Mid. S. C. Barney; Ass^t. Surgeon A. A. Henderson. 6 canoes, 29 Men.

2d. Division, U.S. Brigantine "Jefferson": Passed Mid. Geo. H. Preble Com'dg; Midshipman C. Benham. 4 Canoes, 18 Men.

3d. Division, Marines: 2d. Lieut. R. D. Taylor Com'dg. 3 Canoes, 17 Men.

Recapitulation: 16 Canoes, 2 Lieuts., 2 Passed Mid., 1 Mid^n, 1 Asst. Surgeon, 2 Lts. of Marines, 51 Sailors, 24 Marines, 1 Indian, 1 Negro, 1 Squaw, 1 Papoose. Total, 87 souls.

At 8 A.M. The Expedition started up the Bay to the N^d; at noon entered the Rio Ratones, and followed its very winding course to the Everglades. Both banks of the river lined with mangroves. At 2 P.M. Came to in the grass and dined. At sundown camped in the Canoes under the lee of some bushes.

Monday, Feb. 14.—Valentine's-day; under way at daylight. At 8 A.M. entered New river at its source; followed it down, and reached Fort Lauderdale[5] at 11 A.M., in season to see it abandoned by the army. Procured an Indian Guide, and at 1 P.M. started up river. At 4:30, Came to on the Left-hand bank, and pitched our tents in an open pine barren with palmetto undergrowth.

Tuesday, Feb. 15.—En route again at daylight. At 8 A.M. entered the Everglades and stood to the N^d & W^d, through a generally broad and open trail. At 2 P.M. hauled into the grass and dined. The guide lost the trail several times, and put back to find it. At 7:30 P.M. Hauled into the grass and camped in the canoes for the night. Observed the light of a fire in the S.E., and supposed it at our last night's camp.

Wednesday, Feb. 16.—Underway at 6:30 A.M.; traversed an open trail; saw only two islets. Examined the first, and found that it had been cultivated. Dined under the shade of the second island. Weather disagreeable and rainy. At 5 P.M. Came to under the lee of a small clump of bushes, where we procured a quantity of Crane's eggs, and camped in the canoes for the night. Course during the day to the N^d & W^d. The night silence broken by the screaming of Everglade Hens and Cranes, the bellowings of frogs, and the hooting of owls.

Thursday, Feb. 17.—A cold morning, wind N.E. The word passed to follow on at sunrise. Course to the N^d & E^d through a bad trail, most of which we broke for ourselves through the saw-grass.[6] At 10 A.M., saw high trees bearing per compass N.E. by E. Probably a part of the Alpatioka, or Cypress Swamp,[7] bordering the pine barrens along the coast. Very few bushes in sight during the day. Lat. obs'd at noon 26° 16′ N. At sundown camped in the canoes around a small clump of bushes, and posted sentry as usual.

Friday, Feb. 18.—Warm and pleasant. Light airs from the S.E. At 7 A.M. got the canoes under-

6. A sedge whose leaves have very rough edges, saw grass, grows in swamps and shallow water from Virginia to Florida and Texas, near the coast. Henry A. Gleason, *The New Britton and Brown Illustrated Flora of the Northeastern United States and Adjacent Canada*, 3 vols. (New York, 1952), 1:291.

7. The Big Cypress Swamp is in northeastern Florida. It contains about 2 million acres and is not considered adaptable to agriculture. *Florida Guide*, p. 481.

5. Fort Lauderdale is the seat of Broward County. It occupies the site of the fort constructed in 1838 during the Seminole War. *Florida Guide*, pp. 317–18.

way, and followed a northerly course during the day, but very winding. Our guides caught five Terrapins, and the men obtained several hats full of crane's eggs. Had to break our trail most of the day, the men walking the canoes along. Our route through a portion of the glades plentifully besprinkled with bushes. Camped at sundown in the canoes under the shelter of some bushes, and made my supper off some trout which had jumped into my canoe as we pushed along.

Saturday, Feb. 19.—Warm and pleasant. Started at sunrise, course N.N.W., through an open and generally deep trail, the plain covered with short grass, fields of water-lilies, and low bushes. The cypress in sight to the right N.E. Came to at sundown at a small island showing traces of an old Indian encampment; pitched my *tent* under a tall cabbage-tree,[8] and had a tall sleep. Lat. at noon 26° 38′ N.

Sunday, Feb. 20—Warm and pleasant; wind S.S.E. Passed through open Everglades, no bushes. Cypress to the right. Tracked the canoes all day, and at times forced them through the mud and grass with the assistance of the crews of four canoes to each one. Lat. 26.27; course N.W. Our guides say the water in the Everglades is unusually low. Camped in the canoes in the grass; no fires allowed, and night rainy. To-day officers as well as men have been compelled to wade in the mud, saw-grass, and water, and assist the sailors in dragging the canoes. Saw large flocks of white curlew.

Monday, Feb. 21.—Morning thick and misty; underway with canoes at 7½ A.M. Course generally N.W. to W. Thick, cloudy weather, with heavy showers of rain. Country an open prairie, with the Cypress on our right. Killed a black moccasin-

snake and saw others; they are very numerous. Passed the remains of an old clinker-built canoe, probably an army-boat; broke it up for firewood. At sundown nearly surrounded by woods on the horizon, our course taking us along those to the N.E. The woods bordering Lake Okeechobee in sight in the N.W. Wind during the day, N.E., but shifted about sundown to the N.W., bringing clear and cool weather. Camped in our canoes in the open grass. Saw during the day numerous flocks of wild birds,—curlew, cranes, blue-winged teal, crow blackbirds, swallows, &c.

Tuesday, Feb. 22.—Washington's birthday. Morning air clear, and cold enough to show our breath. Wind N.N.E. At 4:30 P.M. left the Everglades, passed through a narrow belt of cypress swamp, hauled over a sandy ridge, and launched our canoes in the waters of Lake Okeechobee, or "the Bigwater."[9] Camped under what was once Fort Dulany,[10] a cabbage-tree log fortress. The lake spread out before us, and to the W^d when the sun went down no land visible.

Wednesday, Feb. 23.—Launched our canoes upon the lake through a rough surf and heavy swell. One of my canoes was swamped, and capsized, losing everything,—provisions, arms, clothing, and ammunition. Turned back and assisted the canoe to land, bailed her out and started with her again; the other commands ahead; followed them along the coast of the Lake, and landed with them about two miles to the S^d & E^d. Was ordered by Capt. Rodgers to remain in charge of the provisions with the boats of my command, and twelve men and one canoe and five marines, while the remainder of the Expedition, taking provisions for

8. This tree is also known as the cabbage palmetto and the swamp cabbage. It is a semitropical tree growing along the coast of the Carolinas and Georgia, and throughout Florida. Grimm, *The Book of Trees*, pp. 88–90.

9. Lake Okeechobee, the second largest freshwater lake lying wholly within the United States, covers about 700 square miles. *Florida Guide*, p. 477.

10. Fort Dulany was on the west coast of Florida near Sanibel Island. It was used during the Seminole War. Prucha, *Guide to Military Posts*, pp. 140, 141.

six days, continued their cruise along shore. At 9 A.M. the Expedition departed with twelve boats and fifty-eight men, leaving me Mid^m. Benham and four boats, with seventeen men. Commenced securing the provisions from the weather and devising means for our defence.

Thursday, Feb. 24.—Organized our camp, inspected the arms, and exercised the men. Commenced building a log fort of cabbage-trees, and had it three logs high when the Expedition unexpectedly hove in sight and suspended our labors. Before sundown it arrived at our camp, when I restored the marines to their proper commander and took my own division again. Benham shot a crow blackbird and a woodpecker, and with their assistance we made a sumptuous dinner.

Friday, Feb. 25.—My birthday. The canoes underway at daylight. Stood to the N^d & W^d, coasting the Lake under sail. The guide's boat swamped; hauled into the grass and dined while waiting for the guide's boat to come up. At 4 P.M. discovered eight hogs on the beach; sent the guide to shoot one. Heard a noise like wood-chopping (probably a hog rooting); sent the boats in, landed and armed the men, and dispatched each command on a scout. The "Madison's" men going across the country, the marines along the shore interiorly, and my command up the beach to the N.W. in search of Indian canoes. Discovered an old Indian encampment, apparently many months deserted. The guide shot one large hog and wounded another, a sow, which our officers ran down afterwards and captured. On the return of the scouts, Tansall, with twelve marines, was sent out again with orders to scour the country to the Everglades. He returned at 7 P.M., after a fatiguing march through mud and water, but without having effected his object. He reported the Everglades as approaching this portion of the Lake, and his discovery of a stream or river about a mile and a half north of us, and leading apparently into the Everglades. We are

to explore it to-morrow. Camped for the night, and pitched our tents under a grove of cypress, maple, bay, and cabbage-trees. The beautiful moonlight contrasting with the dark recesses of the forest, and our camp-fires' glare upon the gray mossy beards which draped the trees, and our rough and rugged men in their careless costumes and still more careless attitudes, combined to make our bivouac a scene which Salvator Rosa[11] would have been glad to have copied. Regaled on fried pork. Our men went the whole hog, and dispatched both animals to the skin and hoof. Punished one of my men, John Bath, with 18 lashes for drunkenness and insubordination, and for endangering the safety of the whole command by his noise.

Saturday, Feb. 26.—Underway at 6:30 A.M. After refreshing with a "pot of coffee," stood along the Lake to the N^d & W^d. About a mile up entered "Tansall's River," bordered on both sides with large cypress and a young growth of maple and bay-trees; about one-quarter of a mile up reached its head. The Madisons and Jeffersons were ordered to march; and we waded through cypress and willows up to our waists in water and mud about 200 yards, and came to a belt of saw-grass which was at least 15 feet high; waded 50 yards farther and reached the dry land,—a wide plain dotted with cabbage-tree and pine hummocks and a palmetto scrub; dense woods surrounding the entire horizon. Saw ten parroquets. On emerging from the grass the Madisons went off in a S. Easterly direction; the Jeffersons with me to the N.W. Marched six or eight miles over the plain. Examined several hummocks, discovered two long-abandoned encampments; found numerous trails of horse-tracks and footprints,—none of which, our guide said, were newer than three weeks. On our march started four deer; they stood at gaze and looked at

11. An Italian painter (1615–1673), Rosa was born near Naples. His specialty was battle scenes. *Century Dictionary and Cyclopedia*, 9:866.

us. How tantalizing not to be allowed to shoot them![12] Returned to our canoes about one P.M. Turned down river and resumed our course along the coast of the Lake. The Madisons on their march discovered an old encampment. During the afternoon explored five creeks in search of canoes and Indians; discovered nothing to repay our trouble. Passed six or eight large Indian encampments, of old-standing, like those we visited in the forenoon. Our guides are of opinion they were all abandoned at the time the Indians entered the Everglades in 1837.[13] Found the coast this afternoon gradually bending to the S^d & W^d. Crossed a deep bay in the Lake, making to the N^d & W^d. At dark came to in the bulrushes and camped in our canoes; night rainy, coast low and swampy, mosquitoes plenty. Oh Lord!

Sunday, *Feb.* 27.—Warm and pleasant, with light airs from the N.W. Underway at sunrise S^d & S.W. to S. Saw many alligators basking on the water, and immense flocks of white curlew and other birds. The coast of the Lake low and marshy, and bordered with sedges. Lat. at noon 27.02 N. Camped in our canoes around some small lumps of floating land just enough to swear by and make a fire on. During the night saw the reflection of a large fire N.N.W. of us; supposed it the prairie fired by army scouts in that direction.

Monday, *Feb.* 28.—Pleasant and warm, wind

S.E. to E. Coasted the Lake to the S^d & E^d between isolated patches of marsh-grass. Land low and fringed with bulrushes. Lieut. Taylor, in the afternoon, discovered an old Indian canoe in shore, and broke it up. Made sail at sundown and stood E.N.E. about three miles; hauled well into the grass, and camped in the canoes. Killed a moccasin-snake. Made our supper on a "stewzee" of young cranes, water-turkeys,[14] and fried eggs. Lat. at noon 26° 50′ N.

Tuesday, *March* 1.—Warm and pleasant, wind E.S.E.; underway at sunrise; paddled until 10 A.M. to the E.S.E., and landed on a small sand beach. At 10 A.M. made sail and stood to the N^d & W^d on a return trail. Lat. at noon 26.55 N. At 4:30 P.M. reached our camp of night before last, passed it, and entered a creek to the N^d & W^d. Were soon stopped by floating weeds similar to heads of lettuce, and came to with the canoes. The Madisons were sent on a march to the S^d & W^d in search of Fish-Eating Creek,[15] and the marines in pursuit of a fire seen to the N.N.W. Sent five of my men to build a fire to guide their return. After a fatiguing march through saw-grass and water, both parties returned to camp about 9, entirely unsuccessful. At 9:30 heard the report of three muskets west of us; supposed them fired by the guides, who have not yet come up.

Wednesday, *March* 2.—Marines ordered to prepare for a three days' march to the N^d & W^d in search of a fire seen in that direction. Myself, with six men, ordered to trace out a supposed creek. Capt. Rodgers accompanied me. Started, middle-deep, in mud and water, and commenced our wade through the saw-grass towards an island about

12. While there were no laws protecting game until after 1875, it has been suggested that this expedition was shooting only as much game as it could use in a day, because there would have been no way to preserve the meat. It is likely that shooting was forbidden in order to avoid alerting the Indians and possibly also to conserve ammunition. Arthur Howell, *Florida Bird Life* (New York, 1932), pp. 42–43; statement of Mrs. Oliver L. Austin, Jr., curator of the Florida Museum, Gainesville, 20 March 1969.

13. This opinion has no basis in fact. Several groups of aboriginal Indians lived in the Everglades during the colonial period; early Spanish records substantiate their residence. Charlton W. Tebeau, *Man in the Everglades*, 2d ed., rev. (Coral Gables, Fla., 1968), pp. 35–37.

14. Similar to the cormorant. Ralph S. Palmer, ed., *Handbook of North American Birds*, 1 vol. to date (New Haven, Conn., 1962), 1:357.

15. Fish-Eating Creek drains into Lake Okeechobee from the west. It is frequently referred to in accounts of the Seminole War. *Florida Guide*, p. 502.

quarter of a mile distant. Reached it, puffing and blowing with our exertions. Climbed a tree and looked about for the creek; could discover none, though a line of bushes S.E. of us seemed to point one out. Heard the report of one musket, then another, and soon a third. Was ordered by Capt. R. to return and prepare for a push along the coast in the direction of the firing. Glad to escape a damp and tiresome march, turned about and reached the canoes about 9 A.M., and started down the creek, and to the S^d & E^d picked up our guide about three miles down, and turned back, pushing into all the bays and inlets to discover the creek. Capt. R. ordered me to follow up an inlet and examine it; followed it out, pushing through fields of broad-leaved lilies and spatterdocks, and came into the Lake again about a mile to the S^d. Made sail to return. Met Capt. Herndon with the Madisons near an "old cypress," and was informed by him of the discovery of the creek, and that I was to go to the rendezvous and take charge of the marines' canoes, the marines being off on their march. Joined my boats about 5 P.M.

Thursday, M'ch 3.—Still camping in our canoes in the grass and weeds, no dry land neighborly. Read, smoked, and slept. At 11.30 received orders to join the remainder of the scout, and bring the marines' boats along, men being sent me to man them. Got underway and stood up the Fish-Eating Creek to Fort Centre.[16] The creek winding and deep. Arrived at 1 P.M. and found all the canoes there. The large fire still to be seen N.N.W. of us. Sent a canoe and four men to the Island to wait the return of the marines.

Friday, M'ch 4.—Pleasant, fresh breezes from S.E. Appointed Supt. of repairs, and ordered to fill up gaps and put the Fort (a cabbage-tree stockade) in a state of defence. Cut trees and stuck

16. Fort Center was one of the forts established during the Seminole War. It was on Lake Okeechobee. Prucha, *Guide to Military Posts*, pp. 140–42.

them up like the others. Went to the mouth of the creek, 6 miles west, and observed the Lat. 27° 04′ N. On my return found the marines at the Fort, they having marched there. Sent for my boat. The coxswain on his return reported having found on the island several old houses, some pumpkins, and parts of half a dozen saddles, but no signs of *recent* habitation.

Saturday, M'ch 5.—Warm and pleasant. Left the Fort at daylight. Doct. Henderson with fifteen men and marines, and John Tigertail, sick, remaining behind. Proceeded up the creek with great difficulty, pushing the canoes through the weeds, the creek for a space spreading out into a wide swamp. Saturday night remembered absent friends.

Sunday, M'ch. 6.—After hauling the canoes over two troublesome places re-entered the creek, —a beautiful stream, clear, with a beautiful white sandy bottom. Pulled against the current to the S^d and W^d. Saw immense flocks of cranes, pink spoonbills, curlew, and wild turkeys in plenty. Also, a large number of alligators killed; killed two small ones and cut off their tails for eating; caught a soft-shelled and a hard-shelled turtle and had them cooked for supper, with a fry of some little fish that foolishly jumped into one of the canoes. Our camping-ground the prettiest by far that we have had. Two veteran cypress stretched their scraggy arms over our camp, draped in moss to the very ground. The day was rendered harmonious by the warblings of multitudes of feathered choristers, and the night hideous with the splash of alligators, hooting of owls, and screamings of a variety of unquiet night-birds.

Monday, M'ch. 7.—Warm and pleasant. Left our beautiful camp at sunrise, pursuing the windings of the creek, which occasionally spread out to the appearance of quite a large river, but soon returns to narrow bounds. At 11 A.M. reached the head of the stream, which loses itself in a swamp.

Dined and turned back. Permission to shoot was granted, and bang, bang, bang went guns and pistols in every direction. At sundown landed and pitched our tents under a cypress grove, and feasted sumptuously on wild turkey, broiled and fried curlew, plover, and teal, stewed crane, grecian ladies[17] and fried fish, our spoils of the day. The Astor House could not have supplied such a dinner or *such appetites*. Invited Capts. Rodgers and Herndon to our feast, and illuminated our camp with three halves of spermaceti candles. Lat. 27.05 N.

Tuesday, *M'ch* 8.—Warm and pleasant; wind S.E. Breakfasted off the remains of our "Tarkey," as my coxswain called it, and underway at daylight. Passed both haulovers[18] with little trouble, leaving one to the left and the other to the right. Dined in the canoes in the grass. Passed an extent of prairie which had been burnt over since we passed up, and in places yet burning, which accounts for the dense smoke seen yesterday. After dining hauled the canoes through a narrow streamlet into a lily swamp; tracked them across it, and bothered about until after dark searching for the creek; finally struck it and reached Fort Center, where

17. Water turkeys. Howell, *Florida Bird Life*, p. 12.
18. Portages.

only three boats had as yet arrived. Garrison well.

Wednesday, *M'ch* 9.—Pleasant and warm. The marines, canoes, and adjutants did not come in until this morning. Served out thirty days' provisions to the men, and exercised them at Target-shooting. Discovered all hands were plaguey poor shots.

. . . .

Monday, *Ap'l* 11.—Left Fort Lauderdale at 8. Passed over the bar at the entrance of New River without damage, and stood along the coast under sail twenty-five miles. Passed outside Bear's Cut[19] and inside Key Biscayne, and arrived on board the Brig early in the afternoon. Glad to get back and to receive letters and news from home. My boat the first to get alongside; most of the canoes grounded and had to wait the rising of the waters. Thus ended our expedition of fifty-eight days in canoes after Sam Jones,[20] during which Lt. Rodgers says in his official report we had "less rest, fewer luxuries, and harder work than fall to the lot of that estimable class of citizens who dig our canals."

19. The entrance to Biscayne Bay between Key Biscayne and Virginia Key.
20. An Indian Chieftain whose tribal name was Arpeika. Marjory Stoneman Douglas, *The Everglades: River of Grass* (New York, 1947), p. 202.

The Right Reverend John Mary Odin (1801–1870), was born in France and came to New Orleans as a Catholic missionary in 1822. From 1839 onward he was very active in the Texas region, continually travelling the area on horseback. His distinguished service led to his appointment as Bishop of Galveston in 1847 and Archbishop of New Orleans in 1861.[1]

Under this head we will lay before our readers two letters from the Rt. Rev. Dr. Odin, vicar apostolic of Texas. These letters are extracted from the *Annales of the Propagation of the Faith,*[2] and exhibit the labors, hardships and privations which attend the missionary life in that new republic. Since these letters were written, Dr. Odin has been appointed vicar apostolic of Texas, and religion has been on the increase. Churches have been built at Galveston, Houston, on the river Labaca, near the mouth of San Antonio, at Fort Bent,[3] St. Augustin[4] and Nacogdoches.[5] Other ancient churches have been recovered by a grant of Congress.[6] The number of Catholics in Texas is about twenty thousand, out of a population of 250,000. In the following interesting narratives, the reader will judge of the difficulties which religion has to contend with, and of the indefatigable zeal with which the clergy labor for the salvation of souls.

April 11th, 1841.

Last year the holy see having vouchsafed to confide to our Congregation the spiritual direction of the Catholics of Texas, I set out from the seminary of Barrens[7] on the second of May, 1840, to proceed, as vice-prefect apostolic, to explore this new mission. It was not without regret that I quitted Missouri; to separate myself from a people that had become dear to me, and establishments which I had seen in their commencement, was to expatriate myself a second time.

Texas, situated between 26° and 35° of north latitude, and extending from 95° 20′ to 104° 20′ of west longitude, possesses more extensive prairies and more abundant pasturage than any other

John Mary Odin, "Mission to Texas," *The United States Catholic Magazine and Monthly Review* 3 (November 1844): 724–30. Ellipsis in original.

1. *Dictionary of American Biography*, vol. 7, pt. 2, pp. 625–26.

2. *Annales de la Propagation de la Foi Recueil Periodique des Everques et des missionaries des Missions des Deux Mondes*, 103 vols. (Lyons and Paris, 1823–1931).

3. Fort Bend, on the site of the present Richmond in Fort Bend County, was a pioneer blockhouse built in 1821. Walter Prescott Webb, ed., *The Handbook of Texas*, 2 vols. (Austin, Tex., 1952), 1:620.

4. San Augustine is in an area originally inhabited by the Ais Indians. In 1716 Father Antonio Margil de Jesus built a mission for them, known as Nuestra Señora de los Dolores de los Ais. The name of the settlement was changed to San Augustine in 1834. Ibid., 2:547.

5. Named for an Indian tribe which originally inhabited the area, Nacogdoches was visited by La Salle's expedition in 1687. The first permanent European settlement was made in 1819. At the beginning of the nineteenth century it was the second largest city in the state. Ibid., 2:256.

6. An act was passed on 13 January 1841 confirming the "use and occupation and enjoyment of the churches, church lots, and mission churches to the Roman Catholic congregation living in or near the communities in or near the vicinity of the same." John and Henry Sayles, comps., *Early Laws of Texas*, 2d ed., 3 vols. (St. Louis, Mo., 1891), 1:429–30.

7. This seminary was located at Cape Girardeau, Missouri. Carlos E. Casteñada, *Our Catholic Heritage in Texas, 1519–1936*, 7 vols. (Austin, Tex., 1936–1958), 7:4.

country in America. Wood is rare here, particularly towards the west. Several rivers water the country, but there are few of them sufficiently large for navigation. Although the exact number of the Texian population is not yet known, it is generally allowed that it cannot exceed one hundred and thirty thousand souls.[8]

When the first Spaniards established themselves at Texas, more than a century and a half ago, religious of the order of St. Francis came to found here several missions, in order to convert and civilize the savage tribes. The most celebrated missions are those of *San Antonio*, of *Conception*, of *San Jose*, of *El Refugio*, *San Sabas*, and *Nacogdoches;* they all became flourishing, and counted a great number of fervent neophytes.[9] Every year the reverend fathers entered the forests, and gained by their presents, and manners full of kindness, the confidence of the Indians, and conducted them to the stations, where they were gradually formed to piety and labor. In 1812 those valuable establishments were suppressed;[10] at present they are only heaps of ruins. As for the poor savages, being deprived of their fathers, they dispersed: some re-

tired into Mexico, several sank under the attacks of the uncivilized tribes, and others returned to their primitive state. The fervor which I found in the few who still inhabit the country shows sufficiently that they had been formed to virtue by able hands. Two churches, the only ones that have withstood the inroads of time, and of the recent wars, display a beauty that does honor to the taste and zeal of the ancient missionaries.

From Linnville, a small seaport, where we landed, we proceeded to Victoria.[11] I left the Rev. Mr. Estany at this post, and I took the road of San Antonio, accompanied by Mr. Salvo and an assistant brother.[12] The distance which separates these two towns is only fifty leagues; but the numerous bands of savage *Comanches* and *Tonakanies*,[13] that continually rove through the country, render the journey extremely perilous: it is even nearly certain that one will be massacred, if not travelling with sufficient company to intimidate those Indians. We joined then a convoy of twenty-two carts that were carrying goods. All our companions were very well armed; but if, on the one hand, the strength of the caravan secured us against the attacks of the savages, on the other, what miseries had we not to endure! how slowly we advanced! The heat was excessive, and scarcely a shrub was to be met with, under the shade of which we might take a moment's rest. We used to set out in the evening; but frequently, on the first movement, one of the vehicles got out of order

8. The first census in 1847 counted 135,775 inhabitants. Homer S. Thrall, *A Pictorial History of Texas*, 6th ed. (St. Louis, Mo., 1881), p. 765. The 1850 federal census gives the population as 212,592. Bureau of the Census, *Seventh Census*, p. 506.

9. While missions were primarily religious institutions, they also served as agencies of the Spanish government in civilizing the frontier and were not necessarily considered permanent establishments. They conducted agricultural and industrial schools in certain areas. Nuestra Señora del Refugio, the last of the Texas missions, was founded in 1793. San Saba de la Santa Cruz mission was founded in 1757 on the south bank of the San Saba River. Nuestra Señora de la Purisima Concepción de Acuña mission was in the eastern part of the city of San Antonio. Webb, *Handbook of Texas*, 2:215-16, 295, 562.

10. The missions were suppressed by the Spanish government in 1812. John G. Shea, *History of the Catholic Missions among the Indian Tribes of the United States, 1529-1854* (New York, 1881), p. 87.

11. Linnville, three and one-half miles northeast of Port Lavaca, was established in 1831 by John J. Linn. It was destroyed by the Comanches in 1840 and was never rebuilt. Victoria, on the Guadalupe River, was established in 1824 by Martin León. It was incorporated in 1839 with Linn as the mayor. Webb, *Handbook of Texas*, 2:60, 839.

12. Eudald Estany and Michael Calvo accompanied Father Odin to Texas in May 1840. They had come from Spain in 1838. Casteñada, *Our Catholic Heritage*, 7:41-43.

13. This may be a variation of the name Tonkanras; no tribe called Tonakanies could be identified. The Tonkanras lived in central Texas. Webb, *Handbook of Texas*, 2:788.

and we had to pass a part of the night repairing it. These accidents sometimes happened at a distance from springs and rivers; we had then to traverse the solitude, happy when, after great searching, we discovered in a slough some drops of muddy, disgusting water. Besides, we were ill-supplied with provisions, and yet we endeavored to share with our companions, who were worse circumstanced than ourselves; we had even to have recourse to the chase, at the risk of drawing upon us the savages by the noise of our guns.

Together with scarcity, we suffered from fever; I had several attacks of it; but some medicines with which I had very fortunately provided myself, restored us by degrees to health. The relief which I afforded to our poor sick acquired for me a reputation which subsequently embarrassed me very much; for so soon as our carriers had made me known under the name of the father that knows how to cure, all the invalids came to ask my opinion and medicines. Several times during the journey, the cry of *Los Indios* spread alarm in our ranks: it was, I believe, only a mistake of our advanced guard, for we arrived at San Antonio without striking a blow.

This town was founded in 1678 by some Spaniards, who had emigrated from the Canary Islands; it contains a population of two thousand souls;[14] there are some houses built of stone; the other habitations are only miserable cabins covered with bulrushes. It is watered at the east end by the river of San Antonio, and at the west by a very small stream; in the centre of the town there is a canal, of which the plentiful supply of water spreads fertility over all the other gardens; this canal was formerly made by the Indians, under the direction of the missionaries. Nothing can be more beautiful than the Valley of San Antonio: an agreeable climate, pure and salubrious air, a rich

and fertile soil, all would contribute to render it a delightful place of residence, only for the continual hostilities of the savages, who have not allowed of the exploring of its immense resources. There is not a family that has not to deplore the death of a father, a son, a brother, or a husband, mercilessly murdered by the *Comanches*. To the massacre of the colonists these robbers add the devastation of their lands, and the carrying away of their flocks: hence the poverty is extreme in the country; and if ever it had been consoling to me to have some relief to bestow, it would have been on seeing so much wretched indigence.

A few days after our arrival at San Antonio a ceremony took place that filled us with consolation, by proving to us how much the faith is still alive among the Mexicans. A sick man in danger of death was to receive the holy viaticum; we judged it right to carry it to him publicly and with solemnity. At the sound of the bell the people ran to the holy place, in order to accompany our Lord through the streets; tears flowed from the eyes of the old, who, for fourteen years, had not witnessed this homage paid to our religion. Several of them cried out that they did not fear death, now that heaven had sent to them fathers to assist them in their last moments.

Having passed three months at San Antonio, and seeing that all was proceeding according to our wishes, I set out towards Seguin, Gonzales,[15] and Victoria. My stay in these towns was very short, because I could not separate from my travelling companions without exposing myself to be killed by the Indians. Subsequently, I ascended along the river Labaca; a journey which exposes one to less danger, and I found on its banks seventy

14. The population of San Antonio in 1850 was 3,488. Bureau of the Census, *Seventh Census*, p. 504.

15. Seguin, the seat of Guadalupe County, was founded in 1838 as Walnut Springs; the name was changed in 1839. Gonzales, the seat of Gonzales County, was settled in 1825 by De Witt's colony. It burned and was rebuilt several times. It was the scene of the first battle for Texas independence. Webb, *Handbook of Texas*, 2:519; 1:706–7.

Catholics, formerly my parishioners at the Barrens. It was very consoling to me to see them again, and particularly to know that they had lost nothing of their faith and primitive piety, although they had been deprived of the succors of religion since their arrival in Texas. All presented themselves at the tribunal of penance, and had the happiness of receiving the holy communion.

I could only remain with them a week. From Labaca I proceeded to Austin,[16] a small rising town, lately appointed to be the seat of the Texian government. The congress was then sitting; I solicited from the legislators a decision that would confirm to the Catholic worship the possession of all the churches anciently built by the Spaniards. It is true that, if we except the *Concepcion* and *San Jose*, these edifices are nearly all in ruins; however, they might be repaired, and considering the poverty and the small number of the faithful, we could make use of them, whilst awaiting until more prosperous times would give us the means of building new ones. Thanks to the generous intervention of M. de Saligny,[17] *chargé d'affaires* of France, my request was well received.

It remained as yet for us to visit the eastern part of Texas. What difficulties and obstacles did we not meet in this long journey! At one time it was necessary to cross a river by swimming, at another time we had to traverse a vast and miry marsh, where we ran the risk of losing our horses; here we had hunger, and nothing to satisfy it; and besides, torrents of rain and no shelter. It was thus that we advanced from Montgomery to Huntsville, from Cincinnati to Cork and Douglas, from Nacogdoches to San Antonio.[18] It is true that we

were recompensed for our fatigues by the eagerness which the inhabitants of the different localities manifested to hear our instructions; I have rarely seen the word of God listened to with more joy and recollection. This visit although short, has contributed not a little to dissipate the prejudices of the Protestants, and to awaken pious sentiments in the hearts of the faithful.

Besides the Catholic population of Texas, estimated at near ten thousand souls, there are several tribes of savages, to whom it would be necessary to attend: among them are the *Comanches*, to the number of twenty thousand; the *Tonakanies*, the *Lipans*, the *Tankoways*, the *Bidais*, the *Karankanays*, the *Nacocs*, &c.[19] The greater part of these Indians take delight in feeding on human flesh; the feet and hands, in particular, are their favorite dish.[20] I have already taken some steps with the *Karakanays* towards forming them into

16. Austin, the capital of Texas, was established on the site of Stephen F. Austin's "little colony" in 1839. Ibid., 1:85.

17. Alphonse de Saligny served his government in several capacities before being appointed chargé d'affaires to Texas in 1839. He had financial difficulties and was forced to leave Texas after a short period. Ibid., 2:533.

18. Montgomery, named for General Richard Montgomery, a famous figure in the Revolution, was founded in 1837. Huntsville, in Walker County, was established in 1836 as an Indian trading post. Cincinnati, also in Walker County, about fifteen miles north of Huntsville, was founded in 1838. A yellow fever epidemic in 1853 practically wiped out Cincinnati and it never really recovered. Douglass, fourteen miles west of Nacogdoches, was laid out in 1836. Cork could not be identified. Ibid., 2:226; 1:867, 347, 516; 2:256.

19. The Lipans were an Apache tribe who roamed from the lower Rio Grande in New Mexico and Mexico eastward through Texas during the eighteenth and nineteenth centuries. The Tonkawas lived in central Texas. The Bidais lived near the Trinity River; though they were declining by the latter part of the eighteenth century, they were reported to be the chief intermediaries between the French and the Apaches. The name Karankaw was originally given to a small tribe living near Matagonda, Texas; it was later broadened to include several related tribes. By 1840 they were greatly reduced in numbers and were living on Lavaca Bay. The Nacocs could not be identified. Hodge, *Handbook of Indians*, 1:145–46, 657–58, 768–69; 2:778–83.

20. Cannibalism was sometimes performed among the Tonkawas as a ceremony; occasionally it occurred as a result of necessity. Ibid., 1:200–201.

a mission: Mr. Estany has also visited them, and they have expressed to him the desire of having a priest. The *Comanches* will be more difficult to gain. From time immemorial this tribe has been constantly at war with the civilized inhabitants and its neighboring tribes. Able horsemen and active robbers, they handle the arrow and lance with the greatest dexterity; they are incessantly traversing the country in bands of ten, twenty, thirty, or fifty. From the heights they watch their prey, and if they discover a convoy too weak to resist them, they rush upon the travellers with the rapidity of lightning, and murder them without mercy. It would be impossible to tell how many unfortunate persons have fallen under their arrows, or how many women and children they have carried off captives.

A short time after my arrival at Texas, a party of five or six hundred *Comanches* penetrated as far as Linnville. The inhabitants who did not expect this visit, were obliged to take refuge in the middle of the bay of Labaca, to shelter themselves from their arrows; eight persons fell victims; and a young lady, only ten days married, after having seen her husband pierced by her side, became their prisoner. When the savages had pillaged the warehouses, and made a minute search for every thing that could enrich them, they set fire to the town. From Linnville they proceeded to Victoria. The first house they attacked was that in which our colleague, Mr. Estany was lodging. He had the good fortune to pass through a shower of arrows without receiving any wound; but all that he possessed was taken: linen, vestments, books, nothing was spared. There were here also several murders, and women and children carried away. The alarm soon spread, a pursuit was raised after the brigands, and they were overtaken near the rivers *Plomberek* and *St. Mark*.[21] The fight was

bloody; eighty-four *Comanches* lost their lives, without counting those who must have died soon after from the wounds they received. Those unfortunate creatures, on the approach of the Texians, attempted to exterminate all their prisoners. A poor mother, who, with her little infant, scarcely ten months old, had fallen into their hands, had the affliction of seeing the little innocent dashed to pieces before her eyes, and herself then pierced several times with a lance. I have counted, in the space of six months, nearly two hundred persons murdered by this single tribe.

Notwithstanding the devastations to which this country is a prey, heaven has already begun to bless our humble efforts. From the 1st of August, 1840, to the 1st of March, 1841, we have heard nine hundred and eleven confessions, and administered the sacrament of baptism two hundred and eighty-one times; there have been four hundred and seventy-eight communions. The interest of religion would require that we should build at once six chapels at least in the most important parts of the republic; but where shall we find the funds? We are without means, and the people are poor. During my journeys, I pass some of the nights in the woods in the open air; I dress my food myself, and still my travelling expenses are considerable. We should also require schools at San Antonio and at Galveston: but who will pay the first cost? We have no lodging and are obliged to ask hospitality of the Catholics, and often even of Protestants. It is here that one really learns to lead the life of a missionary: I thought that I had already passed a long apprenticeship; but since my arrival in Texas, I have perceived that I was not as yet initiated.

Your most devoted servant,
J. M. ODIN.

21. Plomberek is probably a typographical error for Plum Creek, three branches of which flow into the San Marcos River. This river rises in Hayes County and empties into the Guadalupe River near Gonzales. Webb, *Handbook of Texas*, 2:386–87, 558–59.

I have been for a long time desirous of writing to you; but almost continued travelling, joined to the difficulty of procuring even a table in the places where I made any stay, have hitherto deprived me of this pleasure. I have as yet no fixed abode in Texas; going from cabin to cabin, I employ every moment, either in catechising, giving instructions, or administering the sacraments. At length I have returned to Galveston, where there has been lent to me a little room, and I take advantage of this momentary halt to speak to you concerning our new mission.

Last year, I transmitted to you long details upon our first labors in this republic: I hope you have received my letter. Shortly after having despatched it to you, his lordship, Dr. Blanc,[22] wrote to me to repair without delay to New Orleans, concerning important business that he had to communicate to me on the part of the holy see. What was my surprise, on meeting his lordship, to hear that I was named coadjutor of Detroit! It was the wish of his holiness that I should accept without hesitation so formidable a burden. I was unable to bring myself to do so. The intimate conviction of my unworthiness made me send back the bulls,* and after a short sojourn in the United States, I set out again for Texas. My intention was to pass the summer at Galveston; but after three weeks employed in preparing for the paschal duty those who had not as yet complied with it, it was announced to me that the house which served me as a chapel was going to be occupied by a family newly arrived in the country. Not knowing where to set up my portable altar, after having painfully carried it from garret to garret, I thought that, whilst awaiting the finishing of the little church that I had just commenced, my time would be more usefully spent in visiting the Catholics scattered on both sides of me. I set out then for Houston.

It was the period when the fever shows itself in this city; all those who were attacked with it hastened to be reconciled with God, and many other persons presented themselves at the tribunal of penance and at the holy table. However, at the end of a fortnight, the apartment in which I used to assemble the faithful was converted into an alehouse, and I was obliged to think of proceeding farther. On the banks of the Brazos, at thirty miles from Houston, there live about twenty Catholic families, that emigrated some years since from Kentucky and Missouri; as I had not been able to visit them before, I proceeded towards them, and was much edified by the zeal and eagerness with which those neophytes welcomed me. All, from the child to the old man, confessed themselves. There were sick persons in all the families: I offered then the holy sacrifice in each house, to give to them all the consolation of hearing mass. On Sunday I celebrated it in the most central habitation, where a great number of dissenters came to attend at the instructions. This little flock has the desire, but not the means, of raising an humble chapel to the good Shepherd. May I be able one day to second their wishes! A Protestant, who was a long time sick, sent to request me to go to see him; we had together long conversations on religion, in consequence of which he embraced our holy faith: when I thought him sufficiently instructed, I administered to him the sacraments, and I since learned that his death was most edifying.

I quitted these good Catholics, to proceed towards Mill Creek and Cumming's Creek,[23]

22. Antonio Blanc, Bishop of New Orleans in 1837. Casteñada, *Our Catholic Heritage,* 7:6–7.
*After this, Rev. Mr. Odin was appointed vicar-apostolic of Texas, and was consecrated at New Orleans, on the 6th of March, 1842.

23. There are a number of streams in Texas called Mill Creek. The one referred to here is evidently the one also known as Cummins Creek. It rises in southern Lee County

between the Brazos and the Colorado; but on the second day of my journey I felt myself attacked by a violent fever, accompanied with frequent vomitings. Finding myself then alone, and without any acquaintance, in a part of the country but little inhabited, I determined, notwithstanding the fever, to make my way as far as the river *Labaca*, where there are some colonists who resided formerly in the Missouri. The distance was hardly fifty-five miles, yet I was three days in making the journey. You could not imagine all I had to suffer, both from the rays of a scorching sun, from the want of water, and the burning of the fever. On the second day, particularly, I thought I was approaching my last hour, I stopped at every instant to stretch myself upon the grass, and the violence of the sickness obliged me to mount again on horseback.

I did not well know where I was going, when I discovered a forest, at two or three miles distance. The hope of finding some relief under its shade induced me to direct my course towards the first wood that caught my sight. The improvement that I promised myself was not realized. I was scarcely stretched under a tree when I felt the illness growing worse; my thirst became dreadful, I was then once more on horseback, wandering at random, when Providence showed me in the distance a column of smoke that seemed to indicate a habitation. I hastened in this direction, and had the happiness of finding in the bosom of a family newly arrived from Michigan, all the succor that the most tender charity can suggest. I drank copiously, and passed the night under their tent. The next day, feeling myself a little relieved, I continued my journey. I reached at last my old friends of Missouri. The fever did not leave me until after twenty-four days: there was neither

and flows into the Colorado River. The Spanish called it Benave; it was renamed for James Cummins, who settled on its banks in 1824. Webb, *Handbook of Texas*, 2:194.

physician nor medicine; so I abandoned myself to the kind care of Providence.

So soon as I was a little convalescent, I attended again to the duties of the sacred ministry, although it might have been easy to foresee that preaching and hearing confessions would soon produce a relapse. At this period, having found at Victoria some travellers who were repairing to San Antonio, I joined them, not doubting but that the salubrious air of that beauteous valley of Texas would restore me to my former strength. Excessive rains during our journey, threw me again into a state of illness, which obliged me to continue my sojourn at San Antonio longer than I should have wished. In order not to lose time, I set about directing the repairs of the church, which were already commenced. We found it in a very sad state. Burned in 1828, it had been only partly roofed again, when the war of 1836, so disastrous for San Antonio, ruined it almost entirely. We have finished the ceiling and replastering all the interior; five new doors have been made, also a sanctuary and a communion table; on the exterior we have restored the steeple and front, and closed all the holes made by the cannon balls.

The work has given great joy to all the inhabitants; all wished to take part in it, and their contributions have been much greater than the extreme wretchedness of the country allowed me to hope for. Although the Protestants rivalled the Catholics in zeal, the greater part of the expenses still fall upon me; I have even had to contract debts. On the 5th of December we sung high mass, and had an exposition of the holy sacrament, to thank God for the works which we had finished. The news of this solemnity having been circulated beforehand, we saw flock to it not only the inhabitants of the town, but also those of Rancho, which is thirty miles distant. A great deal of tears flowed from the eyes of these poor people, so long neglected, but their faith is not extinguished.

On the 12th of December, the feast of Our Lady of Guadaloupe, the patroness of Mexico, and of all the Spanish colonies, the inhabitants of San Antonio, who, in more prosperous times, solemnized this day with great rejoicings, felt their ancient zeal for the veneration of Mary revived in seeing their church restored. A good old man, together with some of his friends, wished to bear the principal part of the expenses of the feast; they purchased a hundred and fifty pounds of powder, borrowed all the pieces of cloth they could procure, whilst the women, on their part, lent with emulation their most valuable ornaments for the decoration of their temple.

The image of Our Lady, loaded with all the necklaces and jewellery of the town, was placed upon a bier elegantly adorned. At three o'clock in the afternoon the cannons and bells were heard: this was the hour of the first vespers. A numerous procession was immediately in motion: young girls dressed in white, with torches or *bouquets* of flowers in their hands, surrounded the banner of the Queen of virgins; then came the statue of Mary, raised upon a bier borne by four young persons, and in their train followed the women and men of the city. Sixty of the militia escorted the procession with their arms, which they discharged continually. At eight o'clock in the evening all the town was illuminated; enormous bonfires lighted the two great squares in the middle of which the church of San Antonio rises. We then came forth again from the sanctuary, to the sound of the bells and cannon, with the cross, the banner, and the image of Our Lady of Guadaloupe, and made the circuit of the squares, reciting the rosary, and singing canticles in honor of the mother of God. It was ten o'clock when we re-entered the church. Perfect order prevailed, and I confess that I have seen few processions more edifying. Besides the inhabitants of the town, we had at the ceremony all the Mexicans that reside along the river, together with a considerable number of Americans, that had come from Austin and from other different countries.

The feasts of Christmas have been celebrated with equal pomp and similar marks of piety. There remains, no doubt, much to be done at San Antonio: the reform which the country required is not yet as great and as general as we should desire; however, thanks be to heaven, our feeble efforts have not been fruitless, and already many abuses have been corrected.

I quitted San Antonio on the 27th of December, to visit the stations already formed in the western part of Texas. The Comanchee savages who during five or six weeks, had ceased to trouble the country, had just shown themselves again in the neighborhood, carrying off horses, and murdering without mercy such unfortunate travellers as they could meet. Nevertheless, I set out with one man, reposing more upon the protection of Providence than upon the force of arms. We had scarcely gone twenty miles when we found a dead body: but a few instants before fourteen savages had rushed upon an unfortunate young man, and pierced him with their arrows and lances, in sight of his parents, who from their house witnessed the horrible scene, without daring to come out to his relief. I should have found myself in presence of the savages, if fear had not made them quit the beaten way, to cross the river San Antonio, and proceed towards Medina.[24]

At a few miles thence I met two travellers, who advised me not to advance further; they announced to me that there was a band of sixty robbers encamped upon the banks of the *Cielo*,[25] at the very

24. A town, a lake, a river, and a county all bear the name Medina. However, the town and the lake were not named until some time after this account was written. The county is in southwest Texas; the river, in the same area, empties into the San Antonio River. Ibid., 2:168–69.
25. No Cielo Creek has been located. However, there are three streams named Cibolo, one of which is in the area being described. Ibid., 1:347.

spot where we were to pass the night. The travellers had been smartly pursued by them, and were indebted for their safety only to the fleetness of their horses. I knew not well what to do; nevertheless, resolved not to retreat, we encamped in the place where we were; and for fear the savages might possess themselves of our horses, we hid them at a little distance from us, in the thickest part of the wood; then, wrapped up in our blankets, we passed a rather tranquil night.

At twelve miles from Goliad[26] we received a new fright: all of a sudden we saw issue from behind a little wood, a man with a long beard, a tall figure, and armed with a heavy carabine, pistols, and cutlass, who accosted us with a ferocious air. I spoke to him very coolly. The conversation lasted but a short time. We hastened to take leave of the stranger. He looked after us for a long time, and we were not fully satisfied until we had entirely lost sight of him.

I made but a short stay at Goliad, at the Rancho de Don Carlos,[27] and near the mouth of the river San Antonio, because Mr. Estany had visited these several posts not long before. Five days passed at Victoria gave me all the consolations of the holy ministry. From Victoria I proceeded to the river Labaca, which I ascended as far as its source; thence I went to Bushy Creek, and to Navidad, staying two or three days wherever I met Catholics. During this journey I gave communion to fifteen hundred persons; the number of confessions was much more considerable.

The Rev. Mr. Calvo, at San Antonio, and Mr. Estany, at Rancho de Don Carlos, labor with admirable zeal, and God seems to be pleased to re-ward their efforts, indemnifying them for all the privations they endure by the blessings bestowed on their works. Mr. Estany visits seven posts, thinly peopled, it is true, but destined to become one day very important.

Another missionary, Mr. Clarke, is charged with the chapel of Labaca, and with a small school for the children of that part of Texas: he preaches also from time to time at Victoria and Texana. We have had the affliction to lose, in the month of October, the Rev. Mr. Hayden, who died near the mouth of the river San Jacinto, at two hundred miles from his colleagues. He was of very great assistance to me by visiting the scattered Catholics.[28]

Frightful scenes have occurred in Texas since last year. Without speaking of the savages who murder the travellers, bands of plunderers have committed several murders and depredations of every kind. Thus, in the month of September, sixty-five villains, from Rio Grande, came during the night to attack Refugio,[29] a little village composed of fifteen Catholic families: they surprised the poor colonists plunged in profound sleep, seized the men, bound them, and after having plundered their houses, carried them all captives to Laredo. An unhappy father, awakened by his neighbors' cries of distress, placed himself on the defensive, and when the robbers came to his house, he fired, killed two, and wounded a third. But his courage did not save him: he was taken, tied to the tail of a horse, and dragged over stones and briers, to the distance of nine miles. Seeing him then on

26. Goliad, the seat of Goliad County and one of the oldest towns in the state, was the site of Indian and Spanish villages. Ibid., 1:699.

27. Don Carlos ranch was in the part of Refugio County which in 1841 became Goliad County. Ibid., 1:297, 689; 2:456.

28. Fathers George W. Haydon and Edward A. Clarke were teachers in St. Joseph's College, Bardstown, Kentucky, when they learned that a group of settlers from Kentucky and Missouri were planning to go to Texas in 1839. They went along as missionaries. This group settled along the Brazos River. Casteñada, *Our Catholic Heritage*, 7:30, 43–45.

29. Refugio was founded in 1834 at the site of Nuestra Señora del Refugio mission. Webb, *Handbook of Texas*, 2:456.

the point of expiring, the villains hung him by his feet to a tree. In vain did his wife, with an infant at the breast, throw herself at their feet to beg mercy for her husband: in vain did she follow them with all the women and children of the village: the hearts of those wretches were inaccessible to pity. Judge of the mournful state to which all these poor mothers and unhappy children were reduced! On hearing of their misfortune, Mr. Estany, together with several Texians of the neighborhood, repaired at once to Refugio, in order to bring them consolation and relief. The captives were not restored to liberty until the month of November following.

Be please to accept the respectful sentiments with which I have the honor to be, rev. sir and dear colleague,

> Your most humble and
> Most obedient servant,
> J. M. ODIN.

The Slavery
South at Noontide
1846–1852

In the main this accelerated traveler interest was heightened by such recent developments as the political upheavals of 1848 in Europe, the increase in information, sometimes highly colored, about the "matchless opportunities" for economic and democratic betterment in America, the Mexican War, and the Texas question. Discovery of gold in California, improved transportation facilities, the rising tide of sectional consciousness combined with the curiosity and zeal about slavery brought scores of visitors from outside the South. . . . Others came to enjoy the lavish appointments of American hotels, to see the Indians, and to travel on the much publicized "floating palaces" on the Western Rivers.

Clark, *Travels in the Old South*, III, 197

FRONTIER LIFE IN THE SOUTHWEST

We propose to give the readers of the Courant a few brief sketches of the South West, and we begin with a characteristic scene in a court room. By "the South West," in this communication, we mean a portion of our country situated in that quarter, and immediately upon the Indian territory.

The Indians, who are civilized, have their own courts of justice, lawyers, judges, &c., and administer their own laws and punish their own offenders.[1] But, sometimes it happens that an offender, by crossing the line, subjects himself to trial in the courts both of the Indian nation and of the State bordering upon it—Such a case occurred not long since and an Indian, who was tried for murder in the nation and acquitted on the ground that the offence was committed across the line in the State, was, by the brother and relative of the deceased, arraigned for murder before the tribunal of an adjoining county. The murderer was confined in the county jail, and as the trial drew on, the Indians flocked into the county seat, and a good deal of interest was felt, by the whites, in the result. We went with the crowd. The prisoner, a full-blood Indian, sat in a chair, to answer the charge of the wilful murder of a half-blood Indian, and his negro slave. Through the whole trial he sat unmoved as a statue. On his dark features was an expression of calm resignation and even peace which almost proclaimed his innocence.

"Frontier Life," *Connecticut Courant, Supplement* 17 (24 April, 14 August 1852): 66, 122.

1. One authority has stated that an Indian tribe in this area had "no judicial system other than the individual acts of its members. About the only formal procedure was one that seems genetically related to the calumet idea; for example, certain head men could wave a pipe over contending parties who were then bound to desist or to be set upon by the community." Clark Wissler, *The American Indian*, 2d ed. (New York, 1922), p. 178.

A jury of twelve men sat on the two benches, on the left of the prisoner; and the judge, on his elevated bench, and the lawyers, at their desks, were at his right hand. The court was surrounded by the anxious spectators, and friends of both parties. The witnesses were kept in custody in an adjoining room. An interpreter was placed near the prisoner, and the witnesses, one by one gave in their testimony in their native language which was interpreted by the half-bred, and written down by the lawyers and the judge. The testimony of the prosecution bore hard upon the prisoner. The brother of the deceased Indian, and a number of Indian men and women agreed in all the particulars of the murder, and in locating it across the line in the State, which was a material point. They all testified that they saw the prisoner stab, with his knife, the negro and the Indian, and all the evidence of the prosecution went to prove a cold-blooded, unprovoked murder. It was understood that the poor Indian would either be acquitted or hung, because there could be no mitigation of his offence; and as the interpreter brought out the facts, the attention of the jury was strongly excited, and the earnest listeners looked upon the calm face of the Indian with a mixture of pity and indignation. A knife was brought in by the defence, and identified by the brother of the dead Indian as having belonged to the latter. It was passed along the jury benches, and drew considerable attention. Then a pistol was brought; and the owner, a respectable merchant in town, was introduced, and identified it as his own. He had loaned it to the dead Indian, knowing that he was (as one witness testified), a quarrelsome Indian, who had already murdered two Indians. Another merchant was then called, who witnessed the whole scene. The prisoner, a sober, peaceable man, crossed the river in the ferry boat, and as he left the boat with a small sack of salt on his shoulder, the deceased Indian and his negro servant made an attack upon him, by discharging the borrowed pistol.—It missed its aim; he then told his negro to seize him, and the prisoner, replying "you have begun it," threw down his sack of salt, sprang to the hostile Indian, and took his knife from him; and left the negro and his master dead upon the sand. The witness and the ferryman both testified, that as soon as the pistol was discharged at the prisoner, all the witnesses who had just sworn they were present, and saw the whole affray and the murder, took to the woods, some on horseback and others on foot, and never once looked back to see what happened. At this point of the testimony, there was a general movement through the court; and the prosecuting attorney presented the prisoner with his discharge, and dismissed the jury.

The Indian prisoner rose majestically from his chair, looked round upon the court, and audience; shook hands with the Judge, and passed through the crowd to the door of the court-house, and disappeared.

As he went by me, I shook him heartily by the hand, and congratulated him upon his release, at which, as he returned the pressure, his iron features smiled. I cannot adequately describe the sublimity of the scene, or the feeling, which, for a time, agitated the court room. This whole train of Indians, instructed by the brother of the murdered man, had deliberately perjured themselves for a purpose of revenge. The brother was a good looking half-breed Indian, and spoke English. His whole plot and testimony had been defeated by the introduction of the knife and pistol which his brother bore, for the purpose of murdering, in cold blood, a peaceable, inoffensive, full-blood Indian. But for these silent witnesses with the testimony of the white man, the poor Indian would inevitably have fallen a victim to the vengeance of the

relatives of the deceased; unless Providence had interposed some other means of defending the innocent. It is to be apprehended, however, that the prisoner will yet fall a victim to the vengeance of his enemies, for nothing short of death can satiate the lurking revenge of an Indian. Previously to this acquittal, a noble looking Indian, an half-breed, had been convicted of man-slaughter, as accessory to a murder across the line, and sentenced to imprisonment, in the penitentiary for five years. Unfortunate race! they seem destined to intemperance, crime and misery, and ultimate extinction; but in every criminal process against an Indian justice should begin with the trader who sells the whiskey, and furnishes the weapons.

Murder is a common occurrence along the line, and in almost every case, it may be traced to an intemperate use of ardent spirits, which are freely dealt-out to the idle Indian, in the face of the Law and its penalty, and in defiance of the retributions of our final Judge.

In our next, we will describe another court-scene of a different character. *March*, 1852.

NO. 2

In our last No. we promised to "describe another court-scene" in the South West, on the frontier of our country. The scene however will not be limited to the court room, nor will the present writer be confined to the scene, for some preliminaries are necessary. Sometime in the winter of '50, at a late hour of the night, a drunken man, of the medical profession, or, at least, called "Doctor," forced the door of a peaceable citizen, when he was not at home, and his family alone and unprotected, and with a large knife in his hand, and with oaths and threats, drove the wife and children through the woods to the nearest house. When the alarm was given, the neighbors came in, and were witnesses to the outrage. When the "Doctor" found that he was to be indicted for his offence, he left $5,00 with a friend of his, with which to settle it. The Judge of Probate, and County Judge, who lived near the offender, seemed disposed to excuse his neighbor on a plea of poverty and intemperance.

The prosecuting attorney advised the injured party to bring the witnesses before the "grand jury." Two days were spent in travelling to the seat of justice, and back again, over a road that could not well be worse. The County Seat was in the woods, and the trail was so devious and obscure that the party in the carry-all, lost their way several times. At length, however, after travelling—in going from, and retreating to, the trail about 20 miles to reach a place 12 miles distant, they came upon a log cabin, standing alone in the woods, and discovered two lawyers sitting near in secret consultation. It was the County Seat, and the log cabin was the Jury Room. The plaintiff was desirous of presenting his case, and of departing from this seat of justice, as soon as possible, on the homeward trail. He knocked at the door; and a stern backwoodsman opened it, looked at him a moment, and shut it again, in expressive silence. Some persons who gathered near, said "the grand jury were busy"; and the little party were directed to the house of entertainment. As they rode along, they saw a large ark-like covered wagon, in the woods, with a long table standing near it, and a fire for culinary purposes, at which a woman was frying her bacon, and baking her corn bread for her boarders. Their lodging was in or under the wagon.

The carriage drove up as near as convenient, to the unfinished log-house, fitted up for the reception of Judges, Lawyers, and visitors; and our little party were ushered into "the room." It was a double log cabin, with the usual space between the pens; but no partition to keep the smoke generated in clouds, in the cooking room, from rolling its suffocating columns, under the roof, into "the room." Here were the beds, saddles and saddle-bags of the boarders; and here the party were to lodge for the night. The Court House was another unfinished log-house, at a little distance: with another cabin for "the county poor," and, in these two buildings, some of the City Lawyers slept upon their blankets and saddle-bags, on the floor.—The scene in and around the Court House was peculiarly western; but as no business seemed to be on hand, and nothing worthy of note; we pass on to notice other matters of more interest. The prosecuting attorney promised to examine the Law, and confer with the Judge; and, in the morning, advise the plaintiff as to the presentment of the offender. The morning dawned brightly upon this seat of justice, and the birds warbled in the sun-lit trees. It was one of those western mornings which throw an indescribable loveliness over the wildest scenery; and the only refreshing season of a two day's journey. The Judge and Attorney agreed that there was no indictable point in the case; but the injured party "could go before 'the grand jury,' and see what they would do with it."—They went to the log-cabin, before this august body had convened. A clergyman sat at the table in the capacity of a clerk; and some of "the jurymen," were stretched out on a bed in one corner of the room. One or two were fined 25 cents for late attendance. At length "the grand jury" were convened and the witnesses sworn on the Bible. The testimony was heard, and recorded by the ready pen of the clerical member, and the plaintiff and his party were dismissed. Returning to the boarding house; he had "to gear up" his own horse; pay a tavern bill, equal to that of a New York Hotel; and return home, by another track, no better than the former save that it was more easily found. As to the presentment, he heard nothing for some time; until the clerical member informed him that "the grand jury" *did nothing with it.* Some of the members of "the grand jury," he was afterwards informed, were for indicting the offender; but others were unwilling to make cost for the county and the state, and "the doctor was drunk anyhow." This it appears, was not his first offence of the same kind: probably it will not be his last, so long as he has such influential friends and advocates. The injured party, so far from obtaining justice, and the protection of law; did not get the expences of his witnesses paid. He is advised to "appear before another grand jury": possibly he may: if so—there will be another scene in frontier life.

EMIGRANTS ON THE FRONTIER

This is a brief but vivid account of that element in our population later designated as hillbillies.

Any month of the year, in passing through South Western Virginia or Eastern Tennessee, you may meet the huge and heavily-laden covered wagons of the country, filled with emigrants, the children of the soil, seeking new homes far away. In the depth of last winter I came upon a family among the mountains, where something like a northern winter is known; the father was on the ground in the wet snow and ice, urging on his horses over wretched roads, and the cumbrous wagon creaking lazily along. "An odd time to be moving, isn't it, stranger?" he called out. "How far do you go, my friend, in such weather—not a long journey, I hope!" "Oh," said he, "over in Kaintuck, about sixty miles further, I reckon." By such modes of travelling thousands have changed their homes every year. Every variety of condition in life is to be encountered on the road, but especially those on whom the world has not smiled. They are the hardy descendants, many of them, of the early Scotch and Irish settlers of this mountain region; and the peculiarities of that frontier and com-

"'Movers' in the South-West," *Dollar Magazine* 7 (January 1851): 21–22.

paratively rude state of civilization, are far enough from having vanished to this day. Their ancestors fought well, as King's Mountain in North Carolina, and the fierce fight victoriously maintained there, against British valor in the Revolution, bears witness. At this time these mountaineers are essentially a military population. Naturally they have steady sense and acuteness of mind, and particularly shrewd at a bargain. Their learning is seldom such as is seen inside of school-houses; it may not even include an ability to read and write; but they are pretty good judges of a stump speech, of a sermon, or of an argument at the bar; from these is drawn their education. They are moreover good horsemen, marksmen, and hunters, and capital judges of horseflesh and stock in general; but the men, at least, are not remarkable for agricultural industry, for the patient thrift and intelligent skill that make the successful farmer. They are squatters rather than farmers. It is certain at least that very considerable tracts in the mountain districts of Carolina and Tennessee have been occupied and cultivated in no other way, and the rightful owners of the soil have found it difficult and hardly profitable to dispossess those occupants.[1]

Mark the courteous manners even of the lowest and most ignorant; there is a frank, ready, and kindly address, seldom seen in the same class elsewhere. Withal, the sallow gaunt visage of poverty and sickness is too often to be observed. Some are not too proud to ask an alms as they go on their way. I met a family group near the Cumberland mountains this summer that had travelled on in sickness and feebleness, one hundred miles on foot, and one of the boys asked for money to buy some coffee for his sick sister. The poor girl was borne along in the arms of her mother. "*He*" said the wife,—meaning her husband, "*he* would not take a house or live in one, lest he should have to work." At the next cabin in the woods I called for a moment; "your money will go for liquor," said the man of the house, "I know such movers right well." "Perhaps not, my friend: they may be very honest folk, and at any rate the will and the effort to help them in their want does me some good."

Families make these journies in ponderous wagons, closely stowed with all sorts of culinary apparatus, when they have it, or perhaps in lieu of this, a man or woman of African descent is lodged among the other household stuff, the sole indication of wealth or station on the part of the family that is moving. Some are tramping on foot, the men stepping off straight and erect like Indians, with trusty rifles slung at their backs. At night they camp out in a wood, or under a big tree by the road-side, heap up a huge fire of logs, prepare corn-cakes and bacon for supper, tie up their horses fast to the waggon and soon all are stretched out seeking rest for the night. This is the life of great numbers for weeks together, and the weather is so mild during a large part of the year as to make this pleasant. There is an independence about it that has a charm, and there is good in it, also, for the pilgrims, of a higher kind, if their travels are not protracted too far, or pursued too long; they shake off the effects of poor training and unfortunate associations at home; they develope new resources, impart new energy, and are often the beginning of successful and honorable endeavor. Among their rich neighbors these persons had been neglected, and to some extent depressed and kept down. They were not wanted as neighbors, and were not cared for; they grew up untaught and ignorant. They knew the road to the great man's door in their vicinity, and in some parts could hardly tell another road but the one to the mill. Even the negroes looked down in scorn upon "poor white folks." Their houses were the rude log cabins of frontier backwoods life, sixty and seventy years since, when the Indian was still powerful, and spread over the land. Two rooms is a large allowance in such establishments, each consisting of a square "log-pen," plastered more or less thoroughly at the interstices with the strongly adhesive clay of the country, but few attempting to exclude the air, or starlight: to have them quite close, were it practicable, is not considered healthy. Those who lived year in and year out, contentedly in such tenements, have the same Anglo-Saxon blood coursing through their veins, that beats proudly in the hearts of the wealthy and the great; and, what is better, they possess the mind, and sense, and resolved will of the same bold race.[2] Leaving

1. Tennessee land laws were very complex and made fraudulent sales of land possible. Thomas B. Jones, "The Public Lands of Tennessee," *Tennessee Historical Quarterly* 27 (Spring 1968): 13–36.

2. One authority on the southern mountaineer discusses in some detail the ancestry of residents of this region. He does not limit himself to the "poor whites," and he concludes that there is no information to prove certain national backgrounds. John C. Campbell, *The Southern Highlander and his Homeland* (New York, 1921), pp. 50–71.

behind them their old homes in the upper country of the Carolinas, in Georgia, and Tennessee, they go, a small part of them to Texas, and to Mississippi; they, chiefly, have settled Arkansas and Missouri; there they rise to affluence, in real respectability and consideration; and their children rank often among the truly eminent and noble of the land. From this stock have sprung senators and statesmen whom the whole people have delighted to honor.

STEAMBOATING IN THE SOUTHWEST

This is both a colorful and a factual description of Mississippi steamboating.

NO. I

To institute a comparison between large and small things, New Orleans may be termed the "South Ferry" of the Mississippi, the frequent steamers arriving and departing reminding one of the omnibuses incessantly rattling up and dashing off; and the countless handbills on the posts, and boards upon the boats announcing immediate departure for "Red River," "Bayou Lache," "Little Rock," "St. Louis," "Cincinnati," or "Pittsburgh," in the place of, "Broadway, right up," "Here's the Bowery," and "Bull's Head, right off, sir," of our jarvies.

The steamboat levee presents a strange, unwonted, and amusing sight to the Northern visitor. A hundred, more or less, huge boats all lie with their bows on to the land and pointing to the vast piles of cotton which they have disgorged, or to the unwieldly sugar puncheons or countless coffee bags which they are about to ingulf. In this position they look for all the world like so many mastiffs with their heads reclining upon their paws, quietly but intently watching each his bone. To keep up the illusion, ever and anon a low rumbling or impatient snort of steam answers to the growl or bark in which watchful canines are wont to indulge.

The Western boat bears no more resemblance to its Eastern congener than does the Western man to the Eastern man of business. The Western boat dashes off under a full head, thrusting the water aside from her bows with violence, forcing her way against the opposing current by sheer strength, carrying aloft a murky banner that marks her progress to eyes distant miles and miles, belching forth at regular intervals a shrill yell or a steam huzza, until the old forest rings again, and echo taking up the chorus carries it far away, warning thousands of her coming.

The Eastern boat, on the contrary, like the Eastern man, goes quietly about her business, slips smoothly past all opposing obstacles, accomplishes quite as much as the other, and finally arrives at her journey's end without noise or disturbance, and as if she had done nothing unusual or unexpected.

The passing of a Mississippi boat near a river plantation is the signal for a general *emeûte*[1] on shore. In the foreground of the picture will appear a score of horses of all ages, from incipient colthood to exempt senility, all in a row, heads extended, eyes starting from their sockets, ears and mane

"Every-Day Commerce, Nos. IV and V. Steamboats and Steamboating in the Southwest," *Dollar Magazine* 8 (July, October 1851): 4–8, 148–51. Pages 8 and 151 are omitted.

1. Riot, turmoil, or disturbance.

erect, and feet braced forward in readiness for a sudden bolt.

The youngest invariably sounds the retreat, and with a snort, away scour the entire drove, carrying horizontal tails, wheeling into column every few rods for another look at the deep-throated and smoke-wreathed monster, and then off again for another scamper.

The negroes, hoe in hand, suspend operations, exhibit their ivory, and hat or handkerchief waving, respond to the jovial shout or cheery *refrain* of the firemen, invariably tapering off with the African yah, yah! The overseer dashes down to the nearest point, and hails to know if they want any wood, or perchance, if they will stop on their return trip and take off his sugar or cotton. The planter shouts aloud for news—"Who is President?" "What's cotton worth?" and, if he obtain an answer to his queries, is off in five minutes for the next town— made up of a store "of all sorts" with a post-office attachment, a *grocery*, and a blacksmith's shop—to spread the news, himself an object of extra consideration for the day, while the chances are ten to one that the poor man has been terribly sold.

I mentioned the *refrain* of the firemen. Now, as a particular one is almost invariably sung by negroes when they have anything to do with or about a fire, whether it be while working at a New Orleans fire engine or crowding wood into the furnaces of a steamboat, whether they desire to make an extra racket at leaving or evince their joy at returning to a port, it may be worth recording; and here it is:—

> Fire on the quarter-deck,
> Fire on the bow.
> Fire on the gun-deck,
> Fire down below.

The last line is given by all hands with great voice and volume, and as for the chorus itself, you will never meet or pass a boat, you will never behold the departure or arrival of one, and you will never witness a New Orleans fire, without hearing it.

I have said that steamboats and steamboating in the West are very different from steamboating in the East. The Western boat is built for freight, the Eastern for passengers; at least, these are respectively the first objects to be attained. Speed both seek to obtain; the one by the application of immense power, and the other by a sharp, narrow model. Yet it is strange that the Western boat is immeasurably superior in its conveniences for the accommodation of voyagers, in fact no other mode of travelling can compare with it for comfort and pleasure.

Their first cost is usually much less than that of the boats upon our eastern rivers, but the expense of running—except upon the Ohio—is much greater, and the "wear and tear" at least treble. For instance, the distance from New Orleans to Louisville is some 1,250 miles and a few years since seven days was deemed an extraordinary passage—in fact but few boats could boast of as good;—and although I believe that the "up trip" is now occasionally made in about five, yet the traveller who spends but a week upon the voyage, has no just grounds for complaint. A large eight boiler boat will burn sixty cords of wood per day, at a cost of from three to four dollars per cord, thus incurring the expense of, say 200 dollars per day, or from 1,000 to 1,400 per trip. The expense for fuel in an eastern boat is much less.

To arrive at something near a correct estimate of the number of boats now running respectively upon the eastern and the western waters, we must consult the reports upon this subject of 1849–50, the latest that we have, although, perhaps, before this has left the printer's hands, the returns for 50–51, may be issued.

During the last seven years previous to 1850, 1,211 steamboats have been built in the United States;[2] and, as seven years is about the average

age that western boats attain,[3] or rather as after that age they are generally worn out and useless, good for nothing, but to break up, employ as wharf boats, &c., &c., I think it a fair basis upon which to take the census. There are probably enough running that have passed their grand climacteric to fill the place of those that have fallen victims to snags and collisions, fires and collapsed flues. We will now see what proportion of the number—1,211—are employed on the western waters.

The 208 steamers launched in 1849, were built as follows:—

MAINE.—Furnished 7, all for the eastern trade.

NEW HAMPSHIRE.—None.

VERMONT.—None.

RHODE ISLAND.—None.

CONNECTICUT.—1 for the eastern trade.

NEW YORK.—21; of which 17 were turned out from the ship yards of the Empire City; and the remaining 4 from Sackett's Harbor, Buffalo, and Cape Vincent were for lake navigation.

PENNSYLVANIA.—63; by far exceeding in number her nearest competitor, Ohio. Philadelphia furnished 9; Presquile, 2, for the lakes;[4] while the remaining 53, were from the yards of Pittsburgh; and all are now or have been, upon the Mississippi or Ohio.

DELAWARE.—None.

MARYLAND.—5.

DISTRICT OF COLUMBIA.—None.

VIRGINIA.—2.

NORTH CAROLINA.—None.

SOUTH CAROLINA.—2, both for the river trade.

GEORGIA.—1, for the river trade.

FLORIDA.—None.

ALABAMA.—None.

LOUISIANA.—4.

TENNESSEE.—2.

KENTUCKY.—34, all from Louisville.

OHIO.—44: of which 38 were from Cincinnati; and the remaining 6 from the Lake Shore.

MICHIGAN.—6 for lake navigation.

Thus, of the 208 built in 1849, we have of sea-going steamers, those employed in the coasting trade and in our eastern rivers but 44; and upon the northern lakes but 20; while the large number of 144 have been built for western and south-western internal navigation.

Now, assuming this as a basis, we shall obtain the following result:—

WESTERN BOATS.—Running, on the 1st January, 1850—839.

EASTERN BOATS AND SEA STEAMERS.—(Built since 1842),—256.

LAKE BOATS.—(Built since 1842),—116.

This I believe to be very nearly correct as far as western boats are concerned; but the eastern boats are more durable than they, in fact, on an average they will last twice as long; and we shall not be far from right, in putting their average duration of service at fourteen years. Supposing then, that during the seven years previous to 1842, there were half as many eastern boats built as there were in the seven succeeding, we shall have—

WESTERN BOATS.—839.

EASTERN BOATS AND SEA STEAMERS.—384.

LAKE BOATS.—116.

In all, 1,339 steamboats of all sizes and descriptions, engaged in American commerce. I have not thought proper to add to the first estimate of lake boats, since, as far as personal experience serve, I

2. One estimate for the years 1841–1850 gives the number of boats built on the western rivers alone as 1,133. Louis Hunter, *Steamboats on the Western Rivers* (Cambridge, Mass., 1949), p. 106.

3. No official figures are available before the Steamboat Inspection Act of 1852. It has been estimated that the average lifespan of a steamboat was not much over four years. Ibid., pp. 100–101.

4. The French established a fort at Presquile in 1753. It is now the harbor of the city of Erie, Pennsylvania. *Pennsylvania Guide*, pp. 221–22.

am convinced that, if anything, their number is over-rated, and perhaps 20 should be deducted, and added to western boats.

The first attempt to navigate the great western waters by steam, was made in 1812. A boat named the Experiment was built at or near Pittsburgh, and launched upon her perilous voyage.[5] The pioneers in this enterprise were aware of the dangers to be apprehended from snags and sawyers, eddies and sand bars, but they were to encounter an adversary as dreadful as it was unexpected: an earthquake in this memorable year extended its ravages throughout all the great valley of the Mississippi.[6] It had been the intention of the bold navigators to have run their boat by day-light alone, hoping thus to avoid the snags with which the river literally bristled, but on turning the mouth of the Ohio, they found it even more dangerous to tie up their craft to trees on the bank, than it was to keep on and encounter dangers against which at least they could use some precautions. Banks were caving in upon every side, acres of trees slid into the river, islands of sand arose as by magic in the very bed of the stream, and one morning the mighty Mississippi flowed over what had been a populous town but the preceding night. And so, through fogs and mists, by day and night, threading their course among sawyers and planters, skirting boldly through the eddies, and by the sand bars, they kept on their dangerous path, and at length reached the port of their destination in safety. Things have changed since then, the government has sent snag boats among these waters, and the fangs that have brought destruction on many a gallant boat and her crew have been extracted.[7] These snag boats have a double bottom, like to our ferry boats. They run up to a snag or sawyer, from down stream, force it up straight if it be inclined by the force of the current, fasten to it by a chain, and drawing it on the deck, it is cut by machinery into lengths of perhaps eight feet, and then cast overboard again, to do no more mischief. At Choctaw Point, a mile below Mobile, the shore is covered with these remains of snags, which by some means find their way around there.

Before taking leave of this fruitful subject, I shall have much to say of the various classes of modern boats, but let me here devote a page to a class of vessels now extinct, and of men who are nearly so. In the earlier days of steamboating in the West the Captains and Pilots were men who had served their time and learned their trade upon broadhorns or keel boats, and a rough set they were. Almost born, and really educated upon the river, passing their days either in floating down stream, exposed to the various dangers of the voyage, or wearily working their boat up again in the face of the rapid current, liable at any time to be attacked by some one of the many gangs of robbers that infested all the region through, which they passed, exposed to heat and cold, to snow and rain; plying the oar by day and the whiskey bottle and fiddle bow by night, they formed a class strictly sui generis, and a devil-may-care, roystering ready handed and open hearted one at that.

By these men were the earlier boats officered,

5. The *New Orleans*, under the command of Nicholas Roosevelt, left Pittsburgh in October 1811 and arrived at New Orleans the second week of January 1812. Hunter, *Steamboats on the Western Rivers*, p. 12.
6. Beginning on 16 December 1811 and continuing into the next year, several shocks were felt in the New Madrid, Missouri, area. Numerous changes occurred in the topography of the area; the land in some sections sank from five to sixteen feet, while other areas rose. Reelfoot Lake in southwestern Kentucky and northwestern Tennessee was formed at this time. Adams, *Dictionary of American History*, 2:181.

7. Beginning with an act of 1824, the federal government began to tackle the problem of snags. The first contract for snag removal was awarded to John Bruce, a Kentuckian, in October of that year. Hunter, *Steamboats on the Western Rivers*, p. 193.

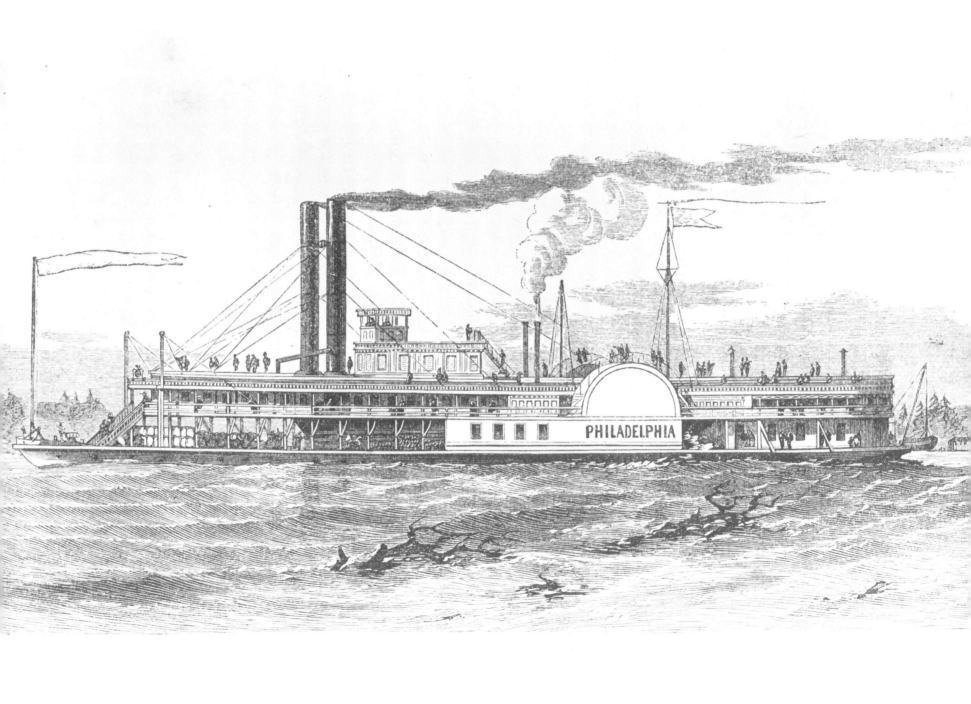

and now for the boats themselves.[8] Differing in every particular from those of the present time. They were built with hulls very clumsy indeed, but serviceable in resisting the attack of the frequent snags. Their engines were all low pressure, and their cabins upon deck. Accidents were then of frequent occurrence, but almost invariably the result of a contact with a snag. Fires and explosions were then not so common as now, but perhaps the greatest proportional sacrifice of human life occurred after high pressure boilers were introduced, and before lower deck cabins were dispensed with. The Captains were a fresh water variety of the old sea kings; doing pretty much what they pleased with boat and passengers, freight and wood yards.

The pilots, then as now, were selected from flat and keel boatmen, and the mates, picked up at New Orleans, had previously filled a similar berth upon sea going vessels. In all cases of disturbance, officers and crew fought for and clung to each other; all steamboatmen were at feud with flat boatmen, but when gamblers or any longshoremen interfered with the rights of either of them, all boatmen made a common cause, leaving the discussion of private quarrels until their mutual enemies were quelled.

Many tales are told of the exploits of these old river dogs, and among them at this moment I recall one of a certain Captain Russel, familiarly known as Dick Russel, who commanded the old Constellation in the palmy days of boating.[9]

Russel was a man of great strength, one of those minor Samsons, that are occasionally encountered in this degenerate age, and his courage was in proportion to his muscular power. The boat which he commanded had stopped at Natchez, under the hill, for the night, and many of his passengers had gone on shore to see the fun going on among the various drinking, gambling, and dancing houses, that made up the town, such as it was. Now the said fun was never over decorous, seldom over safe, and one of the said passengers made both discoveries at his cost. He was robbed of his pocket book, which contained the proceeds of the sale of his flat boat and cargo.

Early the next morning Russel was informed of the robbery, and sending for the loser requested all the particulars.

Having satisfied himself that the money was really lost, and that, too, in a notorious house, immediately opposite the boat, on shore he went, and marching bold as a lion into the den of thieves, demanded the pocket book and contents of the proprietor. Of course the theft was denied, and the denial accompanied with many a threat of vengeance upon Russel, whose prowess, however, they were too well acquainted with to make any overt demonstration.

"I'll give you," said Russel, "until I get my boat ready to go to hand over the money, and then if *they* don't come the house shall." True to his word, just before the boat started, on shore he went again accompanied by a gang of deck hands, bearing the largest cable the steamer possessed.

This was passed around the house and in and out some of the windows, and when all was ready Russel again demanded the book.

No answer but curses being returned, he jumped on board the boat, sung out to the pilot to "go ahead" and to the engineer "to work her slow," and off the boat moved very moderately.

The rope began to tighten, and the house to

8. The first steamboats were rather simple in their appointments, though as early as 1824 they were referred to as "floating palaces" by one traveller, because of the contrast in comfort with stagecoach travel. In 1852 the *Eclipse*, built for the Louisville–New Orleans trade, was said to have accommodations equal to the best hotels of the country. Ibid., pp. 390–96.

9. A side-wheeler called *Constellation* was built at Pittsburgh in 1837 and abandoned in 1844. Lytle, *Merchant Steam Vessels of the United States*, p. 40. We have not been able to identify Captain Dick Russel.

creak. Two minutes more would have done the business for building and people, when the latter signified their surrender, and pitched pocket book and money out of the window.

. . .

NO. II

That steamboat accidents are more common in the United States than in any other part of the world, is unfortunately but too well known.[10] Several reasons may be adduced why this is necessarily the case. Our steamboats very far exceed in number those of any other country, and the navigation of most of our rivers is dangerous in the extreme. The frequency of explosions upon our Western boats is owing in a great measure to their employing high pressure boilers and engines. The steam is generated with great rapidity by this mode, yet as long as the boat is in motion all is safe, but let a boat under a full head stop suddenly and there is always a danger of explosion; so much so indeed, that old stagers will generally be seen hurrying to the stern as soon as the engineer's bell is heard to command "stop her." These high-pressure boilers are long cylinders, resembling the huge smoke-pipes of an ocean steamer—except that the former are placed horizontally and the latter perpendicularly. Through them runs the flue, and if at any time the boat has enough "list" to cause the water to run from the outside boilers into the others— thus leaving the steam in contact with the red-hot flue—an instantaneous explosion is almost inevitable. The steam in this case is resolved into a combination of oxygen and hydrogen gases—and about as effective an agent of destruction as gun-

10. No official statistics exist before the Steamboat Inspection Act of 1852. A Cincinnati newspaper of that year stated that between 1811 and 1851 there were 995 accidents on the western rivers, resulting in property losses of $8,658,776. Hunter, *Steamboats on the Western Rivers*, pp. 270–71.

powder. With regard to the frequent losses of boats by fire, these are too often the result of the manner in which they are built and freighted. The cabin is entirely above the deck, built of the lightest material, and always as dry as tinder, from the constant heat beneath. It only wants a full load of cotton to complete the danger. When a boat is fully freighted with this article she appears like a moving mass of cotton bales, no part of her hull being visible except the paddle-boxes.

Around the bows and upon the guards the bales are piled as high as the "hurricane deck." They almost touch the boilers, which are exposed and unprotected upon the forward deck, and generally surrounded by huge piles of wood, not unfrequently in absolute contact with them. A tier of cotton often adorns the hurricane deck itself, and needs but a spark from the smoke-pipe to convert the boat into a fiery furnace, from which the chance of escape is small indeed.

Travellers descending the Mississippi avoid these boats thus laden with cotton, but no one taking passage at Pittsburgh, Cincinnati, or St. Louis can tell what the situation of the boat will be before she arrives at New Orleans. The lower country boats, the Natchez and Vicksburg packets, and those that ply up and down the Arkansas, Red river, and the bayous during the latter part of autumn and the whole of the winter, all make their "down trip" loaded and overloaded with cotton, and the voyager must perforce submit to the danger and inconvenience attendant upon such a passage.

Accidents to Western boats seem to come in an epidemic form. For a month or two we hear of none, and then again every day's mail or rather telegraph will record some new calamity by fire, snags, or steam.

The list of boats destroyed and injured in 1850 I do not think is comparatively large, although when arrayed in figures it looks frightful enough. During the year there were fifty-three boats lost

upon the Western waters and 107 serious accidents occurred as follows:—

33 boats Sunk.
14 do. Burned.
6 do. Destroyed by Explosion.
64 do. Seriously Injured.

Over 700 *persons lost their lives*, and property to the amount of 1,500,000 dollars was sacrificed. During the summer of 1841 on the Mississippi between the mouth of the Ohio and St. Louis, thirty boats were snagged and sunk, in fact a great part of the then St. Louis fleet was lost. That this was the case can excite no wonder in the mind of any one who has sailed upon the Upper Mississippi in a time of very low water. The river, which at other times presents an appearance of majestic and solemn grandeur, as it rolls its grey waves through the immense and seemingly boundless forests that clothe its sides, then seems equally horrible and disgusting. The once majestic tide retreats into a thousand narrow and sinuous channels, leaving an enormous field of mud and sand literally bristling with the now apparent snags, for the traveller to feast his eyes upon. In every direction he will see wrecks of mired boats, and tremble lest the next hour may add his own to their number. One spot above Cairo is known—and justly—as the "Grave Yard"; and the bottom is paved with the bones of lost steamers.

It may appear singular, but the danger to be apprehended from explosions is much less than that from snagging or fire. A collapsed flue does its work instantaneously, and all is over, but a fire or the sinking of a boat gives the passengers time to see the danger; and then in place of adopting some proper mode of saving their lives, nine out of ten will from fear and want of presence of mind, jump overboard without anything to sustain them in the water, or more probably remain on the boat until too late to escape. The effect of fear upon some men is singular; often ludicrous. Two instances that occurred in my sight are exactly in point.

I was once descending the Mississippi River in the "Brian Boirhoime."[11] The boat was new, and being intended for the Red River trade, had no regular pilots, as the price they demanded to make half a trip and then to be left at New Orleans without a boat, was so unreasonable that the captain determined to steer the boat himself with the aid of a Red River pilot who was on board.

All went on very well until we turned the mouth of the Ohio, and the captain abandoned the wheel to the care of his assistant, with full direction how to run the boat for a few hours. It was a clear starlight night and we were ploughing our way down stream famously, under a full head of steam, when suddenly a tremendous jar threw nearly everybody and everything in cabin on their beam ends, and every one thought or said, "We have struck a snag!"

I am an old stager upon the river, and never enter a boat without fixing my eye upon something that can be used as a support in case I have to swim for it. As I ascended the Brian's cabin stairs, the first thing that I saw was a very snug washstand which was upon the guards and almost against the paddle-box. As soon as I could pick myself up I hastened to my washstand and there I remained until it was discovered that we had met with no more serious disaster than running full against a "bluff bar." A young man of perhaps twenty had previously attracted the attention of all the passengers, from his peculiarly Daniel Lambertish proportions.[12] At the time that we struck, he was

11. A side-wheeler called *Brian Boroihme* was built at Louisville in 1836. It ran between Louisville and New Orleans until it was sunk in 1842. Brian Boroihme was king of Ireland from 978 until 1014. Lytle, *Merchant Steam Vessels of the United States*, p. 22; N. Philip Norman, "The Red River of the South," *Louisiana Historical Quarterly* 25 (April 1942): 426.
12. Lambert was an Englishman celebrated for his size. He was five feet eleven inches tall and weighed 739 pounds.

in a very sound sleep, but being aroused by the subsequent confusion, jumped up and dashed into the cabin in a paroxysm of fear. He looked around him one moment and ran out at top speed upon the boiler deck, then turning around upon the guards rushed past me and ran up the paddle-box to get upon the hurricane deck. From the latter a short pipe carried down the water into the wheel-house. This was painted white and seemed to the terrified sight of my fat friend a sturdy pillar, and just the thing to help his descent. As he seized it his feet slipped, the pipe gave way, and down he rolled, pipe in hand, struck on the guards, rolled over once more, which last turn brought him to the cabin stairs, down these he plunged, struck a fender that happened to hang up at their foot, and landed directly underneath the boiler. The deckhands seized him and drew him from his warm berth, but the moment he was on his feet he made an attempt to jump overboard. When he was brought up into the cabin he presented a very odd appearance, covered with dirt, and yet grasping very tightly his infirm but constant friend, the pipe.

The other case was that of a man upon the small steamer "Mechanic." The boat was making her way slowly up against a very strong current, and when opposite Plaquemine she struck a large log that gave her a pretty severe jar.

It was about midnight, and the man—a Texan recruit—had spread his blanket upon the hurricane deck near the pilot-house, and was fast asleep. The moment the boat struck up he jumped, and without stopping to ask any questions ran the full length of the deck and jumped overboard. Being a very good swimmer he was saved, although such good fortune would have befallen but few. The old river men have a saying, that "the Mississippi never lets go of a man who has clothes on," and it is generally true.

.   .   .

SCENES IN TEXAS

The author of this discerning article on Texas may well be Thomas Wyatt, an American officer who also wrote several historical works of a military nature.

The city of Antonio de Bexar, which was founded more than two centuries past, occupies a fertile plain on the west shore of the Antonio river,[1] and now, even in its curtailed condition, reaches fully a mile along that beautiful stream, while in width it extends perhaps to more than half that distance. It seems to have been regularly laid off in streets, crossing each other at right angles, with an oblong space in the centre, about midway of which stands the cathedral and other public buildings, dividing it into two equal divisions of some eight acres each, the eastern being denominated the civil, and the western the military square. Around the whole extent of these squares are erected, a continuous wall of stone houses, which from the exterior, with their rough walls, their flat roofs, and their portholes, resemble nothing but an impregnable forti-

T[homas]. W[yatt?]., "Scenes in Texas," *Graham's Magazine* 38 (January 1851): 37–40.
1. The present city of San Antonio developed out of the Spanish villa of San Fernando de Bexar. The San Antonio River rises just north of the city. Walter Prescott Webb, ed., *The Handbook of Texas*, 2 vols. (Austin, Tex., 1952), 2:540–41, 544–45.

fication, while on the interior, with their plastered fronts, large windows, and spacious corridors, they present at once an appearance of comfort, uniformity, and security. The other buildings are miserable huts, built of crooked muskeet-logs[2] stuck endwise into the ground, the crevices filled with clay, without windows, with dirt floors, and generally thatched with prairie grass or bullrushes. The surface of the ground being level, the streets, which are without pavement, appear to have been prepared by the hand of nature for the especial purposes to which they have been appropriated by man. The suburbs on the eastern bank of the San Antonio, where a considerable portion of the population reside, yield to the curvitures of the river from the Alamo to the full extent of the city.

The river of San Antonio, which is formed by some half-dozen springs that burst up within a small compass, is perhaps one of the coolest and purest little rivers on the American continent.

Besides affording an abundance of water to supply the numerous diverging ditches for irrigation, it sweeps on with a bold current, and with its flowery banks and its meandering channel winding gracefully through the city, may be considered as its most valuable and interesting ornament. From early evening till the hour of midnight the inhabitants flock to it in crowds, for the purpose of bathing, and then the forms of hundreds of young and beautiful nymphs may be seen joyfully gamboling amongst its limpid waves. It is by no means an unusual sight to behold the forms of three or four young brunettes come dashing down the current, with their dark hair floating over their shoulders, and gliding like dolphins on the sea. The writer describes an incident which came within his notice during his visit to this beautiful river. He says—"As I stood gazing on the various

forms before me, I beheld one younger and more delicate, rolling, curvetting, and sporting among the waves, whose tapering limbs and well formed figure shone amidst the sparkling waters like alabaster when exposed to the sunlight. She was the only female of light complexion I saw in San Antonio, and as she passed her flaxen ringlets fell wantonly about her white neck and half-developed bosom. She seemed artless and sinless as a child of the coral caves of the deep, deep, ocean—but when her full blue eye turned up and its glance met, in wild surprise, with ours, a blush of modest consciousness passed over her cheek, when she darted to the bottom to rise no more till distance had deprived us of the powers of discrimination."

The population of San Antonio is divided into three classes. The third is the connecting link between the savages and the Mexicans, and are termed *Rancheros* (or herdsmen), a rude, uncultivated, fearless race of men, who spend a great part of their lives on the saddle, herding their cattle and horses, and in hunting deer and buffalo, or pursuing mustangs, with which this country so fully abounds. Unused to comfort, and regardless alike of ease and danger, they have a hardy, brigand, sun-burnt appearance, especially when seen with a broad, slouched hat, a red or striped shirt, deerskin trowsers, and Indian moccasins.

The second are a link between the Mexican and the Spaniard, or Castilian, and are somewhat more civilized, more superstitious, owing to the influence of the priest, and yet possessed of less bravery, less generosity, and far less energy than the former. They reside in the city, with but scanty visible means of support, and without the least effort to procure the comforts of life; still they vegetate, and appear to be perfectly independent and contented. Their usual dress is a broad-brim white hat, a roundabout, calico shirt and wide trowsers, with a red sash or girdle around the waist. At an early hour of the day they go to mass, then loiter out the

2. Mesquite is a thorny, deep-rooted tree or shrub that grows in the southwestern United States and in Mexico.

morning, sleep through the afternoon, and spend the night gaming, dissipating and dancing—but they drink but little liquor. Almost entirely uneducated, completely cut off from all intercourse with the world (for except a few paths and Indian trails, there is no appearance of a road to San Antonio), and therefore deprived of the common means of intelligence—they have no enterprise or public zeal, no curiosity, but little patriotism—know nothing of government and laws, and seem incapable of feeling themselves, or appreciating in others, those lofty aspirations which fire the brain, warm the heart, nerve the arm, and burn in the bosom of a free man.

With apparent good nature, and much awkward courtesy, they are yet treacherous and deceptive, and can no more stand the frank honest gaze of a real white man, than a fox can the eye of a lion.

The wives and daughters of the *Rancheros* are as rough and uncouth as their husbands and fathers, and disdain those light and polite amusements that generally amuse their sex. But the females of the second class are agreeable, handsome and fascinating—although not particularly accomplished. They dress plain and tastefully, and in a style best calculated to develope the elegant proportion of their persons.

Generally poor, they of course wear but a few costly jewels; yet with much good sense seem to consider their own natural charms as the richest ornaments that can adorn a woman, and as those surest to attract the notice and secure the attention of the rougher portion of humanity.

This class are the votaries of the *fandangoes* for which San Antonio is so justly celebrated.

Nightly, while yet fresh and buoyant with the exhilarating effects of a *siesta* and bath, they flock by hundreds to those dirt floor saloons which are the scenes of mirth and music.

Conducted with much decorum, and yet without such useless restraints as announcements, bows and introductions, the fandangoes were well calculated to afford rare sport for a company of young volunteers fresh from the United States; and so omnipotent was their influence over the ladies, and so terrible their appearance with pistols and bowie-knives to their brown-skinned neighbors, that the arrival of a single platoon was sufficient to clear the room of every Mexican except a few who stood around as silent and disinterested spectators. The English language is but little spoken at San Antonio, and not much Spanish is understood by a single trooper.

It is frequently diverting to observe the sighs and soft glances of the gentlemen and the smiles of recognition and nods of assent reciprocated by the ladies—and it is still more diverting at the end of the fandango, after each dancer has paid the fiddler, and treated his partner to some simple beverage prepared for the occasion, to see them pairing off by consent, and silently, though not sentimentally, striking off by the light of the stars to every quarter of the city.

The first class, now reduced to a limited number, is composed of the direct-lineal descendants of Spanish dons and Castilian nobles, who, though stript of titles and prerogatives which they enjoyed under a royal government; yet retain their dignity, their royalty, and their fortunes, and keeping aloof from the two degenerate and subordinate classes already described, are content to live in ease and aristocratic retirement. While a bench or two, a *mitato*, for grinding corn, a copper kettle, an earthen jar, and a few cow hides and Mexican blankets spread on a dirt floor, with a shelf of clothes, and a saddle and larrietto, are the articles of furniture usually found in the thatched hovels and stone huts of the two first classes, the comfortable dwellings of the first are supplied with most of the comforts, and many articles of taste and elegance.

In this class may be found gentlemen of education and talents, of polished manners, and refined and hospitable feelings; and if the females in the second class are handsome and fascinating, those in the first class are splendid and irresistibly captivating. Having been educated either in the city of Mexico, the United States, or Europe, they have, with perhaps a very few exceptions, traveled much, seen much of the world—and those superlative advantages with which nature has gifted them, have been cultivated, cherished, and embellished, until they exceed in appearance, and equal in capacity, any women of the present day. And when collected within the luminous walls of a ball-room, as they were the evening preceding our departure, with graceful figures, floating with elegance and dignified ease through the cotillon and waltz, while the flashes from beneath the long drooping lashes of their dark eyes, eclipsed the dazzling lustre of the diamonds and costly crescents that clustered amongst the jet black braids of their hair, the belles and beauties of San Antonio looked like a band of houries from some fabled land of the East, or like an assemblage of young princesses of some romance.

They were all so young, so lovely, and so noble, and yet so very natural and unaffected—they smiled with such exquisite sweetness, laughed with such delight, their voices possessed so much melody, their mien so artless, they danced so divinely, and spoke broken English so prettily, that more than a dozen of our troopers lost their hearts, while the heads of one or two were so completely turned that they have looked westward ever since our return to America.

This city has been the theatre of so many skirmishes, and so many revolutionary scenes, that not a house has escaped the indelible evidences of strife. The walls, windows and doors on all sides, are perforated by thousands of balls, and even the steeple of the venerable church was penetrated by a shot from the ordnance of the Texians during the first memorable action in December, 1835. The noted spots where the lamented Milam fell, where the fearless Ward lost his leg, and where the intrepid Beldin, after rushing out to spike the cannon, was deprived of an eye by a ball from the enemy, were all pointed out to me.[3]

The traces of the ditches across the streets, and along which they advanced from house to house, are yet visible, and the unrepaired wall, then demolished by their hands, yet stands the proud monument of their patriotism and their prowess.

We next visited the Alamo[4] . . . on the east bank of the river, and opposite the northern extremity of the city. It stood in ruins as it was left by the Mexicans, and was occupied by a few hundred soldiers, and as many thousand chattering swallows, forever passing in and out like bees around a hive.

By a broad archway through the centre of a fortress which fronts the south, we entered an oblong square of some twelve acres extent, and turning obliquely to the left, we had passed all but the last of a long row of soldier's quarters, which form a part of the western wall, when our guide exclaimed, "Here perished poor Crocket." We then followed along the wall on the north and east until we came to an edifice of great strength, two

3. Benjamin R. Milan, a native of Kentucky, was in charge of a group of Texans who attempted to capture San Antonio in December 1835. The attack was successful but Milan was killed. Thomas W. Ward, the second commissioner of the General Land Office of Texas, was a native of Ireland who came to Canada in 1828 and then to New Orleans. He went to Texas in 1835 as a member of the New Orleans Greys and lost a leg at the siege of San Antonio. He recovered and lived until 1872, dying of typhoid fever. John Beldon, or Belden, was listed as severely wounded at San Antonio. Webb, *Handbook of Texas*, 2:191, 861; William C. Binkley, ed., *Official Correspondence of the Texan Revolution: 1835-1836*, 2 vols. (New York, 1936), 1:212.
4. The Alamo was a mission fort. At the time of the siege it consisted of an enclosed area containing a barracks, a church, and a convent. Webb, *Handbook of Texas*, 1:22-23.

409

Scenes in Texas

stories high, and divided by thick walls and archways with many apartments, some of which are in good repair and others in ruins. This building stands detached from the wall and it was in one of its rooms that Colonel Bowie[5] was murdered, while confined to his bed by sickness. Extending from its southeastern corner to the wall in the rear, is seen the splendid ruins of the cathedral, a building of beautiful proportions, entered by a large ornamented door fronting on the west, on either side of which, between two deeply fluted stone columns, stands a figure of some holy saint, executed and finished with taste that would do credit to some of the best European sculptors. The roof had fallen in, but the high columns and part of the archway remained, and the cells and chambers that were once the abode of priests and bishops, were filled with Comanche prisoners and mutinous soldiers, while an armed guard stood upon the rear wall, directly over the seat of the holy altar.

Within a short distance, and very similar in appearance to the Alamo, stands the mission of St. Jose.[6] Here, too, the hand of time and destruction is visible, yet the walls and the numerous edifices are more perfect, and the church is in a good state of preservation, although every thing about them is touched with a cast of great antiquity. This establishment, with its towers and steeples, and buttresses and spires, reminds the traveler of an old baronial castle in the feudal times; and as the ditch around its walls, which once served to irrigate the fields around it, answers for the "deep moat," nothing but a drawbridge across the San

Antonio is wanted to complete the delusion.

The front of the church is embellished with a rich vine, within the curvitures of which are hearts and darts, the moon, the sun, and the globe; then there are cherubim and seraphim, with trumpets and garlands, and with mandates[7] in their hands, who seem ministering to the wants, and worshiping around the wrought figures of St. Jose, the Virgin Mary, with the infant in her arms. The whole is cut in stone, and stands out boldly from the wall. Within we found remnants of rich tapestry, fragments of images and crosses, and very natural looking figures of St. Jose, and Jesus, with his bandages and wreath of thorns, as he was seen after he was taken down from the cross. The vase for the holy water is chaste, and must have been beautiful indeed. Like every thing else, it is of stone, and represents four winged angels seated on a rich pedestal, and bearing in their hands a bowl resembling large convex leaves, diverging from the centre, which, with their pointed edges, form a beautiful brim. Here again were the evidences of warfare, which called to mind the events of the bloody revolution of 1835–6. On every side Nature had been bountiful in her gifts—the fertile soil still freshened by irrigation, and the multiplicity of bright flowers and fragrant shrubs flashing among the waving grass, like the rays of a prism whenever agitated by the slightest breath of wind.

The climate was pure, the air sweet, the breeze fresh, and the sunbeams warm, though not sickening—yet the thousands who once lived and moved and were happy upon this spot, had passed away, and wildness extended from the missions to the very walls of the city. It was then we wished for the genius, the fire, and the conception of a Byron, a Scott, or a Stephens, that we might give vent to our feelings, and pourtray the beautiful prospect which surrounded us.   T.W.

5. James Bowie was born in Georgia in 1796; he moved to Texas in 1828 and settled at San Antonio. He was killed in 1836 when the Alamo fell. He is sometimes credited with the invention of the type of knife that bears his name. *Dictionary of American Biography*, vol. 1, pt. 2, pp. 509–10.
6. San José y San Miguel de Aguayo mission, about five miles from the Alamo, was established on 23 February 1720 by Captain Juan Valdez and Father Antonio Margil de Jesus. Webb, *Handbook of Texas*, 2:556–57.

7. A Papal ordinance in an individual case.

GEORGIA LIFE AND SCENERY

The rural "depressed areas" came into being early in the evolution of American life.

Mounted on horseback, with coarse leggings and a heavy blanket to protect me from the weather, saddle-bags filled with clothing and provisions, and armed (as is the custom of those who travel in this section of the country) with pistol and bowie-knife, I set off alone to wander for a few days among the mountains of Georgia, filled with high anticipations of a pleasant and novel excursion.

The first day of my journey was mild and pleasant; unusually so, for January. My road lay along a bold ridge, which sloped in some places gently, now abruptly off on either side, leaving me a commanding view of the surrounding country, dull and uninteresting though it was, seeming like an almost interminable forest. Here and there in the distance might be seen the light blue smoke curling gracefully upward from some "settler's cabin," or a denser, gloomier mass, rising from the black and charred trunks of an hundred trees: still farther in the distance, bordering on the horizon's edge and rising in bold relief against the sky, the lofty snow-capped summits of the "Blue Ridge" appear.

The slumbering echoes of the forest were occasionally awakened by the solitary fall of some shattered trunk, whose noble frame had long resisted the inroads of disease and decay; but now falls with dull and gloomy sound, to rouse the traveller from his reveries, and tell its tale of "passing away."

Toward evening I overtook a man, who from his dress, a homespun suit, mud-color, and a broad-brimmed wool hat, I took to be a "native." We jogged along together, and in half an hour I knew him well: with the frankness and confidence of a southerner, he had, unasked, told me his whole history. He frankly acknowledged that he could neither read nor write; which by the way is no uncommon thing in Georgia, even among people of considerable wealth. And his greatest pride seemed to be his "faculty for a horse swap": in this he considered himself *par excellence*, to use his own expression, "right smart." Yes, and he strode a "right smart chance of a critter," that couldn't be beat in "them diggins," if you'd believe him.

Having ridden ninety miles, over an exceedingly rough road, and through a monotonous country, stopping the first night in Gainsville, the second in Clarksville, I arrived on the morning of the third day at Toccoa Falls, twelve miles from Clarksville.[1]

.   .   .

I lingered here long after the sun had departed, till the mountains were obscured by the thickening shades of evening, and then hastened on to find lodgings for the night. A ride of a mile brought me to a log-cabin, the only house near the falls.

I was soon quite at home in my new and humble habitation, sitting before a blazing lightwood fire, conversing familiarly with mine host: around us were playing four bright-eyed, rosy-cheeked little children, whose names, Tallula, Magnolia, Rolla, and Cherubusco, well bespoke the eccentricity of the father. Think for a moment, reader of Cherubusco Beale! I told the father that it was wicked to

"Interior Georgia Life and Scenery By a Southern Traveller," *Knickerbocker Magazine* 34 (August 1849): 113–18.

1. Toccoa Falls is located on Toccoa Creek in Stephens County in northeast Georgia. It is 186 feet high. *Georgia Guide*, p. 409.

impose such a name upon his child. He replied: "What's in a name?"

After partaking heartily of a venison supper (which no one can cook superior to Mrs. Beale), and drinking a gourd of water, feeling fatigued by the day's exposure, I asked where I was to sleep. They led me into an unoccupied part of the house, and up into the second loft, reached only by a ladder. I did not like its open-work looks, for the night was bitter cold, but as my only alternative was this or nothing, I wrapped myself up in my blanket, piled the bed-clothes over me a foot high, and tried to find the soft side of a corn-shuck mattress.

Lulled by the roar of the distant cataract, I strove to sleep, but strove in vain. I tried to forget my woes by counting the stars which glistened through the many cracks in the roof; but through those same cracks the wind, cold and chilling, came whistling through two holes, cut to let in the light, in which there was no sign of glass. Shivering, shaking, was my song during the whole long night, and happy was I when morning dawned.

.   .   .

It was morning when I left Tallula,[2] and before nightfall I had ridden thirty miles. No pleasant villages, with neat white cottages and ornamented gardens, so many of which one sees in a day's ride through New-England, greeted my vision; but the log-cabins of the "squatters" scattered here and there, with an occasional frame-house of the rudest construction, were seen.

I met no one walking: all ride, however poor. Sometimes two are seen on the same animal; a man

2. Material omitted from pages 115–16 mentions the Terrora River, which Indians called Tallulah (in their language, "awful, terrible"). Near the falls of this river were thick woods, "which stand on the precipice, and send their sombre shadows over the stream." Sherwood, *Gazetteer of Georgia*, pp. 165–66.

and woman, perhaps, on one poor doleful-looking mule, or on some antiquated horse, more cadaverous looking than themselves. I met also large wagons, canvass covered, drawn by four or six mules, and driven by negroes. As night approached, I saw the camp-fires of these drivers, they sitting about the fire, on the ground, cooking "hog and hominy," cracking rude jokes, singing "corn songs" and laughing their loud "Yah! yah!" as the whiskey-bottle passed among them.

Being anxious to see how the poorest class of people lived in the interior, at night I stopped at the door-way of a very small and rudely-constructed hut, and inquired if I could "get stay" for the night. At first I was refused; but upon representing myself a stranger in the country, and fearing to go farther, as there were "forks in the road" and "creeks to cross" before reaching another house, they finally consented to my staying.

The cabin contained but one room, with no windows; the chimney, built of mud and stones, was, as is usual in the South, outside the house. The furniture of the house was scanty in the extreme; a roughly-constructed frame, on which was laid a corn-shuck mattress, a pine table, and a few shuck-bottomed "cha'rs."

I had not been long in this place, before preparations for supper commenced. An iron vessel—a "spider," so called—was brought and set over the fire; in this dish was roasted some coffee; afterward, in the same dish, a "corn cake" was baked, and still again some rank old ham was fried, and the corn-cake laid in the ashes to have it "piping hot." This constituted our supper, which, being placed on the table, three of us sat down to partake, of, while Cynthia, the youngest daughter, held a blazing light-wood knot for us to see by, and the "gude woman" sat in the corner "rubbing snuff," or "dipping," with her infant in her arms. A pet deer stalked in through the open door-way, and helped himself from the table without molestation.

Bed-time coming, one by one the family retired to the corner, and all lay together on the corn-shucks, sleeping as soundly as on "downy couch." Taking my saddle-bags for a pillow, and wrapping my blanket around me, I laid down before the fast dying embers, and was soon in the embrace of "tired nature's sweet restorer."[3] Morning came, and as I was to leave early, all were up "by sun." I asked the hostess for a wash, and the vessel which had served for roasting, baking and frying in the evening previous was now brought; and, "'tis true, 'tis pity, and pity 'tis 'tis true,"[4] I washed myself in the dish out of which twelve hours before I had eaten a hearty supper. I paid them well, and thanked them kindly, for they had given me the best they had. Destitute as they were, they seemed contented and happy: "Where ignorance is bliss, 'tis folly to be wise."[5]

. . .

While in Dahlonega[6] I was interested by visiting the "gold mines." Here I saw the various processes by which gold is collected, both in the "dry" and "deposit" mines, the digging, pounding, quicking, panning, also the various kinds of rock and soil from which gold is obtained.

The people of Dahlonega, like the inhabitants of any town entirely dependent on mining for support, are generally poor, ignorant and licentious; drinking and gambling, like thieving in ancient Sparta, are here considered virtues.

The night after leaving Dahlonega I stayed at the house of a very old and very wicked wretch, who, although worth forty negroes (at the South a man's wealth is reckoned by the negroes he owns), lived in a log-house and could neither read nor write. His family consisted of an idiot son and two daughters, who at supper-time sat down to eat with hat and bonnets on, their faces and hands betokening confirmed cases of hydrophobia, from evident dread of water. Rather than eat the food such hands had touched, I took from my saddle-bags some provisions which I was preserving for to-morrow's dinner, and with a gourd of water, made a palatable meal. Frequent potations from a whiskey bottle served to keep the old man in good humor during the evening, and his conversation was amusing if not instructive.

Hardly had we all retired to our beds, before the "voices of the night" commenced. The geese and hogs in the yard kept up a continual cackling and grunting, which was promptly responded to by a cat and dog in the house; the latter under my bed. These sounds, mingled with the asthmatic snoring of the old whiskey-drinker, and the muttered curses of the idiot, who could sleep no better than myself, served to "make the night hideous."[7]

It was long past midnight, as I lay awake, that I saw the old man rise slowly and softly from his couch, and gradually approached my bed. My heart beat quicker, and I unconsciously grasped my pistol, which was by my side; for I could see no honest purpose to call him up at such an hour. My fears were soon allayed, however, by seeing him pass by me, and take from the shelf just above my head his—whiskey bottle.

3. Edward Young, *Night Thoughts*, bk. 1, line 1.
4. William Shakespeare, *Hamlet*, 2. 2. 97.
5. Thomas Gray, "On a Distant Prospect of Eton College," st. 10, lines 4–5.
6. Dahlonega, the seat of Lumpkin County in the northern part of the state, is an Indian word meaning "yellow metal." Gold fields were discovered in 1828 or 1829 in Cherokee territory. Georgia acquired the land in 1830 and divided it into lots which were sold by lottery. The United States government established a mint there which operated from 1838 to 1861 and coined about $6,106,569 in gold. The Civil War caused the mint to be closed, and the industry never fully recovered, though it had sporadic revivals. *Georgia Guide*, pp. 383–84.

7. William Shakespeare, *Hamlet*, 1. 4. 54.

MARDI GRAS IN NEW ORLEANS

The excitement of the Mardi Gras has been reborn each year for decades.

"Cab, sir?—have a cab?" was the brisk inquiry of a dozen nice young gentlemen, with pointed politeness and coach-whips, as I descended the Alps of stone-steps which led to the vestibule of the sumptuous St. Charles—the most imposing hotel in New Orleans.[1] "Have a cab, sir?"

Impenetrable to either the blandishments of the foreign Jehus, or the obsequious bowing and scraping of indigenous darkies, I mounted the car of "a whip," upon whose face there was so liberal an outlay of court-plaster, that I should have mistaken him for a negro, had not the virtuously indignant exclamations of the exotics against the "*natyve*," "*narteef*," and "*natib*," as they variously styled him, added to his nasal, New England intonation, assured me he was a Yankee.

"Ter tuyfil! von o'dese sometimes I vill preak your head, mine cot!" said one of the cabmen, looking cheese-knives at the American, and exhaling at every breath enough of his country's primest spirit, gin, to poison all the musquitoes within a rod of him.

"*Sacre!* I sall shoot him one day, by gar!" said another, twirling his mustachios fiercely.

"No jabers! but I'll put the spalpane at the expinse iv two or three more shates iv *cort-plasther*, before this blessed day iv *Mardi Gras* has walked herself into to-morrow—that's what I wull!" added a third, shaking his fist.

"No, *gemmun*" (chimed another with an air of offended dignity), "wouldnt *insinnerwate hissef* way he hab, clean agin de principles ob de stand, widout de sufferges ob de entire crowd!"

The rest echoed the sentiment of the last speaker (a smart fellow in a dark skin and light gloves), and the condemnation of my countryman's intrusion upon their stand, was pronounced, in almost every living language, by these motley members of the most peculiarly-piebald population in the world. To all of which my charioteer vouchsafed no reply until he had secured my trunk, mounted the box, and assumed the whip and ribbons, when he addressed them resolutely in this wise:

"Look-a-here, loafers!" said he, "it aint no *marner* o' use! If the hull bilin of ye should light on me agin, and make my picter, like a profile, as black as any face or heart amongst ye, it wouldn't pay, *no haow you could* fix it, and I should make jelly o' some o' ye, depend on 't! I *rayther* guess my right here is *un*-alienable, and if 'taint sot down precisely so in the Bill o' Rights, 'taint none o' your business as I know on, seein' as *haow* it tuck *this* child to be *born* nateralised and civilized *tow*, and that air's more than *ary* one o' you can say, I calculate! I'm a *treue* American from way down there, where *our* yeast makes the sun rise, and all your fat's in the fire, if ye think to make me go meachin' off, though ye do look sour enough to clabber a hull milk-cart. I wont do't! I *hadn't* oughter and I wont—so there!"

The cabmen, thus defied, uttered a variety of "open and strong expressions," and they would have proceeded, perhaps, to the use of something rather more detrimental to bones than hard words, had not their attention happened to be diverted at

A.L.S., "Reminiscences of the South," *Ladies Garland* 15 (May 1849): 109–12.

1. The St. Charles was built in 1837 at a cost of $800,000. It was one of the finest hotels in the United States until its destruction by fire in 1851. *New Orleans Guide*, p. 313.

that moment, by a fine-looking, fat man's ambling the largest and handsomest mule I ever saw, through the portal and over the tesselated marble floor of the spacious bar-room in the basement story of the St. Charles. Glancing into the place, I saw this free-and-easy personage coolly imbibe, while still in the saddle, a scarcely less cool julep and lighting a cigar trot his velvet-footed beast carelessly forth again to pursue his avocations elsewhere.

"I beg your pardon, Mister," said my cabman, when the others had left him; "but them air darned foreigners have been a crowdin' on us so in this town, that they've riz the native-American dander right up, and it's agoin' it oudacious strong from common council to cabmen! Where'll ye be tuck to?"

"To the Pontchartrain Rail-Road," I replied.

"To the Ponchartrain? Wall, I guess yer goin' to Mobile? That aint your hum, I s'pose? Wall, I kind o' thought so. From the land of steady habits, baked beans, and punkin pies, prehaps?"

"Yes!"

"Dew tell! I swow I know'd it! I'm all-fired glad to see ye! The Pontchartrain? Wall it'll take you through Gumbo Taown—that's what we call the French quarter—and ye'll have a chance to see the great show. To-day is *Mardi Gras*, and yender goes one of the maskers, Mister!"

The Yankee pointed, as he turned his vehicle, to a long, lean figure, clad in a rye and Indian suit, and striding a steed which looked as if it were never born in the course of nature, but was some rough wooden frame with a very indifferent hide stretched over it, to season in the sun previous to its transfer to the tannery. Upon the head of the rider was a small, meal-covered, sugar-loaf hat; in front of him a measure of bran, and upon his back a label with the name of "Doctor Graham." Both rider and racker were too thin to sport a shadow,

and compared to them Don Quixotte and his Rosinante might have claimed to *embonpoint*.

As I had time to spare, I directed the downeaster to take me to my destination by a circuitous course, in order that I might see more of the maskers than a direct course would have allowed. Accordingly, he drove into Poydras street, passing the church of Theodore Clapp (a divine of singular power and great popularity),[2] and the magnificent St. Charles theatre,[3] since destroyed, like the American, by fire; and thence to the "Neutral Ground," the division line between the American and the foreign section of the city. Here we encountered the procession of mummers. They had just entered Chartres street, and that popular thoroughfare of the beauty, fashion, wealth and trade of the French population, never appeared so narrow and crowded before. Every window was wide open, and lighted with faces as bright as they were innumerable; and the piazzas and balconies (of which there are so many in this horn of the "Crescent," and where these gay creatures spend so much of their time), were laden with all ages, from the smiling infant to the glad old octogenarian, who chuckled as the fantastic figures passed along, at the reminiscences which they suggested of similar scenes, in which he flattered himself, he had taken no mean part.

These spectators, children and all, were dressed as only the French know how; and the ugliest woman there was so "made up" as to surpass in fascination the most *naturally* handsome *dowdy* that ever lived. Then there was such a continual

2. The Reverend Theodore Clapp, a native of Massachusetts, was the pastor of the Presbyterian church in New Orleans from 1820 until 1830. Ibid., p. 80.

3. James H. Caldwell, an English actor, presented the first English play in New Orleans in 1820. It was such a success that in 1822 he laid the cornerstone of the American Theater. In 1835 he built the St. Charles Theater, which was considered one of the handsomest theaters in the world. Ibid., pp. 26, 313–14, 357.

flashing of tongues and eyes—such an untiring gesticulation with the hands—such a shrugging of the shoulders, that never failing pantomimic epigram, which serves the Frenchman to a whole vocabulary when words are deficient; ay, even when voice is gone, and grim death is at his elbow —such a constant, gushing stream of laughter, clear, and sweet, and silvery as the tinkling of a bell! In good sooth, it was a pleasant sight to see! The *pavé*, too, was covered with spectators and maskers—the latter either on mules and horses, or in vehicles—in some cases superbly *decorated*, in some grotesquely. The characters were chiefly comic, and the French, who are dear lovers of the extravagant and *bizarre*, had evidently tasked, on this occasion, their appreciation of the burlesque "to the top o' its bent"; for every where in the fantastical procession were to be seen the most *outré* caricatures of both man and beast, and to refrain from laughing at the sight required more rigid risibles than any whom I saw appeared to possess. Among them I remarked the lank mummer whom I have before described. Instead of throwing back, as the rest did, the sugar-plums with which all were playfully pelted by the ladies from the windows and piazzas as they passed, he was disbursing his bran-meal in copious showers upon the heads and shoulders of all within his reach.

Chartres street being impassable, the Yankee, when I had become weary of the scene (for which he expressed much contempt on account of its inutility), took me through Royal street, and its squares of tile-roofed, one-story, old Spanish houses, by the way of the great St. Louis hotel, and little "*Theatre D'Orleans*," to that prematurely time-stained and venerable edifice, the Cathedral, in front of which is the *Place D'Arms*,[4] famed for

its Sunday shows of soldiery; and in the rear, the site of the old calaboose, where some excavators had recently fallen upon not a few mysterious little iron arches, which the lovers of the marvelous, and believers in the utter moral turpitude of the holy church, exaggerated, with inconceivable facility and despatch, into cells for human incarceration and destruction. There were tales, too, of bones being found there, and chains, and other relics of guilt, without number, including a cross weighing twenty-eight pounds, *not* gilt, but "all solid gold"! And incalculable were the crawlings and creepings of the flesh, and the risings of hair of all true and pious Protestants, on account of these astounding discoveries. The curious in such matters even went so far as to dive into, and crawl through, many musty manuscripts concerning the early history of the colony, to ascertain if the Inquisition had never contaminated the city. One was so fortunate as to find that during the administration of O'Reiley,[5] the Spanish governor with an Irish name, an imported Jesuit had entertained the *idea* of establishing in Louisiana a branch of that then tender and pining institution. To be sure, the follower of the lowly and loving St. Loyola did not succeed in his public-spirited enterprise, if he ever attempted it, but might not he have "got up" (or *down*, rather, for it was evidently not an open-and-above-board, but entirely an underground affair), a Holy Inquisition on his own account for private speculation? Most indubitably, thought the crowd, who

4. The Orleans Theater, the third to be built in the city, was established in 1809. Lafayette was entertained there in

1825. Several buildings preceded the present St. Louis Cathedral, the first having been erected by Bienville. It was made a cathedral in 1793 when New Orleans became a separate diocese. The site of the Place d'Armes is the present Jackson Square, commemorating the victory of General Andrew Jackson at the Battle of New Orleans in 1815. Ibid., pp. 124–25, 260–61, 255–56.

5. Alexander O'Reilly, an officer in the Spanish army, served as military governor of Louisiana in 1769–1770. *National Cyclopaedia of American Biography*, 10:73.

with pricked up ears, gaping mouths, and wonder-drinking eyes, hung about the spot—like crows over a carcass, between which and their greedy executorship a little life still remains—until the erection of a block of modern houses on the place broke the charm and sent them packing. Matter of fact people believed the mysterious arches to have been intended for sewers, or a similar purpose, but there are dozens of dyspeptics in New Orleans, who still dream of those dungeons (as they persist in denominating them), nothing but *diablerie*.

Next, after giving me a view of the *levie*, already as high as which, the rising Mississippi was rushing on in muddy majesty, my conductor drove through a street, where from almost every house might be heard the rattling of billiard-balls, the expletive *diables* and *sacres* of Frenchmen playing at *rouge-et-noir* and faro, and the monotonous cry, in the deep nasal Gallic accent of *vingt-et-un?* Here I saw a hearse followed by two or three carriages, hurrying on with their dead and living freight to a neighboring cemetery, where the corpse was to be deposited—not among the nameless strangers' graves, of which there are so many melancholy traces there, or there would have been even less show of ceremony, a rough board coffin and a cart are sufficient for them.

Passing a deserted nunnery, which, like the high wall that surrounded it, was crumbling to ruin, and through long rows of Spanish and French houses, almost as crowded as their swarming occupants, I almost forgot but that I was in some ancient city of the Old World. An illusion contributed to, not a little, by the jesting and laughing of a thousand French men, women, and children, talking all together, in squads, or across the street from piazzas, windows, and all manner of nooks and corners, while hundreds of itinerant Dutch or Gallic organ-grinders, with dancing monkeys and squalling *prima donnas*, were aggravating, very superfluously, the diabolical discord issuing from

the open mouths of miserable mules, and a legion of dogs, unfortunately not yet sacrificed to the consumption of sausages. Out of this street (which like many others in the First and Third Municipalities, was too narrow to admit of two vehicles passing each other, unless indeed, they were as diminutive as the fairy one of Cinderella), my driver was in the act of dexterously turning, with the charming prospect of an upset despite his skill, when an unexpected impediment presented itself. Bishop Berkley, with his peculiar notions, would not have considered the obstacle as *material*,[6] but he could not have denied that it bore the shape of a *very* little mule, stooping under the weight of his enormous ears, and drawing a cart-buck of vegetables on the top of which was seated a choleric Gaul with a buccaneer's red cap on the apex of his chubby person, and in his mouth a fierce guttural "*Gare!*" As the Frenchman had only turned the corner, he could have very easily obviated the difficulty by backing out, but his prejudice against every thing American would not allow of this accommodation, and his only reply to the Yankee's "moral suasion," was a gust of expletives, and the frequent repetition of "*Gare!*" (rolling the *r* therein with a forty horse power), as he urged his mule on, and strove to breast back the opposing vehicle by force.

"Look-a-here, old beet-head!" now exclaimed the Yankee, "riling" at this demonstration, "jist you saw off from that, monsus brief, or I swow I'll enymost raise the nation with ye!"

The other persisted in his obstinate course, in which he was egg'd on by other cartmen who had come up in the rear. In a few minutes the street became completely blocked with vehicles, the drivers swearing in every imaginable language at

6. George Berkeley, Irish bishop and philosopher, held a theory that "external things are produced by the will of the divine intelligence." *Century Dictionary and Cyclopedia*, 9:149.

the obstruction. Seeing the odds against my cab-man, I advised him to submit to the other's requisition.

"No, Mister!" he replied, standing up and gesticulating, "you may git *aout*, but I wont *gin* in to a foreigner, no way it *can* be regulated! I'm a true born American, good as new, real grit, and *no* mistake! I stand here on principle, immarculate principle, and so, old carrot-tops, jist you give way there, or I'll upset your apple-cart and spill all your huckleberries."

Better comprehending his manner than his words, the indignant Gaul lashed his poor mule until the quadruped, incensed perhaps at the utter want of reason on the part of the biped who was impelling him to impossibilities, planted his fore feet resolutely before him, with a look which said as plain as words could speak, that the rock of ages was not more immovable. To add to the rage of his adversary, the Yankee, who saw how much better his pantomime was understood than his peroration, put his thumbs to his ears, and alternately lowering and elevating his wide-spread fingers, in graphic imitation of ears asinine, gave vent to a loud and discordant bray, which was echoed by every donkey within hearing, the green-huckster's included. This set the mass of spectators a laughing, a very unnecessary aggravation of the fury of the Frenchman, who thereupon pushed the goad on the end of his stick hard into a tender place on the back of the animal to whom the Yankee had so libelously likened him. This tender spot was one which had been assailed only in extreme cases, and even then, in a manner comparatively gentle, and not unequal to the animal's philosophy, but the present application of the rusty stimulus was so unmeasurably savage, that flesh and blood could not stand it. Suddenly starting from the rather egotistical position which he had assumed of firmness personified, the tortured creature, careless of consequences, sprang (not forward, for the Yankee was in his way, but obliquely) crash! through a tailor's shop window, in the midst of a half a dozen journeymen, who with legs crossed and needles suspended midway in their course, were at the moment making merry at his expense.

If a bomb-shell had fallen amongst them, the astonished snips could not have *scattered* in greater consternation. Then followed such a general closing upon the scene by the crowd, and such a universal laugh, that the green-huckster began to think that he was in what Dickens would call the worst possible of all bad boxes, more especially when the master-tailor (who was a wrong-headed Welchman), issued from his shop with a huge pair of shears, and backed up by his journeymen, wrathfully swore that nothing short of the Frenchman's two ears should satisfy him for the damage to his establishment. Alarmed at the threat, the latter jumped with remarkable alacrity to the top of his load, seized a cabbage in one hand and a bunch of turnips in the other, and swearing that he had fought with *le grand* Napoleon at the Bridge of Lodi, bade the man of shreds and patches to approach him at his extreme peril! Hereupon the Yankee brayed again, and concluded by imitating the other's grandiloquent manner and crowing like a victorious bantum. So peculiarly provoking was all this, that if he had felt assured death would be the immediate consequence, the Frenchman could not have omitted hurling the cabbage directly at the American's head. The horse, however, received the missile intended for his master, and backing suddenly, brought a wheel of the cab rather roughly against the shin of a fat, quashy negress, causing her to change her laugh to a sharp squall of mingled pain and anger, and to pitch the tin-enclosed cargo of ice cream, which she bore upon her head, incontinently down upon the gouty toe of a rum old officer of the *gens d'arms*, who had come up to quell the disturbance.

The projection of the cabbage aforesaid, was the signal for a general *melée*, commenced by the wrathful Welchman's making a pass for the desired ears, and the journeymen pelting the proprietor with his own greens. The crowd, taking sides agreeably to their national sympathies, maintained a pretty general, though scattering fire of the disseminated esculents—the Yankee hurling at the combatants indiscriminately every vegetable that came in his way—until a squad of *gens d'arms* reached the scene of action, and placed themselves under the command of the old officer, who, with tears in his eyes, was grinding his few remaining teeth, and imprecating innumerable negative blessings upon the dark-skinned ton of flesh before him. For her part, she stood regarding alternately her ruined cream, and the swollen foot of the functionary on whom it had been precipitated, and presented a ludicrous spectacle of personified dismay.

Ordering the negress into immediate custody, as a person dangerous to the peace, and a ringleader in the present riot (in which capacity she had assaulted him with intent to kill), the worthy officer who was in a fit mood to arrest every body, made a dive, with his myrmidons, into the midst of the *melée*, and succeeded in securing a superannuated Spanish cobbler and an old fruit-vending Mexican, two persons who had been, much against their intentions, jammed in with the disputants.

Others of the police ordering back the vehicles which blocked the street, cleared the way so efficiently that my cabman was enabled to turn the corner. Not that this was done with any intention to accommodate *him*. For that matter, they would, if it lay in their power, and they had given it a thought, have preserved the obstruction to the end of all time; but in the confusion of the moment, they lost sight of him, and in a minute after of his cab also, for by this time we were rattling away toward the *depot*, leaving the "quarrelsome serpents," as the Yankee said, "to settle the hash," as best they might. Arrived at the Rail-Road, I paid and parted with my cabman, wishing him a more peaceable occupation, and took a seat in the cars, which were already moving.

SKETCHES FROM ARKANSAS

William Graham (1821–1897), born in Pennsylvania, was a Methodist missionary to the Choctaw Indians from 1844 to 1846. Later in his life he was prominent in fostering Methodist religious and educational activities in Indiana.[1]

TRIP TO A CAMP MEETING

In the month of July, 1845, I set out from Fort Coffee[2] for a camp meeting in Arkansas. My traveling companion was Rev. John Page, a native Choctaw of pure Indian blood. He was about twenty-four years of age, had been in a good degree educated at the Indian school in Kentucky,[3] and had come to his people in the West to labor, for their salvation as a missionary in the Methodist Episcopal Church. It was his second year as probationer in the Indian Mission Conference, and he was the most promising native Choctaw preacher in the tribe. Having been taken to the school when a small boy, where he was in constant communication with white people, he had acquired a ready use of the English language, and preached in it with some ease; his enunciation, however, was indistinct, and his language not very correct.

William Graham, "Frontier Sketches," *Ladies Repository* 24 (August, October 1864): 49–95, 619–22.

1. Methodist Episcopal Church, *Minutes of the Annual Conferences, 1897* (New York, 1897), p. 445. Information furnished by the Ohio Methodist Historical Society, Delaware, Ohio.

2. A military post established in 1834 at Swallow Rock on the Arkansas River in Le Flore County, Oklahoma, named for General John Coffee of Tennessee. George H. Shirk, *Oklahoma Place Names* (Norman, Okla., 1965), p. 81.

3. The first school for the education of Indian boys beyond the elementary level was the Choctaw Academy at Great Crossings in Scott County, Kentucky. Established about 1818 at the home of Colonel Richard M. Johnson, it operated until 1846. Ethel Macmillan, "First National Indian School: The Choctaw Academy," *Chronicles of Oklahoma* 28 (Spring 1950): 52–62.

The indefinite, figurative language of his own tongue was constantly in the way of his English, and he habitually omitted the particles, especially the prepositions of our language, which made many of his expressions obscure. This is a defect to which all educated Indians are prone; their native languages are florid and poetic, but less definite and exact than the English, and of much fewer words. Mr. Page seemed fond of language, and was everlastingly studying the theory and rules of grammar, annoying his company with principles and examples of syntax; and yet, in spite of all his diligence, he would leave out the little words in discourse. But notwithstanding these minor defects, every body loved to hear him preach, even in English. He was never embarrassed before an audience, which was greatly in his favor; it is, indeed, doubtful whether he ever felt diffidence, and yet he was not vain. In his vernacular tongue he was said to be eloquent; he was certainly effective as a speaker, and being pious and conscientious, he was quite useful among his people. No one ever equaled him in my experience as an interpreter; one felt perfectly secure that he would rightly construe the discourse; and when the sermon was ended, he would usually continue in a strain of animated exhortation.

Much of Mr. Page's youth having been passed among the Kentuckians in good society, he had acquired their manners, and possessed some of the qualities of a Southern gentleman; but in essential character he was an Indian still. In stature he was under medium hight, spare in person, with slender limbs, delicate hands, and small feet. He had a wide mouth, set with rows of sound, white, irregular teeth, rather thick lips, high cheek-bones, keen, dark eyes, and a scalp well covered with coarse, black hair, which he kept shorn quite short. In dress he was scrupulously neat, even fastidious; his garments were of the best material and neatest fits. He was polished in his manners, rather excessive in politeness, apt to be extravagant in his salutations and lavish in his courtesies, so that his red brethren sometimes accused him of putting on needless airs.

His traveling equipage was in keeping with his general character, and was an amusing mixture of the humors of the white man and the Indian. He rode a fine, large horse, instead of the scrubby pony or sharp-eared mustang which the Indians generally rode—a square-trotter, as the furthest remove from the pleasant, ambling gait of the pony. Instead of the easy, half-finished Mexican saddle in common use, he preferred a highly-finished American saddle, figured, ornamented, and mounted. Under his saddle he used a bear-skin, dressed with the hair and tail on it, trimmed at the edges—the hair side up, and the tail laid on the crupper of the horse. Over the saddle was a buffalo robe, with its caudal tip so arranged as to be on an exact line with the tail of the bear-skin. Then came his well-filled saddlebags, and over all he spread his folded blanket in the most approved manner. Thus mounted on a tall, chestnut sorrel, and being rather short of limb, he presented an amusing figure. Notwithstanding his incumbrances, he was a bold and hard rider, and prided himself not a little on his equestrian skill and hardihood. At the side of such a figure, as may be readily imagined, I made a sorry show with my half-breed mustang and bare, wooden saddle-tree; all eyes were attracted to my companion, particularly after we reached the State. His cheerful humor, vivacity, and amusing whimsicalities made him a very pleasant traveling companion when once we were under way, which always took him a provokingly-long time.

. . . .

We were kindly entertained the first night out at the house of Mr. M., where my red brother was a curiosity in more senses than one. He carried with him shoe-blacking, soap, brushes, and slippers; and his interminable polishing, washing, soaping, rubbing, and brushing was a novelty to a backwoods family. After he was well brushed up, however, and his toilet was made, he took his seat with the family; and feeling animated by his glossy boots and starched linen, he became very agreeable and pleasant. He had a whimsical habit of shaving every few days, vainly attempting to coax out a beard on a face which, as with most Indians, was as innocent of hair as the face of a squaw. As if in revenge for the fruitlessness of his efforts to acquire the masculine mark of an Anglo-Saxon, he shaved part of his scalp above the ears, which gave him a dubious prominence of ear. In spite of all his shaving, and soaping, and scouring, he was one of the darkest of his race, and in feature quite homely to boot. In the morning any man's patience would become exhausted in waiting for him to arrange all the numerous fixtures in his riding-gear, which had to be regulated in the most showy fashion. When, however, he was once astride of his sorrel, he rode off with the dashing speed of Jehu, most "furiously."

We took our lunch and grazed our horses at noon, at the Dripping Spring.[4] In a deep, shadowy glen not far from the road, a wall of stratified, overhanging rocks, some thirty feet high and several hundred feet in extent, projects from a mountain spur in dark and frowning grandeur.

4. Dripping Springs was in the western part of Crawford County, north of Van Buren. John L. Ferguson to Jacqueline Bull, 28 October 1969.

From between the layers of these rocks pure, cold water issues and trickles down in millions of drops, making a silvery stream below. On a small stream near by is formed a natural dam, where stratified rocks are so disposed as to form a perpendicular wall, the rock declining with a dip up the stream, where a large basin of water is collected and precipitated over the wall in a roaring cataract. The vicinity abounds in caves, and the whole region has some marked geological features. Not far from this place we come to Lee's Creek,[5] not a formidable stream ordinarily, but in times of heavy rains it becomes a wild, dashing current of immense volume and force, bearing down every thing in its course. Many a traveler has been deceived by its treacherous currents, and some have found a watery grave in its wild floods. Rusty swords and firelocks have been found imbedded in its rocky channel, the sad evidences of unfortunate soldiers who attempted to ford the turbid stream when this region was first traversed, and but little known.

.   .   .

We reached the camp-ground on Friday evening about sunset. The camps were constructed of light, round logs, and arranged in the form of an oblong square, with a large shed in the area covered with clapboards. The number of tenters was large and well provided, and altogether the arrangements were superior to what I had seen in other parts of the country, and bespoke a people of enterprise and taste, whose religion extended to their temporalities. My Indian *protegé* was the object of general attention and attraction, and the authorities at once asked him to preach that evening; but he declined giving them an answer till he should consult with me. He wanted to know

of me whether I had been asked to preach, and had declined; if so, he was willing to preach, otherwise, he was not. He had put himself under my care when we started for the meeting, and his sense of propriety would not permit him to allow himself to be preferred before me: he was bound that they should respect me. In vain I tried to induce him to preach—it was all to no purpose; he insisted that injustice had been done me, to which he was not going to submit. He was prevailed on, however, to exhort after another had preached. The exhortation was a novelty. He told the people that he had come down into the State out of a heathen country to worship God, and learn some refinement; but he perceived that he was to be disappointed; that instead of the good order and quiet behavior observed among the barbarous Choctaws at a religious meeting, he saw here among the civilized white folks a continued walking about, talking, and smoking in the house of God. After giving them a terrible castigation for their misconduct, he advised them to come up into the Indian country and learn good manners. His scathing rebuke had a happy effect on the order of the meeting.

The religious interests of the meeting seemed to be progressing favorably till Sunday morning, when all religious interest and feeling ended. The presiding elder of the district, who had been a delegate to the Louisville Convention, which effected the organization of the Methodist Episcopal Church South,[6] very imprudently took the popular hour on the Sabbath to defend the action of the Convention, and justify the measure of Church secession. It raised a general buzz and tumult. The old, substantial members of the Church were opposed to the separation, and refused to submit to the new order of things.

5. The road in this area ran from Vineyard, or Evansville, in Washington County, to Lee's Creek. *Langtree's New Sectional Map of Arkansas* (Little Rock, Ark., 1854).

6. This group met in Louisville on 1 May 1845. W. E. Arnold, *A History of Methodism in Kentucky*, 2 vols. (Louisville, Ky., 1936), 2:289.

Nobly did these old heroes stand loyally by the Church with unfaltering fidelity to the last. All honor to their memory! Discussions ensued on all parts of the camp-ground, heated and angry. The traveling preachers favored secession, the lay members opposed it almost unanimously. The spirit of controversy ran high; the laymen rallied under the leadership of Rev. Thomas Norwood, a local elder of piety, standing, talent, and unbending will, and unswerving integrity. He was apt in controversy, able in debate, and rather more than a match for any man on the ground. The movement had been strategic on the part of the pro-slavery cabal; anticipating strong opposition from the honest laity to the new organization, pains had been taken to secure a large attendance of the traveling preachers, who, by a show of unanimous sentiment, might overawe the opposition. But the stratagem failed; and the preachers found themselves confronted by a set of hard-headed and stout-hearted old veterans on whom their sophistries had no effect, except to disgust and excite contempt.

All day long on the sacred Sabbath they argued, and argued, and argued, till the preachers lost their patience and their temper, and the scene became absolutely disgraceful. On Monday Norwood cried out, "Choose ye this day whom ye will serve,"[7] and the meeting broke up in disorder, and the people went to their homes much worse for having come together. Most of these people repudiated the Southern Church as long as they lived; brother Norwood, being an able preacher and ordained elder, administered the sacraments for them, till, at last, he died in peace, an honored minister in the Methodist Episcopal Church.

This was but one of many similar scenes that occurred at the time of our unfortunate Church division, in which the people would have stood by

our Church to the last extremity, had not the preachers taken possession of their churches, incited the fury of slaveholders against them, and cried them down with the odious epithet of abolition. I speak of what I saw. Brother Page was as pro-slavery as the other preachers. As for myself I kept my own counsels. Being young, and without position or influence, I felt that I could do nothing under the circumstances. My mind, however, was made up not to continue in the pro-slavery Church organization into which I had been dragged any longer than seemed unavoidably necessary. To oppose the whole body of the traveling ministry, and run against the inflamed passions of the slaveholding population and their desperate minions, seemed madness.

Having gone to a neighboring farm for my horse on Monday, I found on my return most of the preachers gone, and Mr. Page waiting for me. The presiding elder, who lived some six miles from the place, and but a short distance from our return route, had invited Mr. Page with others to take dinner with him, which he had agreed to do. The elder not having seen me in the morning, failed to give me a formal invitation. When Page learned that I had been overlooked, his indignation became unbounded, and he utterly refused to meet his engagement, declaring that he would teach these men courtesy, if they had not learned it before. "We go to Evansville," he said; "buy dinner, get cigars, smoke like gentlemen"; which we did, all except the "gentlemen." The fact is, they sought to conciliate Mr. Page in every way, as they did all the Indians, for the purpose of wheedling them into the Southern Church.

On our return we preached at a settlement on Lee's Creek, where Page had a good opportunity of indulging his Indian propensity for bathing. Here he preached one of Bishop Morris's[8] best

---

7. Josh. 24:15.

8. Thomas Asbury Morris, elected senior bishop in the

sermons memoriter, greatly to the admiration of the people. He also preached by request at Van Buren, where he administered to the people a severe castigation for growing rich by selling whisky to his people.

THE BORDER TOWN

I know of nothing more calculated to disgust a man with this world than a town on the Indian frontier. Every variety and shade of characters resort thither from all parts of the country, with almost every imaginable purpose in view, and a goodly number without any purpose at all. The population is a singular medley of the genus homo, from that "noblest work of God," an honest man, down to the most graceless vagabond, and the most detestable fiend dishonoring human flesh. The same extremes of character may exist in our large towns and cities; but a decent respect for the virtuous and a wholesome dread of punishment lead to a cautious concealment of the more heinous vices from the public gaze. Not so in a border town. The facilities for concealing deeds of darkness and for screening the vile do not exist there. There are no unfrequented passages through which the un-suspecting are decoyed into haunts of iniquity; no concealed dens of vice, where the deluded victim is sacrificed upon the altar of moral death; no polished sirens to beguile the unwary with artful enchantment, and entice them to ruin by the blandishments and caresses of fashionable deceit; nothing of all this. Capital and economy have had no time to rear edifices of brick and mortar, within whose walls a world of iniquity may exist without coming to the notice of the public eye—whose fair and fashionable exterior conceals sepulchral cor-

Methodist Episcopal Church in 1836, was editor of the *Western Christian Advocate*, published in Cincinnati. He also published a volume of sermons. *National Cyclopaedia of American Biography*, 5:525.

ruption within their secret chambers. All lies open to the generous light of day, and vice is bald and bare to inspection, with no vail to cover its hideous deformity. The susceptible sensibility of modest virtue will at first be greatly shocked at the scenes of vileness; but, alas for the flexibility of human nature, familiarity with these scenes will dissipate the sense of their heinousness—yea, more. Many can attest the truthfulness of Pope's sentiment, thus strongly expressed:

> Vice is a monster of so frightful mien,
> As to be hated needs but to be seen;
> Yet seen too oft, familiar with her face,
> We first endure, then pity, then embrace.[9]

By the operation of this sad law of man's fallen nature, the heterogeneous population of the frontier town gradually assimilates, and on the easy descending scale each character glides un-resisted to a common level. If one should chance to make his advent there whose virtue is too real, and whose principles are too rigidly stern to yield, he must be disposed of in some way; such antagonisms must not disturb the harmony of the place, and some method is adopted, peaceable or otherwise, to rid community of so troublesome a member. A "vigilance committee" warns him to be absent by a given time; or he is spirited away by night, he knows not by whom; or he is dragged from his bed and ducked in the river, he knows not why; or he is stripped, tarred and feathered, and rode out of town on a rail to the music of the Rogue's March. The design is to rid the place of a dangerous intruder, and the manner in which this end is accomplished depends on the character of the person, and on the temper of those who represent the community. Why should the peace of Herod be disturbed by the rebukes of John the Baptist? In this manner the population of the

9. Alexander Pope, *An Essay on Man*, epistle 2: line 217.

border town is kept homogeneous, at least in one respect.

The several professions and industrial pursuits of civilized life are represented in the frontier town. The shrewd tradesman is there, who, after experimenting for a time in traffic with the Indians at profits of a hundred per centum, reports himself as "doing very well." How well he does for the deluded Indians is another question; but he compensates for any distortion in that direction by selling goods to the "parson" at half-price, and by occasionally making him a handsome present besides. No class of men know how to be liberal to preachers so well as these border-town merchants; and these clerical gentlemen usually have the weakness to receive their favors with many thanks. The attorney has found his way there, who, by a sudden transition from obscure mediocrity in some older community, has reached a position of prominence at a single stride of territory. His supposed legal lore, and familiarity with Blackstone, Kent, and Story, place him at once at the head of the "vigilance committee," that popular institution of the frontier, and he is charged with all the political and legal affairs of community. He pleads in the court of that redoubtable personage, Judge Lynch,[10] with the vigilance committee as the grand jury, and then superintends the execution of the penalties which the court awards, that the law may be sacredly carried out to the letter. This court is formidable to all virtue, and especially to religion. Woe to the minister who has censured the popular vices, or in whose hat an abolition pamphlet has been found, or who in any way disturbs the

10. Charles Lynch was a Virginia justice of the peace after whom the term "Lynch Law" was coined, according to tradition. During the time of disruption of justice following the Revolution, Lynch and his associates resorted to extra-legal methods to enforce law. *Dictionary of American Biography*, vol. 6, pt. 1, pp. 519–20.

"patriarchal institution"! The lawyer is pious, always attends church, and, like the fabled Argus, keeps a hundred eyes upon the preacher, that truth may be conserved, and the peace of society not be disturbed.

The disciple of Esculapius finds a lucrative "situation" in a place of such excesses and vices, and practices the healing art with a profusion of pills and powders, and roots and herbs, truly marvelous. Even the Yankee schoolmaster, from "away down East," gets that far "abroad." But as the school is no institution of a border town, he has turned his hand to "something else," which no one knows better how to do than a Yankee. What that something else is does not matter now; it is enough to know that a "down-easter" can turn his hand to almost any thing that pays. As it would not be reputable to the place for the people to disregard religion, a preacher is usually employed to preach occasionally on the Sabbath in the town, who resides somewhere in the vicinity. It is most becoming the sacredness of his character as a messenger of peace, that he should have his residence in some quiet nook out of town, where he may be free from the bustle and annoyance of trade, and be spared the unpleasant sights occasioned by the debauchery, drunkenness, and murders of the Indians who frequent the place. These excesses of pagan neighbors are unavoidable, and it is needless that the righteous soul of the pious parson should be vexed by the abominations of such heathen. The people all turn out to hear preaching, and pay the parson well for his services in shining coin from Uncle Sam's mint, which has come to hand by way of Indian annuities—the sole source of the wealth and prosperity of the town. After paying the preacher liberally, they send him out of town rejoicing, in blissful ignorance of their real character, and the dreadful vices which they practice. He praises them for their benevolence and pious turn, and they laugh at his simplicity, both parties being mutually pleased with one another.

In the towns and at the trading posts of the Indian frontier in the South, all simulate the "Southern gentleman," that character being regarded as the standard of respectability. Nobody works but the slave; every body sleeps late in the morning, dines at a fashionable hour, has servants to wait on him, and apes aristocracy in every thing possible. The people dress well in the latest style, have a few articles of marble-capped mahogany furniture in a wretchedly-leaky log-cabin, whose crevices are stocked with chinches and fleas, together with many similar evidences of "high life down stairs." Every gentleman carries arms, understands the "code of honor," is susceptible to proprieties, high-minded, and chivalrous—indeed, their courtesies and politeness are far in advance of their culture, and out of all proportion with their intelligence, wealth, and virtue.

To give an account of one such border town is substantially to describe them all, so similar are they in general character. Immediately on the Indian territorial line is located one of these trading-places, which may serve as a representative of the rest. Situated on a stream of water, and bordered with open woodland and blooming prairies, it was by no means wanting in natural beauty and attractiveness. Never, however, did nature smile on a more graceless people nor dispense her bounties to more worthless recipients, with only a very few exceptions.

The head-quarters of the town was a large frame barn-like inn, presided over by a mass of unsolid humanity, about two hundred and fifty in the scale of avoirdupois, kept moist by whisky. The outlines which marked the animal form of man had been almost obliterated. He was red-faced, bottle-nosed, and double-chinned, and had lost most of the hair from his head, which had gotten marvelously out of human shape. As he waddled about the bar-room he was followed by swarms of flies, who seem to have anticipated his demise, and were tormenting him before his time. A lank, long-limbed, half-clad negro boy was the landlord's chief of staff and executed his master's orders under the dread of the lash, and with the gracefulness of a baboon. He served as steward, hostler, cook, shoe-black, barber, and chamber-maid, and acted as landlord when his master slept, which was most of the time.

The orderly public house was the head-quarters of several military officers, who were there to keep peace among the neighboring Indians. The dining-room and lodgings of the house were in charge of several ladies whom the army had drifted to the frontier. The most noted inmate of the hotel was a Cherokee sachem of immense physical proportions, aged, gouty, and almost helpless. He had been driven from his country by the party of a rival chieftain; and having plenty of money accruing from Government annuities, he could afford the luxury of living in style in a hotel, and was entitled to swear and pitch his boot at the waiter, while he soothed his sorrows in old age with brandy, of which he drank an incredibly large quantity.

Among the most prominent citizens of the place was "Uncle Jonathan," a genuine Yankee, Southernized, and beginning to be venerable with years. He was engaged in the "mercantile business"—a stilted phrase used to dignify the vocation of an Indian trader—and had acquired considerable wealth. In his New England home he had been a Congregationalist, and no doubt was a pious man; for in spite of his surroundings he still retained many virtues and some relics of a religious character. As his own denomination had no church there, he worshipped with the Methodists, the only church in the place. He had a large and interesting family; but having lived some years in the place, their rigid, Puritanic habits had suffered perceptible relaxation, and their religious principles had become quite flexible. The old gentleman was obliged to have hired help, which in that country could be had only in slaves. It would be better to own them than to hire them of their masters; for then he could have entire control of them, and could treat them religiously, as became a Christian master. Thus reasoned the shrewd Yankee; and from these humane and pious motives he became the owner of a number of bondmen and bond-women; and the patriarchal institution having existed for some time in his family, he had "men-servants and maid-servants born in his house." [11] Thus easy becomes even a Puritan's conscience when liberated from surrounding restraints, and prompted by the love of gain. As might have been expected, the old gentleman's sons fell victims to the prevailing vices of such associations, and, like the sons of Eli, they "made themselves vile." [12] Better a thousand times that he had remained penniless in his New England home, with honest and virtuous associations for his growing family, rather than to have "pitched his tent toward Sodom" [13] on the Indian frontier.

The commercial chieftain and millionaire of the town was a Captain ———, who was a Western man by birth and education, and was trammeled by no Puritanic scruples of conscience. As is generally the case with men of his class, because it is most convenient on the frontier, he was a bachelor. In truth, however, he was a man addicted to fewer vices than many of his neighbors, though his business transactions were controlled by nothing like moral principles. He was the wholesale dealer of the place, regulated the details of trade, and gave the town character abroad in the commercial world.

Dr. ——— was also from one of the Western States, was a man of general ability, and possessed of a thorough medical education. It is a marvel that he should ever have been attracted to the Indian frontier. His active, energetic character gave him a commanding influence, and his skill in his profession admitted of no rival in the place. He, too, was without a family; and though his exterior and address were those of a gentleman, his moral character would not bear close inspection. Personally I was under the necessity of testing his medical skill, and feel under obligation to speak well of his ability.

Miss M. was a well-educated, refined, New England lady, who had come out to visit her uncle Jonathan, already referred to. She was religious, of gentle and engaging manners, and not unprepossessing in appearance, though I guessed her to be on the shady side of twenty. Circumstances brought me into her society considerably, and she frankly opened her mind to me on the affairs of morals and religion in the town, so different from what we both had been accustomed to in the older States. Her fine sensibilities had been greatly shocked at finding her uncle a slaveholder; she could not have believed such a change in him possible, had she not witnessed it herself. But, then, he was her uncle, and venerable with years, and it would not do to say any thing about it except to me, especially as those suspected of abolition proclivities would not be tolerated in the place. But one thing was settled on with her, namely, to return East by the first opportunity, and never return where slavery and its attendant evils existed. We had many confidential interviews on that and kindred subjects, fully entered into each other's views and sympathies, and pledged ourselves not to betray each other's antislavery views. We mutually deplored the state of morals and religion

11. This phrase is similar to several passages in Genesis, e.g., 14:14, 17:12, 17, and to Ecclesiastes 2:7.
12. 1 Sam. 3:13.
13. Gen. 13:12.

in the place; and as they were beyond our power to remedy, we agreed to have as little as possible to do with matters.

My work separated me from the place for something like a year, and I supposed Miss M. had long before returned to her Eastern home. One day I was walking the streets of the town again, when I was accosted by a merchant of a former acquaintance, who cordially invited me to his house, adding that there was a lady there who would be glad to see me. Mr. S. had been a bachelor when I knew him before, and rather superannuated even as a bachelor; but he had made money, which amply compensates a multitude of deficiencies. What was my surprise, when I entered his house, to find the former Miss M. snugly installed as his lawful wife, with a jet black slave-woman trudging at her heels, and numerous younger ones sporting about the premises! Our recognitions were ready but confusing to both of us, and though her husband left us for a half hour to renew former acquaintance, neither of us had the courage to refer to the "peculiar institution," which had been the theme of our conversation at former times, and which we mutually hated. A feeling of sadness came over me as I inwardly asked myself, despondingly, "And is no one proof against the witchery of slavery?" I had reason to believe that Mrs. S. perceived my agitation, and she used every artifice to make me feel at home, sending out her servant that her presence might not annoy me, but all was in vain. The idea that a charming, pious young lady, of New England culture, grace and education, should be in daily association with one of the biggest, roughest, and most uncouth daughters of Ham, was to me a revolting idea, and convinced me that the real "negro lovers" are not the abolitionists, but the slaveholders. And, then, the thought that one so worthy should be united in marriage with such a hard-featured old curmudgeon as her husband was

shocking. A tender, delicate, Christian lady doomed to the fate of matrimonial alliance with a worn-out, dried-up, antiquated bachelor, simply because he had money and negroes, was a representation of connubial bliss which was new to me. My visit was short, and I made it my last, fully satisfied that even a Yankee girl is not always to be relied on in standing up to principle, when she takes a notion for matrimony.

To delineate the several characters which go to make up the motley population of a border town, would transcend the limits allotted to an article like this. Reference has been made to a few of the "higher class." The inferior classes who sell whisky by the drink on commission, who get drunk every day on the profits of their trade, and find themselves in the morning lying outside of their miserable shanties, robbed of the proceeds of the previous day's sales, are hardly worth a description. Two things are indispensable to every trading house—whisky and an Indian interpreter. The traders charge the Indians nothing for the whisky they drink in the stores where they trade, and often fill their jugs besides; or rather, they add the price of the whisky to the goods sold, the Indians being none the wiser for the imposition. When the red-skinned customers enter a store, they are not asked to buy at first, but are invited to sit down, drink and smoke at the merchant's expense —women as well as men drink freely. After they are thus regaled and the effects of the liquor begin to appear, then trades are artfully introduced by the wily merchant. Chance if the group leave the store with a single dime of their annuity or a skin of their peltry—all is exchanged before they are allowed to leave. For a distance of a mile around the town the Indians are scattered about under the trees, with their ponies, packs, whisky jugs, women, and children. They usually remain several days— an Indian is never in a hurry. These camping places are frequented by all sorts of the baser characters from the town, by day and by night; frequent broils occur, sometimes fights and murders. Occasionally some incautious libertine incurs the displeasure of the Indian women, who join together and administer to him a well-deserved flagellation with hickory withes, sometimes tying him with a rope. The men take no part in the affray, but look on with undisguised delight, it being considered by them the depth of infamy to be flogged by women.

TEXAS ADVENTURES

Samuel Adams Hammett (1816–1865) was born in Connecticut and received a good education there. Responding to the wanderlust that affected so many young men of the day, he drifted down to Texas where he lived on the frontier for over a decade. Returning to New York City and a business career in 1848, he promptly began to write articles reminiscent of his experiences, material that was later reworked into a novel, Stray Yankee in Texas, *published in 1853 under the pseudonym of Philip Paxton.*[1]

.   .   .

Let us imagine ourselves upon one of those steamers—such as they are—that ply up and down the Mississippi, and to and fro across the Gulf between New Orleans and Galveston—and after a passage of from thirty to sixty hours, within sight of the latter place.

This city—as every one knows or should know—is built upon that narrow strip of sand which separates Galveston Bay from the Gulf of Mexico.

You will neither perceive island nor city until you are close upon them. The shore, low and destitute of anything that may deserve the name of a tree, presents no prominent landmarks to the mariner; and many a vessel, before the city was built, has sought in vain the inlet to the Bay.

I have always considered Galveston as one of the most charming places—in appearance—that I have ever seen.[2] The regular streets are of dazzling and solid white sand—the houses new and nearly all painted white—the dwellings built in that easy, sans-souci style peculiar to the French and Spanish cottage; and all of them surrounded and embowered with the beautiful shrubbery of the tropics—the several varieties of the fig, the orange, the lemon, the pomegranate, and great numbers of flowering plants, that with us require the greatest care and attention, but there grow to a large size, almost unattended and uncared for—such as the various kinds of jessamine, the tube rose, the oleander, &c. &c.

The wharves present quite a business-like ap-

[Samuel Adams Hammett], "Drafts at Sight in the Southwest," *Literary World* 5 (14 July, 15 September 1849): 21–22, 217–18; 7 (20 July 1850): 46–48. Three other sketches in this series are omitted.
1. *Dictionary of American Biography*, vol. 4, pt. 2, p. 201.

2. The earliest settlement at Galveston was made by Jean Lafitte in 1817. Stephen T. Austin attempted to establish the town as a port of entry in 1825, but no permanent settlement was made there until 1830 or 1831. By 1838 the population had grown to 3,000. Webb, *Handbook of Texas*, 1:662.

pearance—a few foreign ships—three or four Bay steamers that ply between this port and Houston, the Brazos and the Trinity—one or two sea steamers—the packets and cotton ships from New York and Boston—and a host of smaller craft, enjoying the beautiful appellation of "Chicken-thieves," which run up and down the Bay, poking their inquisitive prows into all the small bayous, and driving a profitable trade in wood and charcoal, butter, poultry, and eggs.

To the wharves and to the Strand, however (as the street fronting upon the bay is named), all business is confined, and an air of insuperable dullness reigns over the rest of the city. Not a sound is heard except perchance the bell of a steamer, or occasionally voices raised in mirth, a singer in the streets; it would be the place of all the world for a second edition of the "Seven Sleepers"[3] to luxuriate in, without the slightest danger of a speedy awakening.

Galveston can never be more than a forwarding post for Houston[4] and the Brazos. Portentous circumstances, and the idea that it must soon become a place of importance, alone gave it the position it once occupied, and from which it has already sadly declined.

A few English, French, and German merchants, with some capital, and heavy stocks of goods, emigrated there in the years 1840, '41, and '42,

expecting to supply the up-country planters with their necessary goods, and purchase in return their cotton for a foreign remittance. The Houston merchants soon, however, obtained greatly the advantage over them; the navigation of the Brazos and Trinity being so exceedingly uncertain and dangerous, that planters preferred transporting their crops across the country in wagons to the latter place, rather than incur the risk of loss, injury, and serious delay upon the rivers; and when once in Houston, their cotton was purchased immediately at quite as fair a price as they could expect to obtain for it below. Moreover, the men of Houston being generally old settlers and persons well acquainted with the wants of the Southern trade, offered them stocks of goods, if not so large, yet better assorted and adapted to their wants than those of their rivals of Galveston.

Nor was this all: a planter must at some time require credit; this, those who were deserving of it, could obtain from men to whom they were personally known, and who were familiar with their affairs and circumstances; while on the contrary all foreigners came to the country with the idea that it was the first object of every man with whom they met, to cheat and defraud them if they could.

The "Northers," as the fierce north winds of the coast-country are called,[5] offered another and a very serious impediment to the commerce of Galveston.

The waters of the Bay are little influenced by the tide, but completely controlled by the violent winds. A strong southeast wind forces the waves of the gulf into the bay, while a heavy and continued blow from the north or west nearly empties the latter into the former, leaving the flats bare and the sand bars impassable even to the smallest craft.

3. According to legend, seven Christians of Epheseus fled from the Decian persecution to a cave in Mount Celion. They awoke some 200 years later but died in a short while; their bodies were placed in a large stone coffin which was taken to Marseilles. *Brewer's Dictionary of Phrase and Fable*, p. 817.

4. Though Galveston is not as large as Houston, it is one of the largest ports in the United States. Consular representatives from twenty-four foreign countries and offices of sixty-nine steamship lines are located there. In 1836 John K. and Augustus C. Allen drew plans for a new town. By 1837 the town, now Houston, was incorporated with 1,200 inhabitants. Webb, *Handbook of Texas*, 1:662, 847–48.

5. The whole state seems to be subject to these sudden storms, which may occur from fall to early spring. Writers' Program, Texas, *Texas: A Guide to the Lone Star State* (New York, 1940), p. 11.

It is almost impossible for any planter to visit Galveston in winter, receive and dispose of his crop of cotton, purchase and ship his goods, without being there long enough to encounter a "Norther," and he then has the pleasure of remaining at the "Tremont House," or whatever hotel he may choose to patronize, at a very heavy *necessary* expense, besides the *extras*—generally the more serious of the two, or of being caught in a steamer upon some of the "bars"—Red-fish or Clappers for instance—then and there to lie, wind and mud-bound, from a day to a week, as fate may will it, upon short commons, until a southeast wind may be so minded as to again replenish the exhausted bay.

These and other causes occasioned a rapid increase of prosperity in Houston, and a proportionate decline in Galveston, but not immediately; for strange to say, that very want of a regular and legitimate up-country business produced temporarily the reverse effect. The heavy stocks of foreign merchandise were found unsaleable and unfitted for the market. Men [who] had rushed there as our citizens now are rushing to California, taking with them refuse goods of all descriptions, under the mistaken idea that anything would sell in Texas.

Anxious to dispose of their dragging stocks, they soon commenced dabbling in lands, and exchanging goods at exorbitant prices for lots in or near the city. Nor was it long before soldiers' certificates, headright—as the floating claims of settlers were termed—patents, and even Spanish titles, all found a market here.

Land every one had; a crowd of speculators rushed in, strangers filled the hotels, and their money the landlords' pockets; the livery stables, bar-rooms, billiard rooms, restaurants—all came in for a share; a much larger amount of goods was sold for money; building lots rose rapidly in value; houses and stores were erected; those already in

existence were purchased at an extravagant price, and for a time everything bore an unreal and inflated value.

Affairs went on prosperously for a time, but a reverse soon came.

As long as these stocks of goods lasted, and even longer; while the merchants who had been engaged in this business had credit to purchase others upon their individual responsibilities or by the hypothecation of their land papers; all was well—but when no merchant could be found willing to part with his wares, except for such equivalents as he could again employ for the purpose of replenishing his store, an immediate decline of commerce ensued.

Houses and lots decreased greatly in value; most of those who had been transacting a really legitimate business abandoned the place to seek a better location, and Galveston became what it now is.

It is, in fact, looked upon something in the light of a watering place, where one can spend a few days and a few dollars pleasantly, luxuriate upon the fine oysters and fish of the Bay, sail, ride, and bathe. To look at the town, you would note it for the very residence of Hygeia; the neat and beautiful houses, the cleanly appearance of the streets of hard white sand, the almost constant breezes from the Gulf or Bay, all indicate it.

Unfortunately the reverse is the case. Galveston has been severely and repeatedly afflicted with the fatal epidemics of the South.

There is another great drawback to its prosperity—the danger of submersion.[6] Twice within the recollection of the author has the portion of the island upon which the city is built been under water; once entirely, and once partially.

The first visit of Neptune occurred in 1838 or

6. After the disastrous flood of 1900 the city, aided by the state, constructed a seawall fifteen feet high. Webb, *Handbook of Texas*, 1:665.

9. No lives were lost; all the inhabitants took refuge in a large building, then used as the Custom House. The second story was filled with soldiers and Mexican prisoners, whose weight, probably, prevented the building being washed away. The boards were torn off from the lower part of the building, and the waves had full liberty of dashing through without meeting any opposition upon which to wreak their vengeance, except the posts and supporters. All this occurred at night, and the next day, the waves retreated; but dark and fearful must that night have been to those cabined, cribbed and confined[7] in a slight building, surrounded with a raging waste of waters, stunned by the deep-mouthed roar of the furious waves, and the shrill piping of the northern blast.

At this time Galveston was but a military post, of which Col. Turner[8] was the commandant, and he with his wife and family passed the night in a small open boat, anchored near the Custom House, exposed to the violence of the pitiless storm.

The second invasion of his Marine, or Submarine Highness, occurred in 1842. A church built of brick was blown down or undermined, I know not which; houses upset and shattered; vessels made experimental trips upon their own accounts, without having obtained a regular clearance from the Custom House; some of them became so firmly attached, during their first visit to the streets, that they reluctantly refused all overtures made them afterwards to leave; and one or more lives were lost.

P.P.

7. "Cabined, cribbed, confined": William Shakespeare, *Macbeth*, 3.4.24.
8. Amasa Turner, a native of Massachusetts, went to Texas and was appointed captain in the army by General Houston in 1835. For a time he served as commander of the post at Galveston. He was one of the first to settle there. He served in the state legislature in 1850–1851 and in the state senate in 1852–1853. Homer S. Thrall, *A Pictorial History of Texas*, 6th ed. (St. Louis, Mo., 1881), p. 629.

V. A WEDDING AND A WOLF HUNT

A home on the wide, open prairie for me,
Where waves the rich grass like swell on the sea,
To the breezes of heaven untrammelled and free—
  Where the sensitive rose uncared for grows,
  And roams without fear the wild red deer,
    A home in the prairie for me.

A peep at frontier life and a scamper across the prairie on a half-wild Spanish horse at break-neck speed is far better than a dry dissertation upon bricks and mortar; and so Houston (the city) must bide its time while I try my hand at something more congenial—a wolf hunt.

The first scene of the kind that I ever witnessed was in the days of my pristine verdure—and by the way, here let me drop a word of advice to any and every one who may try his or their fortunes in a new country—to pretend to no knowledge that they do not possess. If everything appears new, and queer, and strange, let them say so. Ask as many questions as they please, the more the better. They will find the backwoodsman is not only willing but happy to impart any information in his power, and that he will take pleasure in showing everything that may amuse and astonish them—but for the man who would play the Indian and refuse an expression of either surprise or pleasure, small pains will be taken for his edification.

I enjoyed my first impressions to the fullest extent. The scene which I am about to describe was in Eastern Texas, in a small settlement not far from the forks of the San Jacinto. The settlement consisted of the members of one family, and thus was it made:

Some years since the R. family resided in Louisiana, but finding the range for their cattle becoming every year worse, one of the sons, Joe, set forth as a pioneer to explore, and locate himself upon the more fertile plains of Texas, taking with him his wife and children. Here in the days of the patriarchs he would have pitched his tent, but having no tent to pitch, or no taste for a life in tents, or being intent upon a more permanent mansion, he set to work, and with the friendly assistance of a few near neighbors, living not more than fifteen or twenty miles distant, put up a log cabin. A sturdy arm, a sharp axe, and a willing heart require but few days to furnish the backwoodsman with a secure shelter. Joe had travelled in a covered wagon, which contained his small family and small stock of furniture—the latter probably consisting of an old chest containing the family wardrobe, a coffee-pot, a few tin cups, a steel mill to grind his corn, a skillet to bake his bread in, a few spoons, knives, forks, pans and pails.

His farming utensils were even fewer in number —a plough, an axe, and hoe, perhaps—nothing else. As for provisions, a supply of coffee and tobacco was indispensable; for everything else, except a little meal for immediate use, he relied upon his stock of cattle, to sell or to kill. Having completed his cabin, he now made a small clearing in the adjoining woods where to raise the corn for his family's bread. The next year his brother came out, the two lived and prospered. Their cattle grew in numbers. Before long rumors of the fatness of the land had reached the ears of the other members, and out they trooped—men, women, children, and negroes, horses and cattle, until Joe began to imagine the population too dense for health and comfort. In fact he complained bitterly to me and expressed a determination of moving further, where he would have room to breathe, and the women could not quarrel about their chickens.

This settlement, whose density of population distressed our friend Joe so much, consisted at this time of five families and not over forty individuals of all hues, ages and sexes. There had been a wedding—Cupid had found his way into the wilds and tempted a young man to commit matrimony with one of the daughters of the family after a very curt courtship, which was perhaps excusable, as the lover had to ride fifty miles every time he would visit his inamorata. Unfortunately for all who anticipated the fun and frolic usually incident to such affairs, death had been busy in the family but a short time previous, having with his remorseless scythe clipped off its head—and in consequence banjo and fiddle were tabooed, and dancing decidedly vetoed. On the wedding morning, the rain fell as it only falls in Texas, and the happy man arriving drenched to the skin, was obliged to change his dress before he did his condition. However, as he had ridden in homespun and preserved his best suit in his saddle-bags intact, he soon made his appearance decidedly renovated. If there was no dancing there was plenty of feasting. The Houston stores had been laid under contribution, a host of fat things were spread before the assembled guests, and although I cannot affirm, as it is customary to do in similar cases, that the tables groaned under their unwonted burden—since according to the very best information I have been able to obtain upon the subject, tables never do groan, but are basely slandered in this respect, yet they certainly creaked—and to make up the deficiency the majority·of the guests groaned in concert before morning. The old lady seemed to have taken an exact measure of each one's capacity, and as long as she imagined a stray corner existed in any one, unoccupied, so long she continued to heap her luxuries upon his plate. In the evening songs and stories, nearly as broad as they were long, intimately mixed with whiskey and water, circulated among us, and long ere midnight the majority of the males at least were in admirable condition for bed.

A bed was prepared rather remarkable for its longitude, as it extended the entire length of the porch, being formed simply by laying down a succession of blankets and counterpanes with anything and everything stuck under the end for "heading"—and upon this the males threw themselves down, each man using his own blanket, which no Texan travels without, for cover.

The next morning all were astir betimes and it certainly appeared to me that had the most of them entertained even a remote idea of the thirst they were to experience, they certainly would have taken a drop more before retiring. A wedding without anything of a frolic connected with it would have been deemed a species of sacrilege, and so "faute de mieux," a wolf-hunt was declared the order of the day.

Directly in front of the house, at a distance of four miles, is an "island of timber," known as Lake Island. It is one mile in length, and through it runs or stands, as the case may be, a narrow, shallow, and muddy strip of water. Four miles again beyond this is another and a smaller "island," called, from its usual inhabitants, "Wolf Island." I would here beg the reader to remark, that in speaking of "Islands," clusters of trees are meant to be implied—the same relative terms being applied to prairie and woodland as we use in speaking of land and water—a strip of prairie extending into the woods is known as a "Cove" or "Bay," while a projecting piece of wood is called a "Point"—a cluster of trees, an "Island," &c.

It appears that among the innumerable wolves that ravaged the prairie, one had acquired for herself a very unenviable notoriety, and had been long marked for destruction. Her size was great; in fact, she was represented as being a monster in her way. She had had the audacity to venture boldly into the cow-pens, and drive off all the dogs of the settlement except one huge old veteran, named Rove, with whom she respectfully declined measuring her strength. Our plans were easily arranged—the caviarde of horses driven into the pen, and we were soon very busy catching and saddling—each man paying particular attention to the fastening of his girth, in the anticipation of a hard race over a hog-wallow prairie. Among the

more prominent actors were our quondam friend "Joe," a younger brother "Dave," mounted upon a fine blooded animal, and a brother-in-law, "Sam," who, being almost as much of a Johnny Newcome as myself, and considering himself "Some punkins" in hunting, must needs bring his rifle into the field, for which he was well laughed at. The rest relied for offence and defence upon their long cow whips—an implement consisting of a short eighteen inch handle, to which a very heavy lash from twelve to eighteen feet long is attached, and usually carried over their shoulder with the lash trailing upon the ground—the "caberos" or hair rope, and, in cases of emergency, their stirrups, which, weighing from three to five pounds, and easily unshipped, as a sailor would say, make a very efficient instrument.

All were ready, and, with a shout, off we started at a dashing pace; but our ardor abating, after a burst of a mile, we cooled down to a steady trot. Bearing to the right of Lake Island is a "marais" almost impassable in the wet season, but at this time in good order for travelling, and as we dashed into its high grass up started as fine a drove of deer as ever gladdened a hunter's eye. The sight was not lost upon our friend Sam, who, driving his rowels into the sides of his young horse, dashed off in hot pursuit. "Look out, Sam!" cried Joe, "look out! that critter won't stand fire—she'll give you fits directly." The caution came too late; a shout of exultation from Sam had brought a fine buck to the right about, anxious, with all the curiosity of his kind, to know what in the world that unearthly noise might mean; and ere he was satisfied Sam was within range, in an instant, without the least check of the horse's speed the rifle was at his cheek, and off went the gun, Sam, and deer, "Unanimous," as Mr. George Christy[9]

9. This may refer to George N. Christy, one of the partners of the Christy Minstrels. *National Cyclopaedia of American Biography*, 7:297.

observes, "upon that last note." The buck evidently had the best of it. With his flag raised in triumph, he scoured over the prairie, throwing himself clear above the high grass at every jump. The rifle, the parent of all the mischief, lay reposing in quiet on the ground, and Sam, well bruised and almost stunned, flat upon his back, was holding on to one end of his "caberos," endeavoring to restrain his horse, who, fastened to the other, was prancing, snorting, and trying his best to escape his human anchor. A fall from a horse being too trivial a thing to occasion anything but a laugh at the expense of the fallen, without more ado we secured the animal, righted the man, and again bent our course to the Island. On arriving there I found it to be a cluster of trees covering about two acres, with a heavy thicket of underbrush—and an admirable place to shelter all kinds of "varmint."

The best mounted men were selected to guard the Island, and if the wolf or wolves should break through our formidable pack of dogs, cut them off from taking shelter in Lake Island. Dave and myself were posted without upon one side; we had dismounted for a moment to tighten the girths, and I was just securing mine, when a shout from him brought me to saddle in an instant, and looking around I espied the identical wolf not more than one hundred yards ahead, making the best of her way across the prairie, and maintaining a running fight with "old Rove," while the rest of the pack of hounds and curs were scouring along after them as near as they might.

We gave chase immediately. It was just noon, on an intensely hot day in the first part of September; the ground we were riding over of the description known as "hog-wallow," being a succession of small mounds and corresponding hollows —the wolf, gaunt and in fine running order. In short, the chances were against us; however, off

we dashed, shouting like madmen, Dave right on the trail of the wolf, and I striving to head her off from Lake Island.

It was an animated scene—the wolf right ahead, running side by side with "old Rove," and gaining upon us every moment; the space between us dotted with dogs of all colors and sizes, and scattered from us to the starting-ground, some twenty riders, every man of them making the best possible use of both lungs and spurs.

Whether it was owing to the heat of the day, the roughness of the ground, or the fact that the wolf was contending for life and we only for her skin, I know not, but in a heat of four miles she certainly beat us fairly over a quarter.

Upon reaching Lake Island not only the old hound, but the smaller fry, abandoned all idea of the chase, and rushed indiscriminately into the water, whence they refused most doggedly to stir. They were completely done over and used up, and most of our horses in no better condition.

After beating the bush vainly for a while, we called a council of war, and determined to ride our reeking, panting steeds homeward, procure fresh ones, and other dogs, and return again feeling very sure that "Sir Isengrim"[10] would not dream of leaving his quarters for some time, unless cavalierly ousted; and that we should find him awaiting us, stiffened with his morning's work, and in no condition to make the same "time" again.

On our homeward route Dave and myself, to whom the escape of the wolf was imputed, caught it finely from all quarters. "Look, heah, Dave, whar's the 'Jack ov Dimins' you war gwine to hunt on, that could give a wolf fits *directly*?" "I say,

10. "The name of the wolf in the ancient and famous animal epos of Germany, 'Reinhard, or Reineche, Fuchs.'" William A. Wheeler, *An Explanatory and Pronouncing Dictionary of the Noted Names of Fiction* (Boston, 1889), p. 184.

stra*nn*ger, that's a powerful smart lookin' chunk ov a poney you've got atwixt yer legs thar, but poneys is mighty onsartin."

"Now, boys, jest cum out squar and say ef yer did run ater the varmint, or if ye took a sorter skear and put out tother way."

"I tell what is, boys," said a fourth, "yer all barkin' up the wrong tree. *I* smell a bug. Dave and that ar stra*nn*ger's ondly playin' 'possum, an want to git a quarter race out on us, but they can't pull the wool over this child's eyes; he's got 'em both skinned."

"Shut up," replied Dave, "and let the stranger and me alone. Thar warnt one ov ye in half a mile ov the tail ov our horses. I'll dar ye now to run a race over that same hog-wallow, and anti ten cows and calves on ither the stranger er me, an I'll bet a plug ov tobacker I hev a saddle cover off that varmint's back afore I camp down."

On nearing the plantation we perceived a number of dark objects perched upon the fence, which at first I mistook for buzzards, but they proved to be a general assortment of all the young negroes in the place, chattering like so many monkeys, their white eyes and teeth glistening in their setting of jet, who had assembled to get an early view of the "varmint" we had gone forth to do battle with.

As soon as we arrived at the house, one of the young darkies was dispatched to the river with an invitation for a man who was there living to come up and bring all his pups; two or three more were mounted, and sent into the prairie in search of the "caviarde" of horses—and we went in to dinner.

To use a very expressive Westernism, "*Dave's tail was up,*" and every possible preparation was made to preclude a failure. The dogs that had returned were cared for, the very best cow horses (horses trained to cow hunting) selected, a complete and well digested plan of the campaign devised and explained. It was, however, thought that the difficulties of the chase had very much increased since morning. In the place of a small island that might be easily drawn, the wolf was now in a dense thicket a mile in length, with a stream of water in its midst, which the cunning old rascal might use to great advantage in washing his trail, and throwing the dogs off the scent.

Four o'clock found us all prepared for a start, and half an hour's sharp riding brought us to the hunting-ground. One person was now stationed at either end of the island, and one on either side, all of them at a sufficient distance from it to permit their glance to take in everything from one outpost to another.

We then commenced operations at the southern end, spreading ourselves entirely across the thicket, and forcing our way slowly and surely, keeping back the dogs; and at the same time three of the party riding even with our line upon the outside.

In this way we proceeded through the island, but no "sign" of wolf could we see. Our dogs started all sorts of strange game, but not the kind we were in search of. Dave was in despair. "The 'varmit's' gone home again," said he. "I rayther reckon not," replied Joe. "I rayther reckon not; hit's clear agin the cunnin of the varmint to think so. He's pretty much used up to begin with, and then he knows we're arter him, and you don't catch him showin' his profile in the perara tell dark, and ef thar's a bright moon he'll keep shady till nigh sun up, and then he'll make a break. I tell you what, gentlemen, he's here. I'll bet a horse on that. The crittur's ben in the lake, and jumpd clar across the path into the bush, and thar he lies— we've been within a rod of him. Ef old Rove would git up and go to work we'd fetch him soon, but these dern no-account pups arn't worth shucks, and so we must do the tracking; so, boys, let's 'light, some on us, and take it afoot, whilst the rest keep along on their critturs."

Joe's advice was taken; he started off on the lead, and, strange to say, within ten rods of the spot where the consultation had been held—stopped, and intimated by a very significant whistle that he saw "sign."

Old hunter as Joe was he for once allowed himself to be thrown off his guard—instead of passing quietly on, giving us "item" as he would have called it, and permitting us to surround the beast, and make a sure thing of it, at the sight of the "footprints in the sand," he first whistled, then peering into the bush, and espying the much-sought-for "varmint," he allowed the exuberance of his joy to evaporate in a yell that would have aroused the dead. The wolf did not move, until Joe very imprudently seized a stick and poked it in her lair. Then with but one spring, she dashed at her tormentor, who, slipping, fell backwards into the water; and without waiting even to crawl out, gave us a succession of shouts that would have done honor to a Commanche.

The wolf had evidently made up her mind that there was nothing left for her but a run for life, and crossing the water made for the open prairie—but her situation was far from agreeable. Seen by three of the outposts, she was immediately headed off, and turning, she had to encounter the party stationed on the edge of the island; her speed was sensibly diminished, and her pursuers now felt sure of her; keeping her right between them they now forced her to a course parallel with the island, by which manoeuvre not only would our whole party be gathered, but she would be driven into the main prairie, without any chance of finding shelter, except by taking the back track, and from that they could easily cut her off. As they passed the end of the island the whole party fell in, and we all obeyed Dave's direction to the very letter.

The chase headed down the prairie; running parallel with the wolf, and at a distance of a quarter of a mile on either side were three riders, while the rest spread out widely, followed at about the same distance behind—the dogs semi-distant between us—thus forming three sides of a hollow square, with the wolf and dogs in the centre.

Riding at half speed, and watching every motion of the animal, we now commenced drawing in, four or five riders leaving the back, and joining the side line, until we felt we had her safe, and then Dave prepared to fulfill his promise. Leaving the line, he took his "caberos" from the pommel of the saddle, passed it underneath his leg, then, unfastening it gathered it in a coil in his left hand, in which the bridle was also firmly grasped. In his right hand was the noose at the end of the rope.

Rising in his stirrups, with an encouraging shout to his horse, he dashed directly at the wolf, who, now maddened with fear, rage and pain, made a rush first on one side and then the other, in hopes of escape, but giving it up in despair, resumed her straightforward course.

Dave approached behind, and driving the spurs into his horse's flanks, was soon parallel with her, and not more than twenty feet off.

Giving the noose three or four twirls around his head, he launched it with the certainty of a bullet at the head of the animal, and without one instant's pause wheeled his horse.

The rope ran out, and Sir Isengrim, jerked suddenly about from his headlong career, found himself heels in air, with a half-broken neck, dragged on his back at a rattling pace over the prairie.

At this very moment the yell of a dog was heard, and "old Rove," lame, tired, half-dead as he was, running on two, three or four legs by turns, made his appearance, and dashing through the throng of his useless fellows, fastened upon the wolf's throat. Over and over they went together, Rove having all the fighting and biting to himself.

Dave checked his speed; found the poor wolf past praying for; and it was with difficulty that he could drive the dogs off, so as to redeem his promise, "that he would cover his saddle with that wolf's hide."   P.P.

VIII. TERM-TIME IN THE BACKWOODS, AND A MESTANG COURT

LAWYERS, scenting prey afar,
Hasten to the scene of war,
Gamblers, parsons, culprits, clients,
Fat men, lean men, dwarfs and giants,
Buckskin shirts and broadcloth coats;
Barefeet, moccasins and boots,
Dress of every and no fashion;
Men from all parts of creation,
Until the town is all alive
And swarming, seems a human hive.

If any one would see the backwoods' character in perfection, let him visit some frontier county town during "court week." One may ride through and through a thickly-settled county, from north to south, and from east to west, until he delusively imagines he has seen every face in it, and that he can count the settlers. But let him be in "town" on the first day of court, and he will soon find how much deceived he has been with regard to the population. He will see them pouring in from every imaginable direction, by every possible road, and some that appear decidedly impossible; wagon roads, main roads, "cow trails," and "blazes," all alive, and with a truly heterogeneous mass. The lawyers from the other counties, who, scenting the spoil afar off, have just dropped in for their share; district attorneys and state attorneys, judges and jurymen, criminals and witnesses, parsons and gamblers, horse-jockeys and hard-fisted planters; peripatetic pie and gingerbread venders, who come with the intent of establishing an extemporaneous hotel, spreading their table under the trees, and cooking their "chicken fixin's," *al fresco*—all swell the throng, and fill up the "town" even to overflowing.

For the time being, not only every house in the village is filled, but the country for miles around is laid under contribution to provide the crowds with food and shelter.

During the day the streets resemble the purlieus of a bee-hive, when something unusual has excited its noisy little inmates; but at night they are again emptied, the lawyers herding together for a frolic, a game of poker, or to ponder over some knotty point; the jovial gentry, who came for the fun of it, either gone home, or far past going anywhere, and everything quiet except at the "groceries," which are usually filled with a jolly set, imbibing "old corn," or indulging in a little "faro" in the back room.

The dress of the *dramatis personae* differs as widely as the persons. Here is a gentleman in broadcloth, with his invariable accompaniment, the gold-headed cane, taking a friendly drink with that rough-looking customer in the buckskin hunting shirt, or perhaps unprovided with the latter article.

Here comes a fellow, hooping and yelling, down the street on a scrub of a mestang. "Captain Whiskey" has taken him in charge certainly; but see, he stops, jumps from his horse, and salutes that grave and quiet-looking gentleman, who might pass for a judge or a clergyman, with a slap on the back, and—"Hello, old hoss, whar hev you been this coon's age?" and *they* go in to "wood up."

The people seem to look upon law as a species of amusement, and to regard "court week" in something of the light that the Down-Easter does the "General Training."[11] The most petty cases, even in the Justice's Court, are ushered in with a formality, and conducted with an earnestness which is but little in keeping with the amount at stake. Some years since a very sensible and worthy

11. The militia system of New England was brought over from England. The "training days" became community affairs. Adams, *Dictionary of American History*, 5:303–4.

Yankee—a physician—was elected "Justice," and in a few days after he had been properly qualified for the office, called upon to decide in a weighty matter, probably involving the value of five dollars. At nine in the morning the Doctor made his appearance, and shortly after, the rival attorneys followed suit, each loaded down with books, as if they were about to be engaged in some such momentous affair as the suit of Mrs. Gaines,[12] or the heirs of Anike Jans.[13] "For heaven's sake, gentlemen," exclaimed the alarmed magistrate, "you do not expect to read them through to me! if you do, I shall tell you once for all, that I am appointed, not to judge of nice points of law, but to give my decisions according to the simple dictates of justice and common sense; and if you do not like *that*, you can take your case out of *my* shop, and carry it up."

To work, the opposing counsel went, and despite the deprecatory prayer of the afflicted magistrate, read page after page, hurled point after point, precedent after precedent, Coke upon Littleton,[14] and Littleton upon somebody else, on his devoted head; until, perfectly bewildered, he allowed them to have their own way. As usual, the "court" adjourned for dinner; and after dinner, at it they went again until dark, and the case was then put

over until the morrow. After the adjournment, and before leaving the house, Dr. ——— turned to Mr. ———, the longer winded of the two pettifogers, and said: "Mr. ———, I have heard you with patience, and have wasted one entire day about this trifling case. If *your* time is worth nothing, *mine* is, and I shall come here to-morrow at nine to give you my decision. If you can possibly have any more to say, you must say it within one hour after my arrival, or you can settle the affair between your-selves, as you best may." Mr. ——— assured the Doctor that he would conclude in a few words and they parted for the night.

At the appointed time the Doctor arrived on horseback, hitched his horse, went in, took his seat, and as he did so, pulled out his watch and laid it upon the table before him.

The case re-commenced, and ——— again went on with his interminable argument. After listening for an hour, the Doctor very quietly put his watch in his pocket, left the room, mounted his horse, and rode off upon his business leaving Mr. ——— con-tinuing his harangue, and supposing the doctor's absence was but temporary. How long he continued I know not, but it was long a standing joke against him; and it is said the doctor was bored with no more tedious trials.

To the town, where—for the time being—the district court is in session, flock all the petty gamblers of the adjoining county. As a general thing, they are men of very small capital indeed. In fact, of the dozen or more of these "*chevaliers d'industrie,*" who are always to be found upon such occasions, it is very seldom that more than one of them possesses enough of the *res pecunia* to com-mence business, with a very moderate *Faro Bank.* Around the bank, when opened, the remainder of the gang cling, until a run of luck shall have made some one of them master of the funds, and broken the pro tem banker.

The *then* holder of their *very* circulating medium,

12. In 1859 Myra Clark Gaines sued the city of New Orleans to recover real estate which she claimed to have inherited from her father. A settlement was not reached until several years after Mrs. Gaines's death in 1885. *National Cyclopaedia of American Biography*, 3:369.
13. Anneke Jans was born in Holland about 1600 and came to America about 1630. At her death she left to her children considerable property, part of which was a farm known as Dominie's Bouwery. It was leased in 1697 to the Trinity Church Corporation for seven years at a rent of sixty bushels of wheat. The lease was annulled by an act of the colonial legislature, and from then until 1847 the heirs were involved in litigation concerning the property. Ibid., 9:433.
14. Sir Edward Coke and Lord Edward Littleton, noted English jurists.

now commences business himself, and continues until tripped up in the same manner as his predecessor, and the game continues to be played day after day, and week after week, reminding one—for all the world—of a flock of hens pursuing the fortunate finder of a kernel of corn, chasing her until she drops it; and then—the loser joining with her compeers in the chase—all hands start after the finder, until the disputed article is usually lost! whereas, had they all attended to their legitimate business, each might have had a kernel of her own.

The "picayune gambler" as he is there called, usually owns a horse and *rigging*, and a floating capital of from fifty cents to one hundred dollars. The horse is his last resource, and only staked when affairs become desperate indeed; when lost, the quondam owner is said to be *flat broke* or *flat footed*, and must beg, borrow, or steal, for a *stake*.

As they never work, and are always hanging about taverns and groceries, it is rather astonishing how they contrive to subsist; but subsist they do, and as each clique about every little town have just a certain amount of money among them, I imagine that stray pigeons are found in sufficient numbers, from time to time, whose plucking serves to keep their expenses from eating up their capital.

The quiet inhabitants do not dare to interfere with the clan openly, but on the contrary, prefer keeping up some pretence of good fellowship with them; and all attempts to uproot them by law have entirely failed.

The town of ——— was more than usually infested with this pernicious vermin, and the judges and district attorneys determined, for once, to put every engine of the law in force against them.

The first attempt was made by Judge J., who was himself fond of a quiet game. Now the laws of Texas punish simple card playing as well as gambling;[15] and towards the close of the term, the judge had a quiet hint given him that he, and nearly every member of the bar had been indicted, and a true bill found against them, for card-playing in their rooms. He was forced to adjourn the court, and not appear there again.

Judge S. followed, but he had been seen to play a game of euker with his wife, by some mischievous or interested person, and to his utter astonishment found his name included among those indicted for gambling. *He*, in a violent rage, adjourned the court upon the spot.

This last affair amused everybody in the county, as much as it did the faro players. The old judge has well earned the sobriquet of "Old Dignity" by his extreme pomposity. He spoke of himself upon all possible occasions as "the Court." One day passing down the main street in H——, a mule that had been hitched to an awning-post wheeled, and nearly kicked him. The judge, apparently furious, gesticulated, and shook his cane violently at the offending animal, and a wag who was passing at the time declared positively that Judge S. had said, in an emphatic tone, "if *that* mule had kicked *this* Court, *this* Court would have sent *that* mule to jail." This story, which obtained extensive circulation, annoyed the old gentleman prodigiously.

Having played the same game twice, the gamblers prepared to turn a new trump at the next session. They had their spies and witnesses about, and when a non-card-playing, but very good-natured judge made his appearance, and the grand jury went to work to obtain proper testimony relative to faro dealing, &c. they got rather more than they wanted, for information was laid against almost every respectable man in the county, including the members of the grand jury, foreman and all.

They let the ticklish subject slip through their

15. A law which prohibited the playing of cards "in any place except a private residence occupied by a family" was still on the books in 1901. Texas, Laws, Statutes, etc., *General Laws of the State of Texas* (Austin, Tex., 1901), p. 26.

fingers, and the whole affair was laughed at as a capital joke.

At last came Judge W., a stern, uncompromising man, who would have had no scruples or remorse in punishing the whole county, had they transgressed the laws, and we thought that the gamblers' game was up.

He actually succeeded in sentencing five of the most notorious to a fine of one thousand dollars each, and an imprisonment of six months. This was all very well, but the next thing was to collect the fine, and find a place to incarcerate them. As far as the fine was concerned, *that* he thought he had fixed, for their imprisonment was to continue until it was paid; and as for the imprisonment, there being no jail in the county, he gave them an order for board and lodging upon a public establishment of the penitentiary—not penitential— order in the next county.

The rogues were a set of jolly vagabonds, and had that species of honor said to exist among thieves. They offered the sheriff to save him the trouble of a ride of sixty miles and back, and deliver themselves up, and the officer trusted them so far, as to accompany himself alone without guard.

He delivered them over upon a fine *Saturday* afternoon, and upon parting, they inquired if he had any word to send home.

On *Sunday-morning* they were back again in time for breakfast, and as our sheriff had fulfilled *his* duty, and the jailor below was glad to be rid of them, they were let alone. This terminated the legal war upon the gamblers, and they were given up as a bad job.

One of the principal amusements of the bar during these sessions of the court, is to assemble in some sufficiently capacious room, after indulging in all the boyish games that occur to them, to institute mock proceedings against some one of their number, for some ridiculous, imaginary offence.

One of these "circuit evenings" is very green in my memory—and I do not ever remember to have laughed so long or so heartily before or since, as I did then, at seeing the wisest and most intelligent men in the county entering with perfectly childish enjoyment and *abandon*, into childish jokes and childish games.

The scene was a log hut, containing one room and some dozen beds, upon which, lying, sitting, or in an intermediate posture, were at least thirty members of the courts.

After playing "Simon," "What is my Thought Like?" and a dozen similar games, one of the company arose and announced in a most funereal tone that a member of the bar had—he deeply and sincerely regretted to state—been guilty of a most aggravated offence against decency, and the dignity of his profession, and he therefore moved that a Judge be appointed and the case regularly inquired into.

By a unanimous vote, Judge G.—the fattest and funniest of the assembly—was elected to the bench, and the "Mestang" or "Kangaroo Court" regularly organized. Impossible as it would be for one to convey to the reader a correct idea of the ludicrous and supremely ridiculous scene which ensued, I will yet attempt it.

The Judge opened the court something in this wise:—"Gentlemen of the Bar, Jury, Witnesses, Criminals and Constables, Clerks of the Court, and Prosecuting Attorneys—It has been a source of deep regret to me and doubtless to many of you, that our bar—of the grocery I mean—has of late fallen into disuse, owing to the great want of criminal fines properly imposed, whereby the pockets of the bar-tenders, and throats of our honorable body have suffered an unprecedented dryness.

"It therefore behoves us all, acting in our several capacities, to do our duty most strictly in this matter. Suffering no criminal to go unpunished—no innocent accused, to escape conviction, but each one striving for the common end, heap up fines to be liquidated in liquors at the bar, payable in a circulating medium, whose circulation has not been above medium in these latter days—and thus evade the deep and heavy mantle of disgrace which is fast settling around our once honored shoulders.

"The case about to be submitted to you is one of an extraordinary and atrocious character—"

SPECTATOR. "Had not your honor better appoint a jury before proceeding to trial?"

JUDGE. "Silence, sir, do you dare instruct the court? Mr. Sheriff, I fine this person 'whiskey straight' for contempt of court, and do you attend to the collection."

SECOND SPECTATOR. "Please your honor, no sheriff has yet been nominated."

JUDGE. "Thomas Jones, you are hereby appointed the High Sheriff of this, our honorable court, and will collect of the contumacious individual who last volunteered his knowledge, a treat all round, as soon as I shall have administered the customary oaths of office. Stand up, sir—take off your coat—now. You, Thomas Jones, in the presence of this hon. body, do most distinctly affirm that you will perform the duties of your onerous office in a worthy and dignified manner; that when sent after a criminal you will never return a non est comeatibus; but in default of the guilty party, pick up the first man you can lay hands on; that when sent to the grocery to collect a fine you will not drink more than half the liquor on your homeward path, that you will never fob any change, without handing over one half the nett proceeds to the court—all this you promise truly and faithfully to perform, as you fear your wife, and love brandy and water."

SHERIFF (looking around and speaking hesitatingly). "If—any—gentleman—will—hold—will hold my hat, while I take a swear—"

JUDGE. "No you don't sir, no swearing here, or I'll fine you—your word is as good as your bond, and neither of them worth a copper. Select a jury sir."

The jury being properly selected his honor proceeded to address them:—

JUDGE. "Gentlemen of the Jury—The case about to be presented to you, as I have before remarked, is one of an extraordinary and atrocious character. One who has hitherto concealed his crime beneath the exterior of respectable age, is now to be stripped of the cloak that has so long shrouded him from a prying world. Mr. Sheriff, trot out the individual."

The sheriff here produced the youngest, most correctly attired, and by far the finest looking member present.

JUDGE. "Ah, well, not so old after all, but gentlemen, it makes no difference, he *will* be, should he live long enough. Who appears upon the part of the Republic? Mr. Clerk, read the indictment:—"

Kangaroo, to wit :—At the special court of Kangaroo county, begun and holden in the very extensive city of Kangaroo, to wit: One old shed for a court-house, two taverns such as they are, one blacksmith shop, with a post-office attachment, six groceries which we mean to leave as dry as an old maid's lips, five banks (faro), and nothing else. On the last Tuesday of pea time, and Anno Domini, not a soul of us can distinctly remember, having very lately dined, although the last is of very little consequence:

The Jurors for the Mustang Republic on their oath, present that JOHN SMITH, of no particular place, calling himself a gentleman, although no one believes him, did, somewhere in the vicinity of the last "cotton scraping time," there or thereabouts, and not much matter when, so he did it—with sticks, stones, guns and pistols, and a pair of instruments called, known, and described, in vulgar parlance—"lips," being the labial protuberances of the human face divine. (Any one, however, who might call the said John Smith's face divine, if not quite a fool, must at least be six degrees the other side of idiocy) inflict upon the right cheek of certain juvenile female colored person, of the age of seventy—there or thereabouts, known to the community in general, as Polly, a kiss of about the size of a dollar, or perhaps a dollar and a half, or perhaps two dollars, thereby injuring the feelings, compromising the character and undermining the health of the said "Polly," occasioning an explosion, which disturbed the slumbers of many citizens who were then enjoying a siesta, intruding upon the majesty of this Republic, and reflecting upon the dignity of a profession, of which, however, the least said the better.

And the jurors aforesaid do further present that they could add any given number of counts to this indictment, but as it would consume some time, the Court will suppose anything found against the said Smith which the said Court may please.

THOMAS JENKINS, *Foreman of the Grand Jury*.
WILLIAM BROWN, *Attorney General*.

The testimony upon the part of the prosecution was upon a par with the indictment. One witness swearing that he saw the woman Polly emerge from the prisoner's room with a large white spot upon her cheek; another, that aroused by a terrific explosion, he saw Polly rushing out; a third, that Polly had applied to him for a plaster to draw "the fire" from the wound; and several testified to the excessively delicate condition of the sufferer's health since the sad accident.

After a flaming speech by the prosecuting Attorney, the prisoner, being called upon for his defence, arose and replied as follows:—

Gentlemen of the Jury:—Suddenly arrested in the midst of a career of usefulness, honor, and happiness; charged with an ignominious crime, it is to me a source of most heartfelt gratification, that I am to appear before a body of men of so much intelligence, so highly favored by nature, with noble forms, and expressive countenances, and endowed by the faithful Schneider's art with such unexceptionable vestments.

The prosecuting Attorney, he, of the petrified heart and revolting phiz, flatters himself that he has macadamized the road which will conduct me to the silent tomb; *which*, gentlemen, he is full well aware would be *my* tenement, should your fateful voices not declare me free from spot or stain.

He has magnetized a rope of sand, and burns me with it; but see, how with one touch of the wand of Truth, potent as Ithuriel's spear,[16] it will fall asunder.

Brought up in my earlier days by a father and mother, I soon was taught

Since innocence is bliss, 'tis the height of folly to do any otherwise,

and have continued to increase in virtue and in size, until a few short years past, when finding my full perfectness attained, I shut down, and have done no more in that line since.

This gentlemen, is the first rude blight that has fallen upon my budding fame; the first cloud that has darkened my brilliant horizon of future promise, but *that* cloud shall be swept away by the breath of your all potent voice. My sun shall shine again in your smiles, the bud refreshed by my fast falling, falling, tears (*applying a handkerchief to his eyes*), shall rejuvenate to its primeval lustre.

SPECTATOR (*interrupting*). T'wont, salt water aint good for plants.

16. In Milton's *Paradise Lost* Ithuriel is one of two angels who discover Satan in the shape of a toad seated near the head of the sleeping Eve and attempting to arouse evil visions in her mind. At the touch of his spear Satan is forced to assume his proper shape. Book IV, lines 788–819.

PRISONER (*resuming*). Silence, Sir, and pity the sorrows of a poor young man. Gentlemen, on that sad day upon which I am charged with the commission of so heinous an offence, having partaken with you of a full, but not sumptuous dinner, I retired to my accustomed room to recuperate wearied nature with a restorative siesta.

My waking senses lapsed soon into forgetfulness. I had been thinking, I remember of our approaching annexation, and busy imagination pictured me to myself, as wrapped to sleep in the folds of the star-spangled banner, while the Eagle of Freedom, with slow-moving wings, fanned my moist, but burning brow. I walked in Elysium, in the vale of Tempe, rare flowers were blooming around me, filling the eye with beauty, and the air with fragrance. Birds of gorgeous plumage flitted to and fro, or rested upon some flower-clad tree, and breathed forth their delicious notes. Fat turkeys that I had *not* dined upon, were swimming before me in a duck pond of cranberry sauce, and gobbling ferociously at a particularly tough and dyspeptic piece of hung beef, upon which I *had*.

A change came o'er the spirit of my dream, the heavens were clothed with black, a peal of thunder burst upon my ear, and rolled in terrific grandeur, echoing from crag to crag. I sprang up in affright, and behold, it was Judge G. saluting my washerwoman. The sufferer, taken at surprise by the rude assault, rushed from the apartment. The culprit quaked with fear, waddled towards the bed, and ducked under it, to hide his diminished head. A companion who had been dozing—joint occupant with me of my bed, assisted me, and we finally, *vi et armis*—

JUDGE. No *Choctaw*, Sir—use plain English.

PRISONER. Well, then, by main force, we drew him from his position, and having lectured him with tears in our eyes, bade him go and sin no more. I now call upon Tobias Wilkins to prove the truth of my statement.

I shall not recapitulate the testimony of Wilkins, which corroborated the prisoner's assertion. After another speech or two, the Judge charged the jury, bearing down upon the prisoner ferociously, and ordering them to give him the benefit of the most severe sentence in their power. The jury, after a moment's whispered consultation, announced by the then Foreman that they had found a verdict.

JUDGE. What say you, gentlemen? Guilty or not guilty?

FOREMAN. We wish to inquire of your Honor, whether Polly is in a state of single blessedness, or a legalized sticking plaster to the side of some respectable colored gentleman.

JUDGE. Married, I believe; although I cannot imagine what that has to do with the case.

FOREMAN. We then find your Honor, Judge G. to be guilty of *piracy* upon the *high seize*, having plundered a smack, and of *counterfeiting*, for your portable imitation of Thunder. You will, therefore, please put your old fur cap upon your head, and sentence *yourself* to pay for all the fluids at the bar, to which we are about to adjourn, the *District Attorney* to find the necessary cigars, and the *informer* the eatables.

WESTERN TRAVELER'S COMPANION.

ROUTE

FROM THE SOURCE OF THE MISSISSIPPI RIVER TO
THE GULF OF MEXICO.

TRAVELS IN THE SOUTHWEST

Unsold copies of the twelve issues published of the Magazine of Travel *were bound up, without the printed wrappers and with a governing title page, and sold as a book. In this guise it appears as entry number 325 in volume three of* Travels in the Old South; *actually it is not a reprint in book form but a bound volume of the periodical.*

CHAPTER III

LITTLE ROCK, Arkansas, Nov. 185-.
Dear R.: In my progress thus far, I have given you two letters, detailing personal incidents, and giving some account of the peculiar features of the country through which I have passed. You may say that should I deal less in the former and more in the latter, you would be the better pleased. Perhaps, as I progress, such may be the case. You know with me nothing is studied, and I write at the moment what may be uppermost in mind, be it what it may.

I have now to give you an account of my journey from the "Bluffs" to the "Rock."[1]

Not wishing to again try the stage, having been fully satisfied with that mode of conveyance, in the journey described in my last, I sought another mode. After much trouble and delay, I procured the consent of the keeper of a livery stable in the place to send me to "The Rock" in a buggy. In traveling in the South, you become astonished at the little attention men pay to their business. The idea appears to be very prevalent, that if a business is once started, it must take care of itself. It certainly must be a poor business that will not do that!

Gilbert Hathaway, "Travels in the South-West," *Magazine of Travel* 1 (May 1857): 231–37.
1. The author travelled down the Mississippi River and continued by boat, stage, and wagon through Arkansas and Texas. His route took him through Pine Bluff and Little Rock, evidently the places referred to here. Clark, *Travels in the Old South*, 3:248.

As an evidence of this, I would remark, that there are two stables at the Bluffs, where it is said horses and carriages are let. I soon ascertained that the entire stock of each consisted of a few broken down nags, and buggies equally out of repair—and so well attended to are they by the proprietors, that I was necessitated to call several times during the day, before I could find either at home. One of them had gone into the "bottom," on the opposite side of the river, hunting wild turkies; while the other was enjoying a social glass at a saloon or "exchange" near by. Drinking houses in this country are universally called "Exchanges," I suppose in imitation of the Exchange at New Orleans, from which place the tone and style of living is derived through this region.

I found it necessary to make several bargains with him, before he would undertake to carry either out, and was then doomed to wait two entire days, before he made any demonstrations of execution.

Money appeared to be his principal object, and as long as there was the hope of extorting an additional dollar, he allowed the time for departure to pass, and then for some flimsy excuse, add to the price already agreed upon.

Monday morning came, but with it no horse or buggy, as I had reason to expect. The entire morning was spent in suspense and expostulations, when I supposed that that day too would terminate as others had done, in disappointment, and at night I be found at the Bluffs. At length I was greeted with the sound of wheels approaching

"White's Tavern," with the cheering intelligence that all was ready. My baggage being readily disposed of, I set out, but before I had really time to take a survey of the equipments, we were brought to a halt, by some part of the harness giving way, letting the thills down about the horse's heels. This break was repaired by the driver bringing his handkerchief into requisition; on we moved; but before leaving the town plat, he suddenly bethought himself of some matters he must then and there attend to, so, stop again was the word; another hour's detention was the result, so that it was about mid-day when we fairly set out.

Our way lay over sterile hills, covered with a stunted growth of oak, and slender pines. No settlements greeted the eye. Not a cabin enlivened the scene. All was dull monotony; a constant succession of sand hills; and to add to my discomfiture, the horse was a poor jaded creature, without flesh or muscle; slowly and wearily he dragged himself along, and this too, when I had agreed to pay thirty-five cents per mile passage.

Sometime after night fall, we arrived at a large log cabin, newly erected by the road side, and not yet more than half finished. The roof was partly on, and the chimney had, as yet, attained but four feet elevation. There was no "chinking" between the logs, and the floor was but partly laid. It could not boast of an "up-stairs," although it was intended for a two story building. At this place they keep tavern, and here, it was my intention to pass the night. A black boy met us at the door, giving the welcome intelligence that we could remain, if it was our pleasure, and that he had plenty of "corn and fodder" for the horse. Wishing to be relieved from the sight of the poor, miserable animal that had brought us thus far, I gladly embraced the opportunity that offered. At first the prospect looked cheerless enough, but a fire being "made on," in the half grown chimney, I found I was in the home of those who had seen refinement, and were not strangers to the luxuries of life. It was the house of widow. Her husband, who had been a man of much energy, died some four months before, leaving the house in the condition in which I have described it. He was the owner of a rich plantation on the bank of the river, six miles distant; but for the sake of health, had commenced a house in the hills, where he expected to make his future home. But he had been called to the spirit land, while his widow and children were left to occupy the unfinished premises.

A warm supper, after so dull a ride, was relished with great zeal. Other travelers made their appearance. A young man, a printer by profession, who learned his business in the office of the Journal of Commerce, of N.Y. city, had launched his bark on the great ocean of life, and was now fairly on his "voyage to see the world," seeking his fortune. I found him quite intelligent, being versed in the ordinary topics of the day, and having, during the past year, "tramped" through six states. A fleshy Scotchman, who resided near the Rock, where he had been some nineteen years, told many anecdotes of the past, and gave much information in relation to the history of the State. A company of horse traders, who were returning from a trip in the "low country" in pursuit of their avocation, completed the company for the night. At an early hour we disposed of ourselves as best we could, for sleep—on beds, on chairs, on the sofa, and on the floor. By keeping up a fire in the chimneyless fireplace, the company were able to get through the night with comfort.

A cup of coffee was very welcome in the morning, soon after which we set out with our scrawny horse, which moved as though he had the rickets. The Rock was thirty-two miles distant, at which place we arrived at the close of the day, having been more than twelve hours in performing what, with a good horse, could have been accomplished in from five to six hours.

Little Rock is located on the South bank of the Arkansaw river, three hundred miles from its mouth, by way of the river, and one hundred and twenty-five by land. It is quite prettily situated, on a high, gravelly bluff, and is ironically named, from the "prodigious size and masses of rock about it." It is a place of no trade, except what the legislature and various courts, by holding their sessions here, bring it. Being the capital of the State, it has an importance which it could in no other way attain. The region of country, for a long distance, both above and below, on this side of the river, is poor, and in many places bordering on sterility.

The capitol, when new, was rather an imposing building, but being in an advanced state of dilapidation, it produces an unpleasant effect on the mind of a stranger. It is built in the Grecian style of architecture, with colonade front and rear; on the bank of the river; or, more properly speaking, where the river used to run, for the water is now so low that it would be really a misnomer to dignify it by that appellation.

The lower part of the main building is devoted to offices, and the second story to the Hall of the House of Representatives and Senate Chamber, with a large two story building on each side, affording rooms for legislative committees, but in a like state of decay. After the State consents to pay the interest on her bonds, I suppose she will repair her capitol, but when that is done will be when a different set of men from those now in office, preside over her destinies. All the streets of the town are wide, and cross each other at right angles; they are generally uneven, very little attention having been paid to improving them. The many little hills in different parts of the town, covered with a natural growth of small oaks and pines, furnish beautiful sites for private residences, and not a few richly embelished with native flowers and exotic shrubbery.

To see fine grounds tastefully laid out, in a place where I had but little reason to expect any thing of the kind, was peculiarly gratifying; but when those grounds, as late in the season as the seventh of November, were all adorned and beautiful with roses, altheas, crape myrtle, and asters, of every hue and shade, a juncture not usually met with, was presented, for pleasing and delightful contemplation.

If "lawyers houses," as the old adage has it, "are built with fools money"[2] (you will pardon my allusion), then indeed there must be many citizens who are placed in that category, for the best, most costly, as well as most tastefully arranged houses are owned and occupied by members of that fraternity.

This place numbers among its residents several members of the profession, whose reputation as sound lawyers, and advocates, is not confined to the limits of the State. Among these distinguished persons, there is one more distinguished still. I need not say to you I refer to the poet-soldier and philosopher;[3] for who has not hung with rapture on his measured strains of melody—lines which breathe the true genius of poetry—or listened to the tales of his chivalry while at the head of his brave Arkansaw band, in one of the most sanguinary battles in the war with Mexico; or with grave attention perused those pages which, amidst his professional engagements he has occasionally thrown off for the benefit of the public.

May be you will pardon a personal description. In stature, he is the ordinary height, with firm and elastic tread, broad chest and shoulders, well proportioned, with high and slightly receding fore-

2. A variation of George Herbert's "lawyers houses are built on the heads of fools," in *Jacula Prudentum*, no. 949. Burton E. Stevenson, *The Home Book of Proverbs, Maxims, and Familiar Phrases* (New York, 1948), p. 1371.
3. Albert Pike, the author, was active as a cavalry leader during the Mexican War. *Dictionary of American Biography*, vol. 7, pt. 2, pp. 593–95.

head, heavy projecting brow, sheltering an eye not remarkable for brilliancy, unless it be lit up in the excitement of debate, but of a soft and pleasing look, a countenance at once expressive of kindness and sympathy.

He is somewhat eccentric in his dress, eschewing all conventional rules, such as are established by the aristocracy of fashion. In fact, he seems to delight in dressing in opposition to fashion, for in him we see the reverse of the picture usually presented by that fickle Goddess. At a time when most gentlemen wear the smooth silken hat, he may be seen with *caput* covering after the fashion of our revolutionary sires, only lacking the three cornered form of brim, his coat after the modern style, while his pants are wide and flowing, when "tights" are the order of the day. His beard and moustache are of most huge dimensions, while a heavy suit of hair hangs in clustering masses on his neck and shoulders. He has recently published an edition of his poems, for private distribution.[4] Happy indeed will be those who receive from his hand so rich a boon as one of these volumes.

His residence is in one of the most pleasant parts of the city, of ample dimensions, with extensive grounds, in a high state of cultivation, shrubbery and exotics of choice varieties are scattered with a profuse hand, adding the charms of blossom and perfume to the agreeable and pleasant scene. Every where, almost, the premises are visible evidences of luxury, ease, and taste. This is indeed the residence of a poet.

The Government has an arsenal here,[5] the situation of which is very beautiful. The plat of ground on which it is built is quite extensive, and very beautifully laid out; yet I think a few more trees, properly located, would add to its beauty. The buildings, like most that Uncle Sam erects, are of a substantial character, and well designed for the purposes intended.

Here resides the celebrated, if not notorious, minister, of Greytown memory,[6] whom the dignified editor of the Tribune, of N. Y. city, calls the "bully of the South." When I first saw him, I involuntarily looked for the mark made by the much noted bottle which is said to have come in contact with the most prominent part of his countenance, while, as he contends, in the faithful discharge of his ministerial duty as the representative of this Government; but as others say (very improperly, no doubt), he was in one of his bullying gasconades. But I could see no mark; if any was ever there, time, the great physician, had quite obliterated it. I presume the impression made by a certain Senator, on the nasal organ of poor Kenedy, was of a more enduring character.[7] I learn he has finished his political career, and is now settled down as plain Dr. B., physician and pharmacist.

The people of the State, considering that not much credit was acquired by his course, either at home or abroad, it is suggested, will allow him to pursue the even tenor of his way amid patent medicines and gamboge.[8]

4. Pike's book of poems, *Nugae*, was printed for private distribution in 1854.
5. In 1836 the United States government established a military post and in 1838 built an arsenal in Little Rock. The area is now a city park. In 1940 the old arsenal was converted into the Arkansas Museum of Natural History and Antiquities. *Arkansas Guide*, p. 186.
6. Solon Borland was born in Virginia, studied medicine there, and moved to Little Rock as a young man. He served in the United States Senate from 1848 until his appointment as minister to Nicaragua in 1853. He occupied that ministry for only six months. While awaiting transportation home at Greytown, he became involved in a fracas surrounding the arrest of Captain Smith of the *Routh*, an American ship. In July 1854 he resumed the practice of medicine in Little Rock. *Dictionary of American Biography*, vol. 1, pt. 2, pp. 464–65.
7. This incident may refer to Borland; it could not be documented.

The Legislature of this State is now in session; all its members, uniting with the citizens of the place, have resolved to give a public dinner to the renowned editor of the Louisville Journal,[9] who happens to be in the city, engaged in rail road business. It will "come off" tomorrow night. I am told the poet above referred to, takes the lead in the matter, and from his well known ability in such things, it is supposed it will be a very brilliant affair.

The public house at which I am stopping, the principal one in the city, is crowded to overflowing, and is very unpleasant in other respects. Methinks the man who leaves his home, and his ordinary occupation, to come to such a place and live after the manner members of the Legislature do here, for three months in the year, must require more than the usual amount of patriotism, or desire for distinction. But so it is. We find men using the most strenuous efforts to be elected to such stations; to be traduced and vilified while seeking them, and abused and complained of while in the discharge of duty.

Office seeking in this country is really a *mania* with some people, and often times proves a rock on which the best minds are wrecked. I consider it a most unfortunate circumstance in the history of a young man, to have him elected or appointed to office. It renders him incapable of giving that attention to business, which it really requires. It makes him reckless in manner, and dissolute in habits, and generally renders him unfit for the ordinary duties of life. To make office seeking a profession, is indeed to launch one's bark on a troublous sea, where the voyager would be likely to be stranded with every varying tide. No person should take a political office until he has seen years enough to have his habits fixed and character fully formed. This rarely occurs until he has seen his fortieth year.

CHAPTER IV. LOWRING'S RANCH

Texas, November 185–.

Dear R.—I have had a long and toilsome ride today, and feel much inclined to take rest, but not having written for about two weeks, I fear you will think I have quite forgotten you, so I will endeavor to send you a line from this remote quarter.

Since my last I have passed over about six hundred miles of country: some accidents have befallen me, and the journey has not been entirely devoid of incident.

I left the Rock by stage, drawn by four small horses, such as are usually found in the South, for similar purposes, inferior in size and poorly fed and cared for. It was not far from two o'clock in the morning when a messenger to my room announced that the stage was ready. I had been previously awakened, in great haste, and brought to the bar-room, where lingered many persons in the far gone stages of inebriation, to be in time for the stage, but as I soon ascertained, for the real purpose of giving my bed to a gentleman, who, without such a device, would probably go bed-less till a late hour. I gladly gave heed to the call and took my position at the coach door, which proved to be a vehicle designed for six passengers. The door was opened, the driver invited me to take a seat, being the only passenger, save a station keeper, whose location was distant, a dozen miles, when to my amazement I found the "coach" filled to overflowing with mail bags. It was with difficulty I could get enough of them removed to enable me to get a seat. I protested that I had had enough of mail riding on

8. An orange or brown resin which becomes bright yellow when powdered. Used as a medicine, it is a cathartic.

9. George D. Prentice was editor of the Louisville *Daily Journal* from its founding in 1830 until its merger with the *Courier* in 1868. The new paper was named the *Courier-Journal*. *Dictionary of American Biography*, vol. 8, pt. 1, pp. 186–87.

the route from Napoleon to the Bluffs. After the usual exhibition of ill temper, and the pouring out of several volumes of oaths and imprecations on the part of the driver, I succeeded in getting some of the sacks removed to the boot, and I took a seat. It was a cold frosty night, the first of the season. I felt it severely. The horses felt the influence of this visitation of the frost king, and as if to bid him defiance, sped away at a rapid rate, up and down the many hills on our route. May be a certain king of another description had something to do with our speed, for my fellow passenger, the driver's boon companion, had been indulging freely in his cups, and suffered much from the chilly air.

The breakfast stew was at Benton, a poor looking place, with the marks of decay visible at every turn, the seat of justice of a very poor county.[10] It was at this place the populace of this and adjoining counties, with mob violence and force, but a few days before my visit, took from the jail a negro, who was accused of some crime, and hung him on a tree near by, till he was dead, the sheriff and a few citizens of the better class, resisting them. The reason of this unlawful act cannot be readily ascertained. The culprit was in confinement awaiting his trial. There was no danger that the law would loose its victim, for he was in safe keeping, and if he was guilty of the commission of any crime, that would soon be ascertained; and if not guilty, no reasonable being would say he should be punished. The only solution that I can find for the violent outbreak, was merely the gratification of a spirit of insubordination to law and good order. Will any one pretend to say that the acts of these parties was any thing short of wilful and deliberate murder, and that the punishment due to the crime should not be meeted out to them?

At Benton I was only twenty miles from the celebrated Hot Springs of Arkansas, of the waters of which we hear so much said, in curing all sorts of maladies. I regretted that my engagements would not permit me to pay them a visit.

I reached the town of Washington[11] on the evening of the second day, and a more dull, barren, and uninteresting country for the same distance, I think it would be difficult to find. The road is one that has been for many years the great thoroughfare to Texas and the Indian Nations on the South Western borders of the State. At an early day many emigrants settled along this road, and endeavored to make "improvements," but after dragging out years of misery, have been compelled to abandon all they had done, and seek homes in more propitious spots. What few remain, eke out a scanty subsistence, by the precarious means of hunting, and getting a few shillings now and then from wayfarers or emigrants.

In the neighborhood of Washington there are some good lands, which enterprising Virginia settlers, taking hold of some twenty years ago, have converted into beautiful plantations. Washington is the retail town for quite an extent of country, containing two hotels, six stores, a school, and some mechanic shops. There are places where religious meetings are held. It has probably attained its maximum in size and importance, as most of the good land in the neighborhood is now in cultivation. It is situate on a hill, where the sand in the street is from six to eight inches deep, but inasmuch as they have left most of the native growth of dwarf oaks standing, it is not an unpleasant place. Here I determined to abandon the stage rout, which would have taken me to Clarksville, Texas, and strike Red River at a more southerly point. My means of conveyance was

10. Located about halfway between Little Rock and Hot Springs, the town of Benton was established in 1836. *Arkansas Guide*, p. 211.

11. In 1824 Elijah Stuart built a tavern at Washington, which became an important point for settlers moving west. The town was the state capital from 1863 to 1865. Ibid., pp. 216–18.

what is denominated in this country a "hack," a species of carriage resembling a common Jersey market wagon drawn by two horses. My driver, a mullato, with the frosts of some forty winters on his locks, was the owner. At a price agreed upon, he was to take me to a certain point in Texas, which would occupy him some three days.

It was a clear frosty morning when we set out from Smith's tavern, which place I left with some regret, for my wants had been well attended to while there.

I was the only passenger in the stage from the Rock to Washington, and now I was about to set out on a long monotonous ride, with no companion but the "boy" who drove the horses. At this place, as well as at all others I have been at since I left Cairo, the theme of conversation with all persons, has been railroads.

At Memphis it was their four roads, but the one in which she was particularly interested, was from that city to the Rock. It appears that Congress has donated lands to aid in the construction of a road from Fulton to Cairo, and a branch from the Rock to Fort Smith, and one from the same place to the Mississippi, the point on the river to be fixed by the Legislature. The citizens of Memphis and those in Arkansas who reside in the North part of the State, are in favor of that route. But Helena and Napoleon!! are putting in their claims for the precious boon, and, of course, much "log rolling" is to be seen about the capitol. The people of Washington are directly interested in the road from Fulton to Cairo, as well as the Gains' landing road, so called, which is to run from that place to Red River, near Shrevesport, La.[12]

Many persons along the routes of their respective roads are taking stock, but I fancy it will be a long time before any dividends will be realized. There is but one of these routes that will elicit foreign capital, and without that aid neither can be built.

But I fear I am detaining you too long with these uninteresting matters. I will hasten on with my journey. I found my boy Charles disposed to be very loquacious. Not having any thing more interesting to do, I listened to him. He was very respectful, and had I not cheerfully given him permission to speak, he would have remained silent. He gave me a bit of his history, and in as much as it tends to illustrate in some degree the workings of the peculiar institution, I will give you a part of it.

He was born a slave in Virginia, near Lynchburgh. His father was a wealthy gentleman of the neighborhood by the name of S——p——n. His mother was a mullato slave, owned by his father; and as he stated, he has, still living near the old homestead, *two half brothers* and the same number of sisters, all wealthy, moving in the higher walks of life. His father always recognized him as his son, and although he was treated as a slave, yet it was with much more kindness than usually allotted to members of the black family.

12. On 9 February 1863 Congress appropriated funds for a railroad from a point on the Mississippi River opposite the mouth of the Ohio, via Little Rock to the Texas boundary near Fulton, Arkansas. The road was to have branches to Fort Smith and the Mississippi River. U.S., Laws, Statutes, Etc., *The Statutes at Large and Treaties of the United States*, 81 vols. (various places of publication, 1845-1968), 10:155-56.

See our note in A Decade of Nationalism *on "Wrecking in the Florida Keys"; things had changed for the better in the interval of ten years.*

THIS position, recently become so important as the *Key* of the United States to the Florida Pass, and the Gulf of Mexico, is little known to the outer world, except as a wrecking station; and is consequently and unjustly associated only with scenes of disaster, distress, and *quasi* piracy. The object of the present paper is to remove these false impressions, by a brief outline of the history of the island, and a summary sketch of its present character and condition.

Cayo Yuesson, or *Bone Key,* was so called from the great masses of human bones which were found upon it, on the discovery of the Island by the Spaniards.[1] The time of the discovery is not exactly known, not having been made a matter of distinct record. It was probably somewhat early in the history of Florida. The accumulation on such a spot of such a quantity of human relics as to give a name to the Island, has not been sufficiently accounted for. Whether, in the remote ages of aboriginal history, it was an isolated and over populous island city, a half-way mart between Cuba and the continent—a Palmyra in the desert of waters, where the canoe caravans of unknown predecessors, met for refreshment, or barter;—or whether, as remote from either shore, it was selected as the common cemetery of the nations both of the islands and of the main land, it is fruitless to conjecture. The tradition, among the

modern Indians, is, that the tribes of the main land, in conflict with those of the Reef, drove them, by a series of conquests, from island to island, and rock and rock, till they reached this, their last and most important hold. Here they made a desperate stand, congregating all their hosts, men, women, and children, from all their deserted and desolated isles. A terrible battle ensued. The islanders were overpowered, and utterly exterminated. Large numbers of the invaders also fell in the conflict. Many more fell victims to a pestilence, occasioned by the sudden putrefaction of so many unburied corpses, while the few that escaped were compelled to flee for their lives, leaving the bones of friends and foes to bleach together on the deserted and sunburnt rock.

There may be some foundation for this story. Indeed it is difficult to account for the facts in any other way than by supposing the island to have been suddenly desolated by war, or pestilence, or both united. It was evidently, for a considerable time, the residence of an important tribe of Indians. They have left behind them the traces of their presence, and evidences of their progress in some of the arts. Several mounds have been opened, which were found to be filled with bones. The figures were all arranged in a sitting posture, and decked with ornaments of gold and silver. Glass beads were also found among them, showing that some of the burials were of comparatively recent origin.

The English name, *Key West,* is a corruption of *Cayo Yuesson.* The name is not appropriate to the place. It is not the western termination of the Reef.

"Key West, Florida," *Merchant's Magazine* 26 (January 1852): 52–60. Reprinted in *Florida Historical Society Quarterly* 8 (July 1929): 48–63.
1. S. W. Martin, *Florida during Territorial Days* (Athens, Ga., 1944), pp. 191–92.

There are several small islands in that direction, with Tortugas, the last and largest of them all, about sixty miles distant.

The Island of Key West is four miles long, by one mile in the widest part. The average width is considerably less than a mile. The entire area, is 197 acres, including the salt pond. It is of oval formation with very little available soil. It is very low and flat, the highest spot on the island being scarcely more than twenty feet above the level of the sea. It is situated in latitude 24° 25' N. and longitude 82° 4' W.

The unoccupied parts of the island are covered with a low stunted growth of wood peculiar to that region. Dogwood, Maderia wood,[2] mangrove, and some other species, are found in considerable abundance, and turned to some account, as timber, for various purposes. The Maderia wood is particularly valuable, when found of sufficient size, being hard and durable, and capable of resisting the ravages of the worms. The prickly pear and the geranium grow wild, in such luxuriance as the scantiness of the soil will admit. The cocoa nut, the orange, and the guava, also thrive well in any spot where there is depth of earth to sustain them. This, however, is so rare and so thin, that a garden is the most expensive luxury in the place, and one can easily imagine, that, like Naaman the Syrian, a resident there, visiting some of the rich valleys of our land, might reject more costly offerings, and ask, as the greater boon, for "two mules' burden of earth."[3]

Cayo Yuesson was granted by the Spanish Crown, some thirty or forty years ago, to John P. Salas.[4] From him it was purchased, in Dec. 1821, by Col. Simonton, who now resides there. He took possession, in person, on the 22nd January, 1822, and erected a small house, the first that was built on the island, in April following. One year after, in April 1823, a Custom House was established there, by the United States Government, and it was made a station for the squadron commissioned for the suppression of piracy in the Gulf of Mexico.[5] The squadron arrived in April, and rendered very important services, in accomplishing the object for which it was sent. In 1827, the season proved a very sickly one. Fever and dysentery prevailed to an alarming extent, and the station was removed in November of that year. It is difficult to account for the sickliness of that season. There has been nothing like it since. It is regarded by those who have tried it, as one of the healthiest places in the world.

In 1832, Key West was made a military station,[6] a very pleasant spot was selected for barracks, which were not completed till 1845. The buildings are large, airy, and commodious, and furnished with all the conveniences which the place and the climate afford. They are placed on three sides of a large quadrangle, the open side being toward the sea. If nature had furnished soil enough for a respectable growth of shade trees, or even for the cocoa nut and orange, her liberality would doubtless be often blessed, both by officers and soldiers, particularly during the intense heat of the summer months.

The first white female that settled on the island, was Mrs. Mallory, the worthy mother of the present worthy United States Senator from

2. Mahogany.
3. 2 Kings 5:17.
4. In 1815 the king of Spain gave the island to Juan Pablos Salas, a young artillery officer, for services to the crown. In 1823 Salas sold the island to John W. Simonton, an American. *Florida Guide*, p. 198.

5. A naval depot and station were established at Key West almost as soon as it was proclaimed United States territory in 1822. Martin, *Florida during Territorial Days*, p. 193.
6. An army post was built in 1831 on the north shore of Key West. It served as a garrison for Fort Taylor, built in 1845. It was abandoned and reoccupied a number of times. Prucha, *Guide to Military Posts*, p. 82.

Florida.[7] She took up her abode there in the year of 1823, and was, for some considerable time, without a single companion of her own sex. As the pioneer matron of the place, she was presented with a choice lot of land, on which she has erected a house, which she now occupies, as a boarding house, dispensing to the stranger with liberal hand, and at a moderate price, the hospitalities of the place.

The first white child born on the island was John Halleck, who was born in August, 1829. He is now a printer in the City of Washington. The second was William Pinckney, born Sept. 1829. He is a clerk in one of the largest mercantile houses in Key West. They are both promising young men, of good abilities and excellent character.

From these small and recent beginnings, Key West has grown to be an important and a prosperous place. From the solitary house, erected by Col. Simonton in 1823, has sprung a flourishing and well ordered city of about 3000 inhabitants.[8] It is now the largest town in Florida. The City is well laid out, with streets fifty feet wide, at right angles to each other, and is under a judicious and efficient administration. There is not a more quiet, orderly town in the United States. Alexander Patterson, Esq. is its present Mayor.

The city contains, at this time (1851), 650 houses, 26 stores, 10 warehouses, 4 look-out cupolas, 11 wharves, and 4 churches. The churches are Episcopal, Methodist, Baptist, and Roman Catholic. The buildings are small, but very neat. They will accommodate from 150 to 250 wor-

shipers. There is a Sabbath School attached to each. The services of the Sabbath are well attended. The Episcopal church numbers fifty communicants, and seventy Sabbath scholars. About five hundred persons attached to the congregation. The Methodist Church numbers 100 communicants and 115 scholars. Congregation 700. The Baptist 82 communicants and 22 scholars. Congregation 300. There are four private schools in the city, and one county school. The private schools average about thirty scholars each. The county school has an average attendance of about sixty scholars. This is far below what it should be, showing a want of a just appreciation of the inestimable benefits of education. Perhaps, however, we ought in justice to observe that the occupations of a considerable portion of the inhabitants are of such a nature as to keep them much away from home. The boys, as soon as they are able to work, are occupied with fishing, sponging, and other similar employments, and soon denied the advantages of a regular school.

The county school is not, like our public schools at the north, open to all. It is free only to *fatherless* children. This provision is a singular and an unfortunate one. Though the orphan has a rich mother, he is admitted to the school without charge; while the motherless child of an indigent father must pay one dollar a month tuition. This rule seems to reverse the natural order of things. A motherless child is much more likely to be neglected in his education and morals, at the forming period of life, than a fatherless one. There are but 17 county scholars in this school. If it were thrown open to all who need its advantages, it would probably number 150 to 200, and would be a source of blessing to the rising generation, which cannot be estimated in dollars.

The tonnage of Key West is not very considerable, but it is very active and profitable. It consists of—

7. Charles Mallory, a civil engineer from Reading, Connecticut, married Ellen Russell. They moved to Trinidad, where Stephen R. Mallory was born, and then to Key West, about 1820. *Dictionary of American Biography*, vol. 6, pt. 2, pp. 224–26.

8. The 1850 census gives the population of Key West as 1,943. U.S., Bureau of the Census, *The Seventh Census of the United States: 1850* (Washington, D.C., 1853), p. 401.

27 wreckers, averaging 57 tons . . . 1,539
8 coasters and fishermen, averaging 90
tons 720

Total Tonnage 2,259

The Harbor is capacious, safe, and easy of access. It may be entered by several different channels, the principal one being at the N.W. angle of the island. Ships of 22 feet draft can enter there with safety.

The principal business of Key West is derived from the salvages, commissions and other perquisites of wrecking. This is a business peculiar to the reefs, and demands a particular elucidation. It is not, as many suppose, and as it was, to some extent, before it was regulated by law and well administered by the courts, a species of relentless piracy. It is a legitimate business, conducted under established and equitable rules, and for the mutual benefit of the wrecker, the wrecked, and the underwriter. The persons engaged in it are men of character, standing, and wealth; men of generous sentiments, and kindly feelings, who risk much and work hard for what they get, and who throw into their calling as much of regard for the rights, interests and property of the sufferers whom they relieve, as is exhibited, in any other department of mercantile business. That there are occasional exceptions to this general rule, cannot be denied. A single instance, of recent occurrence, will serve to show that wreckers are not always pirates, nor always chargeable with heartless rapacity, in the pursuit of the hardy profession. A vessel, with a few passengers, having struck upon the reef, made the usual signals of distress, and waited for help. Impatient of delay, and fearing the ship would go to pieces before relief came, the passengers and some of the crew took to the boat, with a view to finding a safe place of landing. When the wrecker came down, the captain was informed of this fact. He immediately left the vessel, and went in search of the wanderers among the intricate passes of the keys. Another wrecker came down, and pursued the same course, showing more anxiety to save life, than to secure the advantages of an attempt to save the vessel and cargo. A third came down, and feeling that the deserters were sufficiently cared for, went to work, to rescue the vessel, and remove the cargo. So much was this act of heroic benevolence appreciated, that, when the award of salvage was made up, those who first arrived at the wreck, and left it in search of passengers and crew, received the same share as they would have done if they had proceeded, in the usual way, to discharge the wreck and get her off; while their comrades, who came last to the spot, received only the share which would appropriately belong to the third in the race.

The rule in this respect is, that he who first boards the wreck has undisputed control of her, till she is delivered into the hands of the court. He determines who, if any, shall aid him in the rescue, and in what order they shall come in for their shares. He also decides to whom the wrecked vessel shall be consigned, unless the master of the wreck has a choice in the case. The whole matter is then left for the adjudication of the court. The amount of salvage is there determined, each party engaged in the rescue receiving his share of the award, according to the previous arrangements of the skipper who first boarded the wreck.

The amount of the award averages about one-tenth of the value of the property saved. Commissions, expenses, &c., swell this to about one-sixth. The average amount of wrecked property brought into Key West, is not far from 1,200,000 dollars per annum of which there is left behind, for the benefit of the place, about $200,000. This, being divided among the captain, crew, and owners of the wreckers, commission merchants, lawyers, auctioneers, wharf-owners, ship-wrights, carpenters, and store-keepers, is pretty widely diffused, and goes into general circulation. It is the principal reliance of all the business men, mechanics, and laborers of the place.

There is a large amount of auction business done here, employing twelve auctioneers, and paying more auction duties than all the residue of the State. It is established by law, that everything saved from wrecks shall be sold at auction.

The following reports prepared by Capt. Hoyt, the intelligent and vigilant agent of the underwriters, at Key West, will show, in brief, the results of the wrecking business, for the last two years: KEY WEST, January 1st, 1850.

The past year in this latitude has been favorable for shipping, there having been but few severe storms and no hurricane. Notwithstanding this, forty-six vessels have been ashore on the reef or compelled to put into this port.

The value of vessels and cargoes
  wrecked and in distress is nearly. .$1,305,000
The amount of salvage 127,870
Total salvage and expenses on the 46
  vessels 219,160

With but one or two exceptions, the wrecking business for the past year has been conducted with good faith, and it affords me great pleasure to inform you that arrangements have been made and entered into by the merchants during the past month to remove one of the most prolific sources of demoralization connected with it.

STATISTICS FOR THE FIVE YEARS ENDING
JANUARY 1ST, 1850

	Vessels	Value	Salvage	Total expenses
1845	29	$725,000	$92,691	$169,064
1846	26	731,000	69,600	105,700
1847	37	1,624,000	109,000	213,500
1848	41	1,282,000	125,800	200,000
1849	46	1,305,000	127,870	219,160

The last three years show a gradual annual increase, but it is not probably greater than the proportional increase of Commerce, within the same period. The number of vessels engaged in the wrecking business does not vary much from my last report. Various causes are now in operation, which must lead to the diminution of the wrecking business. When the coast survey and the thorough lighting of the Florida Reef,[9] both of which are now progressing, shall be completed, two prominent causes of wrecks will be removed. The Tortugas light has been much improved, but it still needs alterations, which ought to be promptly made. When the light on Gordon Key bears N.E. by E. to E., a large part of the power of the light is lost by a narrow door, and the want of more lamps and reflectors. Several shipmasters, that have struck on the reef when the light bore about E.N.E., judged the light to be ten miles off.

The three light-ships on this coast are faithfully kept, but the power of their lights is by no means what it ought to be. The light ship stationed near Sand Key is old, and the light they attempt to show is miserable. Several vessels have been lost, and much valuable cargo, by the neglect of Government to build a light-house on Sand Key, to replace the one destroyed by the hurricane of 1846. The lights of Cape Florida and Key West are both very good. The materials are on the spot, and the operatives at work erecting the iron pile lighthouse on Carysfort Reef. It is to be placed on the extreme outer edge of the reef, within one quarter of a mile of the Gulf Stream; is to be fitted with a powerful light 127 feet high, and can be seen 25 miles from the mast head of a ship.

I deem it my duty to call your attention to a common neglect of shipmasters to provide themselves with proper charts of this coast. The Messrs. Blunt have published a good one on a large scale.[10]

9. The first Federal lighthouse was built in 1825. *Florida Guide*, p. 201. The survey of the coast in this area was begun in 1822 and completed very quickly. Martin, *Florida during Territorial Days*, p. 193.

I seldom find on board vessels wrecked on this coast suitable boats to take out anchors in case of accident. Key West is naturally a position of no inconsiderable importance. It is a strong and valuable position for a naval station; strong because the Government is now erecting an extensive fort in 10 feet water, which will entirely command the harbor; and valuable, as it is the only fort from Pensacola to Hampton Roads, where a ship of war drawing 22 feet water, would make a harbor and be protected in time of war. It is not only a safe commodious harbor, but it has also several channels by which it may be entered.

The population of the island has considerably increased within the past year. It cannot now be much short of 2,500. It depends entirely upon wrecking, fishing, and the manufacturing of salt, for its support. It has two schools, and Episcopal, Roman Catholic, Methodist, and Baptist congregations and churches, each having its own clergyman. There is certainly a great improvement going on in the moral and social condition of the inhabitants, and they will bear comparison in these respects with any marine town in our country of its size. The Hon. Judge Marvin,[11] through whose court a large amount of property annually passes, has presided on the bench for several years, dealing

10. In 1796 Edmund March Blunt published the first edition of the *American Coast Pilot*. His son, George W. Blunt, continued its publication until he was bought out by the United States government shortly after the Civil War. The father and son also published nautical charts as well as books. *National Cyclopaedia of American Biography*, 21:236.

11. In 1835 William Marvin, a native of New York state, was appointed district attorney for the southern district of Florida by President Jackson. In 1839 he was appointed judge of the district court by President Van Buren, and in 1849 President Polk appointed him United States district judge, which office he held until 1863. Andrew Johnson appointed him provisional governor of Florida in 1865. Among his books was *Laws of Wrecks and Salvage*. Ibid., 11:379.

even handed justice to all, and has given satisfaction to all parties interested.

KEY WEST, December 31st, 1850.
ELWOOD WALTER, Esq., *Secretary Board of Underwriters, New-York:*

Dear Sir:—I would respectfully submit to my employers my usual report, and a condensed report for the past six years, with such brief remarks upon the passing affairs of this part of the United States as will be interesting to commercial men.

The number of vessels that have put into this port in distress, and been ashore on the reef in the past year, is thirty.

Estimated value of vessels and cargoes .	$929,000
Amount of salvage	122,831
Amount of expenses	77,169
Total.	$1,129,000

CONDENSED REPORT FOR SIX YEARS

Number of vessels under the head of marine disasters that have been reported by me	209
Value of vessels and cargoes (low estimate)	$6,602,000
Amount of salvage	647,775
Amount of expenses	259,637
Total.	$7,509,642

Nothing has occurred out of the usual course of events since my last report. The Coast Survey progresses slowly. The light on Carysford Reef will not be finished for some time. Government is building a light-house on Sand Key, near this place. Fort Taylor is now safe from hurricanes, as the foundation is finished, and it is now being filled up. The Government works at the Tortugas are progressing. The health of this place has been good during the year, with the exception of the month of August, when more than half the population were sick. There are in my opinion, more vessels and men in the wrecking business than are necessary. The population of the island is increasing, and unless business should increase, there must soon be a large number of unemployed persons.

In my last report I glanced at the value of this place as a naval station. I have not changed my views. This port ought to be looked after by Government. It is a very important point, and when the Tehuantepec canal or railroad,[12] and other connections, are completed to the Pacific, with the increase of Commerce that must follow, Key West, the only port of safety for vessels of a heavy draft from Pensacola to Cape Henry, should be protected.

Respectfully, your obedient servant,
JOHN C. MOTT.

If the Key-Westers are not entitled to the reputation of pirates, they are among the most remarkable and successful *spongers* in the country.[13] The reefs abound in sponges and large numbers of people are now engaged in collecting them. It is quite a profitable branch of business, so much so that most of the fishermen have abandoned their craft for this new and more lucrative employment. On this account, though the waters abound in many desirable species, a fresh fish is a great *rarity* at Key West, and they who keep Lent conscientiously must practice the abstinence of an anchorite. The gathering of sponges, at the present rates of

sale will pay 40 to 50 dollars per month to the hands employed. It is supposed that the amount of shipments in this article is not less than 50,000 dollars per annum. The sponges, when taken from the rock, are full of life, and are left, for a considerable time on the rocks, putrefying in the sun. They are cleansed with no little labor, brought to town, and spread out, by the acre to dry. They are then packed and pressed in bales, shipped to New York, and there sold mostly for the French market, where they are largely used in the manufacture of felt for hats.

A large portion of the population of Key West consists of emigrants from the Bahama Islands. They are called Conch Men, or Conchs, chiefly from their skill in diving, and the part of the city they occupy is familiarly designated as Conch town.[14] They are a hardy, industrious, economical, honest race, all getting their living from the water, wrecking, sponging, turtling, fishing, diving, &c. In the latter they are very expert, and have been known to find the bottom in seventy feet of water.

Many of the leading merchants are from New England. The society of the place is excellent. The people are very social and hospitable. The ladies are intelligent, accomplished and refined; and no man of taste could fail to enjoy a winter sojourn in the island. Among the young men, there is a Temperance Association, which is large and prosperous, and promises to be of great benefit to the morals and happiness of the place.

In the United States District Court, which has cognizance of all the cases of wrecks and disasters, Judge Marvin presides, with great ability and universal acceptance. William R. Hackley is District Attorney and worthy of a better place. In the State Circuit Court, Judge Lancaster at present

---

12. The isthmus of Tehauntepec is in southeastern Mexico between the Bay of Campeche and the Gulf of Tehauntepec. A railroad was built across it between 1899 and 1907; plans for a canal were discussed and construction was begun but abandoned. *Century Dictionary and Cyclopedia*, 9:983.
13. A few sponges were shipped in the early 1840s from the Bahamas. In 1849 a cargo was exported from Key West, whose export business grew to an annual value of $750,000, with 140 vessels totaling 2,000 tons and employing 1,200 men. In 1904 Greek companies introduced new methods of harvesting sponges, and the business was moved to Tarpon Springs. Jefferson B. Browne, *Key West: The Old and the New* (St. Augustine, Fla., 1912), p. 109.

14. Key West Conchs are descendants of Cockney English who first migrated to the Bahamas from London and then early in the nineteenth century to the Keys, when salvaging and fishing became profitable. *Florida Guide*, p. 197.

occupies the bench, a gentleman of liberal views, large intelligence, and courteous manners—one of your old school gentlemen lawyers. The Jail, a substantial stone building, about 30 feet square, is almost tenantless—the office of keeper quite a sinecure.

Senator Mallory,[15] who, though a decided Democrat, was elected, last winter, by a Whig Legislature, solely because they thought he could be relied upon to support the constitution against the madness of Southern agitators, is a man of mark. Self-educated and self-made, he has, by industry, perseverance, and an indomitable energy of character, risen to his present high position, which it is not doubted he will maintain with honor to himself and dignity and advantage to the State. He is a man of great industry, and said to be possessed of unusual powers of memory.

The first light-house was erected in 1823. It was near the shore, and was carried away, with the house adjoining it, in the great flood of 1846. The entire family of the keeper, consisting of fourteen persons, perished in the ruins, of which scarcely a trace remained on the following day. A new and very substantial one was erected in 1847, standing some distance from the shore, and on the highest spot of ground in the island. It can be seen 16 miles at sea. There is a light-ship anchored on the reef, at the western entrance to the harbor, about 9 miles' distance and a substantial iron light-house is now in the process of erection on Sand Key, about 11 miles S.S.W.

The Marine Hospital[16] is a fine airy building, 100 feet by 45, erected under the superintendence of Col. Simonton, in 1844. It stands close on the shore. It is beautifully ventilated, and enjoys the benefit of every cool breeze that comes along. It possesses every comfort for the sick sailor, and is equal, in all that constitutes a home-like retreat for the invalid, to any similar institution in our land. The plan of the building is peculiarly well adapted to the climate, where the chief desiderata are, a shelter from the sun and a good circulation of air. A central building, about 45 by 20, is flanked by two others of the same dimensions, standing at right angles to the former, and distant from it ten feet. It is in the form of the letter H, the two uprights being a little separated from the transverse. In this space between the central and outer buildings, are the stairs, leading to the upper stories, with a wide gallery, which extends quite round the central building, and is protected, in its whole length, from top to bottom by Venetian blinds. The rooms, throughout, are separated by folding doors, which being thrown open admit the air from any direction in which it may be moving. This building is now, unfortunately, much exposed to the washing of the sea, by the removal of a large quantity of sand, on the west side of it, for the purpose of filling in Fort Taylor. In the event of another such inundation as visited the island in 1846, it will inevitably be carried away unless protected by a substantial sea-wall. It is hardly to be expected that Uncle Sam will think of it, till it is too late. We may therefore confidently predict its downfall, at the next return of that same hurricane.

Fort Taylor,[17] now in the process of construction, under the superintendence of Capt. Dutton, is situated at the north-western angle of the island, just within the main entrance to the harbor. It is

15. Stephen Russell Mallory served in the United States Senate from 1850 to 1861. He later served as secretary of the Confederate Navy. *Dictionary of American Biography*, vol. 6, pt. 2, pp. 224–26.

16. Provisions for the care of ill seamen were so inadequate that in 1835 William A. Whitehead, collector of customs, called for the establishment of a marine hospital to serve Key West and the Caribbean. In 1836 the territorial delegate in Congress introduced a resolution to build such an institution. In 1844 a building was finally constructed. Browne, *Key West*, pp. 147–48.

17. Fort Taylor was begun in 1844 and completed two years later. *Florida Guide*, p. 201.

built on an artificial island, made by the deposit of many thousand tons of stone. It stands about 1,000 feet from the shore. It is 700 feet long in the rear, by 250 deep. The front facade is 253 feet, within the bastions, the curtains being of the same length as the front. It is very substantially built. A large sum of money has been expended upon it already. Before it is completed, it will have drawn upon the Treasury to the tune of a million and a half, or more.

At the eastern part of the island, there is a natural salt pond, covering 340 acres, which with slight arrangements to control and regulate the influx of the water, by means of a canal, 40 feet wide, has proved quite profitable. It was nearly destroyed by the flood in 1846, but has been restored to a better condition than before. Its present enterprising proprietor, Mr. Howe, is doing well with the business. He makes an average of 30,000 bushels of salt, which is worth 20 cents on the spot.[18]

The communication between this little island and the great world, is irregular and unfrequent. The only regular direct communication, is with Charleston and Havana, by means of the steamer Isabel, which touches, leaving the mail on her outward passage, and taking it on her return. This gives them a mail once in two weeks. By this means, also, they are regularly supplied with vegetables, fruit, &c. &c. Besides this, there are occasional vessels, small craft, from St. Mark's, Mobile, New Orleans, &c., but so seldom and irregular, that one may often wait two or three months for a passage.

Transient vessels would touch there more frequently in passing, but for the exorbitant rates of pilotage now charged under a recent enactment.[19] These charges are five dollars a foot for United States vessels. For merchantmen, four dollars a foot for vessels drawing over 16 feet—three and a half, if over 12 feet—and three if less than 12 feet. A large ship, passing in February last, made signals for a pilot. The captain was sick and wished to come on shore. The pilot brought him in and the ship went on her voyage. The pilot charged and received sixty-four dollars for this service. It is hoped that others will take warning from this example, and avoid touching there, when by any possibility it can be done. The harbor is easy of navigation and demands no extra skill, or responsibility on the part of the pilot. The charges are preposterous and abusive.

Allusion has been made several times to the hurricane and flood of 1846. It took place on the 10th of October, and was very destructive. The water, driven in by the violence of the wind, rose over the wharves, flooded the streets, and covered almost the entire city to the depth of several feet. From noon of Sunday till about daylight on Monday morning, it stood three feet over the floors of most of the buildings in Duval, and the adjacent streets. The wind blew a hurricane all the time, and the usurping waters surged to and fro with terrific and destructive violence. Many buildings were unroofed, and many more were entirely thrown down. The Light-House has already been spoken of. The Custom House and the Episcopal Church, both built of stone, shared the same fate. Boards and timber were blown about like shingles. Nearly

18. The original settlers of this area believed that the manufacture of salt from the natural salt ponds in the interior would be their main business; however, they lacked the capital needed to begin it. About 1843 Charles Howe obtained the controlling interest in the Lafayette Salt Company, continuing its operation for many years. Browne, *Key West*, pp. 112–13.

19. The law specified the following charges: all vessels drawing 12 feet and under, $2.50 per foot; all vessels drawing over 12 feet and under 14 feet, $3.00 per foot; all vessels drawing over 14 feet and under 16 feet, $3.50 per foot; all vessels drawing 16 feet and over, $4.00 per foot. Charges for vessels of war were an additional fifty cents for each category. Florida, Laws, Statutes, etc., *Acts and Regulations of the General Assembly of Florida* (Tallahassee, Fla., 1851), pp. 154–55.

all the cocoa nut and orange trees on the island were rooted up and destroyed. A large box, containing muskets, which was in the fort, was found, the next day on Tifft's Wharf, nearly half a mile distant. A grind-stone from near the same place, was found on another wharf, and heavy timber from the wharves was piled up in different places, making the streets nearly impassable. Wrecks and parts of wrecks were found all over the island. The grave-yard which was on the southern shore, was wholly uncovered and bones, and skeletons, and coffins, dashed about, and scattered far and wide. After the storm subsided, one coffin was found standing upright against the bole of a tree, the lid open and the ghastly tenant looking out upon the scene of desolation around, as if in mingled wonder and anger that its rest had been so rudely disturbed.

THE FRENCH GRAVEYARDS AT NEW ORLEANS

We have been unable to establish whether Mrs. C. F. Windle was Mrs. Catharine Forrester Windle or Mary Jane Windle, the author of several volumes of fiction and poetry.

To a stranger in New Orleans, there are no greater objects of curiosity than the French graveyards. With their high walls, *ovened* row above row, and bearing frequent inscriptions wherever a slab marks the last resting-place of a frail creature of mortality, their rectangular walls and towering tombs on either side built adjoining one another, and showing in front the door-like entrances on which are inscribed the names of the occupants, they seem more like miniature cities built for the accommodation of the living, than receptacles for the dead. The animated groups of promenaders in them, at all times and seasons, serve to heighten this impression. Occasionally, only, in some one of them, a bowed form in the weeds of sorrow, kneeling before a tomb, speaks to the mind of death and bereavement. For the most part, the aspect of the place is cheerful, rather than sad. To enter unaware of your locality, you could not, it is true, conjecture its visitants to be its inhabitants; but your thoughts might readily recur to the marble cities of Eastern story, and your imagination might people the tenements before you with a Lilliputian race of beings, paying, perhaps, for the moment, a vow of temporary immurement, and propitiating their deity, by votive garlands cast upon their doorsteps. Alas! these offerings are the fruitless appeals of grief and affection from our own kind, to "provoke the silent dust"[1] of the dead.

The French population take great pride in thus ornamenting the tombs of their deceased relatives with flowers. Bouquets and wreaths, renewed as soon as faded, are perpetually strewn in lavish profusion at their entrances. Some, more expensive in architectural finish than the rest, are surrounded by a railing, enclosing a little garden, where a well-tended bed displays a profusion of ever-blooming flowers.

But it is on the festival of *Tous Saints*,[2] that this taste especially exhibits itself. This is a day con-

Mrs. C. F. Windle, "The French Graveyards at New Orleans," *Sartain's Union Magazine* 9 (December 1851): 432–35.

1. Thomas Gray, "Elegy Written in a Country Churchyard," st. 11.
2. November 1 is All Saints' Day.

secrated by Catholics to all the Saints, and set apart for especial prayers to them for the souls of their departed friends. It is celebrated here in the graveyards. Of these there are four or five, but all lying within an area of a dozen squares. For weeks beforehand, the preparations are in progress; and during a few days previous, those living in the neighbourhood, or having occasion to visit it, may see servants passing at all hours of the day laden with baskets, from which bouquets and garlands of paper, muslin, or wax—flower-pots, containing living flowers, and tapers in silver candlesticks, richly trimmed with cut paper—peep forth. To enter any one of the several graveyards about this period, is to meet all the confusion of preparation incident to a drawing room just before the celebration of a fête. Nor is there said to be wanting the addition of some home preparations likewise—at any rate, among the gentler sex; for it is understood, that, for a fair Creole to appear at the graveyard upon All Saint's Day in any other garb than that of a new dress and bonnet, would be, if not to incur the penalty, at least to repeat the sin of the guest without the wedding garment.

On the arrival of the day, the vicinity, for squares in every direction, is lined with human beings, and a police force is in waiting, for the purpose of maintaining the requisite order and decorum. From an early matin hour, when the bishops and priests are in attendance, and high mass is performed, until the time of vespers—a service which also constitutes a part of the celebration—all the graveyards are thronged with visiters. They pour through each, successively, in such multitudes that the vastness of the crowd resembles that often seen elsewhere at a public fair or popular exhibition: and it is composed of all ages, in every rank, colour and condition—the gates being open alike to rich and poor, white and negro, citizen and stranger.

To a person stationary at the place, this concourse presents a perpetually changing scene in the individual faces and forms of which it is composed; but throughout the entire day it shows no diminution in its numbers.

Like almost all other anniversaries, however, the motive of the occasion seems to be lost in the eclat by which it is surrounded: and, except a few sincere religionists—who recognise, at least, if they do not realize, the presence of the Saints,—none of the visiters seem to have any recollection of the solemnity of the day that brings them together. Some, indeed, who have recently buried a child or other dear friend, wear a solemn countenance; but it is the solemnity of woe, rather than the solemnity of worship.

For the most part, the guests are enticed by the giddy desire for excitement which usually invests a crowd with attractions. They are chiefly natives of the place, to whom the decorations themselves are no novelty, and who repair yearly to the spot for the purpose of seeing and being seen in public. They would attend the opera from motives of the same kind, and with sensations very little different.

A smaller class of visiters are strangers, whom mere curiosity draws to the spot. The opportunity forms a more propitious one for seeing the Creole population of New Orleans collectively, than is presented again throughout the year, and they readily embrace the privilege thus offering itself. They do this, moreover, not by any means to the dissatisfaction of the class alluded to, although their motive is not unsuspected. Animated by the interest of the holiday—decorated with their most becoming habiliments—in company, too, with their relatives and friends—the Creoles seem aware that they hold the observer at an advantage, from which they derive full benefit in the favour which their looks and bearing here find in his sight. In these, if he be not unacquainted with the characteristics of both nations, he traces a union of French and American physiognomy, in which the harsher points of each are softened down or lost.

464
———

The French Graveyards
at New Orleans

The tombs, also afford to the stranger, at this time, a more curious and interesting spectacle than at any other. They present themselves trimmed with flowers of every various kind and colour, both natural and artificial—and generally with much regard to taste—some of them spreading over whole sides of the tombs, after the fashion of vine-covered walls, and others entwined in garlands around their pillars, and projections. A small number of them differ in a modest display of only a few white blossoms or delicate flowers of the same spotless hue. One or two others are unique in being dressed in disdain of floral ornaments according to nature,—doubtless from a consideration of their colour not being indicative of mourning,—and they exhibit specimens of black cut paper, formed (still with some regard to unity) into wreaths, or made up into the shapes of different flowers. Yet another class are hung with a drapery of crape, silk, or velvet, either white or black in colour, and festooned with bows of ribbon to correspond or contrast.

Great rivalry, generally speaking, exists among the owners of the different tombs, in regard to the beauty and expense of these decorations—each one being emulous to excel the rest. Sometimes, too, where the circumstances forbid an attempt to compete with a neighbour, envy will watch its opportunity to destroy or deface the more costly surrounding decorations. But this occurrence is rare, for the precincts are guarded with exceeding vigilance.

In addition to their trimming of flowers, the tombs on All Saints' Day are studded with burning candles, tastefully arranged on their fronts. The light of these is of course greatly diminished by the glare of day, but it has nevertheless a singular and imposing effect.

The impression left upon the mind by the whole scene resembles that excited by some pleasing pageant; and it is only on recalling it to mind after this impression has had time to wear away, that it awakens any ideas connected with the grave. On a calm review of the scene, however, you are led to reflect that it was a benefit, as it were, given to the dead; and the idea is gratifying to one who is moulded in the same likeness, and acknowledges kindred clay. It is pleasing to have learned that so much honour can be paid to the departed; and the vague wish is inspired to lie, when you must bid adieu to earth, where surrounded by decorations and illuminations produced once a year by the hands of those you loved in life, a vast crowd shall assemble to hold an anniversary beside your remains. There, too, is the absence of those "bugbears of a winter's eve, the deep damp vault, the mattock and the worm." [3] No cold earth rests upon the coffin, and only a single slab separates it from the light of day.

There is something unspeakably precious to the mourner, at his first bereavement, in his consciousness that the beloved form from which the soul has fled, lies so ready of access to him; not that he is apt to wish to disturb its repose; but it is a satisfaction to him to feel that he might, if he chose, remove the yielding obstacle and water it with his tears. The body soon moulders, however, owing to the climate and its proximity to the atmosphere—so that, ere long, the conviction arrives that nothing remains within the tomb but dust.

Strangers, who have no friends in the place to purchase or keep up a monument to their memory, are usually placed at their death in the ovens in the walls. One of these may be procured at a cost of fifty dollars, with the understanding that it is only to be occupied for three years—at the expiration of which period it will always be found ready to receive another tenant, the last having some time previous crumbled to ashes.

3. Edward Young, *Night Thoughts*, bk. 4, line 10.

Persons wishing to obtain, either for themselves at their death, or for their friends, an unlimited right of interment as to time in one of the ovens of any graveyard, may do so by paying the requisite cost,—namely, double the sum exacted for the three years' privilege of burial. But where individuals are found willing to meet this charge, they, generally speaking, prefer to give still more for the sake of procuring a lot in the premises, on which they may construct a tomb. One tomb sometimes encloses a whole family, from the venerable grandparents down to their latest descendants. Thus, at each successive death, no additional expense is incurred beyond the cost of the funeral, and that of afterwards inscribing another name upon the marble.

Their inscriptions present to the eye every variety of French nomenclature; and, to such as are able to read these names with their correct accent, they appear to contrast very favourably with those of an American graveyard in their more euphonious sound. It is rare to encounter a single harsh or displeasing appellative. This is true not only of their Christian, but also of their surnames, though of the former it may be said especially. The names of their females, in particular, are exceedingly musical. So much is this the case, that in reading any one of them on a tomb, it is difficult to imagine that it belonged in life to other than a young and lovely being. But a glance at the dates frequently serves to correct an erroneous impression of this sort,—discovering a person who died at an advanced age, and, by the rest of the account, full of infirmities.

As in all other graveyards, there is to be found here great diversity of carved devices upon the different tombs, together with the ordinary abundance and quality of epitaphs in rhyme. It is somewhat remarkable, however, that puerile sentiments appear less trifling in French than in English

verse; perhaps because the one language is not so capable of sublimity as the other, and consequently, less is expected from it.

The freeness of the names and other inscriptions of these graveyards from all settlings of dust, and numberless other defacing marks of Time, is worthy of observation. This is to be attributed to the constant washings to which the tombs are subjected. By undergoing that process continually, they appear ever new. This indication of freshness is considered as important as the show of flowers. Indeed, a single speck of impurity left upon the white surface of the marble is looked upon as a mark of disrespect permitted to the dead; while, in like manner, on the other hand, every attention bestowed upon the tomb is regarded as a tribute paid to the memory of the departed.

Another circumstance that gives an air of peculiar cleanliness to the place is, not so much the excellent keeping of the walks, as the material with which they are covered. Instead of being spread with gravel or sand, they are overlaid with fine shells. These, being of a milky whiteness, suggest the idea of great freshness and purity, besides contrasting agreeably to the sight with the scattered surrounding shrubbery, and the adornments of evergreen and flowers.

In connexion with the subject of the graveyards, it may not be out of place to allude to the Creole manner of attiring the dead. With us of the North, to whom the corpse is usually presented arrayed in the snowy vesture of a shroud, it would appear strangely amiss to view it clad in the garments worn in the flush of existence. Such, however, is the mode of laying out the dead in this city. A man is dressed in the coffin in a full suit of broadcloth, with vest, cravat, and boots. If he be married, the vest is black; if single, it is white. A matron, in the same manner, is attired in a black silk dress, made to fit tightly to her person, while a young female is clad in a fashionably cut frock and bodice of white satin. In so unimportant a matter, custom may very well be the arbiter of practice. But where fashion has associated it with the dead, there appears a peculiar fitness in the shroud. Its spotless whiteness, its stiff frills and pointings, its carefully pressed folds, all seem appropriate and solemn; and it is difficult, after having been familiar with these, to become reconciled to the custom of burial in the ordinary clothing.

It is likewise usual here, on the occasion of a death, to throw open the whole house, and expose the body in state, for the reception of visiters. Through this practice, it becomes an easy matter to discover the amount of mortality existing at any particular period in the place. The custom, though, is less in use now than it was formerly. Indeed, like many more of the time-honoured forms derived from the French and Spanish settlers of New Orleans, it is gradually giving way before the innovations of American manners. In another half century, few or none of these peculiarities will exist; and the Crescent City will possess little to interest the curiosity of the visiter beyond many other places in our country, excepting its size and commercial advantages.

SUMMER TRAVEL IN THE SOUTH

Simms used the opportunity of reviewing two travel books on the South to deliver a blistering attack on the regional loyalty of those southerners who patronized the fashionable watering and vacation resorts of the North. As a background for this attack, Simms delineates the development of the region culturally and economically.[1]

We should only be indulging in one of the commonest of all truisms, were we to protest that there is no such thing as unmixed evil in the world; and all the philosophy may be compassed in a nut-shell, which chuckles over the "ill wind that blows nobody good."[2] It will suffice if we insist that our bitter is, frequently, the wholesome medicine whose benefit is in the future; and what we regard as the mishap of the day, and lament accordingly, becomes to our great surprise, the parent of a necessity that leads to most pleasant and profitable results. To bring our maxims to bear upon our present topic, we have but to remark, that the cholera, which devastated the cities of the North last summer, and the abolition mania,—which is destined to root them out, and raze them utterly from the face of the earth, if not seasonably arrested,—have proved, in some degree, highly serviceable, if not saving influences, for the people of the South. How many thousand of our wandering idlers, our absentees who periodically crave a wearisome pilgrimage to northern regions, instead of finding greater good in a profitable investment of thought and curiosity at home—who wander away in mere listlessness and return wearied and unrefreshed—were denied their usual inane indulgences by the dread of pestilence. And how many other thousands, capable of appreciating the

William Gilmore Simms, "Summer Travel in the South," *Southern Quarterly Review*, n.s. 2 (September 1850): 24-65.
1. Simms was reviewing Charles Lanman's *Letters from the Alleghany Mountains* and T. Addison Richards's *Georgia Illustrated in a Series of Views.*
2. John Heywood, *Proverbs*, pt. 2, chap. 9.

charms of nature, and the delights of a glorious landscape, were, in like manner, compelled to forego the same progress, by the patriotic sentiment which revolts at the thought of spending time and money among a people whose daily labor seems to be addressed to the neighborly desire of defaming our character and destroying our institutions.

The result of these hostile influences has been highly favorable to the development of the resources of the soil. We have, in the South, a race of "Soft-heads," a tribe that corresponds admirably with the "Dough-faces" of Yankee-land. These are people born and wedded to a sort of provincial servility that finds nothing grateful but the foreign. They prefer the stranger to the native, if for no other reason than because they are reluctant to admit the existence of any persons, in their own precincts, who might come in conflict with their own importance. In like manner, and for a similar reason, they refuse to give faith to their own possessions of scenery and climate. Their dignity requires foreign travel for its proper maintenance. It is distance only, in their eyes, that can possibly "lend enchantment to the view." [3] They are unwilling to admit the charms of a region which might be readily explored by humbler persons; and they turn up their lordly noses at any reference to the claims of mountain, valley, or waterfall, in their own section, if for no other reason, than because they may also be seen by vulgar people. To despise the native and domestic, seems to them, in their inflated folly, the only true way to show that they have tastes infinitely superior to those of the common herdlings.

For such people, it was absolutely necessary that they should speed abroad in summer. The habit required it, and the self-esteem, even if the tastes

3. Thomas Campbell, "The Pleasures of Hope," pt. 1, line 7.

did not. It is true that they were wearied with the monotonous routine. It is true that they were tired of the scenery so often witnessed; tired of the flatness of northern pastimes, and outraged constantly by the bad manners, and the unqualified monstrosity of the bores, whom they constantly encountered, from the moment that they got beyond the line of Mason and Dixon. All the social training of a polished society at home, was disparaged by the reckless obtrusiveness by which that was distinguished which they met abroad—the free, familiar pertness of monied vulgarity, or the insolent assumptions of a class whose fortunes have been realized at the expense of their education. A thousand offensive traits in the social world which they sought, added to the utter deficiency of all freshness in the associations which they periodically made, combined to lessen or destroy every thing like a positive attraction in the regions to which they wandered; but, in spite of all, they went. Habit was too inflexible for sense or taste; and possibly, the fear that the world might not get on so well as before, unless they appeared, as usual, at the opening of the season, in Broadway, and found themselves, for a week at least, each summer at Newport and Saratoga, seemed to make it a duty that they should, at large pecuniary sacrifice, submit to a dreary penance every summer.

But the cholera came in conflict with the habit. It unsettled the routine which was only endurable in the absence of thought and energy. It suggested unpleasant associations to those who, perhaps, would suffer under any sort of excitement, the wholesome as well as the pernicious; and the idea of eating cherries and cream, at the peril of utter revolution in the abdominal domain, had the effect of startling into thought and speculation the inane intellect which, hitherto, had taken no share in regulating the habits of the wanderer. When, at the same time, it was found that the pestilence confined its ravages to the North,[4]—that either the climate of the South was too pure, or the habits of its people too proper, to yield it the requisite field for operation,—and that Charleston, Savannah and other cities in the low latitudes, were not within the reach of its terrors,—then it was that patriotism had leave to suggest, for the first time, the beauties and attractions of home, and to make the most of them. Her argument found succor, as we have hinted, from other influences. Our "Soft-heads" no longer found that unlimited deference, and servile acknowledgment, which the societies they visited had uniformly shown, in return for their patronage. Society in the North was in revolution. Old things were about to pass away; all things were to become new. Property was to undergo general distribution in equal shares. Every man, it was argued, had a natural right to a farmstead, and a poultry yard, as every woman, not wholly past bearing, had a right to a husband. The old Patroons of Albany were not permitted to rent, but must sell their lands, at prices prescribed by the buyer or the tenant. Debtors liquidated their bonds in the blood of their creditors. The law of divorce gave every sort of liberty to wife and husband. The wife, if she did not avail herself of the extreme privileges accorded to her by this benevolent enactment, was, at all events, allowed to keep her own purse, and to spend her money, however viciously, without accounting to her lord. If he was lord, she was lady. She was not simply his master, but her own; and a precious household they made of it between them. Churches multiplied, mostly, at the very moment when a restless and powerful party—avowedly hostile to all religion—was denouncing and striving to abolish the Sabbath itself, as immoral, and in conflict with the privileges of labor and the citizen.

In this universal disorder in laws and morals,—this confusion of society, worse confounded every day,—in its general aspects so wonderfully like those which, in France, preceded and properly paved the way for, a purging reign of terror,—all the usual amenities and courtesies were fairly at an end, even in those places, hotels and haunts of summer festivity, in which decency and policy, if not charity and good-will to men, requires that every thing should be foreborne, of manner or remark, that might be offensive to any sensibilities. But the cloud and blindness which every where overspread society, was a madness too sweeping to forbear any subject, in which envy, malice, conceit, and a peevish discontent, could find exercise at the expense of one's neighbor. In destroying, at home, the securities of religion, the domestic peace of families, the inviolability of the laws, the guarantees of the creditors—nay, taking his life, as that of an insolent, when he presumed to urge his bond—these reckless incendiaries (like the French, exactly) must carry their beautiful system to the hearts of other communities. They are by no means selfish. They must share their admirable blessings with others—nay, force them even against their desires, to partake of their drunken mixtures. No situation, accordingly, is sacred from their invasion. No refuge is left for society, unembarrassed by their presence. They rage in all places, fireside, street, exchange, hotel, and not so much seeking to reform and teach, as to outrage and annoy, they studiously thrust upon you, at every turn, the picture of the miserable fanatic, whose vanity prompted him to fire a temple, only that he might be seen in its blaze.

·   ·   ·

4. Contrary to the assertions in this text, there were a number of severe cholera epidemics in the South. In 1848–1849, just before this article was written, such southern cities as New Orleans, Richmond, and Louisville all had severe outbreaks. J. S. Chambers, *The Conquest of Cholera* (New York, 1938), pp. 193–210.

Growling over the popular sentiment at the North, which thus dogs their footsteps and disturbs their equanimity, or grumbling at the sudden invasion of cholera, which makes them tremble for their bowels, it is probable that more than twenty thousand Southrons forebore, last summer, their usual route of travel. Mason's and Dixon's line, that season, constituted the *ultima thule*, to which they looked with shiverings only. Thus "barred and banned,"—almost hopeless of enjoyment, but compelled to look for it where they were and to find their summer routes and recreations in long-neglected precincts, it was perfectly delightful to behold the sudden glory which possessed them, as they opened their eyes, for the first time in their lives, upon the charming scenery, the pure retreats, the sweet quiet, and the surprising resources which welcomed them,—at home! Why had they not seen these things before? How was it that such glorious mountain ranges, such fertile and lovely vallies, such mighty and beautiful cascades, such broad, hard and ocean-girdled beaches and islets, had been so completely hidden from their eyes? By what fatuity was it that they had been so blinded, to the waste of millions of expenditure in the ungrateful regions in which they had so long been satisfied to find retreats, which afforded them so little of pleasure or content? Poor, sneaking, drivelling, conceited, slavish, provincialism never received such a lesson of unmixed benefit before; and patriotism never a happier stimulus and motive to future enjoyment as well as independence.

It is a too melancholy truth, and one that we would fein deny if we dared, that, in sundry essentials, the southern people have long stood in nearly the same relation to the Northern States of this confederacy, that the whole of the colonies, in 1775, occupied to Great Britain. A people wholly devoted to grazing and agriculture are necessarily wanting in large marts, which alone give the natural impulse to trade and manufactures. A people engaged in *staple* culture are necessarily scattered remotely over the surface of the earth. Now, the activity of the common intellect depends chiefly upon the rough and incessant attrition of the people. Wanting in this attrition, the best minds sink into repose, that finally becomes sluggishness. As a natural consequence, therefore, of the exclusive occupation of agriculture in the South, the profits of this culture, and the sparseness of our population, the Southern people left it to the Northern States to supply all their wants. To them we looked for books and opinion,—and they thus substantially ruled us, through the languor which we owed to our wealth, and the deficient self-esteem naturally due to the infrequency of our struggle in the common marts of nations. The Yankees furnished all our manufactures, of whatever kind, and adroitly contrived to make it appear to us that they were really our benefactors, at the very moment when they were sapping our substance, degrading our minds, and growing rich upon our raw material and by the labour of our slaves. Any nation that defers thus wholly to another, is soon emasculated, and finally subdued. To perfect, or even secure, the powers of any people, it requires that they shall leave no province of enterprise or industry neglected, which is available to their labour, and not incompatible with their soil and climate. And there is an intimate sympathy between the labours of a people, and their higher morals and more ambitious sentiment. The arts are all so far kindred, that the one necessarily prepares the way for the other. The mechanic arts thrive as well as the fine arts, in regions which prove friendly to the latter; and Benvenuto Cellini was no less excellent as a goldsmith and cannoneer than as one of the most bold and admirable sculptors of his age. To secure a high rank in society, as well as history, it is necessary that a people should do something more than provide a raw

material. It is required of them to provide the genius also, which shall work the material up into forms and fabrics equally beautiful and valuable. This duty has been neglected by the South; abandoned to her enemies; and, in the train of this neglect and self-abandonment, a thousand evils follow, of even greater magnitude. The worst of these is a slavish deference to the will, the wit, the wisdom, the art and ingenuity of the people to whom we yield our manufactures; making it the most difficult thing in the world, even when our own people achieve to obtain for them the simplest justice, even among themselves. We surrendered ourselves wholly into the hands of our Yankee brethren—most loving kinsmen that they are—and were quite content, in asserting the rank of *gentlemen* to forfeit the higher rank of *men*. We were sunk into a certain imbecility,—read from their books, thought from their standards, shrunk from and submitted to their criticism—and (No! we have not yet quite reached that point,—Walker[5] still holding his ground in the South against Webster), almost began to adopt their brogue! They dictated to our tastes and were alone allowed to furnish the proper regions for their exercise. Above all, their's was all the scenery; and the tour to Saratoga, West Point, Newport, Niagara, almost every season, was a sort of pilgrimage, as necessary to the eternal happiness of our race of "Softheads," as ever was that made, once in a life, to Mecca, by the devout worshipper in the faith of Islam!

But, owing to causes already indicated, a change has come over the spirit of that dream, which constituted too much the life of too large a portion of our wealthy gentry; and the last summer, as we

said before, left them at liberty to look about their own homes, and appreciate their own resources. The discoveries were marvellous, the developments as surprising as those which followed the friction of the magic lamp in the hands of Aladdin. Encountered on the opposite side of Mason and Dixon's Line, by the loathsome presence of Asiatic cholera and African abolition, they averted their eyes from these equally offensive aspects, and found a prospect, when looking backward upon the South, at once calculated to relieve their annoyances, and compensate admirably for all their privations. The tide of travel was fairly turned; and, through the length and breadth of the land, in the several States of Virginia, the two Carolinas, Georgia, and even Florida, nothing was to be seen but the chariots and the horsemen, the barge and the car, bearing to new and lately discovered retreats of health and freshness, the hungering wanderers after pleasure and excitement. For such an event, the country was almost totally unprepared. A few ancient places of resort excepted, the numerous points of assemblage had scarcely ever been indicated on the maps. The means for reaching them were rude and hastily provided. The roads were rough, and, with the vehicles employed to traverse them, admirably adapted to give wholesome exercise to rheumatic joints and dyspeptic systems. The craziest carriages were hastily put in requisition, to run upon the wildest highways. Paths, only just blazed out in the woods, conducted you to habitations scarcely less wild, of frames covered with clapboards,—queer-looking log tenements, unplastered chambers, and little uncouth cabins, eight by twelve—where pride, in the lap of quiet, at all events, if not of comfort, might learn upon what a small amount of capital a man may realize large results in health and independence. It was the strangest spectacle, in Georgia and South-Carolina, to see the thousands thus in motion along the highways, and thus rioting in

---

5. Robert J. Walker, born in Pennsylvania, moved as a young man to Mississippi and represented that state in the United States Senate from 1835 to 1845; he was best known for his sponsorship of the annexation of Texas. *Dictionary of American Biography*, vol. 1, pt. 1, pp. 355–58.

rustic pleasures. Such cars and carriages, as bore the trooping adventurers never figured in fashionable use before. You might see the railway trains, long and massive frames of timber, set on wheels, with unplaned benches, an interminable range, crowded with the living multitudes, wedged affectionately together, like herrings in boxes—sorted, if not salted masses—without covering, speeding through sun by day, and rain by night, to the appointed places of retreat; and, strange to say, in the best of all possible humours with themselves and all mankind. A certain grateful determination to make the most of the novel *désagremens* of their situation, in acknowledgment of the substantial good, in healthy excitement and moral compensation, which they enjoyed at home, operated to make cheerful all the aspects of the scene, and to afford a pleasing animation to the strangest combinations of society. Here encountered, to the common benefit, circles and cliques that had never before been subjected to attrition. The reserved gentleman of the lower country, nice, staid, proper and particular, was pleased to receive a freshening stimulus from the frank, free, eager and salient manners of the gentleman of the interior. The over-refined ladies of the city were enlivened by the informal, hearty, lively and laughing tempers of the buoyant beauties of the mountain and forest country. They shared equally in the benefits of the association. The too frigid and stately reserves of the one region were thawed insensibly by the genial and buoyant, the unsophisticated impulse of the other; while the latter, insensibly borrowed, in return, something of the elaborate grace, and the quiet dignity, which constitute the chief attractions of the former. The result has compassed something more than was anticipated by the several parties. Seeking only to waste a summer gratefully, to find health and gentle excitements—the simple object of the whole,—they yet found more precious benefits in the unwonted communion. Prejudices were worn away, in the grateful attrition; new lights were brought to bear upon the social aspects of differing regions; thought was stimulated to fresh researches; and the general resources of the country, moral as well as physical, underwent a development, as grateful and encouraging as they were strange and wonderful to all the parties.

The *désagremens* of these extemporaneous progresses were not limited to bad roads and clumsy or crazy vehicles, rude dwellings and the absence of the usual comforts upon which the gentry of the low country of the South, trained in English schools, are apt to insist with perhaps, a little too much tenacity. We are compelled to make one admission, in respect to our interior, which we do in great grief of heart and much vexation of spirit. If the *schoolmaster* is abroad, the *cook* is not! Our *cuisine* is not well ordered in the forest country. The "*Physiologie de Goût*"[6] has never there been made a text book, in the schools of culinary philosophy. We doubt if a single copy of this grave authority can be found in all the mountain ranges of the Apalachian. They have the grace and the gravy; but these are not made to mingle as they should. The art which weds the vinegar, and the oil, in happiest harmonies, so that neither is suffered to prevail in the taste, has never, in this region, commanded that careful study, or indeed consideration, which their union properly demands. The rank of the *cuisinier* is not properly recognized. The weight and importance of a grain of salt in the adjustment (shall we say *compromise?*) of a salade, is, we grieve to say, not justly understood in our forest watering places; and, skillful enough at a julep or a sherry cobler, they betray but "'prentice han's" when a steak or a sauce, is

6. Antheleme Brillat-Savarin, French gastronomist, is best known for his book *Physiologie du Goût* (1825), a witty study of the art of dining. *Century Dictionary and Cyclopedia*, 9:184.

the subject of preparation. Monsieur Guizot,[7] speaking in properly dignified language of the common sentiment of France, insists that she is the most perfect representative of the civilization of christendom. Of course, he bases her claims to this position entirely on the virtues of her cuisine. The moral of the nation comes from the kitchen. The "good digestion" which should "wait on appetite" must be impossible where the *chef-de cuisine* falls short of the philosopher as well as the man of science. Now, of all that philosophy, which prepares the food with a due regard, not only to the meats and vegetables themselves, the graces and the gravies, but to the temperaments of the consumers, we are sorry to confess that we have but little in our vast interior. Our mountain cooks think they have done every thing when they have murdered a fillet of veal or a haunch of venison,— sodden them in lard or butter, baked or boiled them to a condition which admirably resembles the pulpy masses of cotton rag, when macerated for paper manufacture,—and wonders to see you mince gingerly of a dish which he himself will devour with the savage appetite of a Comanche! You have seen a royal side of venison brought in during the morning, and laid out upon the tavern shambles;—you have your heart set upon the dinner of that day. Fancy reminds you of the relish with which, at the St. Charles, in New-Orleans, or the Pulaski, in Savannah, or the Charleston Hotel, you have discussed the exquisitely dressed loin, or haunch, done to a turn; the red just tinging the gravy, the meat just offering such pleasant resistance to the knife as leaves the intricate fibres still closely united, though shedding their juices with the eagerness of the peach, pressed between the lips in the very hour of its maturity:—or you see a

7. François Pierre Guillaume Guizot was distinguished not only as a historian but also as a statesman; he served as prime minister of France from 1838 to 1848. Ibid., p. 468.

fine "mutton" brought in, of the wild flavour of the hills; and you examine, with the eye of the epicure, the voluminous fat fold upon fold, lapping itself lovingly about the loins. Leg, or loin, or saddle, or shoulder, suggests itself to your anticipation as the probable subject of noonday discussion. You lay yourself out for the argument, and naturally recur to the last famous dinner which you enjoyed with the reverend father, who presides so equally well at the Church of the St. Savori, and at his own excellent hotel in the Rue de Huitres. You remember all the company, admirable judges, every one of them, of the virtues and the graces of a proper feast. The reverend father, himself, belongs to that excellent school of which the English clergy still show you so many grateful living examples,—men whose sensibilities are not yielded to the barren empire of mind merely, but who bring thought and philosophy equally to bear upon the humble and too frequently mortified flesh. With the spectacle of the venerable host, presiding so gracefully and so amiably—the napkin tucked beneath his chin, and falling over the ample domain in which certain philosophers, with much show of reason, have found the mortal abiding place of the soul—you associate the happy action with which, slightly flourishing the bright steel before he smites, he then passes the scymitar-like edge into the rosy round before him. It is no rude or hurried act. He feels the responsibility of the duty. He has properly studied the relations of the parts. He knows just where to insinuate the blade; and the mild dignity with which the act is performed, reminds you of what you have seen in pictures, or read in books, of the sacrifices of the high priests and magi, at Grecian or Egyptian altars. What silence waits upon the stroke and, as the warm blood gushes forth, and the rubied edge of the wound lie[s] bare before your eyes, every bosom feels relieved! The augury has been a fortunate one and the feast begins under auspices that drive all doubts of what to-morrow may bring forth, entirely from the thought.

With such recollections kindling the imagination, our extempore hotels of the Apalachian regions will doom you to frequent disappointment. You see yourself surrounded by masses that may be boiled or roasted polypi for what you know. But where's the mutton and the venison? You call upon the landlord—a gaunt-looking tyke of the forest, who seems better fitted to hunt the game than take charge of its toilet. He is serving a score at once; with one hand heaping beef and bacon, with the other collards and cucumbers, into conflicting plates; and you fall back speechless, with the sudden dispersion of a thousand fancies of delight, as he tells you that the mutton, or the venison, which has been the subject of your reverie all morning, lies before you in the undistinguishable mass that has distressed you with notions of the polypus and sea-blubber, or some other unknown monstrosities of the deep or forest. But the subject is one quite too distressing for dilation. We feel for our readers, and must forbear. But we solemnly say to our Apalachian landlord, "Brother, this thing must be amended. You have no right to sport thus with the hopes, the health, the happiness of your guests. You have no right, in this way, to mortify your neighbours' flesh. Have you no sense of the evil which you are doing—no bowels of sympathy for those of other people? Is it pride, or indolence, or mere blindness and ignorance, which thus renders you reckless of what is due to humanity and society, and all that fine philosophy which the Roman epicure found essential to reconcile to becoming sensibilities the mere brutish necessities of the animal economy? You must import and educate your cooks. You must appreciate justly the morals of the kitchen. You must study with diligence, night and morning, the profound pages of the Physiologie de Goût; you must forswear those streams of lard, those cruel abuses of the flesh, those hard bakings of meats otherwise tender, those salt and savage soddenings of venison, otherwise sweet, those mountains of long collards, inadequately boiled, and those indigestible masses of dough, whether in the form of pies, or tarts, or biscuit, which need a yesty levity before they can possibly assimilate with the human system. We have often thought, seeing these heavy pasties upon your tables, that, if they could only command a voice, they would perpetually cry out to the needy and devouring guest, in the language of the ghosts to hunchback Richard, 'Let us lie heavy on thy soul to-morrow!'"[8]

So much by way of objurgation and exhortation. We have spoken now of all the disagreeables of travel in the South—all the natural consequences of the previous neglect, by our "Softheads," of the claims of their own country. The change in affairs which shall hereafter keep these at home, will, in a short period, work out its natural fruits; and, with the increased facilities of travel, with better roads and better vehicles, we shall no doubt see such improvements in the Apalachian cuisine, as will leave to the stomach no occasion for revolt.

.   .   .

8. The ghost in Shakespeare's *King Richard III* gives this statement in the singular. Act 5, sc. 3, line 131.

The South
in Sectional Crisis
1852–1860

*Travel literature for this decade constitutes an important body of contemporary materials . . .
the tenor of much of it was of special-interest nature. Some of it was vicious, some was distorted
by lack of information, but most of it reflected the spirit of the age. There are possibly no other
sources to which a historian can turn which will reveal so humanly the anxieties and uncertainties
of this pre-Civil War period.*

Clark, *Travels in the Old South*, III, 340

A TOUR OF THE LOWER SOUTH

Although these are only hasty travel notes, they are of more than ordinary interest, in view of the importance of James D. B. De Bow (1820–1867) in the molding of southern attitudes toward economic and political matters.[1]

Since the last issue of the Review, we have strayed off from our desk at New-Orleans, the labors of which held us very closely during the winter months.

The attractions of the *Lake Shore* detained us a day in our passage to Mobile. The leading hotel is one of the finest in the South. Its rooms are large, light, airy, and of spotless cleanliness. The table cannot readily be surpassed. We enjoyed the pompano, undoubtedly the best fish in the country. Green peas and other vegetables of the early spring abound. Extensive gardens bloom with every variety of beautiful roses. Cool and inviting shades woo us to repose. Indeed it is a delightful retreat from the noise and bustle and dust of the town.

There is much in *Mobile* that is attractive to those who have lived in larger cities. Its hospitalities, its refinement, its intelligence, and its virtues, are conspicuous. There is an absence of ostentation and elaboration, we mean by comparison, which is truly refreshing. The merchants are active and enterprising; the lawyers eloquent and able; the physicians—but who are the superiors anywhere of Nott and Levert?[2] Perhaps at this point we might make a remark about the sex, which neither merchants, lawyers, nor doctors include, though it rules them all—the ladies. All the world over, our preferences are with them. In Mobile, our acquaintance includes some of exquisite beauty of person and character. They have charms which, in dreams, re-visit us. But, enough!

The name of the eminent physician which slipped into our paragraph above, suggests pleasing memories of his beautiful home among the rich and elegant structures of Government st. Here his accomplished, intellectual, and fascinating lady dispenses hospitalities and courtesies to citizen and stranger, and especially the latter, with lavish hand and warm heart. Her home, embellished with all that can contribute to elegance and taste, gathered in every part of the world, is the centre of attraction for a large and polished and intellectual circle. Her receptions are like those of a courtly minister. We are invading, however, upon the sanctuary of private life, and hastily beat a retreat at the very beginning of a tribute which our heart was about to pay.

In regard to the commerce, manufactures, and general business of Mobile, we have had occasion to speak on innumerable occasions. In particular we have commended her lavish bounty in aid of railroads, and especially in aid of her great work, the Mobile and Ohio road.[3] Over this route we traveled more than two hundred miles, to a point

James D. B. De Bow, "Editorial Miscellany," *De Bow's Review* 27 (July 1859): 112–18.

1. *Dictionary of American Biography*, vol. 3, pt. 2, pp. 180–82.

2. Joseph Clarke Nott was the founder of the Alabama Medical College. He was one of the first physicians to suggest the role of insects in spreading such diseases as yellow fever. Owen, *History of Alabama*, 4:1288–91.

Henry Le Vert was a distinguished physician. His wife, Octavia Walton Le Vert, was a well-known author. *National Cyclopaedia of American Biography*, 6:440–41.

3. The Mobile and Ohio Railroad was chartered in 1848 but the main line from Mobile to East Cairo, Kentucky, was not opened until 1861. Dunbar Rowland, *History of Mississippi*, 2 vols. (Chicago, 1925), 2:560.

which is connected by a short stage line to Columbus, and which will soon be connected by a branch railroad. The Mobile and Ohio railroad is a durable structure, and will offer a very convenient passage to the North when it intersects with the Memphis and Charleston road.[4] It is now about 90 miles from such intersection, and is in rapid progress. On the other side, the road is in active operation between Jackson, Tennessee, and Columbus, Kentucky, and every effort is being made to connect the two links, when there will result one of the longest and most important roads in every respect, in the Union. We have some recent statistics in regard to the road, which will appear in our next.

Columbus[5] is one of the largest and most beautiful interior towns in the South, and has long been celebrated for the wealth of its inhabitants, the elegance of its society, and the general intelligence of its people. It is a place of considerable and growing trade, and its merchants conduct business on a scale of largeness and liberality. The private residences are beautiful, and are adorned with choicest gardens. In particular we might mention that of Major Blewitt,[6] which offers a perfect paradise. Here abound, without—

> Flowers of all hue,
> And without thorn the rose;[7]

and within, rich embellishments, elegant garnishing pictures, and rare ornaments. Then, too, the unaffected hospitalities of our worthy friend!

Columbus is more than ordinarily blessed in her dowry of beautiful and accomplished women, and the fact may to some extent be accounted for, when it is considered how admirable are her educational facilities. In company with Major Blewitt, the President of the Trustees, we visited the *Female Institute*,[8] and were introduced to all of the departments, through the courtesy of President Larabee. The whole number of students was 231, of whom 14 were in the senior class. Alabama, Texas, Louisiana, Virginia, and North Carolina, as well as Mississippi, were represented. The buildings are extensive, the system of education thorough, and the faculty large and able; the expenses moderate, and the site very healthful.

Columbus, the seat of justice for Lowndes county, is pleasantly situated on the east bank of the Tombigby, in north latitude 33 deg., 150 miles northeast of Jackson, and 480 miles, by river, above Mobile.

It is regularly laid out upon an elevated plain, the streets crossing each other at right angles, and is a beautiful and flourishing place. Within a few years, in consequence of the sale of the adjacent Indian lands, and the great emigration of the surrounding country, it has advanced rapidly in population and wealth.

The first effort made to settle Columbus was in 1819. In the latter part of the year 1817, Thomas Thomas,[9] a man who had been driven out by the Indian agent as an intruder in the Chickasaw Nation, built a small split-log hut, on the spot now known as the corner of Main and Franklin streets, but there are no signs of its ever being occupied by any person till 1819. The town was first called Shookhuttah-tom-a-hah, a name given it by the Indians, signifying "Opossum Town."[10]

4. The Memphis and Charleston Railroad was begun in 1829 and completed in 1857. Adams, *Dictionary of American History*, 3:372.
5. Although this area was visited by De Soto in 1540, it was not until 1817 that a trading post was built on the site of the present city of Columbus. It received this name in 1821. *Mississippi Guide*, p. 182.
6. The largest landowner in northeast Mississippi was Major Blewitt, a native of South Carolina. Reuben Davis, *Recollections of Mississippi and Mississippians* (Boston, 1889), pp. 304–5.
7. John Milton, *Paradise Lost*, bk. 4, line 256.

8. Columbus Female Institute, established in 1847, was a forerunner of Mississippi State College for Women. *Mississippi Guide*, p. 183.
9. Thomas Thomas built a store in 1817 on the Tombigbee at Luxapalila Creek. Ibid., p. 182.

Columbus was incorporated into a town in 1822.

Made the passage of the Alabama river, on the splendid steamer St. Charles. Delayed but an hour at Montgomery, and then over the railroads safely and pleasantly, and without delay to Atlanta, to Augusta, and to Charleston. From *Charleston*, in steamer Edisto, to *St. Helena Island*, a favored retreat of ours, and one which is blessed by the associations of our boyhood, and with ancestral associations, running back almost to the landing of Port Royal and the settlement of Carolina. On the trip, shake hands with an old friend, Prof. Bache,[11] of the Coast Survey, and making the "outside passage," examine with him bars, and buoys, and headlands. In addition to being a man of great science, he is the grandson of Benjamin Franklin.

From Charleston take the railroad to Memphis. This route we have not before travelled, and is therefore one of much interest. The time occupied between the two cities is about forty-two hours. The *Memphis and Charleston road* is an admirable structure, and under most excellent management. It has conferred great benefit upon Memphis and upon the country which it traverses, besides constituting an important link of Northern and Southern travel. We have never journeyed over a more comfortable road, by day or night.

The route from Atlanta is through Marietta, Cartersville, Dalton, etc., to Chattanooga, a distance of 138 miles, over the Western and Atlantic railroad.[12] The tunnel through which we pass is black as night, $\frac{1}{2}$ of a mile long and 18 feet high, cut through solid rock. From Chattanooga, take the Nashville road for 38 miles to Stevenson, passing some of the wildest and most magnificent scenery in the world. The *Lookout Mountains* rise to the height of 2,400 feet.

Standing on its summit, the tourist drinks a bracing air; his eye wanders over a vast sea of forest and cultivated fields, until its vision is bounded by the mountains, fifty miles distant. The Tennessee meanders in graceful curves beneath his feet—now lost to view, and then the glimmer of its waters breaks out again in the far distance. Awful precipices and mighty rocks are all around; and looking from their dizzy heights, the rushing railway-train hastening along its appointed way, seems a child's toy, a mere plaything, amid the great realities of nature.

Chattanooga, superbly situated amid woods and mountains, and by the side of the beautiful Tennessee, which is always navigable here, is a town of 4,000 inhabitants,[13] and much and growing commerce and manufactures. The mineral resources of the country are inexhaustible. Eventually the whole region will be one of much resort during the summer months, on account of health. Beersheba Springs and Sewanee, the site of the new Southern University, are a very short distance.[14]

Leaving Stevenson[15] the space to Memphis, on

10. According to one authority, the town was named Shuk-ho-ta Tom-a-ha, or Opossum Town, for one of the early settlers, Spirus Roach, who had unusually hard features and peculiar manners. W. L. Lipscomb, *History of Columbus, Mississippi during the 19th Century* (Birmingham, Ala., 1909), p. 29.

11. Alexander D. Bache was a physicist. He became superintendent of the United States Coast Survey in 1843 and held that post until his death in 1867. *Dictionary of American Biography*, vol. 1, pt. 1, pp. 461–62.

12. The Western and Atlantic Railroad was begun in 1836 by the state of Georgia at a place which later became Atlanta. It was opened to traffic in 1851. It was state owned and managed until 1871 and was later leased to the N.C. & St. L. Railroad Company. Adams, *Dictionary of American History*, 5:440.

13. No population figures are given for Chattanooga in the 1860 census. In 1870 the population was 6,093. U.S., Bureau of the Census, *The Statistics of the Population of the United States* (Washington, D.C., 1872), p. 264.

14. Beersheba Springs is in Grundy County, south of McMinnville. The University of the South was established by the southern dioceses of the Protestant Episcopal Church at Sewanee in 1857. *Tennessee Guide*, p. 483.

15. Stevenson, Alabama, was located where the Nashville and Chattanooga Railroad met the road to Memphis. ☞

the Charleston and Memphis road, is 271 miles. The most important points in the route are Huntsville, Decatur, Tuscumbia, Iuka, Corinth, Grand Junction, Lagrange, and Moscow.

Huntsville has a population of 3,200 and is a thriving and beautiful town.[16] It is almost the healthiest region of America, and is the abode of much wealth and refinement. To strangers, this place has the greatest attractions.

The city is one mile square and contains, together with its suburban residents, a population of 3,200. It is laid off at right angles and the streets and alleys graded and Macadamized, while the foot-walks are mostly ornamented with shade-trees. Its principal public buildings are a court-house, located in the square, of Doric architecture, and surmounted by a beautiful dome. It is handsomely fenced in, and surrounded by shade-trees. The Northern Bank of Alabama is a tasteful and attractive structure, of the Ionic order. The various churches, developing beautiful architectural styles, and a theatre, constitute the residue of the public buildings, while the private residences are ample and elegant in structure. Two chartered female schools—the "North Alabama College" and the "Huntsville Female College"—are well patronized institutions, affording enlarged and liberal courses of instruction. Two male academies and free schools, in addition to the aforesaid, evidence extraordinary interest in the progress of education; and constitute a pre-eminent feature of the city's glory.

Decatur is rather an old town for the West; has steamboat communication by the Tennessee, with the Ohio river, and a population of about 1,000.[17]

Tuscumbia, with twice the population, is situated in the healthful and beautiful valley of the Tennessee, about a mile from the river. It abounds with mineral and other springs. The "Franklin," the "Ligon," "Bailey," and "Lauderdale" springs are in this region.[18]

Iuka[19] is of no further importance at present than that it is the point of connection, by stages, with the Mobile road.

At *Corinth*, the intersection of the two roads will eventually be had, and a town of some consequence must result. It is in Tishamingo county, Mississippi, and has already a population of about 1,500.[20] The advantages of location, natural and artificial, are very great.

Grand Junction is the point of connection with the Mississippi Central road.[21] It is growing rapidly in population and trade, and should now have another name. We propose that of "*Jefferson Davis*." Mississippi has yet none of her towns named after this eminent son.

Lagrange, with less than a thousand inhabitants, is a place of healthy and desirable residence.[22]

18. Census figures do not bear out this statement of population, and no figures for Tuscumbia appear in the 1860 census. Bailey Springs is discussed in some detail in a book on resorts of this area but other springs are not mentioned. James F. Sulzby, *Historic Alabama Hotels and Resorts* (University, Ala., 1960), pp. 27–37.
19. Iuka, the site of a Chickasaw village, was settled by white people when the Memphis and Charleston Railroad was built. It was the site of a Civil War battle on 19 September 1862. *Mississippi Guide*, pp. 442–43.
20. The population of Corinth is not given in the census for 1860. The county was named for Tishmingo, an Indian chief. Ibid., p. 442.
21. Grand Junction is the point where the Southern and the Illinois Central railroads cross. *Tennessee Guide*, p. 491. The Mississippi Central Railroad was chartered on 10 March 1852 to operate between Canton and the Mississippi-Tennessee line. It later became part of the Illinois Central system. Thomas D. Clark, *A Pioneer Southern Railroad* (Chapel Hill, N.C., 1936), pp. 86–91.
22. Lagrange was to be the terminus of the Lagrange and Memphis Railroad, chartered in 1836, but when this plan

Gilbert E. Govan and James W. Livingood, *The Chattanooga Country, 1540–1951* (New York, 1952), p. 150.
16. The figure given in the official census for 1860 was 3,634. U.S., Bureau of the Census, *Population of the United States in 1860* (Washington, D.C., 1864), p. 9.
17. No population figures are given for Decatur in the 1860 census.

Moscow[23] connects, by a short railroad, with Somerville, Tennessee, a point which we should delight to visit again, having enjoyed in years long past the society of its excellent and hospitable people.

In regard to *Memphis*, we shall have quite an article in our next number, from the pen of Prof. Stueckrath.[24] We remained there ourselves a day or two, and were amazed with the evidence of its progress since our last visit in 1851. It was charming to meet again and enjoy the hospitalities of many old friends.

Took the steamer "Capitol,"[25] in company with the South Carolina and Georgia delegates, for the Southern convention at *Vicksburg*.[26] In this fast and splendid boat we make the trip, which is 350 miles, in about 24 hours. From the guards of the boat the view for a great part of the way is of nothing but ruin. The old Mississippi has broken the feeble barriers and inundated to the very parlors and chambers of their mansions, hundreds and hundreds of rich plantations. The heart sickens at such a prospect of devastation presenting itself on every hand.[27] Can nothing be done to prevent these enormous and annually increasing losses? In our next we shall present a vast mass of interesting material upon the subject from the pens of very able contributors, and practical as well as scientific men.

The week which we pass at Vicksburg, is associated with memories the heart would not willingly let perish. Suffice it that we could not return too often, or stay too long. In a late number of the Review, we had some interesting notes on Vicksburg.[28]

In regard to the *Convention*, we have spoken in another place. It was clear that the people of Vicksburg looked upon it with some distrust and (with exceptions of course) seemed disposed to keep at a safe distance from its *infected* districts. Some of them had in advance "snuffed *treason* in the tainted air," and our friend, Gov. Foote,[29] was glad to meet "with it and struggle with it, in its own naked deformity." It is an excellent theme in his hands, and we congratulate the governor on so fruitful a one in these piping hot times on the Mississippi stump! The agreeable and companionable editors of the *Whig*, the *Southron*, and the *Sun*, added many pleasures to our Vicksburg visit.[30]

failed to materialize, Lagrange did not develop. *Tennessee Guide*, p. 492.

23. Moscow was a post town in Fayette County, Tennessee, on the north bank of Wolf River. Eastin Morris, *The Tennessee Gazetteer* (Nashville, Tenn., 1834), p. 105.

24. G. H. Stueckrath, "Memphis, Tennessee," *De Bow's Review* 27 (August 1859): 235–39.

25. Built in 1853 in Louisville, the *Capitol* was burned in 1863 in the Yazoo River with ten other large steamers to prevent their falling into the hands of the United States fleet. Norman, "Red River Boats," *Louisiana Historical Quarterly* 25 (April 1942): 427.

26. This was the last in a series of southern commercial conventions which began in 1852 in an effort to bolster the economy of the South. Political sentiments gradually overshadowed economic discussions. Adams, *Dictionary of American History*, 5:129–30.

27. The problem of flood control was attacked on an individual basis for many years, each planter or small group of planters trying to protect small stretches of river bank. This only aggravated the problem, because the more the river was confined within its banks the larger and more destructive the floods became. Perhaps the writer of this article was especially impressed because one of the most disastrous floods of the antebellum period occurred in 1858, the year before the article was written. Sitterson, *Sugar Country*, pp. 20–23.

28. "A New Spirit in Vicksburgh," *De Bow's Review* 25 (August 1858): 229.

29. Henry Stuart Foote, a native of Virginia, moved to Mississippi as a young man. He was governor of Mississippi in 1853–1854. He opposed secession and moved to Tennessee because of his inability to reconcile his ideas with those of the majority in his area. *Dictionary of American Biography*, vol. 3, pt. 2, pp. 500–501.

30. The *Whig* was published from 1839 to 1863 and the weekly *Sun* from 1858 to 1860. Gregory, *American News-*

Take the *Southern Mississippi Railroad*, 46 miles to Jackson. This road is in fine condition, and is being extended eastward to the Alabama line. We trust that the connection will be eventually secured.[31]

Leaving *Jackson*, which has been referred to in the last volume of the REVIEW,[32] fully, we take the railroad to New-Orleans. The distance is 183 miles, and this is the first time that we have traversed it on the road, although having much to do with the incipiency of the undertaking. The New-Orleans and Jackson[33] railroad is in excellent condition, and is well managed and, but for the drawback the present season in the overflow of its lower portions, would be on the high road to prosperity. The evil, however, the president tells us, can be easily remedied, and obviated hereafter. We hope so. The points passed are Byram, Terrey, Crystal Springs, Hazlehurst, Bahala, Brookhaven (the highest point of the road), Bogue Chitto, Summit, Quinn's, Magnolia, Osyka, Tangipihoa, Amite, Tickfaw, Pontchatoula, Manchac, Kenner, etc. These are nearly all the creation of the road, and are advancing with it. The region is for the most part in the piny woods and very healthy, being entirely re-

moved from dangers of epidemics. Large numbers of the citizens of New Orleans are building or occupying handsome country residences at some of the points above named, and the number will greatly increase from year to year. The advantage thus conferred upon New-Orleans will be incalculable. Its citizens can have at their very doors health and rural enjoyments.

At Manchac, in consequence of the inundation, take the steamer for New-Orleans by Lake Pontchartrain. Reach in two hours the terminus of the Carrolton and Lake railroad.[34] Then over the Carrolton road, and we are at the St. Charles Hotel in New Orleans.

New-Orleans, about the first of June, begins to show evidences of waste. People inquire of steam and rail routes, and are buying *trunks*. The hotels look very shabby, and the parlors have lost their lustre. The streets are parched and dry. We remain but a few days, and having passed again over the railroad, are at Jackson, and then 34 miles further on, are at Canton.

Canton[35] is one of the termini of the Mississippi Central and of the New Orleans roads. It is a point of some importance, and is the seat of a refined and wealthy people. Here we meet many old acquaintances, and among the rest, spend a day very pleasantly with that excellent gentleman and popular and able Congressman, the Hon. Mr. Singleton,[36] of this District.

A few miles from Canton we leave the railroad,

papers, pp. 349–50. The weekly *True Southron* was published in 1858. Louis P. Cashman, Jr., publisher of the *Vicksburg Evening Post*, to Jacqueline Bull, 13 March 1969.

31. On a map of railroads in this area in the period 1827–1850 the Vicksburg and Jackson Rail Road is shown connecting these two points. A map of the railroads in the same area in the period 1861–1865 shows this same road extending from Monroe, Louisiana, to Meridian, Mississippi. Adams, *Atlas of American History*, pp. 108, 124–25.

32. "Miscellaneous Department: I—Jackson, Mississippi," *De Bow's Review* 26 (April 1859): 466–68.

33. In 1849 C. S. Tarpley of Mississippi began to campaign for the construction of a railroad to connect New Orleans and Jackson. He was joined by several prominent persons in New Orleans. In 1850 the New Orleans, Jackson and Great Northern Railroad was begun. By 1854 eighty-eight miles had been completed and by 1858 it was completed to Jackson. Merl E. Reed, *New Orleans and the Railroads* (Baton Rouge, La., 1966), pp. 88–100.

34. A map of railroads in the period 1827–1850 shows this road, which ran from Carrollton, Louisiana, via New Orleans to Proctorsville. Adams, *Atlas of American History*, p. 108.

35. Canton was incorporated in 1836. Its prosperity was enhanced by the travel on the Natchez Trace and by the flourishing cotton economy. *Mississippi Guide*, p. 388.

36. Otis Robards Singleton was born in Jessamine County, Kentucky, in 1814. He was admitted to the bar in 1838 and served as a representative from Mississippi in Congress, 1853–1855, 1857–1861, and 1875–1887. He died in 1889. *Biographical Directory of the American Congress*, p. 1817.

and after a stage ride of about six miles are at the celebrated ARTESIAN SPRINGS.[37] They are now under the proprietary and control of a gentleman from Canton, who seems to be admirably qualified for the trust, and is determined in every way to make it one of the most desirable retreats in the South. From its admirable position it should be resorted to by thousands. The accommodations are ample. The grounds are extensive. The water is abundant and highly remedial and medicinal. The terms are moderate. We attended the opening ball, which brought many fascinating ladies from the neighboring counties, and all went merry as a marriage bell.

The following in regard to the water has been furnished for our pages. There are four springs:

NO. 1 SPRING. Base Iron, Muriatic Acid, Gas—suited best for Liver and Spleen diseases generally, or a deficiency of red particles in blood; also good for kindred affections.

NO. 2 SPRING. Free Carbonic Acid Gas—suited for Dyspepsia, Diarrhoea, Dysentery, and Bowel affections generally; Dropsy, Gravel, and kindred affections.

NO. 3 SPRING. Sulphuretted Hydrogen Gas—suited as a general tonic; Cutaneous or Skin affections.

NO. 4 SPRING. Suited for Sore legs, Eyes, &c.

We are again on the railroad, and at its terminus take the stage, and through much dust and heat, but over a fair road, are soon at Lexington, Carrolton, Grenada—the distance being about sixty miles. Over this route we travelled eight years ago, in an open buggy, making speeches at every ten miles or thereabouts, in advocacy of the Great Central Mississippi road,[38] which was then considered a myth or a fantasy, but which is so nearly

now in all its length and extent and predictions, a practical *reality!* But those times are passed and with them the doubting Thomases and Peters, and those who doubted most are often afterward among those who claim the most and carry off the highest honors of the undertaking.

Remain a day at *Grenada*,[39] at the residence of our old and esteemed friend, Col. A. S. Brown,[40] which is just out of the limits of the town, and combines a thousand beauties and attractions. Here resides the Hon. Judge Bennett,[41] who formerly represented the District in Congress, and many other intelligent and interesting people. Grenada is growing very much, and when the railroad passes through it will advance still faster.

Eight miles of staging take us now to the cars again, and after the ride of an hour in them we are at *Oxford*, the seat of the famed UNIVERSITY OF MISSISSIPPI.[42] At the invitation of the estimable and learned President, F. A. Barnard,[43] and his

37. There was at one time a resort hotel called Artesian Springs about fifteen miles from Canton. Mrs. J. H. Frizell, Librarian, Canton Public Library, to Jacqueline Bull, 21 January 1969.

38. This must refer to the Mississippi Central Railroad.

39. Grenada was established in 1836 on the site of two earlier towns, Pittsburg and Tulahoma, which had been laid out by rival land companies. *Mississippi Guide*, p. 383.

40. Albert Spooner Brown, a native of Tennessee, moved to Grenada in 1835. He was an architect and a successful land speculator. He gave the right-of-way across his land to the Mississippi Central Railroad Company. In appreciation the company placed a brass plate carrying his name on its largest locomotive. After the Civil War, Brown moved to Memphis where he died of yellow fever. J. C. Hathorn, *A History of Grenada County* (Grenada, Miss., 1967), pp. 124–25.

41. Hendley Stone Bennett represented Mississippi in Congress in 1855–1857 but was unsuccessful in running for an additional term. He was judge of the Circuit Court, 1846–1854. *Biographical Directory of the American Congress*, p. 840.

42. The town of Oxford was established in 1837 on land ceded by the Chickasaw Indians. One year later there were 400 inhabitants. *Mississippi Guide*, p. 255.

The state university was chartered in 1840 and opened in 1848, when the Lyceum was built in the center of the campus. Ibid., pp. 259–60.

43. Frederick A. P. Barnard, a native of Sheffield, Massachusetts, served as president of the University of Missis-

agreeable lady, we take up our abode for a day or two at his mansion on the College grounds. Here we have presented the subject for an entire article, which will be given to our readers after a while. Suffice it that the University is very prosperous, and under its present control in admirable working condition. The President and Faculty are very able. The grounds are immense. Some new and costly buildings are in course of construction. The new Observatory will be one of the finest in the country. President Barnard devoted much time in exhibiting to us the extensive and costly apparatus, which has been selected under his auspices, and which is not to be excelled in any Southern institution. Some of the instruments, especially the electric machine and the electric clock (his own invention), are not surpassed anywhere in the world. President Barnard presented us several able reports made by himself upon Education, which will be referred to at length when we come to prepare the article which is alluded above. The total number of students in the Law and undergraduate departments is 178, and the number of alumni to this date 198. The faculty consists of

FREDERICK A. P. BARNARD, L.L.D., President.

WILSON G. RICHARDSON, M.A., Professor of Latin and Modern Languages.

WILLIAM F. STEARNS, Professor of Governmental Science and Law.

FREDERICK A. P. BARNARD, L.L.D., Professor of Mathematics, Physics, Astronomy, and Civil Engineering.

EDWARD C. BOYNTON, M.A., Professor of Chemistry, Mineralogy, and Geology.

HENRY WHITEHORNE, M.A., Professor of Greek and Ancient Literature.

————* Professor of Intellectual and Moral Philosophy.

JORDAN M. PHIPPS, M.A., Assistant Professor of Mathematics.

WILLIAM T. J. SULLIVAN, B.A., Tutor in Rhetoric, Logic, Composition, and Elocution.

DANIEL B. CARR, B.A., Tutor in Mathematics.

JORDAN M. PHIPPS, Corresponding Secretary.

DANIEL B. CARR, Recording Secretary.

HENRY WHITEHORNE, Librarian.

Thirty miles further, and we reach *Holly Springs*.[44] Most of our acquaintances here are absent. Meet, however, with Mr. Goodman,[45] President of the Central Road, who speaks encouragingly of its prospects, and thinks that by December next the connection will be made complete, and the stage service entirely discharged. We trust sincerely that this will be the case. We are sure then that this will be one of the most important routes of travel in the Union.

"Holly Springs† is remarkable for its beauty and healthful location, being situated upon an elevated and extended range of table lands. 'Cutler's Well' is near the public square, and its waters possess great medicinal properties.

"The cause of education seems to have received much attention and the schools rank among the most prominent of their kind. The town has two High Schools for males and females respectively. Holly Springs Female Institute and Franklin Female College are well endowed and excellent institutions. St. Thomas Hall and Chalmers Institute rank high as male schools. Between 400 and 500

44. Holly Springs was founded in 1836 by William Randolph of Virginia. *Mississippi Guide*, p. 201.
45. Walter Goodman was one of the original commissioners or incorporators of the Mississippi Central Railroad. Clark, *A Pioneer Southern Railroad*, p. 87.
*This chair will be filled in July next. The duties of it are discharged during the present session by the President.
†We quote in this and in one or two other instances, from the excellent 'Guide Book' of G. B. Ayres.

sippi from 1856 to 1858 and chancellor from 1858 to 1861. He was elected president of Columbia College in 1864 and held this position until his death in 1889. *Dictionary of American Biography*, vol. 1, pt. 1, pp. 619–21.

pupils annually enjoy the facilities afforded by these four prominent institutions, and on which account many wealthy planters reside here solely for the education of their children.

"Fifteen thousand bales of cotton were sold here in 1856. There are about forty mercantile establishments, and which also supply the adjacent country trade. The citizens are known for intelligence and hospitality, and thus evidence the effect of and enjoy the beneficial results which naturally accrue to the fostering of education."

From Holly Springs, to the junction of the Memphis and Charleston road, the distance is 25 miles, which we make in about an hour and a half.

Having still a day or two to spare, we are seized with a strong desire to re-visit *Jackson*, Tennessee,

where once upon a time some happy hours were spent by us. The railroad being completed, and under the jurisdiction of the Mississippi Central, we have little or no difficulty, and surmounting a distance of only 50 miles are at Jackson. The town does not seem to be very thriving, though it is the seat of a wealthy and refined population, which is estimated at 3000 souls.[46] The completion of the Mobile and Ohio road may yet bring out Jackson.

Here the notes of our trip terminate, we hasten on to *Washington City*, and now at our desk there, on this 21st day of June, are completing the July number of the *Review*.

46. The population of Jackson in 1860 was 2,407. Bureau of the Census, *Population of the United States in 1860*, p. 467.

LIFE AND TRAVEL IN THE SOUTHERN STATES

One of a series of articles which relate in detail one of the more extensive trips through the South.

In the autumn of 1853 the writer found himself with his family, at Wilmington, North Carolina, and having a few months of leisure, he concluded to pass the time in an excursion through several of the Southern States. A simple, straightforward narrative of what he saw and experienced during the journey, it is thought, may prove acceptable to the readers of the "Great Republic," and for that purpose they are now written out from notes made at the time.

Instead of taking the usual route from Wilmington to Charleston by sea, we preferred to go by the way of the W. & M. Railroad,[1] as this route, though

less direct, would afford us an opportunity of seeing the interior of the country—a country that flows with "tar and turpentine," if not with "milk and honey."

From Wilmington we were conveyed in a little "cockle-shell" of a steamboat, some miles up the Cape Fear River, to the railroad station. The scenery along the river is beautiful, and the valley lands through which it winds its way are very

"Life and Travel in the Southern States," *Great Republic Monthly* 1 (1859): 80–84.

1. In 1853 the Wilmington & Manchester Railroad had been completed 163 miles, from Eagle Island on Cape Fear River to a junction with the South Carolina Railroad near Kingsville, South Carolina. A steamer connected the train at Eagle Island with Wilmington. This railroad became part of the Atlantic Coast Line system. Richard E. Prince, *Atlantic Coast Line Railroad* (Green River, Wyo., 1966), p. 9.

fertile, and considered as among the most valuable in the State. Here we saw, for the first time, rice-fields, in which stocks of the gathered grain still remained. The rice is grown in low grounds, which are so situated as to be capable of being overflowed with water at pleasure, by means of artificial channels. This kind of grain, though not so valuable or nutritive as wheat, is of immense value to mankind, especially to the inhabitants of low, alluvial lands in warm climates, where the more stimulating food of colder regions would prove uncongenial to the preservation of health, if not inconsistent with the laws prescribed by nature to the different races of men. It is a grain which yields abundantly, at least six-fold more than wheat, and in warm climates two crops may be produced on the same lands in a single year. It grows from one to six feet high, erect and jointed, leaves large and cuspated, and resembles in appearance the oat stalk, with the exception that it usually grows much taller. From the earliest ages it has been much cultivated in the Eastern world—in Egypt, in Greece, and in Hindoostan—and was first introduced, it is said, into Carolina, in 1697. It has now become a staple article of food in the Southern States, and a commodity which enters largely into the commerce of the country. It is not a grain, however, which the Saxon race will ever cultivate to any considerable extent for the reason that the climate best adapted to it is destructive to the health of the white man. It cannot be cultivated in the Southern States except by the negroes. There is evidently a law of climate, which assigns to the different races of men their appropriate zone, with reference to which the natural products of the soil, and their adaptation to the health and wants of man, seem to be regulated. The negroes are a tropical race, and flourish best under the influences of a tropical sun. The Saxon race belongs to northern latitudes, and can never flourish, physically, anywhere else.

On being released from the "cockle-shell" that

conveyed us up the river, we ascended on foot a steep bluff, where we found the cars in readiness, and in a few minutes found ourselves gliding with frantic velocity into a dark wilderness of pines. So dense were the pines that surrounded us on every side that it seemed as if we had entered a realm of sighing and mourning, where nature herself had assumed the "habiliments of woe." All was solitude, and not a sound saluted our ears, except the spasmodic puffings which issued from the distended nostrils of the steam-horse, that bore us along at the top of his speed, flinging

Defiance on his way.

But, as we progressed, we soon discovered that man had left his "footprints" even here, and that these immense pine forests had been allotted into "plantations," which are devoted exclusively to the production of tar and turpentine. Here and there by the wayside appeared a small cabin, or factory, where the turpentine, put up in barrels, is collected. In this region the pines are so dense that they seem to crowd each other. They are tall and straight, and would measure in diameter, I presume, from six to twelve inches. The turpentine is extracted from them by boxing and scarifying the trunks. This process consists in cutting a cavity into the trunk near the ground, and then scarifying the bark above it, so as to conduct the oozing life-blood of the tree into the cavity or box, which is sufficiently capacious to contain a quart or more. This process of scarifying is repeated every year, by extending the incisions higher up the trunk, and is done usually in the month of March. In a few years the wounded tree dies from exhaustion, and is then "hewn down" and consigned to the tar-kiln. One thousand trees, thus boxed and scarified, will produce, for some years in succession, a yield of twenty barrels of turpentine; and one slave can gather, it is said, the product of ten thousand trees in a single season. The turpentine is dipped from the cavities or boxes with a large spoon, and deposited in buckets. It is then stored in barrels, the spirits of turpentine extracted by distillation, and sent to market in the various forms of rosin and spirits. In this branch of industry slave labor is made very profitable, much more so than in cultivating the soil, poor as it generally is in North Carolina.

The somber appearance which is given to the country by its extensive pine forests is by no means cheered by the tar-kilns which meet the eye here and there as you pass, and which resemble burning volcanoes on a small scale, sending up the "smoke of their torment,"[2] like a "pillar of cloud by night and by day,"[3] and surrounded by an unearthly-looking set of black figures in human shape, thrusting long pikes into the agonizing structure. These kilns are constructed of pine knots and the trunks of dead pine trees, cut and stacked in the form of a cone, and then covered with earth in order to secure a slow conflagration. They are then fired at the top, and the tar conducted from the base by a channel or pit, and barreled for market. Though the pine of the South seems too abundant to be valuable, yet it in fact furnishes a source of great wealth. Not only the best of lumber, but the living tree yields turpentine, and the dead one tar—indispensable articles in the long list of human wants.

It is said that the entire sea-coast of the Southern States is skirted with pine forests from one to three hundred miles in width. In fact, the South is not only skirted but crowned with evergreen. When we see dame Nature thus skirted and crowned, and looking into the sky, as in a mirror, to see a reflection of her own beauty, why should the ladies be censured for consulting their mirrors, or for a slight indulgence in wreaths and flowers, silks and satins, scarlets, and velvets, furbelows and flounces.

2. Rev. 14:11.
3. Exod. 13:22.

To copy nature is always in good taste, though art has a way of her own. Whatever may be said of the winning arts adopted by the ladies, it is too true that Fashion is often too much in love with herself to love nature with a practical sincerity, and hence she is apt to run into extremes, and does not care to correct her follies until it suits her fancy, though good taste may point them out, and strive in vain to suppress a smile. Fashion will have her own way; it is of no use to argue matters with her. She delights in ribbons and gewgaws, in ornaments of "gold and precious stones," in satin slippers and crinoline, and loves to go to church to "see and be seen"—never wearies of flirtation, or experiment, and never can be persuaded that there is any essential virtue in humility. Her fertility of invention is truly marvelous; and her sway not less universal than despotic. In short, she is the empress of the civilized world. Judgment, reason, common sense, all bow at her shrine. And yet her mandates, exacting as they may be, are obeyed from choice. Princes and potentates are included among her devotees—

Pleased with a rattle, tickled with a straw.[4]

The soil of the pine lands in the Carolinas is generally light and sandy. As we pursued our way through the "piny woods," as they are called, we caught an occasional glimpse of a plantation shorn of timber, which presented cultivated fields of corn and cotton. But for the most part we were transported through a wilderness, interspersed here and there with swamps, and uncheered by human habitations. Some time after our usual dining hour, and before we were "out of the woods," the train halted at a station which, it was said, might be regarded as the nucleus of a town, yet to be. The favored spot had already been surveyed into lots and a long, low, log cabin erected, which served as a dining hall, and which was the only building in

4. Alexander Pope, *An Essay on Man*, Epistle 2, line 276.

this contemplated city. It was constructed of un-hewn pine logs, without door or window; yet the builders had provided a door-way by sawing out a section of the logs, and for windows had hit upon the expedient, equally primitive in design, by allowing the apertures between the logs to remain open, through which a sufficiency of light and fresh air were certainly admitted. A negro, standing in the door-way of this spacious hotel, announced dinner at the moment the cars arrived. The broad display he made of his ivory showed that he felt happy in the discharge of his duties. "Walk in, Massa," was the burden of his song, and the passengers, generally, did "walk in," and, half famished, achieved brilliant honors in their en-counter with corn-dodgers, yams, bacon, and greens. Every one helped himself, though attended by slaves. The darkies in attendance were raw recruits, taken from the field, who seemed to have lost their senses in the confusion of orders and counter-orders. When the passengers retired it was evident that no baskets were needed to "gather up the fragments."

Soon after leaving this city, so densely built up with a single log cabin, we suddenly came to a terminus of the railway—an unfinished section of twelve miles long—over which we were conveyed, bag and baggage, in stagecoaches. On our way we halted at Marion, the first town we came to in South Carolina, and while the coachman was re-freshing his horses with a sip of water we were compelled to listen to the eloquence of two "fast young men," who stood in the door-way of the hotel, with cigars in their mouths and the *effects* of brandy in their heads, discussing the terms of a bet on a horse-race, which had resulted in the defeat of a favorite nag, and in regard to which they differed so widely in opinion as to induce a settle-ment of the affair by "wager of battle," according to the ancient law. They exchanged blows and oaths for about ten minutes, with the utmost free-

dom. The citizens, as they collected, formed a circle around the combatants, and cried out, "Give them 'fair play.'" If both did not get whipped they deserved it. The coachman relished the fun, but finally drove on by order of the passengers, and we left the valiant heroes behind us, "alone in their glory," not caring which whipped.

It was late at night when we reached the banks of the Great Pedee, one of the largest rivers in South Carolina, and over which we passed in a flat-boat, ferried by an old negro. As I entered the boat I was forcibly reminded of Charon and the River Styx, and in fact began to "consider my ways," hoping to meet with a favorable reception in Elysium, or in some other pleasant place. Though the night was exceedingly dark, the passage over this modern Styx proved a safe one, and the land beyond, if not a land of spirits, gave us cheerful spirits, and induced an expression of mutual con-gratulation. Within a few miles from the river which we had just crossed we stopped for the remainder of the night, at a log hotel in the midst of the pine forest. For supper the passengers were regaled with a bountiful supply of hot rolls, coffee, and broiled chickens. But the hotel was nearly destitute of every thing else; had but little furniture and no beds. After indulging their appetites to satiety, the wearied passengers desired rest, but could not find it. Men, women, and children, as they best could, composed themselves for the night; some prostrated themselves on the floor, some took to the benches, and some to the few rickety chairs which had survived their more useful days.

The weather was summer-like, and the air with-in the cabin oppressive; yet it was relieved some-what, though not very agreeably, by the serenades of an officious band of little winged musicians, who rejected bouquets, and presented "long bills," never to be satisfied short of blood. When the passengers had fully paid the several "bills" presented against them, including the landlord's, they felt in the morning as if they had been pretty effectually *bled*.

But so far as regards myself, I did not attempt to sleep during the night, as I found it impossible under the circumstances. Of course the cabin offered but few attractions by way of comfort or amusement. A bright light within a few rods of the cabin attracted my attention. In approaching it to see what it meant I encountered a circle of slaves singing and chattering like blackbirds as they were, and crowding around a central fire of pine wood. As they sat nearly enveloped in smoke it was difficult to determine whether they were earthly or unearthly spirits. But I soon learned that they came on the same train of cars with the passengers who occupied the "house of entertainment" in which I had attempted in vain to find repose. The master who owned these slaves had taken lodgings under the friendly branches of a pine tree near them, partly from choice and partly from a desire to secure the stability of his "goods and chattels." He saluted me kindly and I found him much inclined to be social. In the course of my conversation with him he informed me that the negroes encamped around the fire which had attracted my attention were slaves whom he had purchased in Virginia, most of whom were females, from fifteen to twenty years of age, and that he was now on his way with them to his plantation in Mississippi. There were some thirty of them, and a merrier or happier circle than they appeared to be I never saw. Their master remarked that he owned a plantation in Mississippi already stocked with three hundred slaves, and as many of them were young men who desired to marry, he had made the purchase of these females in order to accommodate them with wives on his own plantation and thus prevent them from inter-marrying with the slaves of the neighboring plantations. He thought that his project was dictated by sound policy and by due regard for the welfare and happiness of his slaves.

From the River Pedee to Branchville we passed through a region of country more highly cultivated than we had seen during the previous day—a region interspersed with a great variety of timber, and presenting an agreeable interchange of gentle hills and sweeping vales. From Branchville we took the direct route to Charleston by way of the South Carolina Railroad.[5] In this direction we saw cotton fields stretching away on either side as we passed, which were already literally "white unto the harvest."[6] The negroes were at work in the fields, picking cotton, and stowing it in long baskets. They worked in gangs, or companies, men, women, and children, selected and classified according to age and physical ability—each slave being required to pick as many pounds of cotton in a day as his master, or overseer, had prescribed. The task assigned to each is seldom unreasonable, and is generally performed with care and cheerfulness. While at work in the cotton fields, the slaves often sing some wild, simple melody, by way of mutual cheer, which usually ends with a chorus, in which all join with a right hearty good will, in a key so loud as to be heard from one plantation to another, and the welkin is made to ring for miles with musical echoes. Though I could not comprehend the words of the songs or chorus, I concluded that they afforded at least a practical illustration of the sentiment contained in one of our national airs—

Hail Columbia, happy land!

In the vicinity of Charleston the aspect of the country becomes less cheering to the eye, and gives

5. In 1827 the South Carolina Canal and Railroad Company was chartered and by 1833 the track had been completed from Charleston to Hamburg. In 1843 it merged with the Louisville, Cincinnati and Charleston Rail Road Company to become the South Carolina Rail Road Company. In 1899 it became a part of the Southern Railway Company. Samuel Derrick, *Centennial History of South Carolina Railroad* (Columbia, S.C., 1930), pp. 278–81.
6. John 4:35.

but little evidence of cultivation or enterprise. But as you advance, the city, in the distance, presents a bright picture, and looks like a queen seated at the "receipt of customs" by the sea-side, as she really is, with a wreath of palmetto twined on her placid brow. No other city of the South so much resembles a New England city as Charleston. We could hardly persuade ourselves that we were now "strangers" in a Southern city. A Northern man at the South is readily recognized as such, and is usually addressed by the appellation of "stranger." The hotel at which we stopped had but recently been opened to the public, and was truly a magnificent structure. The landlord, who is a perfect gentleman, knew how to do the agreeable in the most unexceptionable manner, and allowed no want to be imagined which was not promptly supplied, at least so far as "creature comforts" were concerned.

In taking a survey of the town, we were particularly struck with the neatness and order which pervades the entire city. Everything in the way of buildings and public improvements displays good taste. Many of the private dwellings are truly elegant, and most of them are furnished with verandahs, which render them cool and pleasant, with shade trees in front. The mercantile business for the most part, appears to be in the hands of men born and bred at the North. The constant application to business required of a merchant in order to succeed is much less a characteristic of the Southern than Northern man.

Charleston is one of the oldest cities in the United States, and yet it wears a youthful appearance. It was founded in 1672,[7] and in early days was known as "Oyster Point." The ground on which it is built is low and level—not more than six or eight feet higher than the waters of the bay. It has been inundated several times in consequence

of violent winds driving the waters of the bay upon its locality. The Battery is a public improvement which does the city great credit, and affords for its citizens a healthful and elegant promenade. It was constructed by filling up with earth and stone a portion of the bay, and cost a mint of money. It commands an extensive view oceanward, and is paved and set with shade trees, and catches the cooling zephyrs that come whispering from the sea. It may be said with propriety that Charleston is a fortified city, it being protected by Fort Moultrie, Castle Pinckney, and Fort Jackson. It is also rich in historical recollections relating to the days of the Revolution, and with which every intelligent American citizen is familiar. Its principal edifices are built of brick; it has many large and beautiful churches, a custom house, city hall, exchange, college, military school, and public library. Its markets are supplied with every luxury which "heart can desire." Its population is about seventy thousand, including all varieties of color.

The women of Charleston are either blonds or brunettes. But to avoid awkward mistakes in regard to brunettes of the pure blood or impure blood, it is said that the city authorities have provided by ordinance that the ladies of "impure blood" shall wear vails over their faces when they appear in the public streets, or in some public places. It is true enough, that some of them are so slightly tinged with an "African sun" as to be easily mistaken for "pure bloods," and hence it is that you will sometimes be surprised to meet with persons of both sexes who, though taken to be white, prove to be slaves.

During our stay we visited "Magnolia Cemetery."[8] It is situated some mile or more from the

7. The first settlement was made in 1670. *South Carolina Guide*, p. 25.

8. Magnolia Cemetery was established in 1850. It was part of a plantation granted to Joseph Pendarvis in 1672. The Vanderhorst tomb of Egyptian-style brownstone may have been designed by Francis D. Lee, Charleston architect. Ibid., p. 299; Beatrice St. Julien Ravenl, *Architects of Charleston* (Charleston, S.C., 1945), p. 223.

city, on low and broken ground, intersected by a winding creek, whose banks are sunny and pleasant. Here and there may be seen a gray old rock, standing erect like a sentinel, within the precincts of this consecrated inclosure, in company with groups of native trees, hung with trailing moss, and looking like gray nuns. The spot seemed indeed a fit abode for those who are called to "rest from their labors," as well as a fit place for the living to indulge in silent meditation. There are several monuments here which are somewhat peculiar in their structure, not only costly, but such as would naturally attract the attention of the most indifferent. The tomb of Mr. Vanderhost resembles a small cottage, having a marble door in front paneled with plates of glass. The other monuments are many of them decidedly unique, yet modeled and finished in excellent taste. Our attention was particularly directed to a beautiful white urn surmounting a natural rock, and on which was inscribed these words—"Our Little Pauline." The idea seemed happily conceived, and the sentiment not more simple than pathetic.

On our return to the city we passed the military school, and saw the young "braves" performing their exercises and evolutions in a style and with an accuracy that would have been creditable to the "regulars."[9] We also caught a glimpse of St. Michael's Church. It has a chime of bells, and was built before the Revolution. In the church-yard we saw the grave of John C. Calhoun, with only a headstone and an urn of flowers to mark the spot.[10] A monument has, since our visit, been erected to his memory. No man of modern times, perhaps, has been more respected as a statesman, or wielded a wider influence in the national councils than John C. Calhoun. His is

> One of the few, the immortal names,
> That were not born to die.[11]

In Charleston almost every thing seems to be just what it should be—a healthful and a mild climate; a place of great wealth, refinement, intelligence; commanding by sea and land an extensive commerce; a city renowned for its beauty, and full of fascinations; and in short, a place where one might wish to live always, nor care to find a more genial spot. Here money is abundant, and virtue its "own reward." Here invalids from the North resort in winter for the benefit of their health, and to enjoy the pleasures of a refined society. It is in this city that you may find the finest specimens of manhood and womanhood—the polished chivalry of the South. In a literary point of view, it is the Athens of the South, and has in fact produced more distinguished orators, poets, novelists, statesmen, and philosophers, than any other Southern city. Here you will find luxury and philosophy associated and regulated by a system of harmonic principles. In leaving the city—the beautiful city—we could not help casting more than "one lingering look behind" of admiration.

9. The Citadel, the military college of South Carolina, was established in Charleston in 1842. *South Carolina Guide*, p. 209.

10. Calhoun is buried in the yard of St. Philip's Episcopal Church. Ibid., p. 203.

11. Fitz-Greene Halleck, *Marco Bozzaris*, st. 6.

Sugar had been made in Louisiana on a small commercial scale before the Louisiana Purchase, but from about 1810 onward its annual production increased rapidly. A commensurate consumption of sugar by the population of the United States developed, and by 1860 the luxury item of earlier times was being consumed at the rate of about forty pounds annually per person. (For a biographical note on T. B. Thorpe, see "Our Visit to Natchez" in A Decade of Nationalism.)

PLANTATIONS OF LOUISIANA

The largest and most important sugar plantations of Louisiana lie, with few exceptions, upon the low lands of the Mississippi and its outlets. The consequence is, that they are beautifully level, and present a different appearance from any other agricultural portion of the Union. The prairies of the West roll like the swells of the sea, but the fields of Louisiana spread out with an evenness of surface that finds no parallel, except in the undisturbed bosom of the inland lake. The soil is rich —it may be said inexhaustible; and vegetation springs from it with a luxuriance that defies comparison:

> A gray deep earth abounds,
> Fat, light; yet when it feels the wounding hoe,
> Rising in clods, which ripening sun and rain
> Resolve to crumbles, yet not pulverize;
> In this the soul of vegetation wakes,
> Pleased at the planter's call to burst on day.[1]

The stranger who for the first time courses the "Father of Waters," at a season of the year when his swelling wave lifts the steamer above the levee-guarded banks, as he looks over and down upon the rich sugar plantations, is filled with amazement, and gets an idea of agricultural wealth and profuseness nowhere else to be witnessed in the world. On every side, the deep green cane-fields spread out in perspective, enlarged to his eye by the ever-retreating lines of the useful plow, that follow their course to the distant forests, which tower up from the swamps, and wave their moss-covered limbs in sullen grandeur, as a contrast to the smiling field, the crowded garden, and the ever busy joy of the agriculturist's home.

One of the most interesting and picturesque portions of Louisiana devoted to the cultivation of sugar, lying off the banks of the Mississippi River, is the country of "the Attakappas."[2] This earthly paradise—for such a name it really deserves—lies west of the Mississippi River, and borders upon the Gulf of Mexico. It would be almost impossible to describe its character, it is so composed of bayous, lakes, rivers, prairies, and impenetrable swamps. To even a large portion of the oldest inhabitants of the State, Attakappas is an unknown region, and so it is destined to remain, except to its immediate inhabitants, if artificial means are not adopted to

Thomas Bangs Thorpe, "Sugar and the Sugar Region of Louisiana," *Harper's New Monthly Magazine* 7 (October 1853): 746–67. Pages 746 through most of 749 are omitted.
1. James Grainger, a Scotch physician, went to the West Indies where he became a sugar planter. He wrote a long treatise in verse about the cultivation of sugar entitled *The Sugar Cane*, which appeared in 1764. *Dictionary of National Biography*, 8:368–70. This verse is from bk. 1, lines 47–52.

2. This area is also known as "Teche Country." It is the region made famous by Longfellow's *Evangeline;* it extends from the south-central part of Louisiana to the Gulf of Mexico. *Louisiana Guide*, p. 312.

facilitate communication. In the spring you can reach the Attakappas in a comfortable steamer; later in the season all direct communication is cut off by the "low water," and you get there, and to all its fruitful adjacent regions, as best you can.

From the mouth of the Bayou Plaquemine, one hundred miles above New Orleans, to a place called Indian Village,[3] a distance of nine miles; the waters of the Mississippi, when they are at their spring flood, pour down with tremendous velocity, and the ingenious navigator descends inland, with his gallant craft stern foremost, the powerful engines being necessary, not to propel, but to act as a drag, by working the wheels up stream, at the same time the boat is going in a contrary direction. A few miles, however, are only passed when the counteracting floods from the sea meet the waters of the Mississippi, and they compromise, by spreading out over the low lands, giving an idea of desolation difficult to imagine by those who have not witnessed the scene. Amidst this waste of waters the steamer pursues its way, sometimes passing through narrow avenues of cypress trees, and then suddenly emerging into vast turbid lakes, the surfaces of which are agitated by flocks of water-fowl, and the ever-vigilant but disgusting-looking alligator, that either floats as a log, or, if too nearly approached, sinks like lead to the depths below. In the course of your voyage, you run across the beautiful sheet of water known as Berwick's Bay,[4] which must have been a sacred place among the aboriginal inhabitants, judging from the mounds, and the remains of rude "Indian temples," that rise from its shores. You change your course, thread innumerable mazes, and in time find your-self upon the Têche[5]—the beautiful and mysterious stream that flows through the Attakappas country, and upon the borders of which are Louisiana's most enchanting scenery and richest sugar farms.

Unlike the Mississippi, the Têche has no levees; its waters never overflow. The stately residences of the planters are surrounded by gardens, the shrubbery of which reaches to the water's edge, and hedges of rose and hawthorn, of lemon and orange, every where meet the ravished eye. Along its shores the magnificent live-oak rears itself in all the pride of vigorous "ancient youth," and gives to the gently undulating landscape, the expression so often witnessed in the lordly parks of England, for the shelving and ever green banks of the Têche seem created rather by art than by nature, and the magnificent lords of the forest are distributed where the taste of Shenstone would have dictated.[6]

Leaving the Têche, you soon come to the broad prairies, over which roam innumerable herds of cattle, and which are also diversified by lakes, their surfaces shaded from the hot sun by the broad-leafed nelumbium,[7] and their depths filled with the choicest fish. Here again is to be seen the live-oak, perhaps in its most commanding form. Rising from the dead level, it towers a seeming mountain of vegetation, and finds a world of room for the extension of its gnarled and shaggy arms. Away off upon the horizon scud the mists of the sea, and the ever complaining surf, alone breaks solitudes even now as primitive as when the red man here held undisputed sway.

3. Bayou Plaquemine flows out of the Mississippi River and was once an outlet of the river. It joins Grand River. Indian Village was the site of a settlement of the Chitimacha Indians. Ibid., pp. 545–46.
4. Berwick's Bay is a widening of the Atchafalaya River. Ibid., p. 392.
5. Bayou Teche in southern Louisiana was the chief avenue of transportation in this area during the early days. The Acadians settled here. It is one of the most fertile areas of the Louisiana sugar region. Ibid., pp. 393–94.
6. William Shenstone, an eighteenth-century English poet, was widely known for his small estate, Leasowes, which he transformed into a miniature showplace that exhibited the newer modes of gardening. Dictionary of National Biography, 18:48–50.
7. A type of water lily.

The pleasant town of Franklin lies upon the Têche,[8] and is the shipping port of the richest sugar parish of the State. Vessels of large size while in the Gulf of Mexico turn aside from the mud-choked mouths of the Mississippi, and floating and cordelling through innumerable bays and bayous, finally work their way into the "interior," and mingle their rigging with the foliage of the forest. Here these argosies, born in the cold regions of the Aroostook, fill their holds with sugar and molasses, and, once freighted, wing their way to the north.

Tradition says that in "old times" (fifty years ago!) a shrewd down-easter found himself hunting for a harbor along the shores of the Gulf of Mexico. His brooms, his soap, candles, onions, and cod-fish were tossed about in uncertainty for days and nights, but, true Yankee-like, he turned his misfortunes to a good account, for, "guided by Providence," he finally found himself after many days in the Têche, surrounded and warmly greeted by a rich agricultural country, teeming with a primitive and unsuspecting population. Here, without a rival, he traded and bargained to his heart's content, exchanging his cargo of "notions" for cotton, fruits, and money; and then bore himself back to the land of "steady habits" a far richer man than when he left it, and the possessor of a secret that gave him the trading monopoly of the land of the Attakappas. For years, his vessel alone continued to visit the Têche, and he increased in wealth and importance beyond all who in his neighborhood "went down to sea in ships;"[9] and it was not until he was about to be gathered to his fathers,[10] that he left to his children and neigh-bors the knowledge of the *secret passes* that led from the sea to the happy land we have so vaguely described.

Running parallel with the Têche are magnificent lakes, that consequently lie upon the rear of the plantations. It is the mists from these inland seas, with those of the rivers, that rise over the sugar cane in winter, and protect it from frosts which in less favored regions destroy the planter's prospects. To the accidental location of a plantation with regard to water, it is often indebted for a comparative exemption from freezing cold. Plantations, sometimes contiguous, will differ essentially in the preservation of cane; on one, it will stand uninjured until the last stalk is cut for the mill; in the other, it will have been blasted by the frost, and rendered almost worthless for the purposes of life.

Upon the large estates of the Têche, having these lakes in their rear, the luxury of bathing is enjoyed in perfection. As may be imagined, the lakes being as clear as crystal, and solid at their bottoms as minute shells can make them, and never dangerously deep near the shore, all become expert in this healthful exercise. We had a lady on a time pointed out to us, whose matronly beauty gave evidence of the once willingly acknowledged belle, who could as gracefully move in the waters of Grand Lake[11] as she once did in the mazes of a dance at the Tuileries. Among her suitors—and she had many—was one fixed up for the occasion, whose age and heartlessness were hidden under artificial appliances, yet whose self-esteem was insufferable. The presumption of this beau piqued our Creole beauty, and while sailing upon the pellucid waters of Grand Lake, the gentleman expatiating upon his disinterested attachment, and his willingness to make ten thousand sacrifices to prove the ardor of his affection—the lady, with her

8. Franklin was founded in 1800 by Guinea Lewis, a Pennsylvanian. Most of the first settlers came from the East and were of English extraction. Probably because of this, the town and parish opposed secession during the Civil War. They submitted to the federal forces early in the war and their town escaped destruction. *Louisiana Guide,* pp. 395–96.

9. Ps. 107:23.   10. A variation of Judg. 2:10.

11. Grand Lake is in south-central Louisiana. The Atchafalaya River flows into it. It was once called Chitimacha Lake. *Louisiana Guide,* p. 427.

tiny foot, struck the plug from the bottom of the skiff, and it slowly began to sink. The astonished lover, with distended eyes, looked into the watery gulf, and thought not of saving his lady-love, but his dress. Down—down went the frail bark, the cause of the mischief apparently an uninterested observer. In another instant the skiff was gone; the beau dissolved into fragments as he touched the water, while the lady, graceful as a naiad, reached the shore; and as she departed in her calash, she made the air musical with her merry laugh.

INDIANS, AND THEIR REMAINS

There are curious ancient traditions about the land of the Attakappas, for the name in the aboriginal tongue signifies "eaters of men." [12] The Indians in this favored land were unquestionably cannibals, and in this were exceptions to all the remaining tribes of the North American continent. In no part of the world could the means of life have been more spontaneous than in Attakappas. As we have already stated, the innumerable streams are crowded with fish, in the fall of the year the air is darkened by a thousand varieties of aquatic fowls, and in early times the prairies, now covered with kine, were then more abundantly supplied with buffaloes. But the old chronicles authenticate the charge, and relate with rare simplicity, of a long-starved, and no doubt naturally lean Frenchman, who fell into the clutches of the Indians, but being unfit for immediate consumption, was put aside, to be fattened for a future feast. In the mean time, he made himself popular and very useful, and not increasing in fat by the cuisine of the cannibals, he was permitted to live, and, an opportunity offering, finally made his escape.

12. Attakappas means "cannibal." The name was applied by the Choctaws to different tribes occupying southwest Louisiana and southern and southeast Texas. Early French travelers reported that these tribes were cannibals. Hodge, *Handbook of American Indians,* 1:114.

The burying-place of the Chatimeches, [13] a neighboring tribe of the Attakappas, is still to be seen upon one of the islets of Grand Lake. Even within the memory of man, there lay undisturbed around the dead the last mementoes of affection deposited by the sorrow-stricken kindred. Earthen pots, cups of various kinds, and the trusty gun, mouldered, untouched in the solitude. There seemed to be departed spirits that still lingered around, to punish the sacrilegious hand; but, alas! the curiosity-hunter and the phrenologist "passed by that way," and the spell was broken, and all that now remains is the *half-completed mound* of the poor Chatimeches. But there can still be seen how those curious monuments of Indian labor were raised—not, it would appear, by rapidity of construction, but in the course of long years and innumerable funeral rites. Upon the ground, within the prescribed circle, were laid the dead of the tribe, as they accumulated from the ravages of disease and the waste of wars. The space completely filled, a thin layer of earth was thrown over the deceased, and in successive years another tier of the dead accumulated, again to be covered with earth, and again to be the resting place of the Indian. In time the mound would be completed, and no doubt was left undisturbed, as the sacred resting place of the bones of the fathers of the tribe. The Chatimeches were cut off in the midst of their work; they have left a monument, the foundations only of which are visible: the only mound perhaps in such a condition that has ever been critically observed by the profane white, as he moves along, consuming nations instead of individuals in his progress, and in his work of destruction not hesitating to disturb the dead.

In digging into the ancient and completed

13. The Chitimachas were first known by the French settlers. They buried their dead in graves; after the flesh had decayed, the bones were taken up and reinterred. No mention of a burial mound has been found. Ibid., p. 286.

mounds, every where to be met with in this particular section of country, there are found the remains of human bones, earthen vessels, and arrow-heads. Here we have a list of the imperishable property of the Indian. Had the Chatimeches mound, that we have alluded to, been finished by its projectors, and a century or two hence opened by some curious persons, there would have been discovered the earthen vessels; and in place of the arrow-heads, the remains of gun-barrels; which would show that the mound was erected by Indians, after they had become acquainted with the white inhabitants of the continent; thus stamping its modern character, when compared with those mounds, that existed long anterior to the discovery of America by European navigators.

PLANTATION LIFE ON THE COAST

Upon the banks of the Mississippi, which are termed by the inhabitants "the coast," may be seen the appliances of plantation life in their perfection. The stately residence rises out from among groves of lemon and orange-trees, of magnolia and live-oaks. Approaching from the front, the walks are guarded by shrubbery of evergreen jessamines, and perpetually blooming flowers. Grouped in the rear, in strange confusion, is a crowd of out-houses; useful as kitchens, store-rooms, baths, with a school-house, and perhaps a chapel. A little farther on is the neat stable of the saddle and carriage-horses, around all of which is drawn the protecting fence, that shuts up the "residence" from the plantation. Passing beyond this magic circle, you find yourself in the broad fields devoted to the cultivation of cane; and, in the distance, you see the village known as the "quarters," formed of a number of one-story cottages, with the more pretending house of the overseer. In the rear of each cottage, surrounded by a rude fence, you find a garden in more or less order, according to the industrious habits of

the proprietor. In all you notice that the "chicken house" seems to be in excellent condition; its inhabitants are thrifty and well-conditioned. Above these humble inclosures, rise many tall poles, with perforated gourds suspended from the top, in which the wren, the martin, and socially-disposed birds, make a home, and gratify the kindly-disposed negro with their melody, their chattering, and their dependence upon him for protection.

But while speaking of the habitations and intelligent beings of the plantation, why should we overlook that companion of man, the dog, that in such extraordinary numbers, finds a home in the parlor, the yard, the cabin, and the fields? As a general thing, the dog in the South occupies an equivocal position, and falls by association into two classes, which may be designated the white and the black. A negro-dog knows his place as well as his owner; and there is a manner and a spirit sometimes displayed by this race toward each other, that is a most painful reflection upon the manners of some of the "lords of the creation." We have seen the "house-dog" surly and overbearing to the "quarter-dog"; the former putting on airs of superiority, and the other submitting, with the best grace possible, to offensive conduct which he dared not resent. That the dogs themselves make a distinction, there can not be a doubt; for one of them adopting a negro for his master, mixes up his fortunes and makes his home with his humble owner. The negroes are fond of dogs, and love their companionship; no litter of "nine blind puppies" was ever ruthlessly thrown into the engulfing stream by the humble African; he has his tradition, characteristic of his heart, that it will bring "bad luck" thus to destroy canine infancy. The youthful planter on his part has likewise a great passion for dogs; and displays it by frequently expending large sums for fancy importations; but excepting deer-hounds, none are really useful or much appreciated. We have seen some few packs tolerably well kept;

but it is too much trouble to keep them up, and game is too plenty in Louisiana to positively need such an expensive organization. We have been much amused when the newly-arrived setter, fresh from the hills and hollows of the North, was turned loose upon the strange alluvial soil of Louisiana, to see with what astonishment the Southern sportsman looked on as he discovered that "Carlo" did not "perform on the instant as well as represented." The poor dog, not yet off his "sea-legs," not acquainted with his masters, not familiarized with any thing, would look about, get confused, be scolded at, and peremptorily ordered to do something, and then take to his heels, his reputation ruined—and we are all familiar with what becomes of a dog with a bad name. The truth is, the Southern planter is too much accustomed to be implicitly obeyed at the word of command, ever to have patience to humor the pets of the Northern sportsman; and the higher breeds of dogs consequently, do not flourish: they degenerate, lose their self-esteem, and become utterly worthless; many, however, with native pride, refuse to go to the "quarters" for protection, and hang on to the skirts of gentility, preferring to be kicked and cuffed in good society, to a savage independence. Mongrel, indeed, are the dogs of a sugar estate; and, as they issue out upon some strange animal that may be passing by, there can be seen curs of every degree, and high-bred dogs of every conceivable price—some useful, some ornamental and many worthless—but all involved in one general cry, all united by one interest.

The stables of a large plantation are among the last things visited: but they are none the less objects of curiosity to the tyro in Southern life. Here are often seen stalls for fifty, and sometimes a hundred mules and horses, arranged with order and an eye to convenience. The vast roof that covers these necessary appendages to a plantation, together with the granary, sheds, and a score or more of useful but scarcely to be recollected structures, form of themselves, a striking picture of prodigal abundance, and suggest the immense outlay of capital necessary to carry on a large sugar plantation with success—But to the sugar-house: the crop has just been gathered; and by the thousand wings of commerce, it has been scattered over the world; the engines of the sugar-house, therefore, are lifeless; its kettles are cold, its storerooms are empty; and the key that opens to its interior hangs up in the master's house, where it will remain until the harvesting and manufacturing of the new crop.

PREPARATORY WORK—
DITCHING, CLEARING

Immediately after the business of one year is closed, and the holidays are at an end, one of the first things attended to, as a commencement of the year's labor, is the clearing out of the ditches, that have become choked up by vegetation in the course of the summer and fall months. The ditches form one of the most important and expensive necessities of a sugar estate; for, with the exception of frost, standing water is the most destructive thing to cane. Rains that fall in torrents in these latitudes, not only have to be guarded against, but also the more insidious and ever-encroaching "transpiration water." To form an idea of what is meant by this term, it must be remembered that the lands on the Mississippi River are protected from annual inundation by embankments known as "levees." In the spring of the year, the Mississippi, as the conductor to the ocean of more than half the running water of the North American continent, rises not only until its banks are full—but would, if left to itself, overflow for a season the whole lower country through which it passes. To remedy this evil, from below New Orleans and up toward the north for hundreds of miles, the river is lined by an embankment, which, in times of flood, confines its waters within its usual channel. These embankments vary from six to twelve feet in height. When the river is full, it will be noticed that there is an inconceivable pressure made by this artificial column upon the water that lies under the soil of the plantations. Consequently, there is a constant percolation up to the surface; and if this were not provided against by the most liberal and scientific method of ditching, although the sun might shine uninterruptedly for weeks, the cane crop would sicken and die, not as we have seen by the descending rains, but by the *ascending* flood that at these particular times literally boils and billows under the earth.

The highest lands upon the Mississippi River are those forming the banks; as you go inland, they gradually sink. In draining a plantation it is customary to cut parallel ditches about two hundred feet apart, from the front to the rear of the plantation, with cross ditches every six hundred feet.[14] This complication of artificial canals requires not only an enormous outlay of capital and occupation of valuable land, but also taxes the scientific engineer to give them their proper levels. In many instances, it is found impossible to accomplish this, and costly draining-machines have to be called into service. The voyager on the Mississippi at the time when the river is "up," will often, in glancing over the fertile fields of the just budding cane, notice, far off in the dark moss-covered swamp, the constantly-puffing steam, that so eloquently speaks of the industry of man. There is erected the steam-engine, that in every revolution tumbles the superabundant water that is running so merrily in the ditches over the *back* levee into the swamp: the waters of which, have, by the unerring laws of nature, found a level with the mighty reservoir of

14. This system of drainage by canals made a great deal more land available for cultivation. Sitterson, *Sugar Country*, p. 113.

the "Father of Waters." The plantations and improvements are now, by many feet, lower than the wall of water that is piled up in their front and rear, and should the frail protection of the levee break, should some intrusive wave, or mischievous eddy, crumble away the rich soil that forms the embankment, the mighty flood that undisturbed or unchecked flows so noiselessly and peacefully along, obeying in its onward course so kindly the gentle checkings of human art—we say, let this flood throw one too many waves over the levee, or force one drop of water too much through its feeble walls, the barrier dissolves away, and the fountains of the great deep seem to be broken up, as they roll undisputed over the country, carrying terror and ruin, with the cry, "*The crevasse! the crevasse!*"

There are plantations on which within a square mile can be found from twenty to thirty miles of ditching. Often the "bayous" of the country are cleared out, and form an important natural adjunct in carrying off the surplus water, but to the labor of man is to be ascribed the making of the most formidable channels; for on some plantations can be seen a regular system of deep and carefully-constructed canals. It may be with truth said, that the industry and capital expended in Louisiana alone, to preserve the State from inundation, have erected works of internal improvement which, united, far surpass in extent, and if concentrated within the vision of a single eye, would be superior in magnificence to the renowned pyramids of Egypt.

This extensive ditching has required the labor of years to accomplish. At first very little was needed, for only the highest lands of the river were cultivated. As plantation after plantation was opened, and the levees increased, this ditching became more important—in fact, the value of the plantation for productiveness depended upon their construction. Where the "plantation force" is large, the negroes do most of this important work, and generally are able to keep all clean when once they are made. But the same hardy and improvident son of Erin that levels mountains at the North, or tunnels through their rocky hearts, that flourishing cities may be built, and railways be constructed, finds his way to the distant South; and with spade and wheelbarrow, is ever ready to move about the rich soil with an energy and ease that finds no rival except in the labors of an earthquake. Dig and delve may the Emeralder among the rocks of the everlasting hills of the North, and the monuments of his industry every where meet the eye; but it is not until the true-hearted Irishman puts his spade into the stoneless soil of lower Louisiana that digging becomes, as it were, ideal, and reaches its perfection. Here the sod and earth come up in the shapes cut by the spade; no envious and resisting pebble, even as large as the imperfect pearl that homes in the oyster, checks its way; all is smooth and glib, as if the digging were in a vast Berkshire cheese.

Never, shall we forget our friend Finigan, who, upon first striking his spade into the rich alluvium, did absolutely, in the course of a few hours, dig himself out of sight, in the very exuberance of his enthusiasm. Finigan is a flourishing man now, and has raised up mementoes in his enterprise that will be as enduring as our State: he has become a "boss contractor" to ditch and levee; and I never see him now without, in spite of his new dignity, thinking of those terrible animals described by geologists, that had their head and feet shaped expressly to burrow in the ground, enabling them to turn up the tap-roots of the might oaks and cedars for food, with all the ease that a gardener would a radish. It was but recently that we met Finigan; he was contemplating a just completed "draining canal" upon one of our largest plantations. This canal was more than a mile long, ten feet deep, and fifteen wide, and could have been no more perfect

in its square sides, even if it had been the product of crystallization. While admiring this stupendous work, Finigan asked us what we thought was the most beautiful thing in nature. While hesitating to reply, he answered his own question by saying he thought a "straight ditch was"; and we could add, if a straight ditch was not the handsomest thing in nature, it is to the planter, at least, one of the most useful things in Louisiana.

While the labor of cleaning out the ditches is going on, which is performed by the most robust of the negroes, another "gang" has been preparing the fields for the plow. When the cane of the "last year's crop" was being cut for the mill, it was stripped of its abundant leaves, and those joints not ripe were cut off. These leaves and cane-tops really form a large proportion of the gross vegetation of the annual product of the soil, and spread out upon the ground, cover it with a thick mat of slowly-decaying vegetation. This "trash" has answered one purpose—it has protected the "stubble," or roots, from the inclement weather of the winter months, but now the spring has come, the danger of frost has passed away, the ground must be prepared for a new crop, and the withering and drying "trash" must be removed from the surface of the soil. Some few planters, distinguished for their success in their pursuits, plant their cane rows ten feet apart, and plow the "trash" under the earth in the centre of the rows, where it is left to decay into a rich compost, to be used at a following spring, but generally it is set on fire as the least troublesome process of getting it out of the way. Of the improvidence of this method of "cleaning up" a cane-field, much has been said; but so long as the present system of cultivation is kept up and the soil shows no immediate injury, so long, we fear, will it be continued.

Of all the preparations that usher in the planting of a new crop, these fires from the burning trash form one of the most picturesque features. Generally lighted at night, the horizon will frequently be illuminated for miles; and as the steamers ply upon the Mississippi, the traveler is struck with the novelty, and with the splendor that every where meets his view. The rolling clouds and the ascending moon are tinged with red, the low landscape assumes mysterious forms, and at every bend in the river some un-thought-of novelty strikes the eye.

PLANTING AND CULTIVATING THE CANE

The ground once cleared of "trash," it is now ready for the plow. A sugar-cane field is sometimes a mile or more in extent, and but for the constant succession of side and cross-ditches, the furrows would run entirely across the field. As it is, they are frequently very long, and made with great precision by the skillful plowman. The field well tilled and harrowed, the furrows are run from six to ten feet apart, according to the notions of the planter. In the furrow, the cane preserved in the "matlays" is laid in two or three parallel lines, and well lapped, so that there will be little danger of not having a "good stand," for it must be remembered that from every joint of the matured cane there comes, if the eye be uninjured, a plant.

The "seed-cane" once deposited in its place, it is covered with earth from three to four inches deep, according to the season; if it is early, and cold may be expected, it is better protected than when the genial sun of spring has already commenced its vivifying influences.

WORKING THE CROP

Nine months from the time that it is planted are required in Louisiana to ripen the cane. Upon its first appearance, it gives indication of strength; there is a dark green about the leaf and a fibrous texture that instantly shows its nature. As it advances in strength, the most careful cultivation is required to keep it free from the weeds that grow so luxuriantly in the surrounding and recently-disturbed soil. Gradually, the once dark and charred fields at a distance, begin to assume a glow of green, and as the cane advances the plow and hoe are used in throwing soil upon the roots to protect them from the heat and drought of the midsummer months, while the leaves are still too delicate to afford a shade.

Difficult, indeed, would it be to give an idea of the labor necessary to complete the crops. The rain and the drought, the cold and the heat, all have to be guarded against. From the time the cane is put in the ground it is the source of constant anxiety. At first slow of growth, the rich soil in which it is hidden, turned up by the plow, revels with rank and quick-growing weeds and grasses, which if not subdued by the most patient industry, would soon choke up and destroy the just planted cane. It is therefore by a repetition of plowing and hoeing from day to day that the tender plant is absolutely nursed;—if it is cold, the earth is placed over the roots to keep them warm; if it rains, and the falling torrent has beaten down the sod, the plow is at hand to break up its compactness; if the water stands in the furrows, they are deepened, that it may run off. At least every two weeks, for nearly half the year, every part of the cane-field is wrought over until it possesses a garden-like neatness that commands the admiration of the person most indifferent to agricultural pursuits. As the season advances, the cane slowly but surely increases in size, and steadily enlarges its leaves, and increases their number, until they cast their own shade about their roots, and thus absorb the whole effects of the life-fostering sun that had previously awakened into existence so many troublesome and noxious weeds; and thus the hand of man becomes daily less and less necessary for the protection of the cane. Soon it takes entire possession of the surrounding earth, and flourishes without a rival in the field.

The Sugar Region of Louisiana

But before this is accomplished who but the interested husbandman can judge of the anxious hours that have been caused by each change of the season, or the varied temperature of the fleeting day? All that was favorable or unfavorable has been noticed, and amid the multiplicity of his cares he feels that—

> The planter's labor in a round revolves;
> Ends with the year, and with the year begins.[15]

But unseen influences are ever at work in the earth and the air to aid him in his pursuits, and at the close of each year he finds, that Providence has rewarded his industry, and that his storehouses are full.

The "growing crop" in Louisiana consists of three kinds of cane: the first is technically called "plant cane," and is that which springs directly from the "seed cane"; the second is called "rattoon," which is the growth from the roots of the previous year's plant cane; the third is called "stubble," which is the growth from the roots of the rattoon cane. In Cuba and the other West India Islands there are but two kinds of growing cane, the plant and the rattoon, for the latter named never becomes "stubble" by degenerating, as in Louisiana.

In going through a cane-field, you can readily discover the different growths. The plant cane is tall and vigorous, and has all the appearance of a new vegetation; the rattoon is more compact in its appearance, the stalk is smaller than that of the plant, there is an evident deterioration; still the joints are juicy and perhaps what they lose in size, they may, in a great degree, make up in the superior strength of their saccharine secretions. The stubble is still smaller, and the stand only indifferently good; it seems to the unsophisticated as if a blight had passed over it. This rapid deterioration of the growth of the cane from the plant to the rattoon,

15. Grainger, *The Sugar Cane*, bk. 3, lines 46–47.

will explain why it is necessary, in Louisiana, that *one-fifth of the crop* be returned to the soil for reproduction, and gives a startling idea of the superior remuneration of the climate of Cuba and the neighboring West India Islands; for in these islands the plant growing almost spontaneously, it is only necessary to manufacture the sugar from the cane juice, the care of cultivation, and providing of seed, being unimportant items. Taking the sugar crop of Louisiana to be three hundred and fifty thousand hogsheads,[16] and each hogshead weighing one thousand pounds, it will be seen that sugar cane is returned to the ground as seed, that would produce the enormous amount of *seventy thousand* hogsheads of sugar; and this is lost to the State by the disadvantages of climate alone, for the soil of Louisiana is superior to any other portion of the world. But for this necessity of replanting, Louisiana would stand unrivaled in the production of sugar. It may be asserted, without fear of contradiction, that only American industry and American ingenuity could have made, under the circumstances, the production of sugar in Louisiana an interest of vast commercial importance.

In the latter part of June, or by the middle of July, the cane has attained a strength and luxuriance that enables it to "take care of itself." The rapidly spreading leaves cast a dark shade upon the ground, that effectually prevents the growth of weeds, and, to use the expressive language of the agriculturist, the crop is "laid by."

PREPARATIONS FOR SUGAR-MAKING

Now commence new and more heterogeneous labors. The mules, worked down by plowing, are turned loose to rest and recover their strength, to meet the heavy work of hauling in the fall, the per-

16. A contemporary report of sugar receipts at New Orleans gives an estimate of 321,931 hogsheads. "New Orleans Produce Receipts," *De Bow's Review* 17 (November 1854): 530.

fected crop to the sugar house. The negroes are divided into "gangs," some to be employed in gathering "fodder," some to secure the crop of corn, now ripe and ready for the granary, some to manufacture bricks, while the sturdier hands are busily employed in cutting wood.

The amount of fuel consumed in the production of sugar is enormous. Three cords are on an average necessary for the manufacture of a hogshead of sugar, of the usual weight of one thousand pounds.[17] Ten years ago, five cords were necessary for the manufacture of a hogshead, but the improvements in the "Setting of kettles" has lessened the number of cords needed nearly one half. This wood will readily sell to the steamboats throughout the sugar region of Louisiana for three dollars per cord, consequently each thousand hogsheads of sugar costs nine thousand dollars in its manufacture for wood alone.

As may be imagined, the primitive forests are rapidly disappearing before this consumption, and already many large plantations are lessened in value because they have little or no timber left upon them. In Cuba, the *bégasse*, or the remains of the cane after it has been ground in the mill, is quite sufficient as fuel to make the crop; but in Louisiana this vegetable matter is destroyed. The *bégasse* is a spongy fibrous mass, composed of the crushed pith and outside covering of the sugar cane. It absorbs water from the atmosphere, and is very difficult to dry. Various ingenious expedients have been resorted to, to make this vast refuse of the crop, as in Cuba, useful for the purposes of fuel, but none, we believe, have been successful. In Cuba and the West India Islands, the dry weather continues for months without the exception of a single wet day; consequently, the *bégasse* is thrown out in the open air, and under a tropical sun soon becomes as dry

as tinder, and burns under the sugar kettles with a vehemence that defies competition. In Louisiana, the climate is damp, and in the fall showery, and the *bégasse*, in the open air, so far from drying, absolutely becomes more incombustible from wet, than when it is first brought from the mill. The necessity of economy in fuel is every where acknowledged, and ingenious men are endeavoring to invent machinery for rapidly drying the *bégasse* by artificial means, so as to render it fit for immediate use; but up to the present time this grand object has not been accomplished, and the *bégasse* still remains a mass of vegetable matter, not only of no use to the planter, but absolutely causing considerable expense in order to get it out of the way.

The various buildings necessary upon every plantation for the manufacture of cane juice into sugar, differ in costlines according to the means of the planter, and the demands of the estate on which they are needed. Generally, they are placed midway between the river and the forests in the rear of the plantation. This is done to divide up as much as possible the distance that must be traversed in hauling the wood from "the swamps," the cane from the fields, and the crop to the river for shipment. Within the last few years the improvements introduced in the appearance of the sugar house are very apparent. Some of them now have, on the outside, quite an imposing appearance.

The introduction of steam engines not only changed the architectural appearance of the sugar house, but, no doubt, saved the sugar crop to the State as an important staple. Under the operation of grinding with horses, portions of the crop are lost, from the imperfect manner in which the cane is ground, and also for want of expedition, for the process is so slow, that before a large crop could be ground, a portion of the cane would be found in the field injured by the frost. There are nearly fifteen hundred sugar plantations in Louisiana,[18] one-

17. It has been estimated that the average mill required twelve to sixteen cords of wood per day or about two or three cords per hogshead. Sitterson, *Sugar Country*, p. 141.

18. According to the census of 1850, there were 1,558 sugar

third of which have "horse-mills," but it is considered profitable to go to the expense of steam, when the produce of the plantation is one hundred hogsheads or upward.

On every plantation the sugar house is one of the most prominent objects. It would be impossible to give a correct idea of the immense amount of money lavished upon these adjuncts to the sugar estate, not only for things acknowledged to be useful and positively necessary, but more particularly for apparatus to be used in the manufacture of the crop. Hundreds of thousands of dollars annually find their way to the coffers of the Northern artisan, in return for his skillful labor in endeavors to improve upon the machinery used in the crystallization of sugar, and so willing are the spirited planters to beautify and adorn their sugar houses, that mills and engines are now erected, that in elaborate workmanship seem rather for ornament than for use. The cheapest sugar house that can be erected, costs at least twelve thousand dollars.[19] Twice that sum will build the house and purchase the machinery for the best class of plantations, that make the common brown or muscavado sugar; such a house as we intend particularly to describe.

Many of the largest plantations in the State are properly "refineries," for they have the means, not only for producing white or refined sugar directly from the cane juice, but occupy a portion of the year in "working over" the brown sugars made on other plantations. Eminent among these large estates is one in the parish of St. James, and the particulars relating to it will not prove, perhaps, uninteresting to the reader.

The tract of land connected with this estate,[20] contains nine thousand acres, one thousand five hundred of which are under cultivation, and divided as follows: eight hundred acres in cane; two hundred and ninety-four acres in corn; one hundred and fifty acres cultivated by the negroes for their own use; ten acres in olives; the remainder of the fifteen hundred acres alluded to as under cultivation, is taken up by potatoes, building lots, pasturage, and gardens; the remainder of the nine thousand acres is in forest, from which is taken the fuel consumed in manufacturing and refining, and the timber for the casks used in packing the sugar for market.

The buildings consist of the proprietor's dwelling and out-houses—twenty-four negro houses with verandahs in front; each cabin is forty feet square, and contains four rooms, and each cabin has a garden and fowl-house attached—a hospital sixty-four feet square containing seven rooms, and an immense verandah—a nursery fifty feet square, store-houses, overseer's or manager's house, stables containing one hundred stalls, two wood houses, each four hundred feet long by one hundred wide, one sugar house five hundred and seventy feet long, by seventy-five feet wide, thirty-four feet high between the floor and ceiling, and a "double sawmill."

The machinery consists of steam saw-mills and pumping-engine at the river for supplying the sugar house with water, steam-engine of eighty horse-power, and sugar-mill for grinding cane, engines, vacuum-pans, and a complete apparatus for making and refining twenty-five thousand pounds of sugar every twenty-four hours direct

plantations in Louisiana. U.S., Bureau of the Census, *Statistical View of the United States . . . being a Compendium of the Seventh Census* (Washington, D.C., 1854), p. 178.
19. A statement issued by the Agricultural Society of Baton Rouge estimated that for the average sugar plantation of 1,200 acres in 1824–1829, the cost of erecting a sugar house would be $22,000. Sitterson, *Sugar Country*, pp. 159–60.

20. St. James Plantation was located sixty-four miles above New Orleans on the Mississippi River. It was owned by James Brown, whose sugar operation was known as the "Paragon Sugar Works." P. A. Champonier, *Statement of the Sugar Crop Made in Louisiana, 1852/1853* (New Orleans, La., 1853), p. 15.

from the cane-juice, and doing this entirely by steam.

The stock upon the plantation consists of sixty-four mules, twelve horses, sixteen oxen, one hundred and forty-five sheep, eighty head of cows and "beeves," two hundred and fifteen slaves—among which are one hundred and seven field hands, two coopers, one blacksmith, two engineers, four carpenters, twenty house-servants, four nurses, eleven old men and women that attend to the stables, and sixty-four children under five years of age.

The cash expenses of this estate are twenty thousand dollars annually, paid to managers, sugar-makers, engineers, and for food and clothing for the negroes, and repairs to machinery and buildings. The weekly rations of each negro are five and a half pounds of mess-pork, best quality, with as much meal and potatoes as they choose to take—in addition to which every one has his pigs and poultry; for all adults have not only the chicken-yard, but also their garden, which they are obliged to cultivate for their own benefit—the surplus of vegetables and poultry being purchased by their master, and paid for in gold and silver, and amounted in the year just past, to one thousand five hundred and sixty dollars—this sum not including the money obtained by the sales of poultry, pigs, eggs, and fruits, to chance customers. In addition still, the negroes annually receive two suits of clothes, two pairs of shoes, a blanket and hat.

The value of the estate of St. James and of its productions for the year 1852, are as follows:

Value of the Estate

Land: 9000 acres at $40	$360,000
Buildings	100,000
Machinery	60,000
Slaves	170,000
Stock	11,000
Total.	$701,000

Productions of the Estate in 1852

Sugar: 1,300,000 lbs., at 6 cts.,	$78,000	
Syrup: 60,000 gallons, at 35 cts.,	21,600	
		99,600
Corn: 9000 barrels for consumption on the estate; wood: 3000 cords for the engine-house. Estimated value	14,400	
Total products of the estate,	$114,000	

This plantation shows the average production of the best class of sugar estates in Louisiana, the largest of which, in 1852, yielded a revenue of one hundred and fifty-two thousand and fifty dollars; but these estates increase the value of their products, by the aid of costly machinery, not used on the ordinary plantations.

And here, it is perhaps pertinent to remark upon the natural dependence of one portion of the Union upon another, as illustrated by the distribution of a large portion of the income of this particular plantation. The bricks and timber of the immense sugar-house, we have noticed, are of home growth and manufacture; but these crude materials form only an unimportant item in the gross expense. The mill, the steam-engines, the complicated vacuum-pans, the bone-black,[21] the wrought iron moulds, the iron of the railway, the mules, the wagons, the carts, the food, the clothing for an army of negroes, and the ten thousand not recollected but expensive items, are all produced at the North and West; and hundreds of families in those distant portions of the country are just as dependent for their living as the planter himself upon the successful cultivation of the sugar-cane crop.

21. Bones or charcoal, used as a decolorizing material in filtering sirups, etc.

The sugar-house, which boils in "open kettles," is the one generally met with throughout the State, and the sugars thus produced are in the most universal use. There can not be a doubt that good brown sugar is sweeter than any other, and that the process which it goes through to deprive it of its dark color also takes from it some of its intrinsic qualities. Some profess to make a distinction between saccharine and sweet; and say that in one sugar the sweet predominates; in another the saccharine. The Chinese make the fanciful distinction of male and female sugar—the former being most saccharine, the latter most sweet. That there is a perceptible difference in the taste of sugars can not be denied; and perhaps it is true that raw or brown sugar is most sweet, and refined sugar the most saccharine. The marked differences in sugar are no doubt owing, in some degree, to the soil and to the season, but more particularly to the consequences resulting from successful and unsuccessful manufacture. The Louisiana planters, beyond any others in the world, have been most successful in crystallizing sugar direct from the cane-juice; and we have therefore, in their method, the most perfect examples that can be given of the primitive, and if you please the natural way of producing sugar.

The preparations for "grinding"—the term generally used when speaking of manufacturing the crop, are the preliminaries of a busy but happy season. The cultivation of the cane, that has consumed the hard labor of nearly a year, has become tedious; and master and servant greet with gratification a change from a severe routine to a rush of work that may be said hourly to yield the most satisfactory evidence of remuneration. The season of harvesting approaches and who does not rejoice? The sugar house is thoroughly examined, and each ramification, or department, undergoes a rigid scrutiny. The kettles, it is discovered at the eleventh hour, need many repairs in their setting; the engine wants several screws, the mill is out of order; the coolers have opened their seams; the purgery [22] wants cementing; the hogsheads are not all made; and the poor planter finds that the work of the leisure hours of summer is now crowded into a few already too much occupied days. Every thing is hurry and bustle; and the negroes, suddenly rising in importance by the multifarious demands made upon them, seem to shine with an extra polish as they pursue their allotted tasks. The day "to begin" has been named, but it is deferred to another "set time" that proves to be inconvenient, because the cane-wagons are not ready, and the harness needs repairs; and so continues a chapter of annoyances which is only by extra exertion brought to an end.

And now may be seen the field-hands, armed with huge knives, entering the harvest field. The cane is in the perfection of its beauty, and snaps and rattles its wiry-textured leaves, as if they were ribbons, and towers over the head of the overseer as he rides between the rows on his good-sized horse. Suddenly you perceive an unusual motion among the foliage—a crackling noise, a blow—and the long rows of growing vegetation are broken, and every moment it disappears under the operation of the knife. The cane is stripped by the negroes of its leaves, decapitated of its unripe joints, and cut off from the root with a rapidity of execution that is almost marvelous. The stalks lie scattered along on the ground, soon to be gathered up and placed in the cane-wagons which, with their four gigantic mule-teams, have just come rattling on to the scene of action with a noise and manner that would do honor to a park of flying artillery.

We have already alluded to the fact that the sugar crop has to be gathered in Louisiana within ninety

22. The part of a sugar house where molasses was drained from sugar.

510

The Sugar Region of Louisiana

days, or else it will be destroyed by the cold; as a consequence, from the moment the first blow is struck, every thing is inspired with energy. The teams, the negroes, the vegetation, the very air, in fact, that has been for months dragging out a quiescent existence, as if the only object of life was to consume time, now start as if touched by fire. The negro becomes supple, the mules throw up their heads and paw the earth with impatience, the sluggish air frolics in swift currents and threatening storms, while the once silent sugar house is open, windows and doors. The carrier shed is full of children and women, the tall chimneys are belching out smoke, and the huge engine, as if waking from a benumbing nap, has stretched out its long arms, given one long-drawn respiration, and is alive.

In the mean while the cut cane is accumulated in the carrier shed; it rises up in huge masses on every side. Enough "to commence" is obtained, and the steam-pipe whistles shrilly, the lumbering carrier moves, the cane is tumbled between the rollers and ground up, its saccharine juice in breaking jets merrily into the receiver. The furnace fires now send forth a cloud of smoke, and by the time night sets in the sugar house is literally in a blaze.

> While flame the chimneys, while the coppers foam,
> How blithe, how jocund, the plantation smiles.[23]

The planter now becomes indifferent to sleep or rest, and often spends a large portion of the night in visiting the different departments of the busy scene, noticing the working of the engine and the mill, but more particularly he hangs over the kettles, to see what the newly-expressed juice promises. As is always the case with that from cane first cut from the fields, it yields only indifferently well, and it seems as if a "strike" would never be made.[24]

The "taking off the crop" has now fairly commenced, and for sixty or ninety days all is hurry and bustle. From morn to night, and night to morn, the unfeeling and powerful steam engine seems to drag along with its untiring industry all within its influence, and the man and beast must be alike insensible to fatigue. Strange as it may appear, under this severe tax every thing thrives; there is something about the season, the peculiar labor, and the constant indulgence in eating the juice of the cane, that produces unwonted health, and consequently the highest flow of animal spirits. But the planter is not exempt from his misfortunes, and they seem sometimes to accumulate at this critical period. The sugar maker does not succeed in producing "the staple" of a favorite color and proper grain; an unusual quantity of cane passes through the rollers for the amount of sugar known to be in the coolers. Frequently the immense pressure brought upon the mill breaks it asunder, and as there is no place nearer than New Orleans in which to get repairs, a delay is the consequence, harassing in the extreme. The "invalid roller" is tumbled down to the levee, and as the regular "coasting packet" comes along, the experienced eye of the captain detects, by the anxious group ashore, that something has gone wrong at the sugar house. There are the negroes rushing up and down, hallooing and waving their arms for signals, long after the announcement is made that the boat will make the landing. Then the planter, with his working clothes on, paces up and down the levee, his hands thrust in his pockets, his mouth grim while he speculates upon his extraordinary "bad, bad luck," when compared with his neighbors and "the rest of mankind."

But the sugar house has other scenes: frequently there are pleasant apartments fitted up for "the

23. Grainger, *The Sugar Cane*, bk. 3, lines 413–14.
24. A "strike" was made when the juice reached the temperature required for crystallization. Sitterson, *Sugar Country*, p. 133.

family," and the socialities of life are displayed in the most delightful manner; the amenities of high civilization and out-door living blend in beautiful harmony. Here, amid the bustle, the family meal is taken, and every appetite is increased by the bracing air of a Southern winter. The invalid, white or black, that has long been confined to the sick bed, hastens to the sugar house, and in the rarefied air and sweetened steam that pervades a portion of the building, finds a balm for the pains in the chest, and a relief to the distressing cough. The bloom of health not only deepens upon those who already possess it, but revives upon the faded cheek.

The healthful influence of the "boiling season" upon the sick and debilitated of the sugar plantation, and the invigorating qualities of the cane juice upon all who drink it from the kettles, or extract it themselves from the plant, has often been noticed and taken advantage of. Grainger, the rural poet of Basseterre, near a century ago, thus apostrophizes:

> While flows the juice mellifluent from the cane,
> Grudge not, my friend, to let thy slaves, each morn,
> But chief the sick and young at setting day,
> Themselves regale with oft-repeated draughts
> Of tepid nectar; so shall health and strength
> Confirm thy negroes, and make labor light.[25]

As the medicinal qualities of the steam arising from the sugar kettles, and the use of the hot syrup as a drink for invalids, are beginning to attract the speculative attention of some eminent practitioners, we should perhaps be remiss if we did not mention a favorite sugar house beverage, very much in demand by those who, from all external appearance, seem to be any thing but victims of pulmonary complaints. A tumbler of cane juice, partially boiled down to the crystallizing point, is well "tempered with French brandy"—such is the

25. Grainger, *The Sugar Cane*, bk. 3, lines 407–12.

term used—and drank with great precipitation, and is generally not considered unnecessary or unpalatable by gentlemen visitors. There are some persons, however, who are obliged to add to this novel libation some of the acid from the innumerable sour oranges that load the trees in the neighborhood of the sugar house. Persons who are good judges have pronounced this mixture as being nothing more or less than "hot punch," but as it is never drank under that irreverent name, but is called "drinking hot syrup," we prefer to use the technical term, and rest satisfied with the popular ignorance of what it is, beyond what its name implies.

To the children, "sugar rolling" is composed of halcyon days. The little masters and misses, including those of every conceivable age, revel among the sweets, as bees buried in honeysuckles; along with them follow a train of every imaginable sized "little niggers," that dabble in and devour the sugar and syrup, until they are literally loaded inside and out.

The interior of a sugar house can be properly divided into the "cooler room," the "purgery," the place for the kettles, and the mill. These differently named places and things are all connected together, so that the cane juice from the mill runs through provided gutters into the receiver that supplies the kettles; the cane juice, by the power of heat brought to the point of crystallization, is thrown into the "coolers," from which coolers it is removed into the "purgery," where it is, as sugar, placed in hogsheads, and allowed to drain of its molasses, or imperfectly crystallized cane juice; from the "purgery" it comes out the article of commerce and domestic use so familiar to all.

The "coolers" are troughs from ten to twelve feet in length, a foot and a half deep, and four feet wide. They are arranged in lines parallel to each other, yet wide enough apart to admit of a laborer going between them. These coolers hold, when conveniently full, from a hogshead to a hogshead and a half of sugar.

The "purgery" consists of a long room, generally one of the wings of the sugar house, at the bottom of which, in the place of a floor, is a hydraulic cement cistern, about four feet deep. Over this cistern are laid strong timbers, on which the hogsheads rest when they are being filled from the coolers. At the bottom of the hogsheads are holes, out of which the molasses drains into the cistern.

The mill used in grinding sugar cane consists generally of three iron rollers, of two feet and a half in diameter and five feet in length. They are placed about five-sixteenths of an inch apart, and are capable of sustaining an immense outward pressure as the cane passes between them. A stalk of sugar cane is heavy and compact, and has a great deal of strong vegetable conformation about it, but let it pass between the rollers of the mill, and it comes out crushed into fragments—literally ground into dust and ribbons. The mill is placed at some considerable height from the ground, so that the expressed cane juice, as it flows from it, will readily run down to the kettles.

Attached to the mill is an ingenious contrivance known as the "carrier." This consists of a never-ending band, about three feet wide, made of chains and cross bars of wood, that runs upon rollers, and is used to bring the cane from the outside of the building up and into the mill. The carrier generally reaches a considerable length beyond the walls of the sugar house, and, as the grinding goes on, is fed with cane by the women and children appointed for that purpose. The primitive method of supplying the mill with cane was for the negroes to "carry" it by armfuls, which is still the general custom in Cuba, and in the West India Islands. But on the introduction of steam, power was easily obtained, and machinery was soon brought to relieve the laborer of this then most unpleasant duty. Now the cane is placed upon the carrier, at a long distance from the mill; it is arranged in parallel lines, as upon a table, and moves quietly to its place of destination. The steam engine, that is the motive power of this machinery, is too familiar to need a notice from us.

A "set of kettles" consists of five deep evaporating cast or wrought iron kettles, arranged in solid masonry, so that they set in a line, with their tops all upon the same level. Underneath these kettles is a furnace, the mouth of which is outside of the building. The furnace is so arranged that the flame from the burning wood passes, in its progress to the chimney, under each kettle. Sugar makers have given to these several kettles distinct names, as follows: the *batterie*, the *sirop*, the *flambeau*, the *propre*, the *grande*. Each of these boilers enlarges progressively, from the *batterie* to the *grande*.

As the sugar cane juice flows from the mill, it runs into a large wooden reservoir, that connects by a cock with the *grande*. At the commencement of making sugar, every kettle is filled with juice, the fire in the mean time has been lighted, and it soon gives out an intense heat. The concentration of flame is under the *batterie*, for this kettle is situated directly over the mouth of the furnace. As soon as the juice begins to boil, there rises to the top a vast amount of woody fibre, and other foreign substances, not before observable, and the attendants commence, with a large wooden sword, to sweep off the scum of the kettles, from the *batterie* toward the *grande*. In this way, the whole line is purified. As might be presumed, evaporation takes place most rapidly at the *batterie;* consequently, while the dirt that gathers on the top of the foaming kettles is swept by the sword to the *right*, the ladle is used to bring the concentrating juice to the *left*, so as to keep every kettle full. Directly over the boiling kettles is what is termed the steam chimney, through which passes the vapor that rises from the rapidly evaporating cane juice. As can be readily

perceived, the concentrating of the saccharine liquid by heat, requires that the several kettles should be constantly replenished, and it is done as follows: the mill fills the reservoir, the reservoir the *grande*, the grand the *propre*, and so on, the liquor passing from one kettle to another, until the *batterie* receives the concentrated juice of three or four charges of the *grande*, after it had passed necessarily through all the named vessels of the entire "set," and had been "tempered" and "skimmed" as much as the process would permit.

At the *batterie* stands the "sugar maker," the important functionary, for the time being, of the sugar plantation. His commands, be he as black as midnight, are attended to with an unquestioning punctuality that shows how much is dependent upon his skill. We have gone through the details of the labor necessary to perfect the crop, and given a vague idea of the immense amount expended, and the care and exhaustion of the mind suffered, to reach the culminating point; and now every thing is in the hands of the sugar maker; upon his experience and knowledge depends in a great degree, the commercial value of the crop.

No tyro can fathom the mysterious wisdom of the sugar maker's mind. He looks into the *batterie*, but sees more than is accorded to the vision of the uninitiated. The dark tumbling mass of liquid sweet, appeals to his judgment in every throe it heaves from its bosom; a large and ominous bubble will perhaps fill him with dismay; if the mass settles down into quietude, he will yell frantically to the old Argus at the furnace, to "throw in more wood"; perhaps the liquid will then dance and frolic, and whiten and coquette, and then comes over the face of the sugar maker a grim smile of satisfaction, as he, with his wooden spatula, beats down and breaks the bubbles, that might otherwise rise too high. Now also the sugar maker observes the syrup as it cools upon his ladle, and also sees if it will string into threads, for the critical moment is approaching, the "strike" is at hand.

We forgot to say that at the head of the sugar kettles, there was a square box that communicates by movable troughs with all the coolers. The moment the contents of the *batterie* indicate that it must soon be thrown off, which cooler is to receive it is decided upon and arrangements are made accordingly.

The sugar maker, now armed with an immense ladle, fastened on the end of a long handle, holds it suspended over the *batterie;* the sugar maker's assistant, likewise prepared, holds his ladle over the *sirop*, or second kettle. The moment the *strike* is ready, the sugar maker's object is to get the liquid as quickly as possible out of the *batterie*. Over he throws it into the adjoining box, and as it lessens in the heated kettle, it boils more and more furiously; he ladles on nevertheless, with insane zeal until his assistant, seeing what remains in the *batterie* would be destroyed by the glowing heat, tumbles over the displaced quantity from the *sirop*, which is in turn replenished from the *flambeau*, the *flambeau* from the *propre*, the *propre* from the *grande*, and the *grande* from the juice boxes or receivers connected with the mill, and then the work goes on to complete another "strike."

The hot liquor from the *batterie* has, in the mean time, pursued its way along the troughs, and distributed itself over the cooler, where, presenting a large surface to the surrounding air, you can see it crystallizing under your gaze, and taking upon itself the familiar form of brown or muscovado sugar.

At stated times the *coolers* are emptied of their contents; stout negroes are appointed to do what is termed, "potting the sugar," which means, carrying it to the hogsheads, which are, as we have already stated, setting upon timbers over the *purgery*. The contents of the coolers form a mass, more or less a mixture of sugar and molasses. If you strike a spade into the centre of a well filled cooler, and remove a portion of its contents, you will see the opening gradually fill up with a rich fluid, that seems to exude from every part of the wounded mass; this fluid is denominated the *bleedings*, and contains, no doubt, much of the imperfectly crystallized sugar, that never finds its way into the molasses. The sugar thrown into the hogsheads, settles down, and becomes thoroughly cool. If the weather in which it has been made was favorable, and the cane was thoroughly ripe, very little drainage, comparatively, takes place; but if the cane were green, the sugar maker inexperienced, or the plant the least touched with frost, these sad truths can be learned by the increasing volume of molasses that is found in the cisterns of the *purgery*, and the planter, in the bitterness of his heart, finds out that he is making an immense amount of molasses, when his energies have been directed only to produce a crop of sugar.

To remedy the defects of sugar making, has called into action the first order of minds, and consumed an almost unlimited amount of money. There are no less than eight different methods of sugar making by machinery, carried on in Louisiana, the object of each of which seems to be, to procure the product without the adulteration or mixture with any foreign substance. The method of sugar making that we have described is the simplest and the most primitive, it is really, simply boiling the juice of the cane down, until all the water in it is evaporated, and then letting it *cool* into sugar. But it is noticeable, that the manner is necessarily very imperfect. The moment that the cane juice has been brought by heat to the point of granulation, it should instantly be transferred to the *coolers*. The most expert sugar maker can not always judge of the exact moment when he should *strike*, and under all circumstances he must commence "throwing off," with the full assurance that

the syrup will be unequally done, for that which is taken from the *batterie* in the commencement of the strike, must be less affected with heat, than that which is taken at its end. Some of the syrup will be at the crystallizing point, some of it burnt, and some in its raw state. Here, then, we find the causes of the brown color of the sugar, and why molasses also is produced.

Chemists and machinists have exhausted their skill, to find out the way to turn cane juice into pure sugar, unalloyed with any other substance. They have endeavored to avoid burning the sugar by evaporating the juice with steam, and by the use of vacuum pans, so that the heat used could be scientifically regulated, the great desideratum being to work up the cane juice into sugar of a pure quality, without loss by imperfect crystallization, as exhibited in inferior sugar and in the production of molasses.

The importance of this can hardly be realized by any one but the producer. A slight difference in the color of sugar, or in the size of the crystals will make thousands of dollars difference in the value of a large crop. Sugar that sells for sixty dollars the hogshead, entails no more expense upon the planter than that which brings him in half that sum; consequently, the "high-priced" sugar costs for freight and packing, just half as much as the inferior article; while the advance of a cent on a pound upon a crop of sugar, may cause a princely return to the planter for his year's labor; or the deduction of a cent on a pound, a trivial sum, when divided among the consumers, may be to the planter the cause of his pecuniary ruin.

With the inducements held out to improve the quality of sugar, it is no wonder that so much money is expended in the purchase of costly machinery. Still, the old-fashioned "open-kettle" method that we have endeavored to describe, maintains its popularity, in spite of the evident waste that attends it. Machinery of the proper kind is difficult to obtain, and the almost human sensibility it displays in its liability to be deranged, causes disappointment and frequent loss, and satisfies the planter that complicated machinery can only be used with advantage in connection with an enormous outlay of capital, and with appliances not always at his command. The great mass of labor that is expended in making sugar is performed by negroes; and only the simplest and most physical methods are with safety intrusted to their care.

As the manufacturing of the crop progresses, the waving cane in the fields continues to ripen, the increasing cold stops the circulation of the sap, and checking the growth of the plant, the juices are perceptibly enriched in a night. Often, indeed, on favorable days, you can break the cane; and as the juice flows down the stalk, you can see it granulate before your eyes, without the aid of any evaporation, except such as comes from the surrounding air. The influence of cold in enriching the sap of plants is observable not only in the cane, but in the sugar-maple trees of the North; for, with them a warm "unseasonable" day ruins the sap, and turns it into a nauseous, valueless fluid; but let the wind chop round to the north, and even while the sap flows it will change, and become rich and valuable for the wants of man. To the planter, in the "grinding season," the fear of the frost and of excessive heat, keeps him in a state of constant anxiety. A warm sun is destructive; a freeze, ruinous.

As soon as the perfected sugar begins to accumulate in the *purgery*, the "sugar broker," armed with a huge auger, makes his appearance on the plantation, and is always welcomed as a guest, if not always popular as a business man. The sugar broker is the antipodes of the planter: one has an interest in high prices, the other in low prices; one is domestic, the other foreign; one is always in haste, the other has unappreciated quantities of spare time. The sugar broker carries with him a mysterious face, and affects to know something about the markets that can not be divulged without agitating the commercial world; he also insinuates to the planter that he has information about the unusual amount of the "coming crop," that renders it very important that the producer should "take advantage of the present ruling prices." The sugar broker is also a singular evidence of the natural incapacity some people have of discovering light-colored sugars; for with the broker they are always dark, if he is purchasing; and he never *can* see a light-colored sugar except when he has it to sell. The sugar broker generally brings the news of the day to the residents of the plantation, and becomes very popular, if he can make himself agreeable at all. A little experience makes you acquainted with the sugar broker; he is peculiar; and if it were not for the fact that he wields such an important influence in the sale of the crop, every body would be amused at his awkward manner of riding, his "on 'Change" look, his city habits, and his bustling manners, which contrast so strangely with the quiet demeanor of the planter.

The novelty of sugar making in time passes away, and the whole affair assumes a business sameness. Each person, by experience becomes familiar with his duty, and things go on with tolerable smoothness. The "planter's family" has moved permanently back to the mansion; and the ladies seldom visit the sugar house, except to accompany visitors, or for the purpose of healthful exercise. The mules are now pretty well "worked down" in hauling the cane from the fields; the negroes are calculating when will come "the finish," and as January approaches the weather becomes unsettled, the rains fall, and the roads are "cut up." And the "last load" of cane, as it is carried to the mill, is greeted with satisfaction; and already hope pictures new pleasures that are to be enjoyed in the time consumed in the production of the "next crop."

HOLIDAY FESTIVITIES

At the close of the year's labor are the holidays, which extend from Christmas to New Year. The negroes now enjoy uninterrupted repose; or rather, have the liberty of indulging their caprices, so long as they are harmless to themselves and others, free from constraint. It is the season of enjoyment and festivity, and the time for settling up their outstanding accounts with each other, and the master and mistress of the plantation. The long running account for chickens, eggs, and vegetables, is liquidated by the good housewife; and the master pays for innumerable things, which have been provided by the slave, without interfering with his accustomed labors. Now it is that crates of cheap crockery and bales of gaily colored handkerchiefs find a ready sale; and the peddlers that infest "the coast" reap a rich harvest, by selling at large profits ribbons and nick-nacks, that have no other recommendation than the possession of staring colors in the most glaring contrasts. Balls have become the order of the day, and the business of the night; and the humble Paganini of the quarters is called into requisition, and elevated into a person of temporary, but still extraordinary importance—because he is master of the violin; while the negroes—

> Responsive to the sound, head, feet, and frame
> Move awkwardly harmonious; hand in hand
> Now lock'd, the gay troop circularly wheels,
> And frisks and capers with intemperate joy.
> Halts the vast circle, all clap hands and sing;
> While those distinguished for heels and air,
> Bound in the centre, and fantastic twine.
> Meanwhile, some stripling from the choral ring,
> Trips forth, and, not ungallantly, bestows
> On her who nimblest hath the green sward beat
> And whose flash'd beauties have enthralled his soul,
> A silver token of his fond applause.[26]

The planter and his family have too their trysting time. The mother and her comely daughters hie to the city of New Orleans, in pursuit of the innocent amusements of the season; and the "Crescent City," at these times, shows a perceptible filling up of joyous, familiar, and Southern-looking faces. The fashionable dry goods and jewelry stores, the Opera, and the "society balls" all feel the genial influence of these holiday times, and it only gradually disappears as the summer heat sets in, and drives residents of the country back to their rural homes.

CONCLUSION

The State of Louisiana produces over three hundred and fifty thousand hogsheads of sugar, of one thousand pounds each, about half of the amount of sugar consumed by the people of the entire Union. By referring to the map, it will be seen, that but a small portion of the cane-producing lands of the State is under cultivation. There can not be a doubt that the time will come, when the importation of foreign sugars into the United States should cease, and that the immense amount of money now sent abroad for this necessary of life, will be distributed among our own people.

Gradually the sugar made in Louisiana passes into "second hands"; the greater portion of it finds its way to New Orleans, from which mart it is distributed over the Northern and Eastern States. But vast quantities are annually sent direct from the plantations, to supply the increasing demand of the "giant West," and long before the spring has come, the contents of the cane fields of Louisiana are widely scattered over the "broad Union," and enter largely into almost every article of consumption that forms a prominent or insignificant object of the social board; it sparkles upon the bridal cake; assumes a thousand forms in the confectioner's

26. Ibid., bk. 4, lines 585–96.

window; neutralizes the acidity or bitterness of medicine; gives life to the fragrant coffee and tea; destroys the unpurified taste of preserved meats; and retains for years the delicate flavor of our choicest fruits; turn, indeed, which way you will, you perceive the ameliorating influence of sugar upon the economy of life, and thanks to the genius and enterprise of the Louisiana planter, it is raised upon our own soil, and at a price that brings it within the command of the rich and poor alike.

VIRGINIA COUNTRY LIFE

George P. R. James (1801–1860), a British novelist with a prolific pen, enjoyed great popularity in the United States. He came to America in 1850 and from 1852 to 1858 served as British consul in Virginia, during which time he maintained an acquaintance with many leading literary figures.[1]

PLANTATION LIFE

Hospitality, in one shape or another, is spread over the whole United States; but its form varies much, according, I believe, to the different races from which the adjacent population sprung. In great cities, indeed, there cannot be much true hospitality shown by any citizen, unless he be enormously wealthy, or one of those benevolent persons who loves to entertain the pertinaceous *dropper-in at dinner-time*. It is a curious thing that the near proximity of human beings, like the approach of the reverse ends of magnets, produces repulsion and not attraction; but so it is. The country is the only real scene of hospitality, and this is very general, I might say universal, throughout these States. In the North, peopled principally by the descendants of the old Lollards after they had gone through the phase of Puritanism, it is a more square and angular virtue, sometimes impinging a little upon other people's rounds and curves. But still, from Maine to Connecticut, I suppose there are few men who would refuse some entertainment to the weary wayfarer. In the far West there is not a cabin where, as long as there was a place left upon the floor, the traveller might not lie down to rest, and be welcome to a meal, if it were to be had.

The Virginians, sprung for the most part from the old Cavaliers, retain the more frank and profuse spirit of their race. They will in general eat with you, drink with you, fight with you, or let you do the same with them, without the slightest ceremony. To them hospitality seems a mere matter of course. There is no ostentation about it, no parade. Every now and then there may be a formal dinner-party, it is true; and it is possible, nay, I think it is likely, that every one at the board feels himself more or less uncomfortable at a certain degree of ceremonious restraint. But the usual course is quite different. In every well-to-do planter's house there is a dinner provided for the family, which may consist of five or six. Now, in this quarter of the world, what will do for five or six will do for five or six and thirty, and there will be no want. There is always *plenty*, though perhaps we could not add *no waste*. There is a lavish abundance, which in some degree smacks of the olden time in the green island,

George P. R. James, "Virginia Country Life," *Knickerbocker Magazine* 52 (September 1858): 269–82.
1. *Dictionary of National Biography*, 10:646–47.

and still farther back was not unknown in England. The day's round is simply this: all rise early; then, in most families, come prayers; then the ample breakfast, to which the household drop in one by one, as it suits them; and then the separation to various pursuits, according to the various seasons of the year. The studious man takes up his book; the sporting man shoulders his gun; the mistress of the house seeks her basket of keys, and puts her household in order; the master or his sons go out to see that the blessed labors of the plough or the hoe are not neglected by the servants in the field; the daughters have the piano or the song. About, or rather after noon, the visitors begin to drop in—sometimes neighbors and intimate friends, sometimes strangers with letters in their hands. Then comes the universal "Will you not stay to dine? Of course you are going to remain the night." It is to be remarked that Virginia houses and Virginia tables are all made of india-rubber, and stretch to any extent. I speak of course of the country, where you are not "cabined, cribbed, confined" by strange masses of brick and mortar.

The walk, the ride, the book, are often varied, it is true, by special business or amusement. It may be a fox-hunt; it may be a drill of volunteers; it may be a public meeting; for Virginians, God save the mark! are not free from the curse of politics, or the drudgery of self-imposed and often infructuous functions. Beside, I think there are some six or seven hundred elections in the year, from watchmen up to Governors, where few men of public spirit would fail to exercise the inalienable rights of American citizens, even were their devotion to cost their health, wealth, and repose. If some wise person had not devised the plan of putting a dozen or two of candidates for various offices upon a party ticket, the poor citizens would have had nothing to do all their lives but to *elect*.

There is no lack of amusement, however, in a Virginian country house. Many, indeed most of the country gentlemen are well read, though not profoundly learned; and the character of the popular mind, discursive and expatiating, renders conversation lively and interesting. There is, beyond doubt, a fondness for abstraction, but it is by no means carried to the extent which some of their Northern fellow-citizens impute to the people of this State; and one great blessing is, that we never find that tendency lead to discussion of *free grace and predestination.*[2]

Thus, in easy toil and pleasant amusement pass the hours of summer day-light. The autumn—the finest but least healthy season of the year—has also its enjoyments. More exercise can be then taken, either on horse-back or on foot, and life runs as smoothly on the large plantations as it does in any country of the earth. True, the intense heat of the summer, musquitoes, and every winged pest that lives, detract a little, especially from the enjoyment of foreigners; and sometimes, toward night, a little dulness comes upon the march of Time. But then, for the gentlemen, at least, and sometimes for the ladies also, come the 'coon-hunt or the 'possum-hunt. Both must be pursued at night, and are full of sport. For the latter, the party must set out in the early darkness. Dogs, gentlemen, negroes, all assemble at the house or near it, and then forth they issue to the spots most frequented by the cunning vermin. On they go upon the darkling path, till suddenly the sharp eyes or sharp scent of the dogs discover the night-wanderer, and they rush after him, tracking every step. The opossum does not usually run far, but betakes himself speedily to the first little tree he meets with, after he has found out that he is pursued. Up he goes to some thin branch above, and clings, well satisfied to think that his four-footed enemies cannot come after him; but there are the cunning bipeds too upon his trail. He is besieged in his fortress; the little tree is either

2. Theological doctrines of the Calvinist tradition.

bent down to the ground, so shaken that he can hold no longer, or cut down by the blows of an axe. Down flounders Master 'Possum, and lies quite still, as if he were killed by the fall: not a sign of life in him—hands, feet, tail, all still—on his back, on his side, just as he fell. But he is only "playing 'possum"; and the negro gourmand or experienced hunter knows the trick right well, and they soon carry him off to grace the spit the following day.

The raccoon hunt is pursued in much the same manner; but good *coon-dogs* are indispensable, and the chase takes place in the early morning. More active and more game, he gives more sport, runs faster and farther, and when brought down from his tree, shows fight, to the detriment of his canine, and sometimes his human pursuers. But 'Coon's fate and 'Possum's are both the same in the end, and the skin is the trophy of the victory.

But a Virginia marriage is perhaps the highest exemplification of the country life in this State. Form, ceremony, are abandoned, though many a good old custom still prevails. Friends, relatives pour in from all quarters: no regard is had to the size of the house or the sort of accommodation. Abundance of every thing is found, and if there be a defect, it is never noticed in the universal hilarity that prevails. Nor are the rejoicings restrained to one day! I have known them last the week, and the whole bridal party cross a broad river to renew on the other side of the water the merriment of the preceding wedding day, with some distant friend or relation.

But enough of plantation life. We need only pause to remark that there is a class of smaller planters, who represent the sturdy yeomanry of England, from whom, in all probability, they spring, as happy probably as their richer neighbors, not so learned, but endowed with that good, hard common-sense which is the best every-day wear in the world. They have competence and ease, if not wealth, and most of them feel with the merry

statesman who exclaimed: "Give me the *otium*, hang the *dignitate*."[3]

There is another phase of Virginia country life, where we do not have *rus in urbe*,[4] but rather where the town finds its way into the country. Let us call this, Village Life. At some particular spot, the crossing of two or three roads, a rail-road depot, the passage of a river, or the neighborhood of a tavern, the solitary house takes unto itself a companion; another and another follow. Then must come a store, generally furnished with a vast variety of heterogeneous articles, such as hard cider and buttons, tape and butter, bacon and pins, to say nothing of needles, thread, and calico. Moreover, there is a little store of the most commonly-used medicines: tincture of ginger, hive syrup, and castor oil, a good deal of laudanum, and a barrel of whiskey. But in the constant mutations of this transitory world, the store is found wanting in some respect for the needs or caprice of the neighbors. Mrs. Perkins declares that she never can get any thing she wants at the store: "Really, Mr. Catskin, who keeps it, should be better supplied." In the end, down comes a rival to Mr. Catskin—"a nice young man, just married." He builds himself a house; and the new store is greatly patronized, especially if "the nice young man, just married," adds the faculty of preaching to that of selling bobbin and other dry-goods. The place becomes popular; more dwellings are added; the tavern grows into a hotel; a bar-room gives the opportunity and inducement to drunkenness; a row or two takes place; and the magnates of the village meet together, and consult as to what is to be done. They are not at all ambitious: they would prefer being in the village condition still; but they are becoming populous; there are at least a hundred

3. The quotation is derived from the phrase *otium cum dignitate*, "leisure with dignity"; used several times by Cicero. *Pro Publio Sestio*, sec. 45; *Epistle to Lentulus ad fin*.
4. Literally, the country in town.

and fifty souls in the place, including women and children; something must really be done to keep order; and nothing can be done, till an act of incorporation is obtained, and the village turned into a town. Now there is not a single legislator in the whole State, who has the least objection to its being a town, the moment that it likes it: but a mighty fuss is made over the matter; the member for the district is intrusted with the passing of the measure; it is brought forward, debated, argued, speeches are made *pro* and *con;* and the inhabitants are delighted with the importance attached to their bill. At length the *measure* is carried, and the good souls obtain the right of electing their own officers, regulating their own affairs, and managing their own business as unto them seemeth good. Next comes the first election; and only fancy the dignity and satisfaction of every man, woman, child, and little dog in the *Town*. There are eight officers to be elected, seven trustees, the chairman of whom is mayor, and one sergeant, and the number of electors is eighteen. But, alas! the contest is neither fierce nor exciting. Good Virginian common-sense comes into play. A gentleman of high literary attainments, a good knowledge of law, and a house with two wings, is the choice of his fellow-citizens for mayor; and after a proportionate amount of mint-juleps, the very best men, probably, who could be selected, are named for the various offices.

It is a very curious fact, and one worthy of notice, that such in Virginia is the virtue of mint, an amount of brandy which would obfuscate the intellect if imbibed in a crude state, is so corrected and directed by the salubrious herb as to acciminate [*sic*] the perceptive faculties. There must not be too many glasses, however; and who shall say that too many are not sometimes drank?

In the mean time, while the election has been going on, neighbors and friends have been pouring into the town of Doodledumville; the evening shades fall round; the bar stands invitingly open,

and sundry minor offences are committed which might call for interference on the part of the mayor; but happily for himself and the public, he is not yet in a position to exercise his magisterial functions. But those functions must soon be exercised; municipal laws are enacted, municipal taxes are determined, and the awful face of justice is unveiled. Now, with the lady of the scales and weights, as with other people, it does not do to show her teeth without biting. Some public assemblage takes place, Heaven knows for what; Mr. Jeremy from the neighboring country gets drunk—very drunk—exceedingly drunk indeed. He becomes pugnacious; sets mayor and sergeant, and even justice of the peace at defiance; he draws a bowie-knife; cares for nobody; swears he will cut somebody's throat—no matter whom. The mayor is determined to do his duty; he will have no throats cut there. The sergeant is equally determined, and after a stout but ill-directed resistance, Mr. Jeremy is arrested. What is to be done with him? Heaven knows. There is neither prison, cage, nor lock-up in the whole place. There is not a house strong enough to keep in a sparrow. The sergeant cannot keep holding on to his neck all night. But a bright thought strikes the mayor. Luckily there is the rail-road hard by, and also the tavern. The mayor, with a grave and determined countenance, walks up to the delinquent and thus addresses him: "Mr. Jeremy, you have committed a serious offence, which cannot be tolerated in the town of Doodledumville. You have got drunk and misconducted yourself: you have damned the chief magistrate, cursed the trustees, and assaulted the sergeant. The majesty of the law must be vindicated. Sir, till you are sober I shall commit you to prison!"

Then responds Mr. Jeremy: "Go to h——ll, you old coon (hiccup). Prison! I should like to see your prison (hiccup); where the devil is your prison? I care no more for you than for that nigger boy (hiccup). You've stolen my knife, or I'd give you four inches of steel medicine. Didn't I fight in the Mexican war?—tell me that (hiccup)—and d'ye think I care a cuss for you or your prisons? Where's your prison? You hadn't got such a thing (hiccup)."

The mayor then replies with dignity: "Sir you stand committed! But as the whole spirit of our laws requires us to temper justice with mercy, I give you your choice, whether you will be incarcerated in the ice-house or shut up in the box-car of this depot."

MR. JEREMY: "I don't care a straw. Shut me up where you like, and keep me if you can."

The box-car is judged preferable, and Mr. Jeremy is marched off with all the honors; but alas! for the impotence of even official will. Mr. Jeremy had not only served in the Mexican war, but he had worked on a rail-road and the next morning the box-car is found empty, and Mr. Jeremy is "over the hills and far away."[5]

Such is one phase of Virginia village life. There are others and fairer ones where the native kindness of heart and true Christian benevolence, which find no where greater room for exercise than in those small communities, are displayed in their brightest light. I must needs hurry on, however, or fail in obeying your behest.

The negro life of Virginia differs very little, I believe, from the negro life all through the South. In return for food, clothing, house-room, medical attendance, and support in old age, about one third of the labor which is required of the white man in most countries is demanded of the black. He performs it badly, and would not perform it at all if he were not compelled. The rest of his time is spent in singing, dancing, laughing, chattering, and bringing up pigs and chickens. That negroes are the worst servants in the world, every man, I believe, but a thorough-bred Southern man, will admit; but the Southerner has been reared amongst them from his childhood, and in general has a tenderness and affection for them of which Northern men can have no conception. Great care is taken by the law to guard them against oppression and wrong; and after six years' residence in the State, I can safely say, I never saw more than one instance of cruelty toward a negro, and that was perpetrated by a foreigner. That there may still be evils in the system which might be removed by law, and that there may be individual instances of oppression and even bad treatment, I do not deny, but those instances are not so frequent as those of cruelty to a wife or child in Northern lands, as displayed every day by the newspapers; and in point of general happiness, it would not be amiss to alter an old adage and say: "As merry as a negro slave."

I must not pursue this branch of the subject farther, for I can pretend to no great love for Doctor Livingstone's friends, the Makololos.[6] There are, beyond all doubt, some very excellent people among them; but, as a race, the more I see of them the less do I think them capable of civilization, or even fitted to take proper care of themselves.

To give any general view of Virginia country life in a brief space, is impossible, on account of the great variety of character which the various parts of the State present. It is only to be done, if at all, by separate sketches, like that which I have attempted to give of the rise and progress of a Virginia village in the east. As a pleasant *pendant* to that picture, I may give you the portrait from more western life in the State, furnished to me by a friend who knows well the district of which he speaks, promising merely that the great Valley of Virginia, stretching nearly from one side of the

5. John Gay, *The Beggar's Opera*, act 1, sc. 13.

6. An African tribe visited by Livingstone in 1853. *Dictionary of National Biography*, 11:1266.

State to the other, is one of the richest districts that the sun ever shines upon. He may be a little prejudiced perhaps; for according to the old Italian proverb,

Ad agne uccello
Sue nido o bello;[7]

but let us see what is his portrait of

THE VALLEY FARMER

The Western and Eastern Virginian, he says, differ as absolutely from each other as either does from the New-England Puritans. Their lineage, their tastes, their habits are directly opposite. A Valley farmer is a noble specimen of the yeoman. He has little Latin and less Greek, having derived his education in an "old field school-house,"[8] from a stern Scotch school-master, who was contented with hammering into his knowledge-box the three great keys to other knowledge, reading, writing, and arithmetic. But though not learned, the Valley farmer is shrewd, sensible, and refined, with just views of human affairs, generous to others, but frugal himself; industrious and attentive to business, but full of fun in his hours of leisure; a Democrat in politics, a Presbyterian in religion, and a colonel in the militia.

As you approach his residence you will be struck with the neatness and cleanliness of his system of farming so different from the more slovenly course pursued on a large Eastern plantation. His gates, his fences, his out-houses, are all substantial and neat. His barn is always three times as large and handsome as his home. He is hospitable without display, and you would wound his feelings to the quick, if you refused to accept it. His table is loaded with abundance, and almost every thing is the product of his own farm. Even his liquor which, though temperate as he is, he presses upon you with no sparing hand, is whiskey, or "*Apple-Jack*," distilled on his own or a neighbor's estate. His dress, too, is made of domestic cloth, unless on Sunday, or on some important occasion, such as court-day, election, or muster. On these he appears with a well-kept blue coat, glittering with brass buttons, and surmounted by one of those immense, stiff collars, which belong to the style of the court of George the Third.

He hardly ever leaves home, except on the occasions above referred to, and now and then to "the store," where, with a few old cronies, he discusses the crops, the weather, and the news from Richmond. On Sunday,

At church, with meek and unoffended grace,
His looks adorn the venerable place.[9]

But the church itself is worthy of some notice. One of the oldest of these buildings, in that part of the Valley which I have in my eyes, is built of the native blue lime-stone.[10] It is large and substantial, and has a great antiquity for this comparatively new land, having been erected more than a hundred years ago. All the iron work, the glass, the sashes, were, they say, carried across the Blueridge from Williamsburgh on pack-saddles: and, situated just on the edge of a noble forest of oak, walnut, and hickory, it presents a very picturesque appearance to the passing traveller. Here, every Sunday, appears the Valley farmer, to thank God sincerely for blessings past, and pray with hope and trust for others to come.

7. Every bird loves its own nest, or there is no place like home.

8. A school located on land not suitable for farming. Adams, *Dictionary of American History*, 4:170.

9. In the original quotation from Oliver Goldsmith's *The Deserted Village*, lines 177–78, the word "unoffended" appears as "unaffected."

10. This reference is probably to a church in Augusta County, Virginia, about eight miles north of Staunton. The first building was erected in 1736. The building at times served also as a fort. J. Lewis Peyton, *History of Augusta County, Virginia* (Staunton, Va., 1882), pp. 80–81.

A remarkable contrast to this quiet life of useful moderation is afforded by the watering-place life of Virginia, and as Virginia has probably more watering-places than any other of the United States, this sort of life is peculiarly characteristic of the people and the country. Some people go to watering-places in search of health, but many more go for change of scene, and still more for amusement. To the Greenbrier White Sulphur,[11] multitudes, especially from the far South, have resorted, during the summer, for very many years. Doubtless, the water of that Spring, is highly beneficial in a number of cases. I cannot, however, think it so to all who drink it; and I imagine that the great amount of advantage is derived from the gay society, the fine scenery, and the pure air—not omitting to mention the enforced hardships which every visitor has to bear. But scattered over the State are springs of every quality, and the searcher for health may always find some suited to his peculiar condition. Not so those who go to the watering-places for amusement. There is a good deal of sameness in the daily life of the Springs, and the variety must be produced by the visitors themselves, and depends somewhat upon the taste and urbanity of the proprietors. The morning walk, the conventional drinking of a certain quantity of water, the idling through the hotter hours of the day, the ball at night, with flirting and coquetry, are common to all watering-places. But certainly the more substantial comfort (the good food, the comfortable rooms, the attention of the servants) varies very much. The most comfortable Springs I have been at are Old Swab and the Fauquier,[12] and as I am at the latter now, I may as well give some account of it as a good specimen of a Virginia watering-place. The house itself is one of the finest buildings I have seen in the country, large, well-built, with spacious and lofty rooms, a splendid ball-room, with large ante-rooms, good parlors, an extensive dining-room, and chambers such as can hardly be found

11. The Greenbrier Hotel was located at White Sulphur Springs, which is still a popular resort. Perceval Reniers, *The Springs of Virginia* (Chapel Hill, N.C., 1941), p. 277.

12. No springs named "Old Swab" have been identified. The name may have been confused with "Old Sweet," a well-known spa in western Virginia, now Monroe County, West Virginia. Fauquier Springs was near Warrenton. Writers' Program, West Virginia, *West Virginia: A Guide to the Mountain State* (New York, 1941), pp. 452–53; *Virginia Guide*, pp. 613–14.

in any gentleman's dwelling in the land. The cabins, too, are much more spacious and convenient than at most of the Springs; and then there is, stretching before the eye, down to the very valley of the Rappahannoe, that beautiful open grove, which, with its herds of fallow deer, has very much the appearance of a gentleman's park in England. The spring is one of sulphur-water, light, easy of digestion, and certainly powerful in its effect; but surely, that which does the most good is the fine, free air, the morning walk to the well or the baths in that octagon building on the other side of the grove.

After the walk, and the drinking of the waters, come the breakfast at one of the innumerable little tables in the dining-hall; and there, every thing that the skill of excellent cooks, served with quiet but unremitting attention by well-taught servants, can do to refresh, is put before you. Oh! the mutton! the excellent tender mutton! would that it could be had in Lower Virginia! Mutton is the favorite food of Englishmen, and a literary friend once aptly remarked, after a visit to the little island where he was received and feted as any American *gentleman*, will, I trust, always be: They ought to call my countryman "John Mutton," rather than "John Bull"; for it is only when he is very much provoked, that he shows his horns.

After breakfast, comes the stroll again, or better still, the ride: and here we know no impediments. Good saddle-horses are to be procured at any time, and in abundance. Mr. A—— is never required to stop till Mr. B—— has done his ride; but the horse is ordered, and the horse comes, so that the exercise of which Virginians are so fond, is always at hand. Games at bowls, and perhaps a little sleep, diversify the day, and then, with the shades of evening, comes the merry dance, with the best music Washington can afford.

To quiet and sober people, whose toes are neither "light nor fantastic,"[13] conversation, light or serious, fills up a part of this time; and happy is he who is permitted to hear the words of wisdom fall from the venerated lips of a Taney—varied, often playful, but always full of that quintessence of wisdom, common-sense. Having mentioned the name of the Chief-Justice in his favorite retreat, I cannot but remark, that two of the most remarkable men whom the United States have ever produced, have sought to wile away their leisure hours at Fauquier. Chief-Justice Marshall's cabin stands nearly opposite that of his great successor,[14] and the good taste and good feeling of the proprietor of the Springs has left it untouched, though it does not altogether harmonize with the plan of the grounds, or the luxurious finish of the other buildings. There it stands, however, with an empty dog-kennel at the door, and brings pleasant remembrances of the simplest but most acute of the great lawyers to which this country has given birth.

In their general outline, the amusements of Fauquier are those of the other Springs, with all those advantages which greater shade, and proximity to Washington, can superadd. One can enjoy one's self here in weather when there is no enjoyment any where else. But there is one peculiarity in the way of amusement, which must not go without notice. It is true, that what is called the Tournament is not confined to Fauquier; but where can such another tournament-ground be met with?[15] A broad, flat arena, of several acres,

13. An allusion to John Milton's "the light fantastic toe" from "L'Allegro," line 33.
14. Both Taney and Marshall went to Fauquier Springs. Whether they occupied adjoining cabins has not been determined. Frances Norton Mason, *My dearest Polly: Letters of Chief Justice John Marshall to his Wife* (Richmond, Va., 1961), p. 246; Bernard C. Steiner, *Life of Roger Brooke Taney* (Baltimore, Md., 1922), p. 375.
15. Tournaments were held in the latter part of the season. The knights "rode at a ring and not at each other." Bright silks replaced armor, and the participants adopted fanciful names, or names that identified their origin. Reniers, *The Springs of Virginia*, pp. 157–58.

surrounded by high banks, shaded by embowering trees, under which the judges and the spectators sit, would inspire to something like the ancient feats of arms, and we might expect to see the lances shivered, and the helmets dashed away, were not the age of chivalry really past. The tournament, however, of the present day, is confined to one of the minor sports of the olden time—mere running at the ring; the amusement of novices and pages. Some opportunity is afforded for the display of good horsemanship; but the really attractive part of the scene is the display of youth and beauty beneath the green boughs, and the happy faces that look on, fondly thinking that they gaze upon the sports of those chivalrous ancestors, whose deeds of gallantry and daring civilized dark ages, and gave the sublime to wars often unjust and barbarous.

I have now, my dear friend, given you what you asked, a brief sketch of my impressions of Virginia country life. Those who know it better, might have done it better, and the only value it can have,

lies in the fact that it is a picture of the impressions of a foreigner. Even I may be prejudiced; for, when one has received so warm and hearty a welcome in every house, hard must be the heart, ungenerous the mind, that does not view every phase of society through a pleasant medium. I would fain have given one sketch more—that of the militia-muster; but alas! I have never seen one; and I dare not venture to go beyond my depth. I remember in years long gone, when I was a mere lad, hearing inimitable old Mathews, in one of his "At Homes," [16] describe most humorously the scene; but times have changed since then, and I little thought, in those days, that the warm-hearted kindness of Virginians, to which he did full justice, would ever be personally witnessed and enjoyed by

Yours ever,

G. P. R. JAMES.

16. Charles Mathews, an English comedian, was especially successful as a mimic. His best-known performances were his "At Homes." *Century Dictionary and Cyclopedia*, 9:664.

LETTERS FROM THE SOUTH

Curtis B. Pyle was a farmer in Chester, Pennsylvania, who became a Mason in 1851; in 1853 he was one of the editors of the periodical from which this selection is taken. He was prominent in local Masonic affairs until his death in 1884.[1]

SAVANNAH, Monday, March 28th, 1853.

Bro. Hyneman: Savannah is a city of trees and gardens. It reminds me of what William Penn

wished that his beloved Philadelphia might be—"a green garden town." In the city plan here a large number of small squares are laid out, and these are planted with trees. In the outer portion of the town a large plot of ground, still covered with the original forest trees, has been surrounded with iron railing, and set apart as a public park. The lots are generally fifty feet front, with a corresponding

[Curtis B. Pyle?], "Letters from the South. By Our Corresponding Editor," *Masonic Mirror and American Keystone* 2 (6 April–25 May 1853): 115, 125–26, 171.
1. R. Baker Harris and Charles S. Baker, Masonic officials, to Eugene L. Schwaab, September 1962.

depth, and each house of the better sort therefore stands amidst its garden, and surrounded with trees. I regretted to perceive that at several points in the suburbs, speculators had taken up corner lots, and built rows of houses facing upon the side, and consequently making lots of but fifty feet depth. When we recollect that Savannah has been very subject to bilious fever, and that frequently yellow fever also appears here during the summer months, we can understand the solicitude of the authorities for separating the houses, and the danger of the new method just mentioned. The public buildings are numerous, and generally handsome. The houses and streets are lighted with gas,[2] and water works are now in process of erection.[3] A building of some pretension is also going up for a medical college, which will commence its operations next winter.[4] The depot of the Central Georgia Railroad covers a larger space than any structure of the kind I have ever seen, and is the most complete I have examined on this side the Atlantic. It is not yet quite finished.

Savannah has a commercial importance far beyond what its population would indicate. What its precise population is I cannot ascertain, not having access to documents. A Charleston gentleman assured me that it was rather under than over 16,000 while the people here call it 23,000.[5] My impression is that the former is nearer the figure. It is a town, therefore, very little larger than Reading, in our State, and yet it enjoys a large foreign trade, employed in carrying mostly cotton and rice. There were five arrivals yesterday from European ports, bringing salt and coals, and which will carry a return cargo of cotton. The wharves have, therefore, a crowded and bustling appearance, strongly in contrast with the almost rural quiet of the back part of the town. Of the people, I have as yet seen too little to say much. All I have come in contact with have been kind and hospitable in the extreme. Such, in fact, is the character of our Southern brethren generally, and makes traveling in the South delightful, notwithstanding many inconveniences. The great number and extreme blackness of the negroes strike a Northerner forcibly. You may see them sauntering about and sunning themselves in the most deliberate manner. Their method of working at any employment whatever would soon drive a Northern employer frantic. It is said that a Northern master or overseer is always noted for severity to his hands, and that planters will employ a "Yankee" driver because he gets more work out of the men than any other. I can very readily believe this, not because the Northern man is more unfeeling, but, because knowing how much work a man can do and ought to do, he has no patience with the lazy dawdling of these sable do-littles. For the rest, they seem fat and comfortable, and the little ones are the most comical monkeys imaginable. One of my amusements is to watch them playing, which they do with a heartiness and *abandon* which you see only in puppies or kittens, and which white children never approach. Two accomplishments they all have—whistling and playing on the bones—both of which are going on under my window at this moment, as they always do. You shall soon hear from me again.

Yours fraternally, P.

2. A Savannah resident in his reminiscences stated that the city was lighted by gas from 1850 to 1881. Charles Seton Henry Hardee, *Reminiscences and Recollections of Old Savannah* (Savannah, Ga., 1928), p. 129.
3. A report in a Savannah newspaper stated that the city council had authorized the mayor "to cause the Bonds issued by the City, for the erection of the Water-works, to be paid at the Bank of the Republic, in the City of New York." *Daily Morning News*, 25 February 1853.
4. The cornerstone of the medical college was laid on 17 January 1853. Ibid., 17 January 1853.
5. The federal census reports the population of Savannah in 1860 as 22,292. Bureau of the Census, *Population of the United States in 1860*, p. 74.

PILATKA, Florida, March 29, 1853.

Bro. Hyneman: By this date, you will perceive that I am now in the heart of the Land of Flowers, breathing the pure air on the banks of the crystal St. Johns. At my last date, I was still enjoying what I could of Savannah, where there was a struggle between physical discomfort and social pleasure as to whether I should go or stay. The citizens of Savannah have always been noted for their courtesy and hospitality to strangers, and well has that reputation been deserved. I can testify to the fact from my own experience. For this reason I am no longer surprised that so many who leave the North in ill health are tempted to remain in Savannah during most or all of the winter, which I regard as a capital mistake. The climate there is one of the dampest I have ever felt. The difference in temperature between the night and day is very great, and with the setting of the sun there comes a damp chilliness, which strikes like a leaden weight upon the chest of any one affected with pulmonary disease. Every thing about my room felt damp, just as it does always at the sea-shore, and I was obliged to have fire there of evenings. The difference between that atmosphere and this is very striking. Here the weather is still cool enough of evenings to render the blaze of a few pine sticks upon the parlour hearth a pleasant sight, but it is cool without dampness.

One of the evidences of the prevailing moisture at Savannah is the quantity of moss that grows upon and chokes the trees even in the public squares of the city. Every where you see the moss hanging in long and slowly-waving masses from the trees, many of which are entirely killed by it. It is particularly abundant at Bonaventure, the former seat of the Tatnall family, but now converted into a cemetery—a place so peculiar in its features that no visitor at Savannah should fail to see it.[6] The house was built before the Revolution, and the avenues were planted at the same time, so that the trees are now venerable with age and of great size. The original proprietor was a tory, and his property was confiscated, but his son remained attached to the republican cause and became afterwards Governor of the State, when the legislature restored to him the estate of his father. The mansion-house was twice burned down, and after the last conflagration, more than twenty years ago, the family entirely abandoned the place. It is situated upon a bluff, overlooking an arm of the river, and is almost entirely covered with wood or shrubbery. The avenues are of great length, and the trees being large, over-arching and perfectly covered with great, dark masses of moss, that hang heavily down like funeral drapery and wave slowly to and fro in the breeze, they give an air of gloomy solemnity to the place, befitting its present use and such as I have never seen elsewhere. It is several miles from the city, and, in going to it, we passed by endless quantities of wild roses, yellow jessamine, and other flowers, whose names I do not know. In the woods, which are mostly of pine and oak, we saw great numbers of the Palmetto tree, of various sizes, giving a really tropical aspect to the scene.

We left Savannah on Saturday morning, and came by a devious passage inside the chain of islands that guard the coast here. They appeared to be mostly mere mud banks covered with a rank, coarse grass, and liable to overflow. On the shore, and on some few of the islands, the eye was relieved by the tall and graceful forms of the pines, naked almost to the summit, and of many very tall Palmettos.

6. First named Bonaventure in 1760 by Colonel Mulbryne, an Englishman, the estate descended to his heirs, the Tatnall family. After many misfortunes, the place was acquired by Captain Peter Wittberger in 1847; his son later formed the Evergreen Cemetery Company. Federal Writers' Project, Georgia, *Savannah* (Savannah, Ga., 1937), pp. 160–64.

In the afternoon we went outside, and had a rough time of it, with a strong easterly wind, bringing with it a heavy shower of rain, just as we again got under the lee of the islands. The sea-sick soon revived, and we all felt better, for our boat, the Welaka, although comfortable and commodious, was not such a craft as one feels disposed to be at sea in. As the lamps were lit, I amused myself with a more minute inspection of my fellow passengers, the majority of whom were evidently inhabitants of this region. Several long-bearded sallow men with long-napped white hats of ancient pattern, were evidently model specimens of the "Cracker" race.[7] One of them, a one-eyed fellow, with a black beard down to his waist like iron-wire, was so truculent-looking that I found myself involuntary giving him a wide berth, until I fell accidentally into conversation with him, when I discovered him to be a good-natured and mild-spoken person, not without intelligence. (By-the-way—why is it that the loss of an eye gives the countenance such a fierce expression?)

These people speak with a strong, drawling accent, evidently caught from the negroes. Others of our passengers were young men, evidently of the buckish sort, doing a good deal in the way of flashy vests and gilt jewelry. I had noticed them in the day, but now I saw nothing of them. I wondered where they could be, until I heard a man advise a friend, who had some lingering qualm of sea-sickness, to go to the "confectionery" and take a little brandy and water—an advice taken with a much more cheerful acquiescence in the wisdom of the prescriber than is generally witnessed. Following in his wake, I found the "confectionery" on the forward deck, consisting of a wash-room, with a row of white basins and towels, *not* white; and at the other end, a bar with a goodly array of bottles. In the intermediate space was a table around which sate the blades I had missed, deeply engaged in some game of cards I did not comprehend. The chair occupied by one of them was evidently a barber's chair, and there were sundry cups and razors on a shelf against the wall. What entitled the place to the title of "confectionery" I cannot imagine, except that sundry oranges and lemons ornamented the spaces between the bottles. Sir Francis Head[8] relates, that in Connaught, he once found in his bill a charge of sixpence for "material" which, on enquiry, proved to be his night-cap of whiskey-toddy. Every place has its peculiarities, so, I suppose Irish "material" is, in Georgia, regarded as "confectionery." I should also imagine that the confectionery business is a very lively one down in the region to which the temperance reformation has not extended much.

The habitual moderate drinking, once so universal in the North, still prevails here, and not always moderate either. It is worse on the Mississippi undoubtedly, but it is bad enough through all the South. A friend who has recently spent much time, and been most hospitably entertained in Alabama, tells the following story, which may be true and certainly is good. He woke the first morning after his arrival at a friend's house, with a very confused recollection of the incidents of the preceding evening, except that the session at table after dinner was very prolonged. While endeavoring to gather his scattered wits, a negro entered with a savoury "cocktail," which he was readily induced to take. In half an hour he re-appeared with another, which was also swallowed. This produced a condition of quiet doziness, when the

7. Residents of Georgia. George Earle Shankle, *American Nicknames: Their Origin and Significance*, 2d ed. (New York, 1955), p. 169.

8. Head made a short trip to Ireland and wrote of his experiences in *A Fortnight in Ireland*, published in November 1852. Sydney Jackman, *Galloping Head* (London, 1958), p. 141.

Ethiopian again presented himself with another cock-tail! To this the victim positively objected as "too soon," when his attendant told him, with an expression of friendly caution, "Better take it, mass. Dat is de last you git now. We never 'lows but three here afore breakfast!"

Yours fraternally, P.

MACON, Georgia, April 17, 1853.

Dear Sir : While we remained at the Cuyler House, I had an opportunity of conversation with a negro-trader (or "speculator," as he is universally termed here), who encamped in our neighborhood. There is a law in Georgia prohibiting the importation of more slaves into the State;[9] but when they are scarce and highpriced, as at present, the law is practically of no force, as the presence of our neighbor proved. He pitched his tent in the pine-woods west of the house, and remained there several days, waiting for his partner, who was collecting their dues in an adjoining county. He was very communicative, and seemed glad of a visit from us. They had been on what seamen call a "trading voyage," through South Carolina, Georgia, and Alabama, going from town to town, buying, selling, and exchanging. They had left the upper portion of North Carolina, eighteen months ago, with sixty hands, and had gradually sold them off, until now they were left with only three children, whom they would take home again, and keep for their next journey. The reason why one of them would not sell, was evident in the scrofulous tumors that deformed her neck. Another was a bright handsome light mulatto boy, of about ten years old, for whom the trader told us he asked $700! He informed us that mulattoes always sold best, not only for house servants, which is natural

9. Georgia, Laws, Statutes, etc., *Acts of the General Assembly of the State of Georgia* (Macon, Ga., 1852), pp. 263-68.

enough, but even as field-hands. The latter he considered a great mistake, being convinced that a pure-blooded negro has twice the power of endurance of heat and toil possessed by one of mixed breed. His maxim was, that the blacker and uglier they were the better they did for the cotton field. I am inclined to believe that this assertion is true. Here, as with us, the mulatto is the victim especially of scrofula and tuberculous disease. Quarteroons are less subject to disease than mulattoes, and so when the black blood predominates.

The road from Cuyler to Macon is just as uninteresting as that from Savannah to the former place, differing only in the country becoming somewhat more elevated and rolling. As we approached Macon, we saw what we might denominate hills, although they are of sand, and were much rejoiced thereat. Our eyes had been so wearied with the eternal flat sameness of all the scenery we had witnessed for weeks past, that anything like a respectable hill was a great relief to them. The quantity of swamp-land passed through was even greater than on our previous journey, and the clearings seemed wider apart. A very peculiar feature of the road is the occasional cluster of tents occupied by the negroes who are at work repairing the track, &c. It is exceedingly gypsey-like. In some pretty shady nook, by the road side, you will see half a dozen tents, with a pot boiling on a lightwood fire before them, and the newly washed garments of the occupants hanging on a line in the rear. Around sits a group of women, black as ink, and dirty as imagination can conceive, while a regiment of half-naked black imps tumble about in the sand, or whoop wildly at the passing train. They look well-fed and hearty, and seem to enjoy their rude mode of life exceedingly. On the plantations the number of women at work in the fields reminded me of what I had seen in Continental Europe, except that there they were much more neatly attired. A peculiarly southern scene, how-

ever, was a negro woman cutting down a tree. She swung her axe with a vigor and precision that would have done credit to any backwoodsman.

Macon is a thriving town, and presents some points of attraction.[10] Placed just where the sand plains cease, and give way to a primary formation, the land around it is quite hilly, and rather picturesque. The town itself is not much, and yet its wide avenues, with their rows of pride-of-china trees, are quite pretty. Outside the town are many very beautiful private residences, surrounded with gardens, now in the very luxuriance of their vernal bloom. I have nowhere seen a greater profusion of flowers than here. The cluster of residences a short distance from the town, known as Vineville, is a collection of gardens, rich in floral wealth.[11] While you are tormented with little April snaps of fair weather, just enough to make you think of spring, and then ending in a frost, here we are surrounded by roses and honeysuckles, and a hundred other sweet-scented blossoms. There is a rural cemetery a little distance from the city, which is already quite a charming spot, and might easily be made much more so. It is shaded by a dark and sombre pine-wood, and yet the open space is covered with flowers. There is something exceedingly Italian in thus sitting under the pine shade, upon a marble slab half lost in foliage and flowers, and over the surface of which the lithe and nimble lizards glide and play. In the course of our rides, we came upon a copious cold spring of delightful water in the heart of a wood, and where the ground was carpeted with flowers. The spot was almost too beautiful to leave. The spring has been walled in, and an appropriate basin made, and men were at work arranging timber for a house to go up on the

premises, for the accommodation of visiters. As soon as it is finished, I fear that the mint-julep will be substituted for nature's beverage, thus liberally provided. If so, the spring will become but an additional inducement to dissipation; only another instance of the facility with which we convert God's blessings into curses. For there is, I must say, too much drinking done in Macon. There is a ludicrous side, as well as a fearful one, to this matter of intemperance, and, as I lounged about in my lazily-philosophical way, I found myself sometimes laughing, and sometimes more disposed to weep, at the unwearied devotion to the bottle exhibited by some of the frequenters of the Lanier House. They seemed to spend the entire day in diving down into the basement bar-room; then emerging to lounge about with hands in their pockets, and, on the first plausible excuse being offered, diving down again. Occasionally the monotony of the day appeared to be broken by a little billiards, or a short ride, but the chief occupation was what I have described. It is no difficult matter to predict the end of such a career.

The Lanier House, where we are stopping, has a high reputation throughout the South, and certainly is a very good hotel for the place. It is large, commodious, and well-arranged, and the table is very good. Nothing, however, can reconcile me to negro-waiters. This may be prejudice. I know that it is asserted that we Northerners have this prejudice of color more intensely than the people of the South; that we are much more prone to treat the negro personally with a mingling of contempt and abhorrence; and I am afraid there is too much truth in it. Colored people are certainly addressed more kindly and treated more familiarly here than is general with us. But, admitting it to be a prejudice, I cannot as yet get over it, and would rather have a white man to help me at table. The very perfection of waiting, however, all must confess to be the chubby-cheeked English girl, with a deeply

10. Fort Hawkins was constructed in 1806 to protect the state against Indians. In 1821 it became Newtown and in 1822 received its present name. *Georgia Guide*, pp. 225–28.
11. Vineville is now part of the residential district of Macon. Ibid., p. 225.

ruffled cap bordering her merry face, who brings you your chops and mug of ale in some cozy country inn, and has no objection to chat a bit with you while you are disposing of them. This we cannot expect here, and the best we can do is to secure a brisk, vigilant, and good-natured Irishman, as coming nearer to the standard than anything else.

In a few days more, we will turn our faces homewards by way of Savannah, and the steamer State of Georgia [12]—the recollection I have of which is so pleasant that I will travel northward in no other boat so long as she is on the water, and in her present hands. Towards the 1st of May I hope to see you again, and talk over matters personally.

You perceive that in these letters I have said nothing about the Masonic fraternity and its doings. I have met with many Brethren, and have large arrearages of indebtedness for kindness and courtesy, which I fear I can never repay. But the condition of my health keeping me in the house of evenings, I could attend no Lodge meetings, even when the opportunity was presented, which was very rarely.

Fraternally yours,
P.

12. The *State of Georgia*, a side-wheeler of 1,204 tons, was built in Philadelphia in 1852. It was lost in 1866. Lytle, *Merchant Steam Vessels of the United States*, p. 179.

SCENES FROM LYNCHBURG

Although the voice of "King Cotton" came to be dominant in the economic life of the Old South, the chant of the tobacco auctioneer was also heard in the land.

Those who sing the songs of Virginia, have long been familiar with "Lynchburg Town," [1] and those who indulge in the finer kinds of manufactured tobacco, know that it comes rather from Lynchburg [2] than Richmond. Hence, although away off—considerably more than a hundred miles —from the seaboard, Lynchburg has a renown that is universal. The South Side Railroad, with its connections to Richmond, Petersburg, and City Point, has its terminus here, connecting again with the Virginia and Tennessee, which forms a portion of the near route to New Orleans. A branch road to Alexandria is soon to go into operation, which will very much shorten the distance to Baltimore and the cities of the North. Cotton has already been received over the Virginia and Tennessee road, giving promise that large quantities of this great staple will eventually seek this course of transportation to market. [3]

J. Alexander Patten, "Scenes in the Old Dominion. Number Two—A Tobacco Market," *New York Mercury* 21 (5 November 1859): 8.
1. This is probably the song "Goin' Down to Town," the chorus of which is "goin' down to town,/goin' down to town,/goin' down to Lynchburg town,/to carry my tobacco down." Carl Sandburg, *American Songbag* (New York, 1927), p. 145.
2. The legislature of Virginia authorized the establishment of a town on the land of John Lynch in 1786. *Virginia Guide*, p. 265.

3. The South Side Railroad, chartered in 1846, ran 132 miles from Lynchburg to Petersburg. The Virginia and Tennessee, chartered in 1848, ran 204 miles from Lynchburg to Bristol. The Orange and Alexandria, also chartered in 1848, ran 148 miles from Lynchburg to Alexandria. Angus James Johnston, Jr., *Virginia Railroads in the Civil War* (Chapel Hill, N.C., 1961), pp. 3-4.

Lynchburg is located on a series of hills, running back from James River. Each of the long, parallel streets is on an elevation, getting higher and higher, until the loftiest hill is reached. Then, you look down upon the river, canal, and a most picturesque grouping of buildings. It seems as if some day a great land-slide might sweep everything, from the rookeries to the stately mansions, in chaos to the bottom. Indeed, from the way many of the buildings are secured by walls, some such idea seems to have pervaded the minds of those constructing them. One dwelling may serve as a description of many. It was a large double brick edifice, elevated not less than ten feet above the street. Along the whole front was a covered piazza or porch, of wood, resting on a stone wall, built up from the street, and, evidently, mainly intended to keep the hill from giving way under the weight of the building. This was extended beyond the house some forty or fifty feet, facing even with the surface of the garden, and overhung at the top by a profusion of blooming vines. The entrance was by some clumsy wooden steps, rising between the side foundation-walls of the building and an outer wall, still necessary to keep the hill in its place. Reaching a level, paved landing, you can step upon the porch, or ascend to another story, by another pair of break-neck steps. Out from the wall the street is paved with cobble-stones.

On almost any of the lower streets this untasteful and inconvenient arrangement is to be found. Altogether, there is such a curious adaptation of buildings to locations; such walls, such overhanging porches and gardens, that the stranger cannot but be profoundly impressed with the ingenuity and perseverance thus evinced by the inhabitants.

Main street is a long, straight thoroughfare, lined with stores, and active with business. Great wagons, drawn by four and six horses and sometimes by both horses and oxen, make their way slowly along, loaded with tobacco, and wheat from the neighboring counties. These wagons are curiosities. To very heavy wheels, necessary for the rough road, is added a high, cumbrous body, over which a cover is drawn in bad weather. The driver is mounted on one of the horses, and thus pursues his tedious way, coming to town with some produce, and going homeward with supplies. One individual is said to drive an ox, a mule, and a horse. A yoke of oxen and a team of horses are frequently seen. Some of the teams, however, are fine, noble horses, and as the driver goes along, he cracks his huge whip, not so much to increase the speed, as to draw attention to his animals. Very many of the wagoners are white men from the mountain districts. They have coarse, tow-colored hair, high cheek-bones, sunken eyes, and whisky breaths. They are clad in home-spun—few of them can read or write. In their manners, they are very near to the swine upon which they feed so greedily; their language is merely a dialect, and quite inferior to the vulgarisms of the negro; they are utterly corrupted with brutish vices and a[re] completely deadened to the influences of any noble virtue. With the forms of men, they seem to belong to some lower order of brutes.

A colored individual may be noticed at one of the corners of Main street, with a long tin horn. This he applies to his lips, and discourses "sweet sounds" for tobacco buyers. It is a notice that there is a "beck" or public sale of the article at some neighboring warehouse.[4] Immediately, a procession of gentlemen is seen hastening from other

4. As late as 1904, sales of tobacco in Lynchburg were announced by a Negro who stood on the street and played a trumpet. Joseph C. Robert, *The Story of Tobacco in America* (New York, 1949), p. 187. The marketing procedure, particularly the auction system, is described in some detail in Robert's *The Story of Tobacco*, pp. 86–92, and in his article, "Rise of the Tobacco Warehouse Auction System," *Agricultural History* 7 (October 1933): 170-82.

warehouses, eager for a chance at the new lots. The tobacco is generally sent by the planter to his commission merchant, who employs a crier at the day of sale. The crier receives ten cents per hogshead, the factor one dollar, and sometimes two and a half per cent. In the warehouse, the tobacco is inspected, weighed, the hogsheads broken and duly arranged for examination. Some of the tobacco is sent in loose, but it commands a better price when prized and duly arranged for examination. The warehouses are large buildings, with room for several hundred hogsheads, and yards adjoining, convenient for unloading the wagons and feeding the horses. The whole air is redolent with tobacco, and every man about seems an inveterate chewer of the weed. The crowd at the sales is made up of the buyers, planters, warehouse-men, commission merchants, and idlers. Some are in conversation, some bidding, some smelling, some leaning on the piles of tobacco, some sprawling over the emptied hogsheads, and all—black and white, bond and free—chewing.

The crier is a person with a stout stick, good lungs, and a glib tongue. He mounts first one pile and then another, accumulating many dimes in the course of a day. His thought, from morning to night, is tobacco; it makes him eloquent, and it makes him daily heard. Every lot is *the* lot, and every bidder is frowned at, persuaded, coaxed, and implored to buy, until the gentleman seems to conclude that he has given ten cents worth of breath. The commission merchant hops from pile to pile, after the noisy crier. The tongues of the two run races, and if there is any shrewd exaggeration on part of the one, the other comes gallantly to endorse it; and thus they reciprocate favors of this kind profitably, and from hour to hour. Now the crier makes a noise to please the commission merchant, and the commission merchant to tickle the planter, who looks daggers at him if he does not

keep up the excitement; but the cool coons who do the purchasing are but very little moved by it. They pull the bundles from the top and the bottom, they lift the leaves, they examine, smell, and chew, as attentive to their own interests—guided by experience and judgment—as they are deaf to the eloquence of the crier, and the pleading of the commission man. The stick is shaken over their heads—there is wit, there are tones of anger, and there are tones of satisfaction as the bids come brisker. The commission merchant pulls his hat down and pushes it back, he drags at his pants, and he plunges into his pockets; he holds the tobacco aloft, and he dashes it down; he taps his friends on their shoulders, and begs them not to think of losing such bargains; he smiles cheerfully to encourage the planter, and grows morose as the prospect of obtaining a high price becomes "small by degrees and beautifully less."[5] Thus go the "hogsheads," and the "loose," the "manufacturing," and the "shipping." Thus do the manufacturers glean out the fine qualities for the choice brands of chewing; and thus is selected the heavy, coarser article which is destined for the foreign market.

All leaf-tobacco is disposed of at these public sales, and there is quite a number of warehouses. When the "breaks are heavy," as it is called, the tin horn is sounding continually, filling the street with a wild, but not unpleasant sort of music. The yards and streets will then be crowded with wagons, and the greatest excitement exists among the buyers. And another class of very interested people will be the planters themselves, who, to some extent, attend the sales of their crops. The length of time required in the growing and preparation of this crop, its continued liability to injury, and the care which must be bestowed upon it,

5. The original has the word "small" instead of "fine." Matthew Prior, *Henry and Emma*, l. 430.

together with the fact, that, after all, it is an extremely profitable product, always saleable for the ready money-vendors, the final disposition of it is a matter of much importance to the grower.

Tobacco is the idol of the Lynchburgs. In it are their fortunes, and in it are beggars' graves. If there are movements in the firmament, the only concern is to know how they will affect the tobacco crops and market. If the earth is shaken by wars and trodden by pestilence, they care nothing, should the idolized staple come regularly to their town. They take the planter by the hand, they press him to their bosoms, and inquire, with almost tearful solicitude, how the crop stands the wet—the drought—the heat—the cold—how it ripens—has he cut yet—has he manufacturing or shipping? They talk about the last crop; they grow wise over the prospects of the market; they are full of calculations as to the tobacco still growing in the fields. A merchant may be in the port or whisky lines, but he knows that he will not sell much of either, if any undue misfortune should befall the tobacco people; another may be in the dry-goods way, and yet, if this crop fails, he may hang up his yardstick. Consequently, these interests, and all other interests, are linked with the ups and downs of the weed itself. It is hardly possible to buy a Bible or a tea-kettle, without either falling into a discussion on the crop, or at least being affectionately invited to partake of a reviving quid. The article of "cut tobacco," used out of the southern country, is laughed at here, and nobody is anybody unless he carries a plug as broad as his hand. With this he scents his pockets and his person, and having it, he drips the juice from the corners of his mouth, and, at convenient intervals, spouts out a spray like a fountain.

You can hardly turn into a street without seeing tobacco-factories.[6] They are often old, tottering

6. Lynchburg at this time was in Campbell County. There

buildings; but sometimes substantial structures of brick. Here, too, the air is strongly impregnated with the aroma of tobacco, made more delicate as the article passes the process of manufacturing. Out in the streets, and in yards, are long, shallow boxes, containing thousands of the newly-made "rolls"—called, after prizing, "plugs"—undergoing the drying necessary before being prized. There are shops for preparing the various kinds of boxes in which it is finally packed. In the factory which we visited, the hogsheads were taken to the second story for "sorting," and all the other successive stages, until ready to be "stemmed" and "rolled." These operations were performed in some cramped-up rooms on the second and third floors. On either side were high, double tables; and as fast as the leaves were separated from the stems, by workpeople standing on one side, they were tossed over to others facing them, and busy making the rolls. The operatives are all slaves— male and female, adults and children. Their nimble fingers do not stop, although, upon your entrance, every eye wanders to your face, and the younger frequently indulge in a broad grin. The tobacco was prized on the lower floor. In this operation, it is placed in enormously thick iron chambers, closing with hinges. Upon each of these comes a screw, turned by an iron lever, which requires four men to lift and a dozen to work it. The bar is no quicker in its place, than the whole gang lay hold of it; and first by short jerks, and then by more powerful efforts—in which they exert every muscle—the screw is turned tighter and tighter. Then four of them pull it out, trot back with it, thrust it into the socket, and in a moment the measured jerks begin again. With all this tremen-

were forty-seven tobacco factories in the county producing $2,081,149 in products. U.S., Bureau of the Census, *Manufactures of the United States in 1860* (Washington, D.C., 1865), p. 609.

dous power, the tobacco sometimes requires to be prized a second time. After this operation, it is packed in the stout but tasteful boxes in which it is sent over the world.

The superintendent, not only of this but two other factories, was an intelligent slave.[7] He was a man some forty years of age, large-framed, and seemingly of an amiable disposition. He could read and write; and, we were informed, wrote letters of business for his master. He was not only perfectly familiar with the qualities of tobacco, and all the details regarding its manufacture, but he gave a clear and interesting account of the whole operation. Withal, we did not see that he ever forgot that he was a slave. He spoke, with some pride, of the factories owned by "master"; and applied the same term to the gentleman who escorted us. His politeness seemed to be a study. A humility was expressed as well in his tone as in his manners. He spoke to the other negroes as if he expected or intended to be obeyed; but he was neither rude, nor unnecessarily severe. With the women, his directions were more in the form of suggestions than of commands.

Of course, there is a very large negro population in Lynchburg.[8] During the day, not so much is seen of them; but early in the evening, they are unpleasantly numerous. The sidewalks, at the best, are narrow and uneven; and the pleasures of a walk are not increased by the crowds of blacks, who intercept your way. They are generally polite, but sometimes run the risk of a kick for the satisfaction of a little insolence. They hang about the corners, they perch on the fences and walls; and, when not asleep on the steps of the porches, keep

up a continual whistling. All along the streets, come the notes of this boy-beloved music. From the dark corners, where some chap is getting himself to sleep; from groups, where they have made wagers as to harmony and wind; from the kitchens, and away down to the river bank. Moreover the Lynchburg blacks have genius, as well as lips; and whistle in a manner well calculated to "soothe the savage breast."[9] It is the tunes of the plantations where they were born, and hope to die; of the factories, where the song lightens their labor; and each is given with an accuracy, and even sweetness, which the instrument cannot always achieve. The negroes stand with their backs to the palings and walls, their hands in their pockets, and braced by their extended legs, whistle away the evening hours. Other gangs pass, whistling their loudest and best, which incites the first to displays of their fullest capacity; and thus the concert goes on. At an early hour, however, the whistling is hushed; and the streets are deserted by the negroes for their blankets in outbuildings and garrets, from which the earliest dawn will call them.

At the Norval House lives "Ned"—undoubtedly related to the person of the same name who "died long ago."[10] We saw a model porter down at the railroad, who said that he was Ned; and after that, we had Ned to light us to our chamber; Ned, to bring us our boots; Ned, to wait at the dinner table; Ned, to run our errands; Ned, to receive quarters, and Ned, to bow to the ground as he bade us farewell. Ned was everywhere, Ned did everything, and what is more, Ned did it well. Ned is a tall, yellow fellow, as straight as an arrow, and as supple as an eel. He certainly never sleeps, and he never sits. His whole life is devoted to the traveling

7. Much of the labor in tobacco factories was performed by slaves hired on a yearly basis. As a rule they were managed by white overseers. Robert, *The Story of Tobacco*, pp. 86–92.
8. There were 3,051 Negroes in Lynchburg in 1860, of whom 357 were free and 2,694 were slaves. Bureau of the Census, *Population of the United States in 1860*, p. 519.

9. William Congreve, *The Mourning Bride*, act 1, sc. 1.
10. Composed by Stephen Collins Foster, the song "Uncle Ned" was published about 1848. John T. Howard, *Stephen Foster: America's Troubador* (New York, 1934), p. 139.

public, and especially that portion allured by his politeness to the Norval House. When the stage rushes to the cars, Ned's face carries a smile as serene as a saint's; and when it rumbles back, loaded with travelers, he hangs on to the door, conversing like a gentleman. He hands out the males, he is delicate with the females. He takes the babies; he lugs baskets, he gathers up shawls and umbrellas; he backs in at the front door; he bows at the foot of the stairs; he lingers at the parlor; he brushes the gentlemen; he sympathizes with exhausted mothers, and caresses squalling infants. But Ned is an example of politeness when you reward him. His hand closes over the coin, his countenance is lighted with the beams of a celestial smile, he places his closed fist upon his heart, and he bows his graceful and grateful thanks. Friend of the weary traveler—man of many accomplishments—thou yellow-hued Chesterfield, may your own journey end "where good darkies go."

There are so many kitchens, stables, and other outbuildings in and about Lynchburg, that the good people are continually apprehensive of fire. Such a calamity happened in July last. As the thermometer ranged something over ninety, and we had witnessed fires rather larger than any likely to occur in Lynchburg, we did not propose to go. But business seemed pretty much suspended, and most of the population—white and black—repaired to the hill where the fire raged. We, accordingly, took our way thither. We found four frame buildings in flames, and the people in a frantic state of excitement. The only means of obtaining water was in pails, from a reservoir not far off, and in this way they expected to check the devouring demon. That wily scoundrel, Richard III., on a certain occasion very much desired a horse;[11] but the cry of the Lynchburgers was for buckets. (In Virginia, all vessels of this kind are

11. William Shakespeare, *Richard III*, 5.4.7.

singularly called "buckets.") Buckets they demanded of the housekeepers and the shopkeepers; buckets! they cried, rushing down the hills, and buckets was their demand as they came perspiring back. New buckets and old buckets, those with hoops and those without; those with holes in the bottom and those with no handles. Everything that day of any description went for a bucket; and every public-spirited citizen ran home to gather all that belonged to him. They formed water lines, and began the battle. Old gentlemen threw water, looking for the object through their spectacles, and young gentlemen threw water around at the fire, but ducking the old gentlemen. Tall fellows ran up ladders and got in the way of other tall fellows, while some youthful but ambitious workers lost half of the water in hauling it up, and then proudly tossed many of the most venerable buckets from the roofs to the ground. There were ladies in full fashion, and influential citizens on horseback; there were ancient Virginians with pipes in their mouths and sadness in their hearts; and there were juvenile negroes, who danced and stood on their heads for very joy at such a frolic. After wasting as much water as they could, smashing up most of the pails, and each man had worked himself up to the standard of a hero, the fire had burnt itself out, and the labors were happily suspended.

Near us was an old negro woman. On her head was a kind of sun-bonnet, and her sleeves were rolled up very nearly to her shoulders. She had a loud voice, knew everybody, and was overwhelmed at the scene before her. "King of Israel," she exclaimed, "dis am thy judgment. Oh, golly! oh, golly!" Another aged negress approached, and desired to talk with this one. "You, Aunt Chloe," said the first, angrily, "la, sakes now, ain't you ashamed to open you mouf, when de King of Israel am in de elements. Get along, get along wid ye." "La, Aunt Dinah," was all the second seemed to dare to say. "I doesn't want dese yer niggers speaking to me," continued Aunt Dinah, for the edification of the crowd of blacks standing about her. "Dis am a day of wrath—de Lord Jesus am aggrivated at sinners. Oh, golly, child'en, oh golly."

The old woman raised the corner of her apron to wipe the big tears which now started from her eyes. Presently she burst through the crowd with uplifted hands, and exclaiming, "Great King of Israel!—g-r-e-a-t King of I-s-r-a-e-l!"

A PEDAGOGUE IN GEORGIA

This tongue-in-cheek autobiographical narration, written by a self-confessed Yankee schoolmaster, hardly could have endeared him to southern readers.

In one of the back numbers of "Pea Green," a feminine hand touched, gently and skilfully, a few items of the experience of a school-mistress in Texas. The famous picture of Shenstone's[1] is not at hand to verify her words by quotation; perhaps, with all his sympathy for the character, the Texan adventuress could teach the poet, if living, some things out of the circle of his observations. Her narration carries internal evidence of truth to the mind of any one who has cast an eye occasionally, out of a southern school-room. The following jottings have been instigated by her description, and so far as they coincide in spirit, their features must be accorded to her as the first gleaner.

Some of the good people of the Middle States, and a portion of New England, now and then, humorously sketch a Yankee teacher, in the words of the quasi proverb, that he comes up from the east with a spelling book in one hand, and a halter in the other, prepared for either extreme, of "teaching a school or stealing a horse." This was once so generally true, that the caustic saying of a quiet wit embraced the experience of neighborhoods. Beyond the latitude of those States, the equipment has changed in appearance, though not in reality. Halters are exchanged for patent medicines, or new inventions. Within a range of a score of miles, are five Yankee teachers, now the heads of good schools, formerly the hawkers of pills, lightning-rods, tooth-ache drops, and various syrups. Laying aside their peripatetic Galenships, they assume the stole of a master and dispute the palm of encyclopaedic knowledge with the lawyer and priest of the vicinage. Besides, they teach no schools—nothing less than an *academy*, ye shades of Attick doctors. The reply of Boswell's father, the Scotch "Laird of Auchinleck," to an inquirer was printed: "There's nae hope for Jamie, mon. Jamie is gaen clean gyte. What do you think, mon? He's done wi' Paoli—he's off wi' the land-louping scoundrel of a Corsican; and whose tail do you think he has pinned himself to now, mon? A *dominie*, mon—and auld dominie; he keepit a schule, and cau'd it an *acaademy*." Old Auchnileck had an eye for the pretension of his day, and has stamped well the full-grown humbug of the present—the one humbug which overshadows all others of whatever marvellous presumptions. Schools no longer exist in the towns and villages, rarely in the

[H. Hodges], "A Pedagogue in Georgia," *Putnam's Magazine* 5 (February 1855): 187–92.
1. William Shenstone's poem "The Schoolmistress," which appeared in 1742, was an idealized portrayal of his first teacher. *Dictionary of National Biography*, 18:48.

fields; academies and colleges supplant them. All this in a parenthesis.

Finding that a magisterial port and learned way procured more respect and dollars than peddling elixirs and panaceas, the change is effected in the moulting of a snake. Some found it to their pecuniary advantage, or the stepping stone to sudden competencies. Others followed, enticed by the glittering narratives of teachers, who married young heiresses or witching widows, with much land and many negroes. The romance is still alluring enough to draw yearly its supply of ready-made teachers. Within a few years the proverb above has become acclimated at Southern hearths; so that the reception of Yankee masters is on the wane.

Such was the state of the field when your informant came hither; a change for the better quality of instructors was the quotation of the public feeling, and nothing less than "a graduate" was received. Yet some of the old regime then existed, and still rule the benches. This immigration, in spite of prejudice, was in many things much the best, as far as conscientious faithfulness was concerned. They knew the "spelling-book" and taught it; now the spelling-book is nearly effete. An illustration; a few evenings since, one of New England's originals, half actor, half tailor, who has wandered hither, under the half-spent force communicated to him by his progenitor Ishmael, became excited in a conversation with the installed schoolmaster, and exclaimed—"I reckon I know its spelling right; look in Webster; there you'll find it—in the spellin' book—I didn't teach school three months in New Orleans for nothin'—and when I quit, I was a dab at spellin'."

Would that more of both instructors and pupils were orthographical "dabs." For reasonable hope might then be entertained that the present woeful tortion of the alphabet would be exchanged for a knowledge of English letters, at least, superior to the "elegant extracts" exhibited in Dutch ad-

vertisements, and on the signs of cross-roads groceries. When the present generation of active business men has passed away, their sons may advance with capacities better trained to estimate the curriculum of a choice instruction. Advancement has been made, and further improvement in the attitude of the general understanding cannot be checked. It must come, like the wave climbing to the breast of the cliff, at whose foot the spray of the on-coming waters is now hardly cast.

This half prophesy could not have been uttered years ago, as the writer lamentably felt, at his entrance upon the soil of Georgia. I had been placed in school for years—long enough to acquire, by moderate industry, some of the outlines of the wide fields open to the eye of judgment and imagination; a stubborn rust of habit had overgrown the body, and seemingly tended to the inertness of a reading life. A sudden misfortune as suddenly acted upon, wrested me from the shadows of the Green Mountains, and impelled me southward, where I expected to find rolling Savannahs instinct with majesty and quiet power, but where were found neglected fallow-grounds, overlaid with pine-knots and alive with lizards. An early frost had cut short the hope of the planter, and laid low the luxuriant beauty of Georgian vegetation. The climate seemed but the slow fever of a wasting land. Its mildness was a contrast to the repulsive features of the soil. Imagination had formed a false picture of perpetual blooms and the never-ceasing song of birds—falsely; ay, *how* falsely, he only can tell, who has never witnessed the fierce heats of noonday suns firing the air with tropic rays, whose vertical shafts are red-hot arrows, while a bastard simoom sweeps the land. How, then, can even a blown imagination reproduce the lithe vine, the tangled green of the thicket, the overheaped baskets of flowers wildly thrown by the early year broadcast over forest and glade?

Vivid fancy and plastic form collected the

shattered beauty of the Venus de Medicis; but, when Nature drops withered remains in Autumn's lap, what spirit shall call back the once unchallenged grace of her painting to the anatomy of the skeleton, save the revolution of that stern god, Time, that binds and unbinds, creates and destroys, delighting in the change and interchange of the circle of things? My eager appetite for novel forms of natural loveliness kecked at the inferiority of the landscape of a Southern autumn, to the checkered livery of the Northern dolphin.

Perhaps, this disgust was increased by the ways of some of the people inhabiting the red hills and sandy bottoms of the arable lands. Quere: Reader, how would the top Pelham or Beau Brummel[2] have felt, once thrown into the society of Squire Westerns and Commodore Trunnions?[3] Similarly, in manner, if not degree, did I feel, in exchanging the precise and select demeanor of teachers for the naturally fresh, though seemingly uncouth ways of planters. Like many others, I came well laden with introductory letters, serviceable only for the moment, valuable only in forming speaking acquaintances, as the experience of many will testify. As the hunter for schools passes about among the people, a somewhat intimate knowledge is gained of the habits of the sturdy landlords. My first essay was by no means encouraging. The resources of introductions being exhausted, and

with little benefit, I determined to conceal or not exhibit an equally large bundle of testimonials of capacity. Well, that I did. I have since seen some ludicrous receptions given to these wordy and cheap papers of ability, and had cause to thank prudence in this matter.

Throwing these into a corner of my trunk, I mounted a clay-bank colored nag, and rode to the hunt, thinking that fortune would smile upon the first effort—that the attempt would be of a Caesarean type, "*veni, vidi, vici.*"[4] My visions of personal importance and overweening assumption were thoroughly dissipated in the course of two days. My horse proved worse than the rocking horse once used as a penalty for minor felonies.[5]

This mode of conveyance for twenty or thirty miles was novel to me, and the novelty became the greater as observation showed it to be a general custom. Light vehicles are more in vogue now, but not sufficient to destroy the custom. Every one has his horse, like the Arab, however poor he may be, even if he wants the Irishman's more serviceable companion, the cow. Has the reader ever noticed the journey of Peverel[6] on horseback through the west of England, which the masterly hand of the great Scotch novelist has illustrated with his usual fascinating colors of national customs. If he has been lead by his curiosity in this matter, he will be pleased to note the correspondence between the times of the Commonwealth, and our own day in this trivial point. The custom, and the rate of daily travel confined to an easy walk, are the same—thus continuing a journey of days and weeks in the unvarying jog.

2. Pelham, a character in a novel by Bulwer-Lytton, aspired to be the model of the complete gentleman. George Bryan Brummell, known as Beau Brummell, was a leader of fashionable society in London. William S. Walsh, *Heroes and Heroines of Fiction*, 2 vols. (Philadelphia, 1966), p. 296; *Century Dictionary and Cyclopedia*, 9:189.

3. Squire Western, a character in Henry Fielding's *Tom Jones*, was the epitome of the coarse, rustic, English squire of the eighteenth century; Commodore Trunnion, who appears in Tobias Smollett's *Adventures of Peregrine Pickle*, was an eccentric retired naval officer. They may be said to typify crudeness and lack of sophistication. Walsh, *Heroes and Heroines of Fiction*, 1:364, 382.

4. Julius Caesar is said to have used these words in his *Letter to Amantius* announcing his victory over Pharnaces.

5. In Massachusetts a person accused of drunkenness was forced to ride a wooden horse while holding an empty pitcher in one hand. Adams, *Dictionary of American History*, 4:382.

6. A character in Walter Scott's novel *Peveril of the Peak*.

My day's ride ended in a hamlet called the "dark corner," with more of truth than poetry. Morning showed what the fatigue of the previous night had hid from view—the hotel—perhaps its repute in the vicinity was equal to that of metropolitan hotels, or those of fashionable watering-places. My attempts to procure a school were limited to a few inquiries —being satisfied with appearances, often worse than the actuality.

Here was another innovation on old ideas—the day being Saturday, divine worship was held in the neighborhood on this and the succeeding day. Accepting the invitation of the landlord, with others, I went to the meeting-house, prompted more by curiosity than devotion. The results of inquiry only quickened curiosity.

My lot was in the midst of "Hard Shell Baptists." This term "Hard Shell" has no reference to political divisions, whether of Northern, Western, or Southern origin; but was given to the denomination because, professing the same general creed as other Baptists, they withhold all support to foreign evangelical missions, against which they set their faces like flint. They are generally very plain people, indulging in no ostentation or luxury, mostly with moderate means, and for their proverbial honesty and promptness in paying debts may be called the Quakers of the South. They ape no style, are led away by no fashions, hate all popular innovations upon manners and beliefs, and esteem strong common-sense, unaided by disciplinary instruction, in its disconnected utterances, as superior to all the lumber of books and graces of schools. (Hence my efforts to teach were rationally durable.)

The meeting-house, whither we walked, was built of hewn logs, unceiled and unplastered, with sliding window-shutters of plank, having long benches placed, as in a school-room, for seats; it was situated in a grove, a short way from the hamlet, near a pleasant spring of water. Hither, in the course of a few hours, came numerous planters with wives on pillions, now a horse, now a mule bearing two or three girls or boys—none coming in light wagons, or provincially "buggies."

Honest, quiet, and cordial greetings seemed perfectly natural to them all as they met in groups, intentionally or by accident, as by second nature, under the broad trees. Stranger as I was, I yet received the cordial grasp and the conversational coin of the day. After the discussion of planting interests and kindred topics was exhausted, a white-locked father stood in the door, and proclaimed—"The hour for service is cum, bretheren." Instantly, the buzz and laugh outside ceased, there was a smoothing of hair, cleansing of throats, brushing of clothes, a unanimous start for the doors, women to the right and men to the left. The staid members of the church took their seats near the pulpit; others in regular bench platoons, according to grade and age of piety and years; while the frolicsome fell back in the rear seats, behind whom were the slaves. When once within, and the eyes were cast about, the interior brings to mind the quaint conceit of old George Chapman:—

> If ever I be worth a house again,
> I'll build all inward; not a light shall ope
> The common out-way; no expense; no art,
> No ornaments, no door, will I use there;
> But raise all plain and rudely, like a vamuria
> Against the false society of men,
> That still batters
> All reason piece-meal, and for earthly greatness
> All heavenly comforts rarifies the air,
> I'll therefore live in dark; and all my light,
> Like ancient temples, let in at my top.[7]

7. These lines are spoken by Pompey in *The Tragedy of Caesar and Pompey*, 5.1.205–15. George Chapman, *The Plays of George Chapman*, edited with introductions and notes by Thomas Marc Parrott, 4 vols. (New York, 1961), 2:392.

The Elizabethan poet was a "Hardshell" in his style of architecture—perhaps a little more of a non-comformist than his modern brothers. However, the present house seemed more suitable to a warm climate than to English dampness.

If the "Hards"—or as they designate themselves, the Primitive Baptists—discard all claim to fashion in other matters, as sincerely as in the conduct of "service," there seems to be no place for future in-break upon idiosyncracy of the sect. How the patriarchs regulated antediluvian worship, in their wide pasture-lands, may be a mooted question among Biblical antiquarians; yet conjecture might receive some hints touching the question, among the modern worshippers in the woods. Form consists in the want of all forms; ceremony is only a traditional rule to follow general impulses. The fashionable choirs of cathedrals, the stiff routine of a village band of singers or the fire-side songs by family voices, differ from the ragged surges of forest airs, ebbing and flowing with individual caprice, monotone, quaver, slide, slip, and burst, in the same degree, manner, spirit and originality, as Jullien's orchestral triumphs[8] differ from the banjo tune of a negro, in the back room of a "piney-woods" grocery. Bob Acres[9] would describe them as perfect "masters and mistresses of flat and sharp, squallante, rumblante and quiverante."

Thus far, as being but a poor singer, my judgment was liable to err; in the remainder, this deponent wishes to be understood as conforming to

8. Louis Antoine Jullien, a French conductor, was best known for his concerts in London, which were usually planned to reflect contemporary events. A very colorful person, he was the subject of many cartoons in *Punch*. *Grove's Dictionary of Music and Musicians*, 5 vols. (New York, 1927), 2:797-98.

9. Bob Acres, a character in Sheridan's comedy *The Rivals*, is a mixture of the country squire and the London man-about-town. Walsh, *Heroes and Heroines*, pp. 4-5.

historic accuracy. After the songs, expectation labored through a deep silence of ——— minutes for the uprising of the preacher. He uprose—a man of hard aspect, a covenanter in blood and deed, not a mark on him of silken orthodoxy, but clad in home-spun, hybrid cut, between the full Quaker's dress, and the sportsman's roundabout. His locks were trimmed like the Puritans, who used to cut their hair along the rim of a basin turned over their heads; his low projecting forehead hung down on a large flat nose, nearly concealing the eyes beneath a shag of brows; a close shaven chin was dappled with the blue roots of a veteran beard; around the neck a cavernous stock, into which at times the chin sunk like a log swaying in deep waters; his narrow shoulders jerked, his long arms became violently excited, and twirled around and around in the loud parts of his sermon. Excitability no one would expect, who saw him stand peering over the seats, then contracted in a stolid mood, and predestinated hump, not deigning to speak, hardly to move, save the rolling eyes. Suspense was broken by an asthmatic note; he rasped his throat with another phlegmatic retch, raised the book high in the long arms, took a long look around—and laid the Bible down. He placed the handkerchief, which is usually esteemed the peculiar banner of priesthood, under the lid. The preacher rested his arms on the desk, and breathed audibly. The chin fell within the rim of the open-mouthed stock. Again he stood erect, took out a purse, laid a bit of money on the desk, and paused; again lifted up the book, read two verses from the Testament, replaced the book, wiped his mouth, and replaced the handkerchief in the consecrated spot, and spoke:

"Breethereen, I came to this text in a sing'lar way—I determned that I'd take hold of no text that didn't take hold of me—I read one text, and it didn't take hold of me; I read another, and it didn't, and so on and on, till I cum to the *twelfth*, and as it didn't take hold of me, *so I took hold of it.* Here it is, in the good book. Now breethereen, do ye read yer Bibles? I want to see how many knows where them verses is found. Now, I'll bet this here dime" (showing the silver coin in the tips of his fingers) "none here kin tell me where them verses is found"—and the venerable preacher clenched the bet against the house, by a blow on the desk that would have felled an ox.

Does the reader need any comment other than his own manufacture? Make no illicit comparisons; comparisons have no place in such emergencies; wonder alone locks the senses in a pulseless, breathless rest. There is no buzz or mark of astonishment exhibited by the audience, other than the ordinary turn of the head. All seemed right; yet they looked as though they hoped some one would name the text rightly. The look showed nothing but a curiosity as to who would be the lucky one that could uphold the claim of "Hard Shells," touching their familiarity with the Bible. It was a challenge from the clergy to the laity. Would, *could* any dear brother or sister meet the preacher on his own ground? Curiosity began to slacken, to waver, became uncertain, finally came doubt, settling down into defeat. The preacher had the day and in triumphant note would berate them for slothfulness, and send them home stung with his sarcasm. Hope was gone, when a lank, bony frame rose near the desk, buttoned up a blue over-all, that fell to his feet, and shrugged his angular shoulders. After all eyes were centered on him, he turned up his face to the preacher, and said "Brother, it is a small bet, *but I never let 'em pass*"; he referred the passage correctly, and sat down. "The money's yourn."

The preacher had met his match, and carried no flag of triumph. The sermon which followed, was spoken languidly—energy, life, pointed and pert, were fled—the repulse given by the lay brother to the clergy had broken the charm of the preacher's speech—his brain was pressed down with the incubus of chagrin. The war-note was changed for the evening hymn; the bugle gave place to the shepherd's pipe. The sermon closed; the announcement was given out that the "ord'nance of feet-washin' ud take place" on the morrow, in connection with the administration of the Lord's Supper. What? Did I hear aright? Feet-washing? —what did it mean? Silence again was the best resort, through fear of exposing myself to laughter, by inquiring into the matter, or confession to a scoffing spirit if found in error. My perplexity was broken by a short discussion in the course of the day, during which a "Hard" quoted the passages of "Scripter" taken as authority by the sect, for the institution and performance of public "feet-washing," as a religious rite.

Here was an episode in a school-master's life, unforeseen by Henry Brougham,[10] when he sent the pedagogue "abroad"; for which, perhaps the great reformer is unaccountable, as the rite is out of the establishment, and would be looked upon by High or Low Church with the same amazement as the old Roman Flamens[11] portrayed, when told of the barbarous ritual of interior Germany.

On the next day, the concourse of people at the "meetin' house" was larger than the day before. A new brother was expected to hold forth, causing some little bustle. His sermon, when begun, was original beyond the possibility of a doubt. His object seemed to be to delineate some of the proprieties of familiar intercourse and check such of the practices as were unauthorized by "Hard Shell" usage. Several of the popular reforms and

10. Brougham was a celebrated British statesman, jurist, and scientist. One biographer has said, "His attainments were manifold, and he wrote and spoke as a teacher on almost every subject under the sun." *Dictionary of National Biography*, 2:1364.
11. Special priests devoted to special duties. Harry T. Peck, ed., *Harper's Dictionary of Classical Literature and Antiquities* (New York, 1863), p. 675.

associations were bluntly rebuffed, or scouted as "in folly ripe and reason rotten." Maine Liquor Law [12] was not then known as a political measure; yet the same ultimate end was foreshadowed by Temperance Societies and Sons of Temperance; this was enough for the spirit of the speaker, who levelled his heaviest guns against their batteries and felt himself successful in planting some stunning blows. He was a prose Anacreon [13] in his adherence to Bacchus, as a duty in acknowledging the good things of the world, by a moderate use, reproving their abuse, keeping the golden mean and avoiding all extremes. Excess and Tee-totalism were his Scylla and Charybdis. To show that he was within the pale of the "Primitives" in this matter, he narrated a case of discipline in which Brother Dupeasy had been reproved by the church for over-indulgence in peach-brandy; and upon the assertion of Brother Dupeasy that he would never touch another drop as long as he lived, he was again reproved for rejecting the manifest gifts of mercy, and, moreover, the brother was ordered to continue his occasional glass but never to be overcome by the use. "That's the Primitive doctrine, isn't it breethereen?"—a nodding of heads and bonnets on right and left fortified the worthy laborer in his exposition of tenets.

The General Mission spirit was slightly touched, as being a subject of too much magnitude to be embraced in a single sermon; still there was promised a future hour of reckoning against this Gorgon of Hydras. [14]

12. The only Maine liquor law that could be found was one passed in 1835 which prohibited the sale of liquor to Indians. Maine, Laws, Statutes, etc., *The Revised Statutes of the State of Maine* (Bangor, Me., 1857), p. 316.
13. A Greek poet (563–478 B.C.) who sang chiefly of love and wine. *Century Dictionary and Cyclopedia*, 9:53.
14. In Greek mythology the gorgons were three sisters whose heads were covered with writhing serpents instead of hair, and the hydra was a large serpent or dragon having nine heads. Ibid., 3:2579; 4:2931.

As a final shifting of pulpit light, notice was taken of colloquial expressions, by the censor of public morals; in his appeals to the congregation for confirmations of his positions, he frequently turned to his associate in the desk, who sat behind him, and asked if such and such an assertion was not true—and was uniformly answered in the affirmative. His objurgations were mostly hurled towards idle words, cant forms of speech and popular slang: he was distressed in this matter, and labored loudly, dogmatically, and hotly, for thorough reform in these particulars. There was considerable room for complaint, as his reception exhibited.

"Breethereen, it won't do, this talk ain't primitive; we must give up them worldly remarks—must we not brother? must we not sister?" The appeal direct was answered by a favoring nod from said brother and sister. "Yes sir-ee and no sir-ee is slang terms and is forbidden. I don't like 'em, nor no brother don't like 'em; they despise 'em—they jeest 'bhor 'em, kind o' naturally (and wheeling to his clerical brother in the back of the pulpit exclaimed)—I'm determined to set my face agin 'em, now and for ever, like them brothers and sisters, ain't you brother?"

"Yes sir-ee, hoss!" replied the tripping divine. There was need of "line upon line," &c., [15] to such a waiting people.

Exhortation finished the exercise; then followed an actual general *washing of feet*, by the members of the church; the women occupying one side, behind a screen; the men openly and boldly presenting themselves for cleansing. They advanced in couples; one took his seat and bared his foot and leg to the knee, while the other laying aside his coat, girding himself with a towel, kneeled at the basin and washed and wiped the ready member; offices were then exchanged, the couple retired, and

15. Isaiah 28:10.

another brace of the unwashed came up to the water. Four or more couples were busy together—exhorting each other with good counsel, and flattering unction, familiarly quoting the words of "Brother Peter and Brother Paul." Day's worship being closed, all went homeward, the young pairing off in couples through the woods.

My object in visiting this region was fruitless in direct benefit, but indirectly of much instruction and a little new insight into human nature. My attention was called the next day to a "notice" stuck up with wafers on the walls of the piazza. Ye great national educators and Smithsonian Rectors, read:

> WANTED, A teacher with a family, whose services are worth 500 dollars a year. Come and you will be as a light in a shining land. Our county contains over 1000 adults who do not know their alphabet. Come and we trust a halo of success will crown your efforts. We appeal to the ladies of ——— for assistance.

"Our county" was in my route; thither I went, and may possibly detail hereafter its incidents, if these "present presentments" please.

GENERAL HUNTER'S TEXAS LETTER

John Lingard Hunter (1794–1868) was born in Charleston, South Carolina, of English-Scotch descent. He graduated from South Carolina College and became a planter and a military leader in the Creek Indian Wars, ultimately achieving the rank of major general in the militia. In 1835 he sold his two large plantations in South Carolina and moved to Eufaula, Alabama. In addition to creating a major plantation of his own there, he played a principal role in converting what hitherto had been merely an Indian village, into a prosperous town, Irwinton. He became a trustee of the University of Alabama and was elected to the state legislature in 1841.[1]

In introducing Hunter's article, James M. Chambers, the agricultural editor of Soil of the South, *wrote: "General Hunter has made an extensive examination of Texas and has generously communicated . . . information which has cost him many days of laborious travel, and coming as it does from one of so much intelligence and integrity cannot fail to be read by all those who are feeling any concern about that vast and growing country."*

Messrs. Editors: Be pleased to excuse my desire to make a medium of your very interesting and widely circulating journal to communicate to the public a brief and imperfect sketch of Texas in general, and middle western Texas in particular, after several months travel and sojourn in that country. I am induced to take this course in response to numerous applications upon the subject of Texas, as well as to disabuse the public mind in many particulars concerning that interesting and lovely country.

In doing so, I shall endeavor to say nothing incompatible with truth and justice.

My travel was through the low country from

John L. Hunter, "Gen. Hunter's Texas Letter," *Soil of the South* 4 (September, October 1854): 258–61, 291–95.
1. Owen, *History of Alabama*, 3:872.

Galveston to the gulf, where I landed from New Orleans, across the Brazos, near San Philipe, and to the middle country across the Colorado near Bastrop, and west to the San Marcus and surrounding country; continued north to the city of Austin, the seat of government and its surrounding country. As for other more extensive portions of Texas, the writer's information is derived from reading, intercourse, and conversation with intelligent citizens from various sections of the State.

The State of Texas is an inclined plain, gradually sloping from north-west to south-east, as shown by the rivers taking that course and direction to the sea, the most elevated portion of her territory and mountains, if high and wide spreading hills can be called mountains, being situated in the former.

The territory is vastly extensive, embracing every variety of soil and climate, and holds a very thin population and a small agricultural community. It may be properly divided into two grand divisions of eastern and western, or the wooded and prairie region and subdivided into the low country, commencing at the sea-coast and the middle and up country, as you go into the interior. There is a very interesting portion of country on the waters of the Colorado and the eastern part of the Gaudalupe, which may be termed the mixed region of wood and prairie. The eastern or wooded region is the smallest of the two, and extends from the Sabine, the eastern boundary, west to the Trinity and Brazos, a distance of several hundred miles.

The lands and country in eastern Texas are not very dissimilar to those of the other Gulf States, with the exception of having more large and extensive bodies of level and rich soil interspersed with small prairies, otherwise a well timbered country. That portion situated on the waters of Red river and the bayous of Louisiana are very convenient and accessible to the great cotton market of New Orleans—advantages at this time superior to any other portions of the State, and which has on that account attracted the notice and motivated the earlier settlement of the emigrant in pursuit of good cotton lands. This country does not bear a name distinguished for health, although it is said by the old settlers to have proven to them as healthy as the rich bodies of land in the other Southern States.

In settling a new country covered with trees, the emigrant must expect from clearing for cultivation, and the consequent decomposition of timber and vegetable matter, more or less sickness. As the traveler bends his way west, the country exhibits more extensive prairies—less wood, although mixed till he reaches the Guadalupe and San Antonio, when it becomes with the exception of matts and small groves of live oak, scattering musquit trees and narrow skirts of timber, on the water courses, an entire open prairie region. The land is a rich soil of deep black mould, covered with luxuriant growth of the most nutricious grass, called musquit, after the tree of that name, so abundant in that section; a tree and grass that only grow upon the richest soil and not found east of the Colorado. This country from its deficiency of wood must be doomed, and set apart almost exclusively to the stock raising business, till from density of population and rising value of land, a resort will be had to hedging, wire fences, and the use of coal which may be discovered convenient.* The range for cattle is said to be inexhaustible in the neighborhood of San Antonio, one of the oldest towns in America, it has been grazed upon for more than a hundred years, and still to this day, affords sustenance and good pasturage for cattle; stock in western Texas is the most profitable business that can be pursued, yielding upon the capital invested more than fifty per cent per annum.

.   .   .

The farmers are so well satisfied of the adaptation of the country to stock raising in the mixed

*Beds of Coal have been discovered in the middle and up country.

551

*General Hunter's
Texas Letter*

wooded and prairie region, that they devote a large portion of their capital to stock in connection with the cotton culture. The writer has observed with astonishment the smallness of the cotton crop growing,[2] with the largeness of their stock roaming the rich prairies. He had formed an opinion that the sale of their beef cattle (for they never sell breeding cattle only as a matter of favor and that in small numbers) would be attended with much difficulty, trouble and expense, but he was informed and afterwards became acquainted with the fact that purchasers came to their doors to buy at very remunerating prices for California, the home, and New Orleans markets, and they had the trifling trouble of driving their beeves not many miles to a place selected by the purchaser for collecting and making up his drove to carry off.

The raising of cattle is not the only stock raising —some make it an exclusive business to raise horses and mules and have large cavyards or droves of horses which they get from Mexico at a low price, taking care to improve the breed by crossing with American stock. But there are few planters or farmers who have not a number of Mexican Mustangs* to breed on. The writer has seen large droves of hogs in fine order roving the woods, which he was assured had never seen corn but to keep them gentle, that they found abundant support from the mast of the oak, pecan, wild peach and plumb and roots with which the woods and prairies abound.

The prairies of western Texas present a scene picturesque and romantic, of surpassing beauty and loveliness, such as nature rarely exhibits to the admiring gaze of the traveller. Her natural lawns covered with rich grass and a variety of flowers, interspersed with matts or small groves of wide-spreading live-oak and rivulets of water, with a gurgling noise rushing down a small cascade of rocks, remind him of the groves, parks, and pleasure grounds of the country of Old England, and every stride he takes, his imagination is beset that he is approaching a nobleman's palace, or castle sheltered from public gaze, by clusters of wide-spreading trees; the latter (England) to a large extent, is the adornment by the skill, the art and taste of man, at the cost of countless millions, to gratify the pride and pleasure of the Magnates and noblemen of the land, with a million revenue at their command; whilst the former (the prairies of Texas), are the handy work of nature to please nature's noblemen, the sovereign people of a glorious land.

The Editor of the *New York Mirror*, has lately

2. In 1849 Texas produced 58,073 bales of cotton. Ten years later this figure had risen to 431,645 bales. New lands had been opened up for cultivation by the removal of Indians. The introduction of barbed wire and the building of railroads also stimulated the production of cotton. Webb, *Handbook of Texas*, 1:420.

*The Mustang, or Mexican poney, is in general something larger than the English donkey, or South Carolina Marsh Tackey, tough and durable as either, but not so docile and submissive. The Mexicans and Americans have but little mercy upon the Mustang, they are travelled all day long, I am told, 50 or 60 miles a day, and staked out at night upon the prairie—staking—a sharp pointed stick driven in the ground, with a rope, one end of which is attached to the stake, and the other to the Mustang or other animal.

The writer was amused with the extraordinary skill of the Mexican in the use of the Lasso, a long cord made of three or four strips of cowhide plaited together with a slip knot at one end, and the other, if he be riding, is fastened to his saddle. With surprising swiftness, he takes after the horse (or other object he wishes to catch) singles him out from the herd and away they go, until arriving at a proper distance, he whirls the lasso once or twice around his head, then with unerring aim he throws it, and the horse is caught around the neck, or sometimes it happens, that they cannot separate them from the drove, they then resort to a tree, which he climbs, and having fastened securely one end of the lasso to the limbs, he then hides from view, awaits the drove which is driven by the tree, when his practiced eye alights upon the right one passing, he throws it and checks, and holds fast, the animal unconscious from whence it came.

visited the prairies, I presume, of far western Texas, and says, the best possible idea of a prairie may be obtained by imagining a rich, smooth, luxuriant and highly cultivated English meadow, expanded beyond the line of vision, without trees, without fences, unobstructed by any object that rises above the surface of the soft and gently waving verdure. Instead of wilderness, they present the appearance of a sort of Titanic culture, as if the Gods themselves had rolled out these infinite lawns whereon the children of the assembled universe might have ample room to run and play.

In ascending into the interior from the seaboard, the country for 40 to 60 miles is remarkable for its extreme level surface, approaching to apparently a dead level, and forms or makes the low country of Texas. From limited observation, and information otherwise derived, it is a very rich and fertile soil, and upon the Brazos and Colorado, may be found large bodies of level land, not surpassed in richness of soil and beauty of scenery, by any portion of the habitable globe. From the extreme level surface, after heavy rains and fall of water, but for its being an inclined plain, I would presume that this section would be slow to drain, and a portion of the water have to pass off by solar evaporation. It is fortunate for the health and comfort of this low country, that dry weather most particularly in the west, greatly preponderates, heavy rains, seldom occur in the summer season. The low country of Texas, like the low country of all the Southern States, has the reputation of being sickly; great and numerous have been the reports of the ravages of cholera and other diseases, no doubt, greatly magnified and exaggerated. Many of the losses and misfortunes which befall emigrants to this region, or in passing through it, may be attributed to their own imprudence and indiscretion in the management and government of their slave property as regards not providing proper diet, suitable clothing and comfortable quarters against bad and wet weather and

crowded apartments. Those who can afford the time, might find it to their advantage to go by land, provided they can start in October, so as to reach their place of destination before the rising of the waters of the rivers and creeks, and in time for preparing and setting the crop. Here the cane, cotton and corn are cultivated with eminent success— from 60 to 80 bushels per acre of corn, and more than a bale of cotton, making no uncommon return.

I am disposed to consider this the sugar region of Texas; better adapted to the culture of the cane.[3] In the course of time, in such a low latitude and level country, I would not be surprised if cotton when the land wears, became subject to worms and diseases—the cotton crop very uncertain and abandoned to the culture of the cane.

To the large planter, more in pursuit of wealth than health and comfort, this region from the low price of land and great natural advantages, offers great inducements to the emigrant. As regards the remarks upon the sickliness of this region—they were intended to be general; that there are many healthy and beautiful situations, particularly upon the seaboard, he does not deny; one such place has been represented to him almost as a paradise.

In leaving the low country, the surface becomes gently undulating, and in some places slightly hilly, and continues gradually to rise for 60 to 70 miles, and may be called the middle country of Texas, and regarded as the most certain cotton country and most comfortable and healthy, particularly the western portion of it. The soil, although not to compare with Oyster creek, Brazos or old Caney Colorado, in the low country, is in general, a rich

3. Stephen F. Austin was probably the first (1829) to experiment with the cultivation of sugar cane in Texas. Cultivation of cane continued in the following years, reaching its peak in the 1850s. A series of severe winters and droughts, coupled with the loss of slave labor, forced its abandonment. Webb, *Handbook of Texas*, 2:684.

black mould of great depth and fertility. It has been fully tested in the neighborhood of Washington and Independence, on the Brazos and Bastrop, and LaGrange, on the Colorado, as well as upon the San Marcos, Trinity, Red River, and other parts of Eastern Texas and proven very productive in cotton and corn. "The undulating or rolling lands, says a writer, have obtained and deserve a very high character; they are what in any part of the United States, east of the mountains, would be called deservedly rich lands, well watered, healthy and productive in corn and cotton." Although the health and water may be good in general, there are localities unfavorable to both.

The mixed or wooded and prairie region, extending from West Brazos to East Guadalupe, in the middle country in and about 30 degrees North latitude, attracted the notice and attention of the writer, as a most interesting country, offering fair prospects of health, competence, and pleasure to the cotton culture emigrant, particularly of moderate property, or limited means; here he can cultivate a soil that will amply remunerate him, and at little trouble and no expense, raise stock, not only for the use of his plantation, but as a source of revenue also, and if he desires to go further up on the stock business, he can have his cotton and stock farm separate, and at convenient distance, that the overseer and proprietor can superintend both.

The San Marcos exhibited a rich and beautiful country; the banks are high and said not to be subject to inundation; the inhabitants live on the banks and use the river water and appear to enjoy good health. The tracts are laid off by the Mexican authorities in a shape inconvenient and ugly; the same being done upon all the rivers. One tract which the writer particularly examined, with a view of purchasing, was width on the river 869 varras Mexican equal to about 320 American acres, length 6,650 varras or about 2,000 acres, 250 of which was fine rich valley soil, of a light chocolate color, exhibiting the presence of a large preponderance of shell lime, then running into a rich black mould; the general character of the prairies off the water courses, all open prairie except about one hundred acres of timber and wood just on the margin of the river, too small to keep up the plantation with very moderate improvements, a few indifferent small houses and a clearing of about 60 acres, the owner offered for eight dollars per acre, which the writer regarded as too high with the present want of market facilities. The Colorado exhibited a similar appearance with high banks. The writer passed through Webbers plantation 20 miles below Austin, immediately on that river and admired the rich black soil and level surfaces, perhaps too level for pleasant cultivation, and he would suppose an unsightly and unsuitable site for the inhabitants to congregate in a town. The village is called Webbersville,[4] situated a few hundred yards from the river. If the river was a good navigable one, which it is very far from being, he would think the object of the location was to enjoy commercial facilities. He passed in a very rainy spell and was astonished to find so many would reside in a place at that time so uncomfortable, when by going to the hills or elevated grounds, a mile or two, a more dry and comfortable place could be found. Many places in the middle country on the Colorado can be found higher and drier, and if not so rich as Webber's prairie, rich enough for all practical purposes. As it is a dry country or dry weather greatly preponderates, the inhabitants are reconciled to their situation in a wet or rainy spell, which but seldom occurs, and does not last long in order to be convenient to a very rich and productive soil, which it exhibited in cotton and corn. The soil over this whole region, says a writer, is a dark vegetable mould, slightly mixed with sand and

4. First called Webber's Prairie, this village was established in 1839. When it was bypassed by the railroad, it failed to grow to any extent. Webb, *Handbook of Texas*, 2:875.

shells; warm and fertile in the highest degree, and a depth that must render its fertility inexhaustable. The dry atmosphere and the undulation of the country, are said to render the prairies more pleasant for residence and cultivation, than those of any other prairie country.

The soil of this section may be divided into hog-wallow and smooth prairie; both kinds of soil are frequently found on the same tract of land, the former as the name indicates, is of a very uneven surface, and in wet weather holds water; it is said to be very rich but hard to bring into cultivation, and slow in making returns, taking several years before a full crop can be realized. About four or five yokes of oxen are required to break it up and will cost, if you prefer to have it done, about $4 per acre. It is preferred by some as the richest and most productive land, holding moisture an antidote against drought; rejected by others who prefer a lighter soil, and who are not willing or able to wait for returns. The latter (smooth prairie) is very highly esteemed, and has proven to be very productive in corn and cotton. I visited the purchase of a gentleman of a tract of rich hog-wallow land and smooth prairie soil in Caldwell county, about six miles from Lockhart, with a post oak ridge convenient, where he intends to locate the residence and quarters for which place he paid $2.75 per acre cash.

The post oak prairie valley soil is mixed with sand, and although not so rich and durable is esteemed for its easy and light cultivation. If it produces less and wears out sooner, more can be planted to the hand, and as the price is and ought to be considerably less, the proprietor can afford to purchase more land than he wants for immediate culture, so as to be able to alternate and rest his land.

To the small planter with moderate means, such lands address themselves as suitable and appropriate; post oak lumber is convenient and upon the creeks adjacent, the walnut, pecan and other growth abound, but deficient in water facilities. Wherever wells have been dug in the post oak lands, water of a tolerable quality for a lime or prairie country has been found. The creeks in the neighborhood of the post oak ridges go dry in the summer and hold water only in holes; some dig, what in Mexican language they call tanks or holes, in the bed of the deserted water course which they say afford them and their stock water.

Middle western Texas is a dry country, and as far as his observation goes, free from wet swamps, lagoons or waste lands, holding water upon the rivers and creeks; the lands lie sufficiently rolling and the water courses with their rapid currents are amply sufficient to carry off the surplus water in a day or two after a spell of rain, for some days. Although this country is in general, dry, it is said not to suffer for the want of rain, such is the fertility of the soil and the rapid growth of vegetation, it is said, but two or three seasons are required to make a crop.

I have lived in the low country of South Carolina, but prefer a residence for health and comfort in the middle country. The price of lands varies; near populous neighborhoods and towns the price is much higher, and smaller improvements enhance the value beyond what a traveler for land thinks reasonable, considering the want of good market facilities.

North-west of Austin, is a ridge of flat mountains, north-east of which is an elevated and undulating country of extensive prairies; portions mixed with wood and prairie and other portions deficient in wood, until you reach the more eastern portion where it becomes a well timbered country.

It was my good fortune to meet with several intelligent gentlemen at Austin, who represent this region as the choice portion of Texas, very important for stock-raising and the culture of wheat, although cotton is now successfully planted in many parts of it. This may be appropriately designated as the wheat region of Texas although the southern and more eastern portion may be well adapted to cotton, the more northern and western part will be confined to the culture of wheat from its elevation and latitude; altitude having great influence upon cold. In the course of time, when the lands become worn and loose, those vegetable gases that give heat to the soil and climate, will be regarded as too cold, and the season too short, and as better adapted to wheat, and flour will be the most profitable and remunerating crop. It is represented that large bodies of rich valuable lands can be obtained at a very low price, from two to five dollars per acre; the population being very thin, and the lands vacant and unoccupied; it is said that the State Government owns large bodies as well as many individuals, who selling by wholesale, no doubt would take a lower price. This section affords to the capitalist a great field for speculation, which is enhanced in interest and importance, on account of the line of the great Pacific Road passing through it, about 32° north latitude, and about 120 miles above Austin city.[5]

As has been said, Texas has a great variety of soil and climate, and more rich land generally than any State in the Union to its territory. Western Texas is so different and so much more picturesque and romantic in scenery than any other country, that a visit to it would not fail to reward the curious, and the admirers of the grand display of nature.

An emigrant who is in pursuit of a rich country to raise wheat successfully, need but bend his course to the north east of the city of Austin, the up country of Texas.

If he is in pursuit of a good and rich cotton country where he can raise cotton and corn to great advantage, and enjoy in many places, health and comfort, we would point him to the middle country. If he is desirous to connect stock-raising, and cotton planting together, we would direct his course to the mixed wooded and prairie region in middle western Texas, west of the Brazos and east of the Guadalupe rivers, and north to the city of Austin.

If he is in pursuit of large bodies of the richest soil, more particularly adapted to the culture of the cane, although at this time producing large quantities both of sugar and cotton, I would direct him to the low country of Texas; and if greater wealth from large capital be his all absorbing object, I would point him to the Brazos and Colorado bottoms, in the low country of Texas.

If he is in pursuit of the best stock country in the world, he will find it in the open and extensive prairies of far western Texas, west of the Guadalupe and San Antonio.

In giving a true and faithful description of Texas, it will be right and proper to present to the reader the charges, or chief objections raised to this country.

There is no country without its advantages and disadvantages; and the admirers of God's infinite justice, and benevolence, in his enthusiastic zeal, is almost induced to believe in the equality of God's blessings over the Universe. Freely must it however be admitted, that there is a greater equality of God's mercy over all sections of his lower world, than at first sight, man is disposed to imagine, still we are forced to perceive a great difference between the frozen region of the north, and the sunny regions of the South, not only in its influence upon vegetation, but upon the character of man.

The objections to Texas are: First, a want of market facilities: Second, a scarcity or want of

5. As early as 1846, meetings were being held in Texas to discuss the building of railroads whose ultimate goal was California. The gold rush gave added impetus to such construction. Congress discussed and debated at least three routes. The one referred to here, the Texas and Pacific Railroad, was to go through El Paso and the Messila Pass. S. G. Reed, *A History of the Texas Railroads*, 2d ed. (Houston, Tex., 1941), pp. 95-96; Adams, *Atlas of American History*, p. 138.

wood and water in many places: Third, the variableness of the weather and the northers: Fourth, the want of health in many sections: Fifth, the want of building materials. These are serious objections and shall be duly weighed and considered. The want of market facilities as has been previously said, is a great drawback to the prosperity of this country; which checks emigration, and retards the settlement of the country, and must have an influence upon the price of land for the culture of cotton. The rivers afford but poor navigation; the cotton has to be transported on wagons, drawn by oxen, which are exclusively supported on the prairie grass; but for the circumstance, and a level and good road, the expense of transportation, at a very low or reduced price of cotton, would consume the profits.

The country from its level surface, is admirably adapted, to the building of rail-roads, and a great saving made in the grading and leveling of the Texas roads; a very important item in all the roads built which has been estimated at 10,000 dollars per mile.

The State of Texas has been aroused to the importance of the subject, and has passed a very encouraging act, for the promotion of rail-road improvements, and the raising of companies for that purpose, in a proposition of a magnificent donation of lands, which it is supposed will refund the companies for their outlays, and reward them besides for their spirit of enterprise.[6] The Pacific Railroad to pass at or about the latitude of 32° north latitude, is about being surveyed, and that it will in a very few years, be built, I regard as a settled fact.

And I cannot entertain a doubt, that roads to connect the low, middle, and up country in close proximity to each other will follow in short order. The latter may be considered as State policy, to direct and facilitate the trade, and business within her own borders; build up her seaboard cities, and fill the country with population, which will add to the revenue, and importance of this State, and will be advantageously felt, when the State comes to raise taxes from the property of her citizens. It is easier to find fertile bodies of land, but more difficult to find wood and water, although many places can be had advantageously and conveniently situated, as regards both.

The post oak and cedar, most generally used for fencing, lasts much longer than the rails of Alabama and Georgia, and in a warm latitude of 30° less wood is wanted for fuel. In the mixed region of wood and prairie, the emigrant will find no difficulty in getting an abundant supply of wood and water. Although he may fancy a beautiful place, deficient in both, and regret the circumstance; or he may as some do, to avail himself of such a location, be reconciled to but little wood for fuel, and to haul his rails some distance. The large prairies deficient in timber, give the emigrant, advantageously situated near them, the most bountiful pasturage for his cattle, and other animals, richer than the art and industry of man could make it, and will keep him from the nuisance of too close

neighborhood and give him ample room for hunting and exercise. As regards water, I understand in the eligible situations of the post oak and prairie, wherever wells have been dug, they have afforded moderately good water, for a lime or prairie country. The rivers running with rapidity a short distance from the mountains afford a good supply of water, which might be improved, although the streams are limpid and clear by the use of filters. Cisterns that cost but little more than superficial wells, are getting in use, the water from them, is the most wholesome, and a preventive, say the learned of the medical faculty, against cholera.

It has been observed that where cistern water has been exclusively used, no cholera has made its appearance; the heat of cistern water raised as an objection, is obviated, so it is said, by catching the water during the time between November and March. In time a resort will be had to artesian wells as in some parts of Alabama, where and when the emigrant can afford the expense.

The atmosphere is in summer very hot and sultry in latitude 30°, rendered however less oppressive by the constant sea breeze, that blows from about 8 o'clock, A.M. to midnight and longer, as strong as on the margin of the ocean.

The norther is a wind from the north, which produces a great and sudden change, from heat to cold, when the weather becomes very hot and sultry, the wind suddenly shifts round to the north, and in a few minutes blows up severe cold, which is more seriously felt on account of the sudden change from heat to cold. The wind is cold and piercing, in coming from the snowy mountains, unchecked by the flat low mountains of Texas, and has full sweep and masterly control over extensive open prairies. Woe betide the man, who in dead of winter, is traveling in a large prairie destitute of a single tree, or bush, who meets a norther, unprovided with thick clothing, and his overcoat and cloak or Mexican blanket; they last but a few days

6. In 1852, in chartering the Henderson and Burkville Railroad, the state of Texas made a grant of eight sections of land for each mile of road built. These grants were increased to sixteen sections in 1854 and were continued until prohibited by the state constitution of 1869. Webb, *Handbook of Texas*, 2:430–31.

and are only severely felt, for a few hours, and occur about every fortnight or three weeks, and some winters not so often; they are only severe a few winter months, and are pleasant and acceptable in summer. They are represented by some as a curse, by others as a blessing, a purifier of an over-heated atmosphere. In conversing with residents of one or two years, the writer has not heard of any serious injury or sickness, arising from them. The Texan is on the lookout and as soon as they appear, betakes himself to his house, with a comfortable fire, and if required to attend business in the open field, or to go a journey, is provided with thick clothing, and his Mexican cloak or blanket. The writer never spent a winter in Texas, therefore cannot speak of them in that season from personal observation and experience, but he has felt them in travelling through the country during the months of April and May, and observed that the norther was a very sudden change of the weather, more sudden than in Alabama or Georgia, but of shorter duration, and had to resort to his overcoat or cloak; and received no injury, and but little inconvenience from them. A young gentleman traveling with him frequently, did not resort to overcoat or cloak.

Middle western Texas about 30° north latitude, is a dry country or in other words, dry weather preponderates. It is said that the crops do not suffer for the want of rain, such is the rapid growth of vegetation, they require but two or three seasons to make them, except far west, beyond San Antonio, where droughts are seriously felt some seasons.

From the undulation and dryness of the country, and the rapid current of the rivers and creeks; there is no stagnant water. Judging also from the appearance of the settlers, and their families, I believe that middle western Texas, in general, is entitled to a character for health although there are no doubt sickly localities. Indeed the banks of one of the creeks was pointed out to him as such; as regards eastern and other portions of Texas, he has

anticipated the subject in previous remarks. Many localities are deficient in building the materials for fine houses; there is plenty of post oak for common buildings, some few are convenient to what they call cedar brakes or the mountains and creeks where cedar and walnut timber can be procured. There are a few spots of pine trees or timber, where steam mills are erected, called pineries, at which pine lumber is sold enormously high. In the neighborhood of Austin, and above, are found granite, marble, and lime rock in great abundance, of which the capital is built, a large, substantial and beautiful house. For economy a resort is had to put up what they call concrete buildings, the materials being shells, rocks, lime and soil, mixed; the walls built up in a wooden case which is removed when they acquire strength from the atmosphere to preserve them erect. The Episcopal Church at Austin is a concrete building, upon a high eminence commanding a most majestic view of the city—the river and surrounding country—wood and prairie.[7] Some houses in Charleston are built of the same material, which they call tabby.

Texas is thinly populated, but is destined, some day or other, to hold a large prosperous and wealthy population. There are a number of flourishing little towns, and many respectable country neighborhoods.

The writer found more men of intelligence and a high standard of private and public morals, than from report, and a newly settled country, he had reason to expect, and which will not lose by comparison with older western States; the laws are efficiently administered for the protection of the rights of persons and property; and the various denominations of christians appear to vie with each other, in usefulness and moral excellence. He re-

7. St. David's Episcopal Church, whose parish was organized in 1847 and whose building was consecrated in 1855, is the second oldest Protestant church in Texas. *Texas Guide*, pp. 172-74.

ceived on his journey and sojourn among them, such hospitality and kindness as have made a lasting impression upon him, of the character of the population of Texas.

The writer with no bad feelings, would observe, that the high price of land, too high in many places, when the want of market facilities is considered, checks emigration and retards the settlement of the country. To those persons owning large bodies of land, he would suggest if they would not consult their interest in selling a portion at a fair or reduced price, they would promote the improvement of the country, and thereby enhance the value of their lands in reserve.

In conclusion, Texas offers many advantages to the emigrant who is doing badly, or has been unfortunate in the country where he lives and is in pursuit of a new country, she offers such advantages as no other country does.

And when the country is filled with a more dense population, and a way is opened for the travel of the iron horse, who never tires nor stops to rest, driving weight and distance into the very shade with his numerous cars laden with travelers and the products of her rich valleys and prairies, Texas will become, what her destiny awaits her to be, the empire state not of the South only but of the whole union. Whether she will accomplish these things in a short or long time depends upon the public spirit and energy of her people, and public men; her monied resources are great and will be greatly enhanced and increased as her great natural resources are developed.

In writing so long a letter, where brevity would have answered a better purpose and saved so large a tax upon the patience of my reader, I am induced to use the words of Dr. JOHNSON by way of apology, that "I had not the time to make it shorter."

With my thanks for the use of your columns, and with high consideration and respect, I subscribe myself your most obedient servant,

JOHN L. HUNTER.

AN ENGLISHMAN IN SOUTH CAROLINA

This intimate, but objective, portrait of South Carolinian aristocracy on the eve of the Civil War was written by an Englishman with a knowledge of history.

CHAPTER FIRST

"The happiest people on the face of the earth, sir!"

I had heard the assertion in almost all of the slave States, and knew something of the institution on which it was based: I was now listening to the familiar sentence at an epoch that has become

"An Englishman in South Carolina, December, 1860, and July, 1862," *Continental Monthly* 2 (1862): 689–94; 3 (1863): 110–17.

historical. I sat in Charleston, South Carolina, during Secession time, December, 1860.

"They are better fed and better treated than any peasantry in the civilized world. I've travelled in Europe and seen for myself, sir. What do you think of women—white women—working in the fields and living on nothing better than thin soup and vegetables, as they do in France, all the year round? And a man, with a family of nine children to support, breaking stones on the high road, in winter, for eight English shillings a week? Such a thing couldn't happen in South Carolina—in all the South, sir!"

"Perhaps not!" I didn't add that worse social wrongs might and did occur daily, in the eulogized region; knowing the utter unprofitableness of any such discussion, not to mention its danger at a period rife with excitement.

"You are an Englishman," continued my interlocutor—a portly, middle-aged, handsome man, to whom I had been introduced just before the hotel dinner, toward the close of which our colloquy occurred—"and therefore a born abolitionist—as a matter of sentiment, that is. You know nothing at all about the workings of our institution, excepting what the d——d Yankees please to write about us, and the word *slavery* shocks you. Call it servitude, vassalage, anything else, it might be endurable enough. One of the advantages, by the way, that Secession is going to bring with it is, that the world will be brought into direct contact with us, and thus see us as we are, not through the eyes of the North."

"You are in earnest about Secession, then?"

"In earnest! by —— I should think we were! Don't you *know* we are, from what you have seen here?"

I did, and a moment's reflection might have checked my thoughtless inquiry. I said so.

"Yes, South Carolina's going out of the Union, with or without backers, and she intends to stay out, too; never were people more unanimous. The North has got so far toward being abolitionized as to elect a man avowedly hostile to our institutions, and we are only providing for our safety by seceding. It's quite time. Essentially we are a different people: we shall be the best friends in the world separate. It's all a question of difference of opinion about labor; the North prefers a system regulated by the mercenary dictates of traffic, ruled by capital, and subject to the chronic difficulties of strikes and starvation; the South, a simpler rela-

tion, binding master and slave together for their mutual benefit, abolishing pauperism, and dividing society into two unmistakable, harmonious classes —the well-fed, well-cared for, happy negro, and the wealthy, intelligent slave-owner."

I thought I had read something very like the speaker's sentiments in that morning's *Mercury*,[1] but didn't say so. I thought also of the existence of another class at the South, besides the two so favorably characterized, of which I had seen a good representative in a coarse, half-inebriated, shabbily dressed individual, who, just after breakfast, had reeled through the crowd always assembled in the large hall of the hotel to exchange and discuss the news, boasting that a son of his had "cut a man's throat the other day, down on the island," and admiringly wondering whether it was the paternal or maternal side that he got his bravery from. I deemed it, however, advisable to be reticent on this head. And my reward followed.

"Come, Mr. ———, you have been in most of the Mississippi States, I believe, but were never in the Carolinas before, so you don't know how we old-fashioned folks live on our plantations. Suppose you pay me a visit at my place on ——— Island, and see? I come of English blood, myself; my grandfather was a Tory in the Revolution"—with a laugh—"and you'll find us a good deal more British than you think possible here in America. England and South Carolina are mother and daughter, you know; and under the influence of free trade, we're bound to be very intimate. All we of the South ask is that our institutions shall speak for themselves, and I can trust a Britisher's proverbial love of fair play to report us as he finds us. What do you say? I'm going down to the island for a week on Wednesday; will you spend your Christmas with me?"

1. The *Mercury* was founded in Charleston in 1822 and continued until 1868. Gregory, *American Newspapers*, p. 640.

The invitation was given with an off-hand cordiality decidedly prepossessing. Expressing my thanks, I at once accepted it in the spirit it was offered.

"That's right! you're my guest, then"; and the Colonel—he had been presented to me by that military designation—shook me by the hand. "Will you walk?" And we strolled out together into the hall before mentioned.

If I were writing an article on Charleston in Secession time, now, here was an opportunity for description. What a strange, what a memorable period it was! involuntarily reminding one of an historic parallel in the roseate aspect presented by the early days of the first French revolution, when everybody hailed as the dawning of a celestial morrow the putrescent glow of old corruption blending into the lurid fire of the coming *sans-culottic* hell. In this case also an infernal *ignis fatuus* had arisen to tempt its deluded followers toward a selfish fool's paradise, only to be obtained by wading through seas of fratricidal blood. And how they believed in this impossible future in the "cradle of the rebellion!" Only a minority of darker conspirators apprehended—hoped for—war, thinking it necessary to precipitate the remainder of the Southern States into revolution, and the establishment of a separate nationality; the great majority of South Carolinians accepting Secession with an enthusiasm (or rather self-exaltation) and confidence astounding to witness. There would be no collision; the North could not and dared not push it to the extreme issue; she must endure the punishment due to her "fanaticism" in inevitable bankruptcy and beggary, while the South, the seat of "a great, free, and prosperous people, whose renown must spread throughout the civilized world, and pass down to the remotest ages" (I quote from the ordinance of Secession), had infinite possibilities before it. Jack Cade's commonwealth, Panurge's "world, in which all men shall be debtors and borrowers," Gonzalo's imaginary kingdom in the *Tempest*,[2] were not a whit more extravagant than what was hourly talked of and expected from this longed-for slaveholding confederacy at this time in Charleston. But enough of digression on a subject merely incidental to this narrative.

Three days after my conversation with the Colonel, when the city was jubilant with the passage of the act of Secession, I accompanied him to the plantation spoken of. It involved a little steamboat journey, sundry rides in chaise or buggy, and the crossing of more than one of the many creeks or rivers intersecting the low, sandy, swampy coast. I purposely abstain from particularizing the locality. It was toward the close of a mild, humid day when we reached the Colonel's residence.

Suppose an old-fashioned two-story house, one of a very common pattern in this region, built of wood, and standing on an open foundation of brick, with a tall, formal chimney projecting at either end, a broad piazza, and a great flight of wooden steps in front and rear, the latter looking seaward. Like the house of Chaucer's Reeve, in summer it must have been all "yshadowed with greene trees,"[3] the cedar, the cottonwood, the liveoak, fig, mulberry, and magnolia, growing in the sand or light soil accruing from vegetable decomposition; and as the evergreens predominated, its winter aspect was yet pleasant and rural, notwithstanding a certain air of dilapidation and decay, so common in Southern dwellings that the inhabi-

2. John or Jack Cade was born in Ireland and was killed near Heathfield in Sussex, England, on 12 July 1450. He was the leader of a group of Kentish men in an action known as "Cade's Rebellion." He appears in Shakespeare's *Henry VI*. Panurge is a character in Rabelais's *History of Gargantua and Pantagruel*. Gonzalo is described as an "honest old counsellor" in Shakespeare's *Tempest*. *Century Dictionary and Cyclopedia*, 9:201, 779, 447.
3. Geoffrey Chaucer, *The Canterbury Tales*, General Prologue, line 606.

tants seem to be unconscious of it. Adjacent, beyond the short avenue of orange trees by which we had approached, was a double row of negro huts, with little gardens between them, forming a rustic lane; farther on, corn and cotton fields. The geography of the island might be stated as follows: interior woods, girdled by plantations, with houses on the seaboard or shores of the river or inlets; a road circumscribing it, and one running across it.

We were welcomed by the appearance of two or three decently clad house servants, mulattoes, and an athletic negro, of average nigritude,* every tooth in whose head glistened, as his black face rippled into a laugh, when his master favored him with some familiar and approving jocularity. Officiously taking charge of the horse and buggy, he conveyed them to a spacious but dilapidated stable (the door of which, I remarked, hung only by its lower hinge), while the servants were equally zealous in transporting what little baggage we had into the house. There the Colonel presented me to his daughters, two tall and rather handsome girls of the ages of eighteen and twenty, dressed in deep mourning (their mother had died but recently), their aunt, a staid, elderly matron, who seemed installed as housekeeper, and a fat, careless gentleman in short sleeves, with a cigar in his mouth, who impressed me as an indolent and improvident poor relation of my host, as indeed, he proved. There was present also, the child of a neighbor, a little fair-haired girl, called Nelly, who, hearing my nationality mentioned, would not approach me, which the Colonel accounted for by surmising that she had received "Tory" impressions of Britisher's from her parent's negroes.

A sincere, if a quiet welcome, and an excellent dinner, comprising fish, game, chickens, bacon, hominy, corn and wheaten bread, and sweet potatoes of a succulence and flavor only attainable in Dixie, all served by decorus and attentive negroes, made me feel very contented with my position. Nor were the surroundings inharmonious. We sat by a wood fire, burning in a fireplace which contained, instead of a grate, old-fashioned iron dogs: most of the furniture, with the exception of a handsome piano, was ancient, and the room ornamented with books, pictures, and mineral curiosities. Among the former I noticed a row of volumes of British parliamentary debates in old print, contemporary with the age succeeding Johnson. Really, as my host had boasted, his household goods were decidedly English—*colonial* English; and I began to understand the peculiar, ante-revolutionary, patrician characteristics on which he and his class evidently prided themselves. He showed me a portrait of an ancestor who held high office in the days of Governor Oglethorpe, an old-fashioned miniature on ivory, charmingly painted, in the style of Malbone,[4] and one could easily recognize in it the features of his descendant. In conversing, too, on the early history of the State, of which he had much to say that I found interesting, he always assumed that a popular, democratic form of government was rather a mistake than otherwise,* and, without absolutely condemning the Revolution, implied that South Carolina had been moved to her limited share in it against her direct interests, by a high-spirited patriotism and sympathy with the at present ungrateful and venal North. I do not think that the fact of my nationality influenced him in this; he evidently spoke his convictions.

The ladies were at first reserved, acting, I believe, under the impression that their father's brief

*An inquiry instituted by Gen. Hunter, at Hilton Head, S.C., during the past summer, for eight negroes of unmixed African descent, resulted in the total failure of discovery of even one. So much for practical Southern amalgamation.

4. Edward G. Malbone (1777–1807) was an American portrait painter. *Century Dictionary and Cyclopedia*, 9:645.
*It was generally credited in Charleston, that, subsequent to Secession, the convention had debated the advisability of attempting some monarchical experiment.

knowledge of me hardly warranted my introduction to his family; indeed, I am sure it was exceptional, from all I have since learned of South Carolinian society. The casual mention, however, of the names of a few mutual acquaintances, of unexceptional "blue blood," and the fact that both ladies had visited Europe, establishing topics of conversation, they presently warmed into cordiality. I found them well informed and agreeable, less demonstrative in their self-assertion than their Northern sisterhood, but latently wilful, and assumptive of a superior elevation hardly justified by their general air of languid refinement. It reminded me, on the whole, of what I had heard complacently eulogized in Charleston as a tendency toward "Orientalism" on the part of the women, of which the characteristics were repose, fastidiousness, and exclusiveness—one of the many admirable results of the fundamental institution.

The ladies were, of course, ardent secessionists, expressing themselves with a bitterness, an acrimony, an unreasonableness, which might have astonished me, had I been capable of such a feeling on the subject. Inevitably we slid on to it, when I learnt that their only brother was away doing military duty on Sullivan's Island,[5] and so zealous in the discharge of his assumed obligations that he intended to spend his Christmas in camp, not, as usual, upon the plantation.

"You'll be sorry to hear that, Pomp," said the Colonel to an evidently favorite servant, who had waited upon us most assiduously, and who was then kneeling before the fat gentleman, and putting a pair of slippers on his feet. He, by the way, had contributed very little to the conversation, only assenting, smiling, and looking the picture of ease and good humor, as he sat lazily beaming behind a

5. An island in Charleston harbor on which Fort Moultrie is located. It was named for Captain Florence O'Sullivan, captain of the *Caroline*, the English ship that first brought settlers to this area, in 1670. *South Carolina Guide*, p. 390.

tumbler full of Bourbon whiskey and water.

"Yes, sar!" the negro answered, "too bad, mass' Philip not come home for de holidays. All de people 'spect him."

"That's a first-rate boy," said his master, as the negro left the room to fetch something; "I wouldn't take two thousand dollars for him." (Every one familiar with the South, must have heard similar encomiums hundreds of times: each household appears to pride itself on the possession of some singularly admirable negro, whose capacity, honesty, and fidelity are vaunted with an air of conscious magnanimity edifying to witness. The desired inference is that the institution, productive of so much mutual appreciation, *must* be excellent. It never seems to occur to the eulogists that the good is exceptional, or that the praised characteristics might be alleged as an argument for emancipation.)

"That boy has been North with me," the Colonel continued, "to Washington, Philadelphia, and as far as New York. The abolitionists got hold of him at the last place, and wanted to run him off to Canada, but Pomp preferred old Carolina. You don't want to be free, do you, Pomp?"

This was a leading question. The slave hesitated a moment, grinned, and evaded it.

"'Pears like de colored people at de Norf was mostly a mis'able set," he answered: "*can't shum!*"

"You can't see it!" said his master, delighted, and translating a very popular negro phrase for my benefit. And incontinently he launched into a defence and eulogium of slavery, which I shall not oblige my readers to skip by recording. The topic is one on which Southerners are never wearied; and a more uneasy people on the subject than South Carolinians it would be impossible to imagine: long before Secession, they existed in a state of chronic distrust and suspicion about it amounting to monomania.

Next day I accompanied the Colonel over his

plantation. It was a large one, somewhat over seven hundred acres, inclusive of forest land, about two thirds being reclaimed upland swamp soil growing sea island cotton. An old family estate, most of the negroes belonging to it had been born there or in the immediate vicinity; there were about two hundred of them, some living near their master's house, as has been mentioned, the rest in a sort of colony at the other end of the plantation, under the eye of the overseer. These negro settlements merit a paragraph of description.

Their huts were of wood, separate, and standing in little gardens in which each family enjoyed the privilege of cultivating patches of corn, sweet potatoes, and such vegetables as they chose, a street of about a hundred feet wide dividing the houses. Midway, under the shade of a magnificent liveoak, whose branches were mournful with the funereal moss (always suggestive to my fancy of the "little old woman," whose employment in the nursery legend is "to sweep the cobwebs out of the sky," having executed her task in a slovenly manner), was a simple apparatus for grinding corn, consisting of two heavy circular stones, placed horizontally in a rude frame under a shed, to be worked by manual power, by upright wooden handles. This served as a mill for the entire negro population. Entering their huts, you were first conscious of a large brick fireplace, in which a fire was almost constantly burning, though it scarcely lit up the generally dark interior, always much more picturesque than comfortable, for negroes have little if any notion of ventilation, and can hardly be too warm: they will kindle great blazing fires to lie down by or to heat their food, in the open fields in summer. A few roughly fashioned seats and tables, and a ladder staircase, leading upward to an attic or cockloft, completes the inventory of the interior.

We had passed the inhabitants of these huts, at work in the fields, under the direction of the overseer, a strong, spare man, in a suit of homespun, who rode about among them on a horseback, carrying in his hand a cowhide whip, which he exhibited to me with a smile, and the remark that "that was the thing the Yankees made so much noise about." It was a sufficient instrument of punishment, I thought and said, adding that I trusted he found infrequent occasion for the exercise of it.

"Well, they're a pretty well behaved lot generally," he answered, with that peculiar accent derived from almost exclusive association with negroes common throughout the South; "but sometimes it 'pears as if the devil had got in among 'em, and I has to lay on all round. A nigger will be a nigger, you know."

The subjects of this ethical remark were rather raggedly dressed, the men in coarse jackets and trousers, the women in soiled and burnt gowns of indefinite color, generally reefed up about the hips for convenience in working. (Their dilapidation, it may be remarked, was due to the close of the year; they would get new clothes, the Colonel remarked, at Christmas.) They seemed, however, well fed, not too hardly tasked, and, from a sensual point of view, happy and contented. The Colonel spoke to those nearest him patronizingly, asked about absent or sick members of their families, joked about the coming Christmas, and the "high time" impending and inquired how many marriages were to come off on the occasion—the negroes generally deferring their nuptials till the great holiday of the year. He was answered by a perfect shout of negro laughter, hearty, infectious, irresistible.

"Come, how many is there to be?" he repeated, joining in their mirth.

"Six!" the overseer responded, seeing that the negroes did not reply except by continued guffaws.

"Yes, sa! *ya! ya!* bound to have high old *Secesshum* time dis Christmas! *ya! ya!*" added a gray-headed old darky, quite overcome with merriment.

"Why, you'll ruin the young ladies in finding

frocks for the girls!" said the Colonel; "who are these future happy couples, eh?"

"Sal's Joe, sa!" "Polly's Sue!" "Big Sam!" "Pinckney!" "Cal!" "Peter!" "Jule!" and a variety of names were shouted out, not by the owners of them. With a great deal of shyness and simpering and half-suppressed grinning and real or affected modesty on the part of the women, and equal mirth and awkward self-consciousness on that of the aspirant bridegrooms, the candidates for matrimony—or at least such of them as were present, one couple and a "boy" being away—were got together and ranged in a row before us, hoes in hand, where they stood, to their own confusion and the boisterous delight of their colaborers. They appeared generally young, healthy, and well-looking negroes, some of them handsome in an African sense. The Colonel surveyed them with much good nature and satisfaction; he was evidently gratified at the prospect of so many marriages among his own negroes; unions "off the plantation" being looked on with disfavor by proprietors, for obvious reasons.

"Well," he said, after addressing a few remarks to them, individually; "I must talk with the young ladies, and see what we can do for you. If Bones (the sobriquet of a negro-preacher, belonging to the estate) won't be jealous, I think I'll try and get Mr. —— over, to marry the whole batch of you in high style, eh?"

The prospect of a white clergyman, an honor generally reserved only for the marriages of favorite house-servants, seemed to afford unmitigated satisfaction to the field hands. They laughed again, thanked their master, assured him of the perfect willingness of their colored pastor to resign his functions for the time being, in view of the superior dignity accruing to the occasion from the presence of Mr. ——, and we rode off amid a chorus of jubilations.

"What would an abolitionist say to that scene, do you think?" asked the Colonel, as we galloped homeward to dinner.

"Probably he'd admit that slavery has its pleasant side, but insist on looking at both," I answered.

II

"MORNIN', sa! De Cunnel send dis with his compliments. Merry Christmas, sa!" Such was the salutation arousing me on the anniversary of the birth of Him who came on earth to preach the Gospel of love and fraternity to all men—or the date which pious tradition has arbitrarily assigned to it. And Pomp appeared by the bedside of the ponderous, old-fashioned four-poster, in which I had slept, bearing a tumbler containing that very favorite Southern "eye-opener," a mixture of peach brandy and honey. I sipped, rose, and began dressing. The slave regarded me wistfully, and repeated his Christmas salutation.

I knew what the poor fellow meant, well enough, and responded with a gratuity sufficient to make his black face lustrous with pleasure. All through the South the system of *backsheesh*[6] is as prevalent as in Turkey, and with more justification. At the hotels its adoption is compulsory, if the traveller would shun eyeservice and the most provoking inattention or neglect. His coffee appears unaccompanied by milk or sugar, his steak without bread, condiments are inaccessible, and his sable attendant does the least possible toward deserving that name, until a semi-weekly quarter or half dollar transforms him from a miracle of stupidity and awkwardness into your enthusiastic and ever-zealous retainer. This, however, by the way.

My present had the usual effect; Pompey became approbative and talkative:

"You come from England, sa?" he asked, looking up from the hearth and temporarily desisting

6. Tipping.

An Englishman in
South Carolina

in his vigorous puffing at the fire, he had already kindled for me to dress by.

"Yes," I answered.

"Dat a long ways off, sa?"

"Over three thousand miles of salt water, Pompey."

"Golly! I 'fraid o' dem! didn't tink dere was so much water in de world!" adding a compliment on the supposed courage involved in crossing the Atlantic. Negroes have almost no relative ideas of distance or number beyond a very limited extent; they will say "a tousand," fifty or a hundred "tousand," with equal inexactitude and fluency. Presently Pompey began again:

"Many colored people in England, sa?"

"Very few. You might live there a year without meeting one."

"I'se hear dey's all free—dem what is dar? dat so?" he asked curiously.

"Yes, just as they are at the North; only I think they're a little better treated in England. We don't make any difference between men on account of their skin. You might marry a white woman there, Pompey, if you could get her to have you."

Pompey honored this remark with as much ready negro laughter as he seemed to think it demanded.

"I'se got a wife already, sa," he answered. "But 'pears to me England must be good country to lib in."

"Why so?"

"All free dar, sa!"

"Why you'd have to work harder than you do here, and have nobody to take care of you. The climate wouldn't suit you, either, there's not enough sunshine. You couldn't have a kinder or a better master than Colonel ———, I'm sure."

"No, sa!" with a good deal of earnestness; "he fus-rate man, sa, dat a fac; and Mass' Philip and de young ladies, dey berry good to us. But—" and the slave hesitated.

"What is it Pompey? Speak out!"

"Well, den, some day de Cunnel he die, and den trouble come, suah! De ole plantation be sold, and de hands sold too, or we be divide tween Mass' Phil, Miss Jule, and Miss Emmy. Dey get married, ob course. Some go one way, some toder, we wid dem—nebber lib together no more. Dat's what I keep t'inkin ob, sa!"

What answer could be made to this simple statement of one of the dire contingencies inevitable to slave life? perhaps that most dreaded by the limited class of well cared-for house servants, of which Pompey was a good representative. He knew, as well as I, that his poor average of happiness was fortuitous—that it hinged on the life of his master. At his death he might become the chattel of any human brute with a white epidermis and money enough to buy him; might be separated from wife, children, companions and past associations. Suggesting the practical wisdom involved in the biblical axiom that sufficient for the day is the evil thereof,[7] I turned the conversation and presently dismissed him. I experienced some little difficulty in accomplishing the latter, for he was both zealous and familiar in my service: indeed, this is one of the nuisances appertaining to the institution; a pet slave seems hardly to understand the desire for privacy, and is prone to consider himself ill-used if you presume to dispense with his attendance. His ideal of a master is one who needs a great deal of waiting on in trivial, unlaborious ways, who tolerates all shortcomings and slovenliness, and bestows liberal gratuities.

Descending to the breakfast parlor, I received and responded to the appropriate salutations for the day from my host and his family, who had already recognized it, English fashion, by the interchange of mutual presents, those of the Colonel to his daughters being jewelry of a handsome and expensive character. The trinkets were submitted to my inspection and duly admired.

7. Matt. 6:34.

"I must tell you something about these knick-knacks, Mr. ——," said the evidently gratified father. "You wouldn't suppose, now, that these mercenary girls actually asked me to give them money instead of trinkets?"

His tone and looks involved some latent compliment to the young ladies, and I said as much.

"They wanted to give it to the State, to help arm and equip some of the military companies. I couldn't let 'em suffer for their patriotism, you know; so I had to advance the money and buy the trinkets, too; though I'll do them the justice to say they didn't expect it. Never mind! the Southern Confederacy and free trade will reimburse me. And now let's have breakfast."

The Southern Confederacy and Free Trade! During secession time in Charleston, there was displayed in front of the closed theatre, a foolish daub on canvas, depicting crowded wharves, cotton bales, arriving and departing vessels, and other indications of maritime and commercial prosperity, surmounted by seven stars, that being the expected number of seceding States, all presented as a representation of the good time coming. It remained there for over a month, when one of those violent storms of wind and rain variegating the humidity of a South-Carolinian winter tore it to pieces, leaving only the skeleton framework on which it had been supported. May not this picture and its end prove symbolical?

"Did you observe that our Charleston ladies dress very plainly, this season?" continued the Colonel as we sat at breakfast. "There are no silks and satins this Christmas, no balls, no concerts, no marriages. We are generally economizing for whatever may happen."

"Why, I thought you didn't expect war?" I answered.

"No more we do; but it's well to be prepared."

"There's to be no race ball, I understand," said the lazy gentleman, who had appeared later than the rest of us, and was having a couple of eggs "opened" for him into a tumbler, by Pompey. "The girls will miss that. Can you tell me how the betting stood between *Albine* and *Planet*?"[8]

I could not, and observed that the Colonel changed the subject with some marks of irritation. I learned afterwards that his indolent relative had an incurable passion for betting, and when carried away by it, was capable of giving unauthorized notes upon his opulent relative, who paid them in honor of the family name, but objected to the practice. He himself affected to discourage betting, though his state pride actually induced him to risk money on the "little mare" *Albine*, a South-Carolina horse, who subsequently and very unexpectedly triumphed over her Virginian opponent. But this by the way.

Breakfast over and cigars lighted (the Colonel imported his own from Havana, each one enwrapped in a separate leaf, and especially excellent in quality), we strolled abroad. The negroes were not at work, of course; and early as it was, we found their quarters all alive with merriment and expectation. Some of the younger men, dressed in their best clothes—generally suits of plain, substantial homespun, white or check shirts, and felt hats—went from house to house, wishing the inmates the compliments of the season, blended with obstreperous broad-mouthed laughter; in some

8. Albine, a mare bred in South Carolina, was victorious over Planet, a Virginia horse and the favorite, in a race on 6 February 1861. Accounts of the race point to the fact that although the ball and dinner, usually a great event of the season, had to be cancelled, the races were held. The reporter commented, "The turfmen of the South...are keeping up their spirits remarkably well in the midst of the general gloom that surrounds them." Wilke's *Spirit of the Times* 3 (9, 16 February 1861): 360–81. Albine was captured by Sherman's army and taken to St. Louis where she died in the fall of 1865, while in training for a race. E. B. Cantey, *Sketch of the Racing Mare Albine* (Columbia, S.C., 1913), pp. 11–12; S. D. Bruce, ed., *The American Stud Book*, 2 vols. (New York, 1873), 1:160.

instances carrying nosegays, received, in common with the givers, with immense delight and coquetry on the part of the females. These wore neatly-made, clean cotton dresses, with gaily-colored handkerchiefs arranged turban fashion upon their heads. Many of the old men and not a few of the old women were smoking clay or corncob pipes; the children laughed, cried, played with each other, rolled upon the ground, and disported themselves as children, white, black, or particolored, do all the world over; the occasional twang of a banjo and a fiddle was heard, and everything looked like enjoyment and anticipation. Of course, the huts of the future brides constituted the centre of attraction: from the chattering of tongues within we inferred that the wedding dresses were exposed for the admiring inspection of the negro population.

The Colonel had just arrived at the peroration of the eloquent eulogium of the scene, when the overseer appeared at the end of the avenue of orange trees, and presently drew rein beside us, his countenance exhibiting marks of dissatisfaction.

"I've had trouble with them boys over to my place, Colonel," he said briefly, and looking loweringly around, as though he would be disposed to resent any negroes listening to his report.

"Why, what's the matter with them?" asked his employer, hastily.

"Well it 'pears they got some rot-gut—two gallon of it—from somewheres last night, and of course, all got as drunk as h———, down to the old shanty behind the gin—they went thar so's I shouldn't suspicion nothin'. They played cards, and quarrelled and fit, and Hurry's John he cut Timberlake bad—cut Wilkie, too, 'cross the hand, but ain't hurt him much!"

"Hurry's John! I always knew that nigger had a d———d ugly temper! I'll sell him, by ———! I won't have him on the place a week longer. Is Timberlake badly hurt?"

"He's nigh killed, I reckon. Got a bad stick in the ribs, and a cut in the shoulder, and one in the face—bled like a hog, he did! Reckon he may get over it. I've done what I could for him."

The Colonel's handsome face was inflamed with passion; he strode up and down, venting imprecations of an intensity only to be achieved by an enraged Southerner. Presently he stopped and asked abruptly:

"Where did they get the liquor from?"

"I don't know. Most likely from old Whalley, down to the landing. He's mean enough for anything."

"If I can prove it on him, I'll run him out of the country! I'll—I'll—d———n it! I'll shoot him!" And the Colonel continued his imprecations, this time directing them toward the supposed vender of the whiskey.

"These men are the curse of the country! the curse of the country!" he repeated, excitedly; "these d———d mean, low, thieving, sneaking, pilfering, poor whites! They teach our negroes to steal, they sell them liquor, they do everything to corrupt and demoralize them. That's how they *live*, by ———! The slaves are respectable, compared to them. By ———, they ought to be slaves themselves—only no amount of paddling* would get any work out of their d———d lazy hides! I almost wish we might have a war with the Yankees: we should get some of 'em killed off, then!"

*The paddle has superseded the cowhide in all jails, workhouses, and places of punishment in South Carolina, as being more effective—that is, painful. In some instances it is used on the plantations. It consists of a wooden instrument, shaped like a baker's peel, with a blade from three to five inches wide, and eight to ten long. There are commonly holes in the blade, which give the application a percussive effect. In Charleston this punishment is generally administered at the guardhouse by the police, who are all Irishmen. Any offended master or mistress sends a slave to the place of chastisement with a note stating the desired amount, which is duly honored. Like institutions breed like results the world over: in Sala's "Journey Due North" we find the same system in operation in Russia.

How little Colonel —— thought, as he uttered these words, "so wicked and uncivic" (as Gellius[9] says of a similar wish on the part of a Roman lady, for which she was fined the sum of twenty-five thousand pounds brass), that in the future lay such dire fulfilment of them! Apropos of the subject, what fitting tools for the purposes of rebellion have these hated "poor whites" proved themselves!—their ignorance, their vices, their brutality rendering them all the more appropriate instruments for the work in hand. It would seem, almost, as if a diabolic providence had prepared them for this very result.

"I must ride over and see about this business at once," resumed the Colonel. "Mr. ——, I can very well suppose you'd rather be spared accompanying me, so make yourself at home for an hour or two. I won't be a minute longer than I can help. Perhaps you'd better not mention this unfortunate affair up at the house until I return; it'll shock the girls, and I'm very careful to keep all unpleasant things out of their way. It's the first time such an atrocity has occurred on this plantation, believe me."

And ordering his horse, he rode off with the overseer. I should really have preferred visiting the scene of the recent tragedy, but my host's wish to the contrary was evident, and I knew enough of Southern sensitiveness with respect to the ugly side of their "institution" to comply. (I had been advised by a fellow countryman not to attend a slave sale in Charleston, lest my curiosity might be looked upon as impertinent, and get me into trouble; but I did it, and I am bound to say, without any evil consequences.) So I retraced my steps toward the house, presently encountering the lazy gentleman, and one in black, who was introduced to me as the Reverend Mr. ——, an Episcopal clergyman of Beaufort, also a resident on an adjacent island.

The lazy gentleman inquired after Colonel ——. Judging that my host's caution, as to secrecy, was only intended to apply to his daughters, I made no scruple of relating what I had heard. My auditors were at once more than interested—anxious. Whenever a negro breaks bounds in the South, everybody is on the alert, a self-constituted detective, judge, inquisitor, and possible executioner. Eternal vigilance is the price of—slavery![10]

"That boy born on the plantation?" asked the clergyman, when the affair had been discussed at considerable length.

"Yes! he's a valuable hand too; I've known him pick seven hundred and fifty pounds of cotton in a day—of course, for a wager."

"The Colonel will have to sell him, I suppose? he can't keep him after this."

"Reckon so, though he hates to part with any of his hands. This trouble wouldn't have happened, if it hadn't been for the whiskey, I've no doubt. The rascal who sold it ought to be responsible."

"Are crimes originating in drunkenness common among the negroes?" I asked.

"Well, no!" answered the clergyman, deliberately; "I can't say that. But most of them will drink, if they get an opportunity—the field hands especially; and then they're apt to be quarrelsome, and if there's a knife handy, they'll use it."

"That's so," assented the lazy gentleman, nodding. "You Englishmen and Yankees—excuse me for coupling you together!—know very little of negro character; and, because the darkies have a habit of indulging in unmeaning laughter on all occasions, you think them the best-tempered people in existence. In reality their tempers are

9. Born about A.D. 130, Gellius was a Roman grammarian. His *Noctes Atticae* is valuable for information on archaic literature and language, law, philosophy, and natural science. *Century Dictionary and Cyclopedia*, 9:429.

10. An ironic variation of the saying "Eternal vigilance is the price of liberty," which has been attributed to both Thomas Jefferson and John Philpot Curran.

often execrable—infernal!" And he complacently blew a ring of tobacco-smoke into the mild, humid morning. The clergyman looked on assentingly.

"They can never be trusted with any responsibility involving the exercise of authority without abusing it. They ill use animals on all occasions—treat them with positive brutality, and sometimes whip their children so unmercifully that we have to interfere. I don't know what would become of them without us, I'm sure!"

"What do you think of their religious convictions?" I asked of the clergyman, when the speaker had arrived at his comfortable, characteristically Southern conclusion.

"Our negroes are unquestionably pious," he answered; "and some of them have a very earnest sense of their duties as to this life and the next; but I regret to say that a good deal of what passes for religion among them is mere excitement, often of a mischievous and sensual character."

"Heathenish! quite heathenish!" added the lazy gentleman. "Did you ever see a *shout*, Mr. ———?"

I responded in the negative, and inquired what it was.

"Oh, a dance of negro men and women to the accompaniment of their own voices. It's of no particular figure, and they sing to no particular tune, improvising both at pleasure, and keeping it up for an hour together. I'll defy you to look at it without thinking of Ashantee or Dahomey;[11] it's so suggestive of aboriginal Africa."

I had an opportunity, subsequently, of witnessing the performance in question, and can indorse the lazy gentleman's assertion. Inheriting the saltatory traditions of their barbarous ancestry, the slaves have also a current fund of superstition, of a simple and curious character. But further ethical

11. Ashantee was a kingdom in West Africa north of the Gold Coast. Dahomey was a French colony in West Africa extending from the Slave Coast inland to the French military territories. *Century Dictionary and Cyclopedia*, 9:84, 303.

disquisitions were here cut short by the appearance of the Colonel's daughters, when the conversation was at once changed, as by tacit consent of all three of us. What their father had told me, relative to his solicitude to keep them in ignorance of all "unpleasant things" accruing from the fundamental institution, was in perfect accordance with Southern instincts. I had observed similar instances of habitual caution before, reminding me of the eulogized tendency toward "Orientalism" alluded to in the previous chapter. And, of all people, South-Carolinians possess the equally rare and admirable faculty of holding their tongues, when there is occasion for it.

We joined the ladies in a walk. As the elder had much to say to the clergyman about mutual acquaintances, while her fat relative strolled carelessly by her side, her sister naturally fell to my companionship. With a rather handsome and intelligent girl I should have preferred to converse on general topics than the one with which I had been already nauseated in Charleston—secession; but she was full of it, and would not be evaded. Very soon she asked me what I supposed would be the sentiment in England toward the seceding States, in the assumed event of their forming a confederacy.

I told her, as I then believed, that it would be adverse, in consequence of the national hostility to slavery, appealing to her own British experience for confirmation.

"Yes," she said, "they were all abolitionists in England, and could hardly credit us when we told them that *we* owned negroes. They thought all Southerners must be like Legree in *Uncle Tom's Cabin!* But papa, who went to the club houses, and mixed with the aristocracy, says that *they* are much better informed about us; that they were opposed to emancipation in the West Indies, and have always regarded it as a great mistake. And, England must have cotton, you know."

"If there's a war between the North and South, won't you find it very difficult to retain your negroes?" I asked, waiving the immediate question.

Miss ———— responded by the usual assertion of the fidelity of the slaves to their owners.

"What if the new Government resorts to emancipation as a weapon against you?" I made this inquiry, thinking it possible that this might be done *at the outset*. Like other foreigners, though familiar with the North, I had not supposed that nearly two years of civil war, with its inevitable expenditure of blood and treasure, would be needed to induce this direct and obvious means of subduing a rebellion. Englishmen, it is known, have ferocious ideas on the subject, as witness India.

"If the slaves rose, we should kill them like so many snakes!" was the answer. And the young lady's voice and flashing eyes showed that she was in earnest.

Our promenade lasted until the return of the Colonel, who presently took a private opportunity of informing me that the wounded slave would probably survive, and that he had sent for a surgeon from an adjoining plantation, expressing some apprehension that delay or indifference on his part might involve fatal consequences.

"It's Christmas time, you see, and perhaps he won't care about coming," said my host. I may add that his anticipation was in part verified by the result, "the doctor" not appearing till the following morning. Thanks, however, to a rough knowledge of surgery on the part of the overseer, aided by the excellence of his constitution, "Timberlake" recovered. I will mention here, in dismissing the subject, that "Hurry's John" was subsequently sold to a Louisiana sugar-planter, a fate only less terrible to a negro than his exportation to Texas.

Within an hour of our return to the house, we partook of an excellent and luxurious Christmas dinner, to which birds of the air, beasts of the earth, and fish of the sea had afforded tribute, and the best of European wines served as an appropriate accompaniment. The meal was, I think, served earlier than usual, that we might attend the event of the day, the negro weddings.

These were solemnized at a little private church, in the rear of which was absolutely the most enormous live-oak I have ever seen, its branches fringed with pendent moss, literally covering the small churchyard, where perhaps, a dozen of the ———— family lie buried—a few tombstones, half hidden by the refuse of the luxuriant vegetation, marking their places of sepulture. The plain interior of the building had been decorated with evergreens in honor of the time and the occasion, under the tasteful direction of the young ladies, who had also contrived to furnish white dresses and bouquets for the brides. These, duly escorted by their future husbands, clad in their best, and looking alternate happiness and sheepishness, had preceded us by a few minutes, and were waiting our arrival, while all around beamed black faces full of expectation and interest.

We walked through a lane of sable humanity—for the church was too small to contain a fourth of the assembled negroes—to the little altar, before which the six couples were presently posed by the clergyman, in front of us and himself. That done to everybody's satisfaction, the Colonel stationed to give away the brides—an arrangement that caused a visible flutter of delight among them—and as many lookers-on accommodated within the building as could crowd in, the ceremony was proceeded with, the clergyman using an abbreviated form of the Episcopal service, reading it but once, but demanding separate responses. I noticed that he omitted the words "until death do ye part," and I thought that omission suggestive.

The persons directly concerned behaved with as much propriety as if they had possessed the whitest of cuticles, being quiet, serious and attentive; nor did I detect anything indecorous on the part of the spectators, beyond an occasional smile or whisper by the younger negroes, whose soft-skinned, dusky faces and white eyeballs glanced upward at the six couples with admiring curiosity, and at us, visitors, with that appealing glance peculiar to the negro—always, to my thinking, irresistibly touching, and suggestive of dependence on, humility toward, and entreaty for merciful consideration at the hands of a superior race. Perhaps, however, the old folks enjoyed the occasion most, particularly the negresses: one wrinkled crone, of at least fourscore years, her head bound in the usual gaudy handkerchief, and her hands resting on a staff or crutch, went off into a downright chuckle of irrepressible exultation after the closing benediction, echoed more openly by the crowd of colored people peeping in at the doors and windows.

The ceremony over, the concourse adjourned to a large frame building, part shed, part cotton-house, ordinarily used for storing the staple plant of South Carolina, before ginning and pressing. The Colonel had sent his year's crop to Charleston, and the vacant space was now occupied by a triple row of tables, set out with plates, knives and forks, and drinking utensils. Here, the newly married couples being inducted into the uppermost seats, as places of honor, and the rest of the company accommodated as well as could be effected, a substantial dinner was served, and partaken of with a gusto and appreciation only conceivable in those to whom such an indulgence is exceptional, coming, like the occasion, but once in a year. Upward of a hundred and fifty persons sat down to it, exclusive of those temporarily detailed as waiters, who presently found leisure to minister to their own appetites. Their owner surveyed the scene with an air of gratification, in which I could not detect a trace of his recent serious discomposure. I am well persuaded, however, that he had not forgotten it, as that the cause of it was known among the negroes; I thought I observed evidences of it in their looks and deportment, even amid the general hilarity.

The ladies had returned to the house, and we were about following them, when the clatter of a horse's hoofs was heard without, and the officious voices of the negroes announced the arrival of a visitor or messenger for the Colonel, who stepped forward to meet him. A young man, clad in a coarse homespun gray uniform, scantily trimmed with red worsted, and a French military cap, alighted, and addressed our friend in a faltering, hesitating manner, as though communicating some disastrous intelligence. I saw the Colonel turn pale, and put his hand to his head as if he had received a stunning blow. Instinctively the three of us rushed toward him.

"My God! what's the matter? what has happened, ———?" inquired the clergyman.

"Philip! Philip! my boy's dead—shot himself by accident!" was the answer.

A very few words explained all. The young volunteer had fallen a victim to one of those common instances of carelessness in playing with loaded firearms. While frolicking with a comrade, at his barracks, he had taken up his revolver, jestingly threatening to shoot. The other, grasping the barrel of the cocked pistol, in turning it round, had caused its discharge, the bullet penetrating the breast of the unfortunate owner of the weapon. Conveyed to the hospital, he had died within an hour after his arrival.

Our holiday-making, of course, came to a sudden termination. Next day I accompanied the Colonel to Charleston, to claim the body of his deceased son, and not long afterward parted with him, on my return to the North.

INDEX

This book has been set in 'Monotype' Ehrhardt,
a late-seventeenth-century design attributed to Nicholas Kis,
originally cut by 'Monotype' in 1938.
Composed by William Clowes & Sons, Limited, London.
Printed on Warren's Olde Style by
Edwards Brothers, Ann Arbor, Michigan.
Designed by James Wageman